North Korea

In this historically grounded, richly empirical study of social and economic transformation in North Korea, Hazel Smith evaluates the 'marketisation from below' that followed the devastating famine of the early 1990s, estimated to be the cause of nearly one million fatalities. Smith questions preconceptions about North Korea; charting the development of a distinct northern identity prior to the creation of the Democratic People's Republic in 1948 before analysing the politics, economics and society of the Kim Il Sung period. Smith shows how the end of the Cold War in Europe and the famine ushered in a process of marketisation that brought radical social change to all of North Korean society. This major new study analyses how different social groups in North Korea fared as a result of marketisation, transforming interests, expectations and values of the entire society, including Party members, the military, women and men, the young and the elderly. Smith shows how the daily life of North Koreans has become alienated from the daily pronouncements of the North Korean government. Challenging stereotypes of twenty-five million North Koreans as mere bystanders in history, Smith argues that North Koreans are 'neither victims nor villains' but active agents of their own destiny.

HAZEL SMITH is Professor of International Relations and Korean Studies and Director of the International Institute of Korean Studies at the University of Central Lancashire.

North Korea

North Korea

Markets and Military Rule

Hazel Smith

University of Central Lancashire

CAMBRIDGE
UNIVERSITY PRESS

CAMBRIDGE
UNIVERSITY PRESS

University Printing House, Cambridge CB2 8BS, United Kingdom

Cambridge University Press is part of the University of Cambridge.

It furthers the University's mission by disseminating knowledge in the pursuit of education, learning and research at the highest international levels of excellence.

www.cambridge.org
Information on this title: www.cambridge.org/9780521723442

First published 2015

Printed in the United Kingdom by Clays, St Ives plc

A catalogue record for this publication is available from the British Library

Library of Congress Cataloguing in Publication data
Smith, Hazel, 1954–
North Korea : markets and military rule / Hazel Smith, University of Central Lancashire.
    pages cm
ISBN 978-0-521-89778-5 (Hardback) – ISBN 978-0-521-72344-2 (Pbk.)
1. Korea (North)–Politics and government. 2. Korea (North)–Economic conditions. 3. Korea (North)–Social conditions. 4. Kim, Il-song, 1912–1994. 5. Kim, Chong-il, 1942–2011. 6. Kim, Chong-un, 1984– I. Title.
DS935.S57 2015
951.9304–dc23 2014039862

ISBN 978-0-521-89778-5 Hardback
ISBN 978-0-521-72344-2 Paperback

Cambridge University Press has no responsibility for the persistence or accuracy of URLs for external or third-party internet websites referred to in this publication, and does not guarantee that any content on such websites is, or will remain, accurate or appropriate.

To Mihail – from Mount Myohyang to God's own county . . .

Contents

Acknowledgements

The subject of North Korea generates a lot of heat, but not a lot of light. To the extent that this book illuminates anything about North Korea it is because I have been lucky enough to have worked, over the years, with a number of people who have been generous with their time and expertise. Colleagues, some of whom I am twice lucky to count as friends, have shared information and ideas and many times organised fora, especially in Washington, DC and Seoul, that allowed for critical but constructive exchange and dialogue that helped me enormously in the rethinking, refinement and sometimes rejection of ideas that is utterly necessary in any process of research and writing.

This book has been a long time in the making and I have a lot of people to thank. In the United States, I learned a lot and continue to learn from those in the policy world who, despite the vagaries of the political cycle, continue trying to avoid the histrionics and grandstanding that surround so much of the public discussion about North Korea, to try to find a sensible policy that will contribute to denuclearisation, a stable peace and a future that will bring prosperity and freedom to North Koreans. The sterling work of Ambassador Donald Gregg, who has worked tirelessly to promote peaceful policies, even as these have become unpopular options in DC, provides a wonderful example of someone who still sees public service as important and whose obvious integrity underpins what is a highly knowledgeable and nuanced understanding of Korean politics. Jon Brause, Bob Carlin, Alexander Mansourov, Mark Manyin, Patrick McEachern and James Person are global authorities on North Korea; whose work I respect as providing consistently high-quality research and analysis.

Contrary to outside caricatures about the US government (which is far from monolithic) there are a ton of people in State, Defense and other agencies who can see a way in which serious policy development vis à vis North Korea, in the United States national interest, could evolve, but these folk rarely talk the loudest, and are often drowned out by those who know nothing about North Korea but everything about how to get their name out there on the internet and in the press. I would like then to record my experience of the highly professional and genuinely reflective analysis that takes place in DC; in the Congressional Research Service, the United States Agency for International Development (USAID), the Bureau of Intelligence and Research (INR) and the Bureau of Conflict and Stabilisation and in Defense. The pity is that this knowledge and expertise does not seem to permeate top-level decision-making.

In the US, the East-West Center in Honolulu and the Woodrow Wilson International Center for Scholars in Washington, DC provided me with congenial surroundings and a hugely stimulating work environment. I thank Pohang Steel Company (POSCO) for the award of the POSCO fellowship which made it possible for me to carry out research in Hawaii in 2008, and the Woodrow Wilson Center for honouring me with the award of a nine-month visiting fellowship for the year 2012/13. Bob Hathaway is an exemplary scholar on Asia. I count myself lucky to have worked with him at the Woodrow Wilson Center.

In South Korea, I benefited from 'outings' of parts of this book at seminars organised by Professor Yoon Young-Kwan at Seoul National University, and Professor Moon Chung-In of Yonsei University at the East Asia Foundation. Both of these occasions were incredibly helpful to me; forcing me to abandon a descriptive approach to regional differentiation in the former and propelling me to rethink what was becoming a monocausal explanation of marketisation in the latter. Dr Lee Suk provided many formal and informal ways in which we could discuss the march of marketisation in North Korea; quite properly and helpfully forcing me to ensure that the empirics were rigorously investigated. Professor Kim Yongho provided a home-from-home in his Institute for the Study of North Korea at Yonsei University. I can't thank him enough for his kindness and generosity. My four former PhD students, Choi Yong-sub, Kim Ji-young, Moon Kyung-yon and Sung Ki-young, whom I am proud today to acknowledge as colleagues, continue to provide a day-to-day reminder that the future of the study of North Korea, and perhaps the future of inter-Korean relations, depends, crucially, on the new generation of scholars and analysts.

In North Korea, I have two or three colleagues and friends with whom I have maintained contact since I first worked in the DPRK in 1998. I don't intend to name them here as it could cause them to suffer negative consequences. My hope is that when North Korea and North Koreans are free, a very minor consequence of that development would be that I could name those many souls who I know have tried hard to improve the lives of their compatriots, despite all the obstacles that the system puts in their way.

In Europe, I want to acknowledge the work of Ruediger Frank, Jim Hoare, Georgi Tolorya and Alexander Zhebin; all who know what they're talking about when it comes to North Korea and all with whom I have had the pleasure and privilege of working over the years.

Thank you, Marigold Acland and Lucy Rhymer and all at Cambridge University Press for commissioning the book and then bearing with me through my awful delays in delivering the manuscript; it is much appreciated. I also very much appreciate the work of the anonymous reviewer, whose rigorous analysis was at my side as I edited the manuscript.

I want to thank my closest collaborators and friends on this book, who have constantly inspired me to carry on, even as this project seemed to be taking up far too many years. John O'Dea, resident nutritionist and senior humanitarian worker based in North Korea for nearly ten years; thanks for the continued swapping of ideas – it helped a lot. Fred Carrière – a constant source of ethically founded, highly intelligent, highly informed analysis: thank you. Henry Em, thanks for reviewing Chapter 2 to save me from myself. Jong Park and Hyun, for the years of comradeship, thank you.

Inevitably, age brings the necessity to thank those who are no longer around to receive the appreciation they deserve. In my case, I could not have ever conceived of writing anything professionally were it not for the support and comradeship of Fred Halliday who remains an example of what it should mean to be a scholar, not just to me but to many others. I miss the friendship and acuity of Jacob Bercovitch who worked all his life in seeking to improve our understanding of how to make peace and avoid war.

Finally, all of the work in this book was only possible thanks to the continuing support, in many different ways, of my wonderful family, and especially my husband, Mihail. We were more or less in this together from the beginning, since we met in Mount Myohyang in May 1990, twenty-five years ago, and his judgement on what's important and what isn't has been invaluable in the decisions as to what needed to stay in and what could be left for now. Thanks for reading, commenting on, finding typos and reviewing almost every page of this book, often numerous times. The better bits are probably down to him; the rest is definitely down to me.

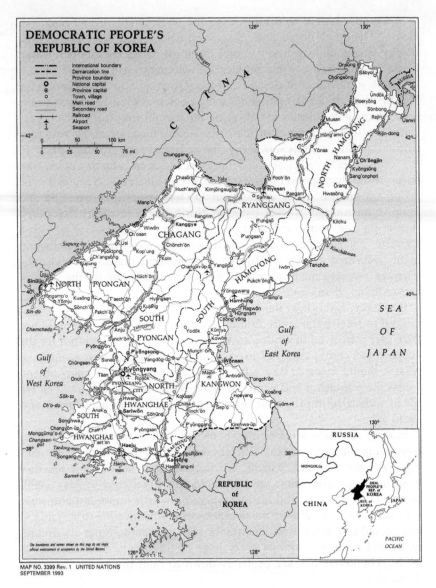

Map of North Korea (Map No 3399 Rev 1. UNITED NATIONS.
September 1993. The boundaries and names shown and the
designations used on this map do not imply official endorsement or
acceptance by the United Nations.)

Introduction: North Korea: politics, economy and society

North Korea is mad, bad and sad.[1] The government is uniquely evil, malevolent and belligerent. The North Koreans are planning to fire missiles armed with nuclear bombs on Alaska. North Koreans are politically indoctrinated robots whose highest ambition is for their children to serve the fatherland in a life of endless privation and unsmiling devotion to a God-like figure in the person of the state leader, Chairman of the National Defence Commission, Kim Jong Un.

The conception of the Democratic People's Republic of Korea (DPRK – more commonly known as North Korea) as so far off the planet that it might as well be in outer space prevails in almost any report about North Korea in the so-called quality press from round the world. This is despite the fact that many of the claims about North Korea are as bizarre and illogical as the picture they are supposed to portray. There are over 24 million North Koreans – do they really all think the same? The dominance of the 'conventional wisdom' on North Korea drowns other perspectives to the extent that it would be surprising if the average, reasonably well-informed member of the public did not automatically view North Korea as alien and inexplicable.

Yet North Korea is far from unique and not a very difficult country to explain. North Korea has an authoritarian government that rules over an economically struggling society. North Korea is not a pleasant society to live in if you are poor, old, ill-connected, religious and/or a political dissident. Should North Koreans be brave enough or foolish enough to engage in political criticism of the government, they face brutal treatment, including imprisonment and internal exile.

North Korea, like many other countries in the early twenty-first century, is undergoing a transition from socialism to capitalism.[2] This

---

[1] The reference here is to Hazel Smith, 'Bad, Mad, Sad or Rational Actor: Why the "Securitisation" Paradigm makes for Poor Policy Analysis of North Korea', *International Affairs*, Vol. 76, No. 3, July 2000, pp. 593–617.
[2] The book expands on cause and consequence of marketisation from Chapter 8 onwards. A good summary of economic transformation is provided in Phillip H. Park (ed.), *The*

fitful and somewhat reluctant process nevertheless represents a vc profound transformation of society. The country's economy is irrever ibly marketised even though the government's political philosophy an rhetoric hangs on to some vestiges of its foundational socialist rhetoric As in many poorly functioning states, North Korea's leaders struggle to maintain authority and legitimacy as they continue to rule over a disillusioned population, tired of political rhetoric and economic hardship. Externally, the government faces a new, hostile world in which communist authoritarian states in one camp and capitalist authoritarian states in the other are no longer protected by the bipolar division of the world led by the former Soviet Union and the United States.

The pivotal moment of social and economic change in North Korea was the catastrophic famine of the mid-1990s. Individuals, families and social groups learned to look after themselves as the government could no longer guarantee a living wage or reliable food supplies. The spontaneous activity of the population created a marketised economy 'from below' where the price of goods and services became determined by the relationship between supply and demand. Internationally determined market prices replaced government-dictated prices as the foundation for all economic transactions. Many of these transactions took place through non-state channels and even when state mechanisms were utilised, price and supply of goods could no longer be controlled by the government. From the late 1990s onwards, a gamut of market operations, some legal, some illegal, some in-between, together provided the main source of supply of food and other goods for most North Koreans.

Post-famine marketisation 'from below' did not produce political liberalisation nor did it result in the emergence of an organised political opposition. The struggle for economic survival, combined with authoritarian politics that savagely repressed political dissent, meant that North Koreans did not have the time, energy or opportunity to engage in politics or protest. Individuals made the rational choice. Regime change activity was risky and much less likely to achieve transformation of daily life compared to the marginal improvements that could be gained by engaging in 'grey market' activity. Everyday lives of North Koreans became increasingly detached from a government that publicly professed arcane ideologies about self-reliance or fighting imperialism and whose priority was regime survival through the development of nuclear weapons.

Dynamics of Change in North Korea: An Institutionalist Perspective (Boulder, CO: Lynne Reinner Publications, 2009).

The seamless dynastic succession from founding president Kim Il Sung to his son Kim Jong Il in 1994 and to his son, Kim Jong Un in 2011 belies the fact that North Koreans aged up to about 30 have grown to adulthood in an economically and socially very different world from that of their parents and grandparents. The Kim Il Sungist era is as historically distant to young North Koreans today as the colonial period was to their parents who grew up after the liberation from Japan in 1945.

The focus of the book

The aim of this book is to show how and why social, economic and political change took place in North Korean society since the now well-known external and internal shocks of the early and mid-1990s.[3] This book is a new venture although I have discussed many of its themes in previous work published in monographs, edited books, scholarly articles, policy reports for international organisations and governments, and media outlets.[4]

[3] Studies that use substantive data to interrogate aspects of economic and social change in the DPRK include Nicholas Eberstadt and Judith Banister, *The Population of North Korea* (Berkeley, CA: Institute of East Asian Studies, 1992); Stephan Haggard and Marcus Noland, *Famine in North Korea: Markets, Aid and Reform* (New York: Columbia University Press, 2007); Suk Lee, 'Food Shortages and Economic Institutions in the Democratic People's Republic of Korea', doctoral dissertation, Department of Economics, University of Warwick, January 2003); Hazel Smith, *Hungry for Peace: International Security, Humanitarian Assistance and Social Change in North Korea* (Washington, DC: United States Institute of Peace Press, 2005); on political transformation see Patrick McEachern, *Inside the Red Box: North Korea's Post-Totalitarian Politics* (New York: Columbia University Press, 2010).
[4] For selection see Hazel Smith, *Food Security and Agricultural Production* (Muscatine, IA/ Berlin: Stanley Foundation/German Council on Foreign Relations, June 2005); Smith, *Hungry for Peace*; Hazel Smith, 'The Disintegration and Reconstitution of the State in the DPRK', in Simon Chesterman, Michael Ignatieff and Ramesh Thakur (eds.), *Making States Work* (Tokyo: United Nations Press, 2005), pp. 167–92; Hazel Smith 'North Koreans in China: Sorting Fact from Fiction', in Tsuneo Akaha and Anna Vassilieva (eds.), *Crossing National Borders: Human Migration Issues in Northeast Asia* (Tokyo: United Nations Press, 2005), pp. 165–90; Hazel Smith *Caritas and the DPRK – Building on 10 Years of Experience* (Hong Kong and Rome: Caritas, 2006); Hazel Smith 'Analysing Change in the DPR Korea', working paper (Bern: Swiss Agency for Development and Cooperation – East Asia Division, November 2006); Hazel Smith (ed.), *Reconstituting Korean Security: A Policy Primer* (Tokyo: United Nations Press, 2007); Hazel Smith, 'North Korean Shipping: A Potential for WMD Proliferation?', *Asia-Pacific Issues*, No. 87, February 2009; Hazel Smith, 'North Korea: Market Opportunity, Poverty and the Provinces', *New Political Economy*, Vol. 14, No. 3, June 2009, pp. 231–56; Hazel Smith, 'North Korea's Security Perspectives', in Andrew T. H. Tan (ed.), *East and South-East Asia: International Relations and Security Perspectives* (London: Routledge, 2013), pp. 121–32; Hazel Smith, 'Crimes Against Humanity? Unpacking the North Korean Human Rights Debate', in Christine Hong and Hazel Smith (eds.), *Critical Asian Studies, Reframing North Korean Human Rights*, Vol. 46, No. 1, March 2014, pp. 127–43.

The book aims to provide an empirically supported analysis of how and why the economy and society of North Korea has been transformed in the post-Cold War era, while the government has hardly changed its political trajectory. This is not therefore a book about North Korea's foreign policy, international relations or historical origins, although I do review these topics in the context of the overall explanation of social, economic and political change.[5] The key questions at the heart of this investigation are 'how and why has the radical dissonance between everyday life and government pronouncements and policy come about and what are the implications for the future of North Korea?'

In this book, I challenge the media mythology that the DPRK is an unknown quantity and aim to shift the debate on from that based on tired and unhelpful stereotyping that characterises so much of the analysis of North Korean politics, economics and society.[6] This includes assumptions that the government controls every action of every human being in North Korea; that North Korean society never changes; that North Korea is nothing more than a monolithic aggregation of persons with identical interests and outlooks; and that the country cannot be studied

---

[5] For a representative selection of writings on foreign policy and international relations see Marion Creekmore, Jr., *A Moment of Crisis: Jimmy Carter, the Power of a Peace-maker, and North Korea's Nuclear Ambitions* (New York: Public Affairs, 2006); Yoichi Funabashi, *The Peninsula Question: A Chronicle of the Second Korean Nuclear Crisis* (Washington, DC: Brookings Institution Press, 2007); Chae-Jin Lee, *A Troubled Peace: US Policy and the Two Koreas* (Baltimore, MD: The Johns Hopkins University Press, 2006); Leon O. Sigal, *Disarming Strangers: Nuclear Diplomacy with North Korea* (Princeton University Press, 1998); Joel S. Wit, Daniel B. Poneman and Robert L. Gallucci, *Going Critical: The First North Korean Nuclear Crisis* (Washington, DC: Brookings Institution Press, 2005). For well-researched and authoritative historical analyses see for example Charles K. Armstrong, *The North Korean Revolution, 1945–1950* (Ithaca, NY: Cornell University Press, 2003); Bruce Cumings, *The Origins of the Korean War, Vol. I: Liberation and the Emergence of Separate Regimes 1945–1947* (Seoul: Yuksabipyungsa, 2002); Bruce Cumings, *The Origins of the Korean War, Vol. II: The Roaring of the Cataract 1947–1950* (Princeton, NJ/Oxford: Princeton University Press, 1990); Suzy Kim, *Everyday Life in the North Korean Revolution, 1945–1950* (Ithaca, NY: Cornell University Press, 2013); Don Oberdorfer, *The Two Koreas: A Contemporary History* (London: Warner Books, 1997).

[6] Including the light-hearted and perhaps therefore forgivable anecdotal narrative of Michael Breen, *Kim Jong Il: North Korea's Dear Leader: Who he Is, What he Wants, What to Do about Him* (Chichester: John Wiley and Sons, 2004); the more serious account of the North Korean famine by Andrew S. Natsios, *The Great North Korean Famine: Famine, Politics and Foreign Policy* (Washington, DC: United States Institute of Peace Press, 2001) in which the author makes claims about famine figures that are not substantiated by way of the data; and the adjectival, apocalyptical prose in Nicholas Ebertstadt, *The End of North Korea* (Washington, DC: The American Enterprise Institute (AEI) Press, 1999) in which North Korea has (excerpt taken at random from the book) 'a fearsome arsenal of weapons of mass destruction'; the government presides over a 'starving, decaying state'; its weaponry has 'killing force'; the country has 'extortionist diplomacy'. The government's plans will 'only provide more of the ghastly, deepening twilight in which the regime is already enveloped' (pp. 21–2).

in the same way as any other country.[7] These clichés are factually misleading. No state or society is ever homogeneous or unchanging and no government, however effective, can control every aspect of its citizens' lives. Where the stereotypes are most misleading, however, is in the myopia about the dramatic social and economic changes that have constituted the fundamental fact of life for every North Korean for the past quarter century. The most basic tenet of social science is that all societies change – even if their governments do not. One conventional assumption about North Korea is that because political philosophy has not changed much since the creation of the state, then North Korea must be a society that does not change or in which social change is insignificant. In North Korea, where people experienced cataclysmic social upheaval during and after the famine of the early 1990s, the assumption of a static society is especially untenable, verging on the fatuous.

North Korea can be compared fairly straightforwardly to other Asian societies, societies in transition from communism to capitalism, and other poor societies. The book shows that the DPRK can be understood through conventional approaches to knowledge, using conventional or 'positivist' notions of social science that seek to assess factual data through a logical evaluation process.[8] The further premise is that North Korea can be understood best through situating the contemporary social and political environment in a historical and cultural context. This historical framing is crucial in explaining the commonalities with South Korea as well as the major differences between the two countries.

In policy terms, this work is underpinned by an old-fashioned liberal trope: better analysis may produce better policy.

North Koreans as agents of change

In this book, I show how and why the society and economics of North Korea changed from a command economy to one that is marketised and in which the population became more and more disassociated from their government. I demonstrate how the political system became delegitimised as the government continually failed to deliver on its promises and as the people of North Korea became aware of the fact that they were poor and their neighbours prosperous. I also show how the government was unable to accommodate the socio-economic transformation that took place in North Korea 'from below' and how it failed to provide

[7] For an exception and for analytically acute comments on social life see Andrei Lankov, *North of the DMZ: Essays on Daily Life in North Korea* (Jefferson, MO: McFarland, 2007).
[8] Alan Bryman, *Social Research Methods*, fourth edition (Oxford University Press, 2012).

credible, effective and sustainable policies to provide secure futures for the population. North Korea is not a democratic state but, like all societies, is made up of different social and political groups with different interests, values, histories and opportunities. I explain and show the heterogeneity of experience of North Koreans as defined by social class, occupation, geographical provenance, gender and age.

This book unpacks the caricatures that have become the conventional 'wisdom' about North Korea, including that of all North Koreans as helpless targets of an all-powerful, omniscient government. From this perspective North Koreans are only either villains or victims. An aim of the book is to introduce North Koreans as the complicated subjects of history that they are. The ethical and political focus is on the potential of North Korean people to make their own history, separately from those in charge. North Koreans, in other words, are the agents of change in North Korea.

The data

The book draws on my twenty-five years of research on North Korea that is in turn very largely based on data from publicly accessible sources, including reports from governments, international organisations and non-governmental organisations (NGOs). I have been aided by the perhaps surprising propensity of the North Korean government to translate and publish huge amounts of books, reports and newspaper articles into English. I obtained these in the DPRK over the years but these days some specialist importers are marketing this material on websites and at Korean studies conferences. The total control of publishing by the government implies that all of these publications convey an official line of some sort and therefore this data has helped to provide representative data about government perspectives on various aspects of history, culture, politics, society and economics over time.

Thousands of reports on different aspects of North Korean society have been published and circulated by international organisations, as well as various governments and NGOs that have worked in the DPRK since the start of the on-going food and economic crisis in the 1990s.[9]

---

[9] See references throughout the book. NGO sources, for example, include field reports such as Action Contre la Faim, *Nutritional Programme: North Hamgyong Province DPR of Korea, November 1999* (Pyongyang: Action Contre la Faim, 1999). DPRK government data is used if the information and analysis is undertaken with supervision and collaboration of international organisations, for example, EU, UNICEF and WFP in partnership with the Government of DPRK, *Nutrition Survey of the Democratic People's Republic of Korea* (Rome/Pyongyang: WFP, 1998); Central Bureau of Statistics, *Report on*

Valuable reporting comes from the Food and Agriculture Organisation
(FAO), the United Nations World Food Programme (WFP), the United
Nations Children's Fund (UNICEF), the United Nations Development
Programme (UNDP), the World Health Organisation (WHO), the
European Union (EU), the International Federation of the Red Cross
(IFRC), the Swiss Agency for Development and Cooperation (SDC)
and Caritas Internationalis, among others. These data resources are
surprisingly under-used, even by the organisations themselves. The
UNDP, for instance, categorises the DPRK as one of the few states for
which there is insufficient reliable data to offer any but the most basic
global comparisons of socio-economic development.[10] At the same time,
since 1995, the UNDP has acted as the coordinator of a huge volume of

the DPRK Nutrition Assessment 2002 (Pyongyang: Central Bureau of Statistics,
20 November 2002); Central Bureau of Statistics, DPRK 2004 Nutrition Assessment
(Pyongyang: Central Bureau of Statistics, Institute of Child Nutrition, February 2005).
A wealth of usable data is contained in the major inter-governmental agency reports,
several thousands of which are freely available on the 'Reliefweb' site hosted by the UN
Office for the Coordination of Humanitarian Affairs (UNOCHA) as well as on
individual UN agency websites. See http://reliefweb.int/country/prk?f[0]=field_country
%3A74, accessed 29 May 2014. For examples see International Fund for Agricultural
Development (IFAD), Upland Food Security Project, Report of Interim Evaluation Mission
Agricultural Component (Pyongyang, April 2008). See also the almost twice yearly FAO/
WFP food and crop assessment mission reports since 1995; for example FAO/WFP,
Crop and Food Security Assessment Mission to the Democratic People's Republic of Korea,
Special Report (Rome: FAO/WFP, 8 December 2008); FAO/WFP, Crop and Food Supply
Security Assessment Mission to the Democratic People's Republic of Korea, Special Report
(Rome: FAO/WFP, 12 November 2012). The WFP webpage on the DPR Korea hosts
a number of extensive reports, including the 2012 national nutrition survey, which the
WFP records as 'the result of a joint collaboration between DPRK Government,
involving the Central Bureau of Statistics, the Child Nutrition Institute, the Ministry
of Public Health and the National Coordination Committee as well as WHO, WFP and
UNICEF'. See www.wfp.org/node/3498/4564/402630#, accessed 26 July 2013. See
UNOCHA, Report (Pyongyang: UNOCHA, 6 August 2002); UNDP, Report of the
First Thematic Round Table Conference for the Democratic People's Republic of Korea
(Geneva: UNDP, 28–9 May 1998); UNDP, Report of the Thematic Round Table
Conference for the Democratic People's Republic of Korea (Geneva: UNDP, June 2000);
UNICEF, Background Situation Analysis on DPRK (Pyongyang: UNICEF, April 1998);
UNICEF, Situation Analysis of Women and Children in the DPRK (Pyongyang: UNICEF,
1999); UNICEF, DPRK Social Statistics (Pyongyang: UNICEF, 1999); Central Bureau
of Statistics/UNICEF, The Democratic People's Republic of Korea Multiple Indicator Cluster
Survey Final Report 2009 (Pyongyang: CBS, 2010); United Nations, DPR Korea Common
Country Assessment 2002 (Pyongyang: UNOCHA, February 2003); WFP, 'Emergency
Operation DPR Korea No. 5959.02, Emergency Assistance for Vulnerable Groups'
(Pyongyang: WFP, 2000); WFP/FAO/UNICEF, Rapid Food Security Assessment Mission
to the Democratic People's Republic of Korea (Bangkok: WFP/FAO/UNICEF, 12 March
2011), available on www.wfp.org/content/democratic-people-s-republic-korea-
wfpfaounicef-rapid-food-security-assessment-march-2011, accessed 25 July 2013.
[10] UNDP, Human Development Report 2004: Cultural Liberty in Today's Diverse World (New
York: UNDP, 2004).

research undertaken by the United Nations in North Korea, some of which it has published itself and some of which it has disseminated, including very detailed evaluations of the nutrition, food and agriculture sectors.

South Korean analysis and data provide another key resource. South Korean analysts and scholars have been, however, periodically constrained by domestic politics and law, which prohibited, by criminal sanctions, any form of activity that could be inferred as sympathetic to the North. The North–South rapprochement of the 2000s eased these constraints but from the late 2000s, the renewed confrontational environment on the Korean peninsula served to inhibit, partly through self-censorship, an efflorescence of research on North Korea.

I have been informed in the writing of this book by many hundreds of conversations with North Koreans in and out of North Korea. I have visited the DPRK regularly since 1990 and lived and worked there for nearly two years between 1998 and 2001. I cannot cite these sources because I do not have their authorisation to use these conversations as material for this book and to a great extent my observations are just that; my observations. In social science that doesn't count as verified data. I have not, however, refrained from using some of this background data in my analysis if I could not provide an alternative source and if I thought the information was important to the reader. I have tried to minimise these interventions as I am conscious that this could make me guilty of the failings I criticise in other work on the DPRK. To as great an extent as I can, however, I have tried to guard against bias and to ensure that no large generalisations are drawn from isolated or unsubstantiated data.

The book does not rely on unsourced leaks from intelligence agencies, defectors and foreign visitors although it does occasionally refer to these sources. Intelligence agencies clearly have multiple agendas, not all of which include transparent and objective analysis. I do not develop an analysis based on defector information even though defector accounts help us understand aspects of North Korean society about which outside observers have next to no first-hand experience. Defector accounts, for example, provide the major source of information on the penal system, which North Korean governments closed to external scrutiny.[11]

North Korea's defector/escapee/migrant community had historically only been given a mediated voice via South Korean intelligence agencies, foreign and South Korean non-governmental organisations and co-writers

---

[11] Chol-Hwan Kang and Pierre Rigoulot, translated by Yair Reiner, *Aquariums of Pyongyang: Ten Years in the North Korean Gulag* (New York: Basic Books, 2001).

from abroad.[12] Recently, however, the self-organisation of North Koreans in Seoul and the publication of unmediated blogs and writings by North Koreans are offering far more useful insights into the nuances of North Korean politics than we have seen before in the public arena.[13] Professional analysis and interviewing of North Korean defectors also has produced useful factual information but unfortunately this material jostles in the public arena with unscientific 'surveys' of defectors as well as anecdotal, unverifiable and sensationalist 'information' that is regularly picked up by global media anxious to increase their circulation.[14] Defector anecdotes bring 'colour' to reporting but because this book is attempting to provide generalizable analysis, these sources are for the most part eschewed.

I do not rely on the plethora of first-hand accounts and trip reports from individuals who have visited the DPRK and stayed there for periods of up to several years. At best, these inform the reader about the author's personal experiences and draw directly from direct observation and qualified comment – resisting claims to overarching knowledge; the weaker ones provide derivative accounts of Korean history cut and pasted from newspaper and other sources that are sometimes not credited.[15] Accounts by former diplomats and officials provide a sub-genre

---

[12] Roy Richard Grinker, *Korea and its Futures: Unification and the Unfinished War* (London: Macmillan, 1998), pp. 225–55.

[13] The well-informed blog *New Focus International* aims for an international audience and bases its news and comment on a network of correspondents inside the DPRK. It was established and is run by former DPRK counter-intelligence officer, Jang Jin-Sung. See http://newfocusintl.com/breaking-north-koreans-ordered-return-state-postings, accessed 28 May 2014.

[14] A good example of the use of defector-based information that is careful to acknowledge the limitation of these sources and to triangulate information from defectors with other data is Gary Samore, *North Korea's Weapons Programmes: A Net Assessment* (London: Macmillan Palgrave, 2004). Another example of professional research based on defector surveys is Byung-Yeon Kim and Dongho Song, 'The Participation of North Korean Households in the Informal Economy: Size, Determinants, and Effect', *Seoul Journal of Economics*, Vol. 21, No. 2, Summer 2008, pp. 361–85.

[15] The memoir by the British citizen Michael Harrold, who spent seven years between 1987 and 1994 working as a translator in the DPRK, is somewhat disappointing as it fails to offer anything other than the most minimal observations of North Korean society, remaining focused on the expatriate community experiences of life in the country. See Michael Harrold, *Comrades and Strangers: Behind the Closed Doors of North Korea* (Chichester: JohnWiley and Sons, and 2004). A book containing some nice vignettes based on visits to the DPRK is Bradley Martin, *Under the Loving Care of the Fatherly Leader: North Korea and the Kim Dynasty* (New York: St. Martin's Press, 2006). A slight but illuminating account and less sensational than the title would suggest, is Nanchu with Xing Hang, *In North Korea: An American Travels through an Imprisoned Nation* (London: McFarland and Company, 2003). A very engaging account of life in Pyongyang that has verisimilitude in respect of the day-to-day life of the now hundreds of Westerners who have lived in Pyongyang for periods ranging from a few months to

of their own and these are often, perhaps surprisingly, absent of crude partisanship and can provide valuable empirical insights into daily life in Pyongyang.[16]

A roadmap through the book

This book is written for a broad audience. It is not theory-laden nor does it presume any knowledge about North Korea or social science concepts. For the scholar or student, however, the book is fairly extensively footnoted. The historical chapters provide familiar material for a reader who is a historian of Korea but they are necessary for my explanation of contemporary politics given the historically laden conceptions of national identity that shape contemporary North Korean politics. They also provide information for the reader whose main interest is to understand more recent North Korean history but who may be unfamiliar with the historical context.

Chapter 1 shows that 'common knowledge' assumptions need to be examined critically as they provide a distorted and misleading picture of North Korea and North Koreans in the twenty-first century. Chapter 2 shows how historically referenced understandings of ethnic and national identity, including ideas that Korean people share a common past, a common culture and a common nation, are naturalised by citizens of North Korea and South Korea. These politically powerful conceptions are shared by leaders of the two Koreas, even as they disagree as to how to reach a common future and a re-unified state. This chapter also introduces the political, economic and social distinctiveness of the northern part of the peninsula, even prior to the partition of Korea in 1945. North Korean historiography often downplays northern distinctiveness in order to stress the official line of the homogeneity of the Korean people although, at the same time, claims are often made about a supposed historically based northern superiority over South Korea.

The next six chapters evaluate the rise and fall of Kim Il Sungism as an integrated system of authoritarian politics whose ambition was

four or five years is the beautifully drawn cartoon book by Guy DeLisle, *Pyongyang: A Journey in North Korea* (Montreal: L'Association, 2005).

[16] An account that remains grounded in observation and guided by analytical acuity is J. E. Hoare and Susan Pares, *North Korea in the 21st Century: An Interpretative Guide* (Folkestone: Global Oriental, 2005). Erik Cornell provides a fascinating account of his time as a Swedish diplomat in the DPRK; his musings on the theory of Marx and Lenin are less successful. See Erik Cornell, *North Korea under Communism: Report of an Envoy to Paradise* (London: RoutledgeCurzon, 2002). See also John Everard, *Only Beautiful, Please: A British Diplomat in North Korea* (Stanford, CA: Asia/Pacific Research Center, Division of The Institute for International Studies, 2012).

nothing less than complete hegemony over the behaviour and thinking of the population.

Chapter 3 explains how the period of Japanese colonialism (1910–45) engendered a pan-Korean national identity and how rapid industrialisation of the north facilitated the growth of radical thinking and Communist ideas. The chapter shows how colonialism was hugely formative for contemporary North Korea as it provided the milieu for the rise of Kim Il Sung, who was to base so much of his political thinking on lessons drawn from his experience in the anti-Japanese colonial struggle. This chapter shows how the external division of the Korean peninsula into two separate political entities after liberation in 1945 allowed for the massive ideological and territorial rupture that established two separate Korean states in 1948 and provided the enabling environment for the rise to power of Kim Il Sung in the north.

Chapter 4 discusses how the devastating Korean War that pitted Korean against Korean and killed an estimated three million Koreans – about 10 per cent of the peninsula's population – provided the rationale and crucible for Kim Il Sung's post-war reconstruction policies based on permanent, mass-mobilisation of the entire population. Chapters 5, 6 and 7 evaluate how Kim Il Sung constructed a political project that aimed to control and organise, respectively, the political system, the economy and the society. The order of these chapters is deliberate. The Kim Il Sungist project was driven by political priorities. Chapter 8 demonstrates how Kim Il Sungism came to an end with the pivotal period of trauma in North Korean history that was marked by famine, economic collapse, political isolation from former allies and government failure that forced 'marketisation by default'.

The remaining chapters analyse the military-first era as characterised by marketisation and the institutionalisation of military rule that embedded regime security politics at the heart of strategic thinking, planning and policy. Chapter 9 charts how marketisation evolved as a social process that engulfed the Party, law and order mechanisms and the family. Chapter 10 shows the priority given to regime security in the military-first era and the contradictions of economic policy that accepted marketisation as an operational necessity but was not prepared to adopt strategic or fundamental reform. Chapter 11 shows how social policy evolved as a function of military-first priorities and market realities. The priority was food security and public health and results were mixed; malnutrition rates sharply decreased in children but the health of women, especially mothers, remained precarious. Chapter 12 examines what marketisation and military-first rule meant for the social structure in North Korea and examines which social groups did well and which did not and why. Chapter 13 evaluates how military-first governments 'went nuclear' in the pursuit of regime survival. Chapter 14 considers how the world, especially the United States, interacted with military-first governments in failed campaigns to avert nuclerisation of the DPRK and encourage human rights reforms. Chapter 15 ends the book with a brief afterword that summarises the argument of the book and looks, tentatively, to the future.

Core concepts

I refer very often to the idea of 'marketisation' and also use the idea of the 'institutionalisation' of marketisation as a way to think about North Korean society. I provide a brief aide-memoire as to what I mean by these terms.

Marketisation

'Marketisation' in North Korea is *not* primarily indicated by the presence of markets as physical locations. *Marketisation in North Korea is better understood as the institutionalisation of market dynamics throughout the society.* Marketisation in North Korea should be understood as both a principle of economic operations and an economic process.[17]

Marketisation provides an underlying economic principle in North Korea in the sense that, since the 1990s, price is no longer determined by the state but by the relationship between supply and demand. Marketisation is also a process, in that different aspects of the economy are marketised to a different extent and the degree of marketisation changes over time. Buying and selling of goods has been fully marketised since the government's economic reforms of 2002 authorised market pricing as the fundamental principle of economic organisation. On the other hand, the buying and selling of labour is only partially marketised in that official wages remain virtually nominal despite some attempts in the 2002 reforms to raise wages. North Koreans are thus propelled into earning income from market-driven activities. Land and property are not officially marketised in that they cannot officially be bought and sold

---

[17] Those interested in the theory and practice of marketisation should consult Taras Kuzio, 'Transition in Post-Communist States: Triple or Quadruple?', *Politics*, Vol. 21, Issue 3, 2001, pp. 168–77. See also Jieming Zhu, 'Urban Development under Ambiguous Property Rights', *International Journal of Urban and Regional Research* , Vol. 26, Issue 1, 2002, pp. 33–50.

privately, but a grey area has grown up where asset transfers take place (illegally) at a price determined by what the market will bear.

Institutionalisation

'Institutionalisation' in this book refers to the establishment of a set of norms, practices and procedures that guide behaviour. These do not have to become formalised in a physical organisation, formally codified or even articulated; they may, however, be highly durable and powerful. Institutions in this sense are constituted by a set of practices understood by a social group as providing the structure for activity. They are 'systems of established and prevalent social rules that structure social inter-actions'.[18] When I refer to the institutionalisation of marketisation in this book, it is in this specific sense of institutionalisation.

The chronological frame

I identify two key periods for comparative analysis. These are *the Kim Il Sungist era*, from the postKorean War up until the early-1990s and *the military-first era*, from the late 1990s onwards. I characterise the mid-1990s as an important period of political, economic and social transition.

These are analytical frames, meant to help in telling the story of change in North Korea. They do not, therefore, represent hard or fast breaks in chronological or descriptive terms. The Kim Il Sungist period includes, for example, a period in the 1980s when Kim Jong Il, his son and eventual political successor, was already playing a leading role in political decision-making. The book also understands the Kim Il Sungist era as ending more or less with the end of the Cold War in the early 1990s, before the physical demise of Kim Il Sung in 1994. Similarly, the categorisation of the military-first era by its eponymous doctrine does not at all imply that economic and social practices were determined by the military-first policy of government and the state. Indeed, the story of this period is how government-directed military-first politics sought and failed to shape the social and economic dynamics of the military-first era. Nevertheless, the analytical distinction provides a useful heuristic device to organise and frame the explanation of how, to what extent and why socio-economic transformation took place between these two eras in North Korean political, economic and social history.

---

[18] Geoffrey M. Hodgson, 'What Are Institutions?', *Journal of Economic Issues*, Vol. 40, No. 1, March 2006, p. 2.

In summary, both eras were constituted by domestic and international markers. The Kim Il Sungist era was constituted domestically by the development of a socialist, anti-imperialist and Korean nationalist political project. Internationally, Kim Il Sungism was framed by bipolar Cold War international politics. The military-first era was constituted domestically by the politics of regime survival and aspirations for economic redevelopment. Internationally the salient factors explaining the military-first era was the globalised international system in which North Korean society became permeable and permeated by foreign goods and ideas.

The analytical frame

This book distinguishes fundamentally between the *government* of North Korea and the *society* of North Korea. The North Korean government rules over a people who may or may not agree with government policy and practice but they are analytically a separate identity. This is true of any society and it is true of North Korea. In empirical terms, if government and society were not separate entities, there would be no need for a government to make and implement policy or to use security services, police forces and judicial systems to enforce its will over society.

A less important distinction in this book but one which will be made occasionally is that between *state* and *government*. A state in the classic social science understanding is constituted primarily by the institutions and means of coercion (the military and police) and the bureaucracy that function within a defined territory and over which rules a government. In North Korea, as in all communist governments, the boundaries between state and government are blurred.

Finally, and very importantly, this book uses the term nation to refer to a group of people bound by a sense of common culture, history and destiny. In this book the term nation is most definitely not synonymous with that of state. Again, it is only by distinguishing these two ideas that one can begin to explain how Koreans consider themselves of *one nation* forced to live in two separate *states* since 1948.

Language and anachronisms

I use North Korean Romanisation of Korean words unless I am quoting directly from a source that uses alternative transcriptions. If appropriate and it adds clarity, I refer to alternative transcriptions as well as the North Korean version. North Korean Romanisation is sometimes complicated by the fact that it has been flexibly used by both North Koreans and interlocutors. One northern DPRK province, for example, is sometimes referred to as *Chagang* in North Korean texts written in English and sometimes as *Jagang*. I have aimed for consistency throughout, so unless I am using a direct quote, I use the most common version of a Romanised word.

In this book, I sometimes refer to places in North Korea whose names have changed over time. Administrative reorganisation in the DPRK also means that the same place name sometimes refers to different geographical locations in different years. Where relevant I specify the difference. The default position in this book is to refer to contemporary place names unless this would cause confusion. I am therefore occasionally anachronistic in the use of place names where the narrative would become very clumsy and the explanation is not relevant to the point I want to make. Where there is a possibility of confusion over location names, relevant supplementary descriptions are given. There is, for example, a Kangwon province in today's North Korea and also in today's South Korea. This is, however, a book primarily about North Korea so the default position is that Korean place names refer to locations in North Korea, unless specified differently.

I write the given name first and the family name second for Korean names, even when the publication uses the Korean syntax of family name first. This is purely for the sake of consistency. The exception is where names are so familiar in their Korean form that it would look silly to write them differently.

Part I

Jettisoning caricatures: understanding history

Part 1

1   Beyond the clichés

The global media remain fascinated with North Korea's supposed weirdness. 'Common knowledge' portrays a monolithic state and society that is hermetically sealed from knowledge of the outside world. The government controls a robot-like 'million-man army' willing to sacrifice itself for the ruling Kim family, which is further protected by its willingness to use nuclear weapons as a first-strike capacity in mad policies of aggression. The omniscient government thinks nothing of starving its population and callously diverting foreign aid from the hungry and the vulnerable to the affluent and the privileged. The entire state is little more than a criminal enterprise. North Koreans are unlike any other people in the world in that they believe everything their government tells them and indeed constantly express heartfelt devotion to the ruling family for the poverty in which they live.

Yet, on the face of it, the North Korean government is neither uniquely authoritarian nor the population uniquely economically badly off. From Laos to Turkmenistan in Asia; Equatorial Guinea to Zimbabwe in Africa; and Syria to Saudi Arabia in the Middle East, political dissent is brutally suppressed and freedom still to be won.[1] In economic terms, North Korea's gross national income per capita of $583 in 2012 made it the twentieth poorest country in the world but it was not uniquely poverty-stricken.[2] North Korea's military and security apparatus remained opaque to outside scrutiny but that was not unique to North Korea. The military and the security sectors remain more or less closed to

---

[1] There are numerous ways of defining 'freedom'. The countries mentioned here are, however, not controversial or arbitrary choices. All, including North Korea, are listed in the United States government-funded think tank Freedom House's 2012 list of unfree countries. See Arch Puddington, *Freedom in the World 2012* (Washington, DC: Freedom House, 2012), available at www.freedomhouse.org/sites/default/files/FIW%202012%20Booklet_0.pdf, accessed 9 December 2012.

[2] United Nations Statistics Division, 'Per Capita GNI at Current Prices in US Dollars (all countries)', National Accounts Main Aggregates Database, available at http://unstats.un.org/unsd/snaama/dnllist.asp, accessed 30 May 2014.

public scrutiny, even in democratic societies. Why then is North Korea considered so exceptionally difficult to understand? Is North Korea really unique?

In the end, it is the North Korean government that benefits from the perpetuation of the myths of North Korean strangeness. Myths of military superiority, fearsomeness and unpredictability help in persuading adversaries to take them seriously. The perpetuation of the 'common knowledge' assumption that North Korea is uniquely inexplicable inhibits more sober analysis that would expose the vulnerabilities, weaknesses and frailties of the regime. This unhelpful stereotyping that shapes too much of the writing and conventional assumptions about the country needs to be jettisoned.

Caricaturing North Korea

Caricatures of both government and society have been remarkably pervasive and persistent during the post-Cold War era in their shaping of 'common knowledge' about North Korea. Caricatures work because they contain an element of truth or perceived truth. They are persuasive because they ignore nuance, change and detail and portray a broad-brush picture in order to convey a simplistic message, often designed to support denigration of a particular target and avoid careful analysis. In the case of North Korea, the major caricatures provide accounts that are so oversimplified and distorted that they do not provide a helpful or accurate picture of the aspects of state or society they purport to describe. Caricature also provides the staple of racism and ethnic stereotyping and is dangerous in its dehumanisation of entire peoples by reducing them to a small number of allegedly shared characteristics.

The reasons for the development of caricature as the dominant prism though which to think about North Korea are manifold. For a start, political analysis of North Korea has been heavily shaped by military planners who are by nature cautious. Responsible military planners assume worst-case scenarios as the foundation for contingency planning. The problem, however, is when worst-case scenarios are used as a substitute for factual reporting. Another reason for the acceptance of claims about North Korea's supposed uniqueness and strangeness is an ignorance of Korean culture. Many of the issues considered culturally singular to North Korea are just as relevant to South Korea; including the strong sense of ethnic unity and ethnic nationalism.[3] South and North Koreans

---

[3] Gi-Wook Shin, *Ethnic Nationalism in Korea: Genealogy, Politics, and Legacy* (Stanford University Press, 2006).

are both taught, for example, that the Korean 'race' has an unbroken genealogy that can trace its origins to 'the dawn of human history'.[4]

Observers also sometimes fail to comprehend the politically significant and pervasive suspicion of Japan that to a greater or lesser extent informs the world view of North and South Koreans. North Korea cultivates an outright anti-Japanese mentality, which is not the case in the South. The sometimes still raw memories of colonialism mean, however, that both North and South Koreans remain sensitive to activities by Japan that could be interpreted as reflecting an absence of repentance for its colonial occupation of Korea in the early twentieth century or as signs of a potential resurgent and aggressive foreign policy.

Korean suspicions of Japanese intentions are mirrored in Japan by a swathe of domestic opinion where it is not uncommon to find views that portray Koreans in a racist manner.[5] Such racism finds a 'legitimate' outlet in the day-to-day vitriol in the mass media directed ostensibly at the North Korean government but which often comes close to caricaturing the entire North Korean people as inexplicable, to be feared, distrusted, even hated. Racism and prejudice thrive on stereotypes; the existence of race-based animosity thus provides another part of the explanation as to why the media mythology is so powerfully persistent.

Rigorous and careful evaluation of aspects of contemporary North Korean state, society and economy exists but these nuanced accounts have failed to make much of an impact on dominant global discourses and the popular global consciousness.[6] Unless they have a very specialist

---

[4] Foreign Languages Publishing House, *Korea Guidebook* (Pyongyang: Foreign Languages Publishing House, 1989), p. 26. The same source goes on to state that 'The racial characteristics of the Korean people have been formed over thousands of years from the Neolithic era to the ancient races and developed later. The ancient Koreans were formed into some races with kinship and united into the ancient races which became the ancestors of Koreans around the end of the primitive age' (p. 27). A South Korean historian argues something similar. 'The ethnic stock of these Neolithic men has continued unbroken to form one element of the later Korean race. It is believed that in the course of a long historical process these Neolithic people merged with one another and, together with new ethnic settlers of Korea's Bronze Age, eventually constituted Koreans of today.' See JinWung Kim, *A History of Korea: From 'Land of the Morning Calm' to States in Conflict* (Bloomington: Indiana University Press, 2012), p. 9

[5] Economic and Social Council, 'Report of the Special Rapporteur on Contemporary Forms of Racism, Racial Discrimination, Xenophobia and Related Intolerance; Doudou Diène, Addendum, Mission to Japan', in Commission on Human Rights, *Sixty-second Session Item 6 of the Provisional Agenda, E/CN.4/2006/16/Add.2* (Geneva: Economic and Social Council, 24 January 2006), available at http://web.archive.org/web/20061214115324/http://imadr.org/geneva/2006/G0610396.pdf, accessed 14 September 2013.

[6] Book-length treatments include Heonik Kwon and Byung-ho Chung, *North Korea: Beyond Charismatic Politics* (Lanham: Rowman and Littlefield Publishers, 2012); Patrick McEachern, *Inside the Red Box: North Korea's Post-Totalitarian Politics* (New York:

interest, most people do not have the time or the motivation to check sources and interrogate the assumptions of the things they read in the press. Most would not feel a need to do so as they might reasonably assume that the information given to them is reliable. They are not aware that many common knowledge assumptions of North Korea are based on surprisingly little evidence and are very often illogical and/or self-contradictory.

North Korea is a dangerous and irrational military power

North Korea is routinely portrayed as a militarily fearsome state that poses a serious military threat to its neighbours and to the world's only superpower, the United States. This assessment is based on the alleged military capacity, aggression and irrationality of the government and the threat of proliferation. These threats are exaggerated and they also shift focus away from the real military threats from North Korea that arise from geography and politics. The proximity of Pyongyang to Seoul means that any type of weaponry could be used to cause mass destruction. In 1995 in Rwanda in one of the most intense killing sprees in recent history, over half a million people were hacked to death by machetes in just ten days. The risk of war comes about, not because the Democratic People's Republic of Korea (DPRK) is inherently irrational but because the underlying conflict between North and South Korea remains unresolved.

Military capacity

North Korea's military spending absorbed a very large proportion of economic resources – at about 20 per cent of its gross national income of US$22.4 billion in 2009, yet compared to its adversaries, North Korea's military spending was derisory.[7] North Korea's prioritisation of

Columbia University Press, 2010); Narushige Michishita, *North Korea's Military-Diplomatic Campaigns, 1966–2008* (London: Routledge, 2010); Phillip H. Park (ed.), *The Dynamics of Change in North Korea: An Institutionalist Perspective* (Boulder, CO: Lynne Rienner Publishers, 2009); Sung Chul Yang, *The North and South Korean Political Systems: A Comparative Analysis*, revised edition (Elizabeth, NJ: Hollym, 1999).

[7] Defence spending figures from International Institute of Strategic Studies (IISS), *The Military Balance 2011* (London: Routledge, 2011), p. 249. GNI figures from Ministry of Defense, *2010 White Paper* (Seoul: Ministry of Defense, 2010), p. 341, available at www.nti.org/media/pdfs/2010WhitePaperAll_eng.pdf?_=1340662780, accessed 8 November 2014. The White Paper compares the defence spending of seventeen countries including Japan, China, Russia and the United States to that of South Korea but leaves out information about North Korea.

national resources to the military could not achieve the goal of military parity with South Korea given the huge disparity in economic capability between the two countries. North Korea's conventional weaponry and hardware is obsolescent, its military infrastructure decrepit and its armed forces hungry and disaffected. The consequence of North Korea's military expenditures was to substantially contribute to economic fragility. These structural military and economic weaknesses were the reason for the decision to build nuclear weapons; the intention was to use North Korea's limited resources to develop the ultimate deterrent against invasion or coercive regime change.[8]

Military analysts are taught that risk of conflict increases when a state increases its military capacity, even if that state does not indicate offensive intentions.[9] This is because other states become nervous about relative military weakness and in reaction increase their own military capacity. This cycle of defensive/offensive arms build-up is sometimes called the security dilemma of states or, more colloquially, arms racing. Military analysts were, therefore, concerned that North Korean governments allocated a high proportion of national resources to the military. North Korea's adversaries worried especially about the government's capacity to use advanced weaponry including nuclear weapons. The ballistic technology programme could potentially produce nuclear tipped missiles that could target all of East Asia and maybe in future the United States. North Korea's continuous efforts to increase military capacity therefore raised alarm bells for military analysts.

North Korea's potential nuclear capacity provided the core of its military threat from 2006 onwards when it conducted its first nuclear test but the Central Intelligence Agency (CIA), global intelligence agencies and academics differed over how many nuclear bombs the North Koreans possessed and how successful it was in engineering usable nuclear weapons. In 2011, the International Institute of Strategic Studies estimated that North Korea may have four to eight operational warheads, although it pointed out that 'North Korea's ability to produce a deliverable nuclear weapon remains in doubt'.[10] North Korea's military technology and nuclear capacity, however, remained insignificant compared to the level of sophistication and production capacity of the United States, which in 2011 possessed 2,200 operational nuclear warheads.

---

[8] Chung-in Moon and Sangkeun Lee, 'Military Spending and the Arms Race on the Korean Peninsula', *Asian Perspective*, Vol. 33, No. 4, 2009 pp. 69–99.
[9] For an introduction to various aspects of security analysis see Paul D. Williams (ed.), *Security Studies: An Introduction* (London: Routledge, 2008).
[10] IISS, *The Military Balance 2011*, p. 469.

The main military threat from North Korea comes from its low-tech but high-impact armaments.[11] The 'neutral' or 'demilitarised' zone dividing the territories of North and South Korea is heavily mined and militarised. North Korea has tens of thousands of artillery pieces dug in and facing Seoul on its border with South Korea. When North Korean negotiators have indulged in bravado by threatening to turn Seoul into a 'sea of fire' it is this conventional military hardware that makes that threat feasible. South Korean military planners take these threats seriously but their assessment of threat is tempered by the knowledge that this conventional hardware has not been systematically updated. The continuing economic crises of the last two decades imply that much of this equipment is probably in far from optimal condition.

In contrast to its adversaries, North Korea's scope and scale of military investment is pitifully small. It is nowhere near South Korean defence forces in terms of the quality and quantity of modern armaments. In 2009, North Korea's defence expenditures amounted to some US$4.38 billion. South Korea on its own outspent the DPRK on defence by a factor of nearly four to one.[12] When South Korean defence capability was combined with well-resourced Japanese and United States armed forces, the DPRK's military capacity was dwarfed.[13] In 2010, the United States and Japan had, respectively, defence budgets of $692.8 billion and $52.8 billion dollars, the first and fourth largest in the world.[14]

An aggressive and irrational military posture

The occasional statements from the wilder edges of the international media that North Korea was preparing to rain bombs down on Alaska can probably be discounted, as the government has never demonstrated an expansionist strategy outside of the peninsula. The more serious consideration is whether North Korea's arms build-up is for defensive purposes or composes part of a strategy of aggression, particularly directed against South Korea. North Korea argues that it is using its

---

[11] Soon-ho Lee, 'Military Transformation on the Korean Peninsula: Technology versus Geography', doctoral dissertation (Department of Politics and International Studies, The University of Hull, 2011), available at https://hydra.hull.ac.uk/catalog/hull:5360, accessed 15 September 2013.

[12] Moon and Lee, 'Military Spending and the Arms Race on the Korean Peninsula'.

[13] For an inventory of missile and other military capabilities of Japan, North Korea and South Korea see IISS, *The Military Balance 2011*, pp. 245–54.

[14] Ibid., p. 469.

military capability, specifically the nuclear capacity, to underpin a military doctrine focused on defence and deterrence, while critics have argued that North Korea's military strategy includes the aim of offensive operations against South Korea.

Much has been made of the North's alleged offensive military posture with its million-man army stationed close to the North–South border – only 30 miles away from Seoul. It is inconceivable, however, that North Korea would not have as much artillery as it can muster in this location, given that its capital, Pyongyang, is situated less than 100 miles from the border with the south. Numerous military analysts have pointed out that it is hard to think about where else these troops might be situated. To defend Pyongyang, North Korea's troops must be situated between Pyongyang and the North–South border, therefore, they are positioned within striking distance of Seoul. The same applies for the South Korean troops located between Seoul and the border; the defensive positioning of South Korean troops could equally be interpreted as constituting an offensive posture towards Pyongyang.

Another well-worn example of North Korea's alleged aggressive intent is its 'brinkmanship' in international diplomacy.[15] Brinkmanship is, apparently, the art of negotiating successfully from a weak hand while refusing to go along with the direction of the stronger partner in an adversarial relationship, in this case the United States. It is very difficult to discern what might be the difference between the notion of brinkmanship from what in less politicised terminology might be understood as the art and skill of classical diplomatic practice. Classical diplomacy is the ability to achieve agreements through non-military means with other states. Success in diplomacy is conventionally understood as giving little and gaining a lot. Labelling North Korean diplomats as engaging in 'brinkmanship' can look very much like a complaint by out-manoeuvred negotiators who cannot quite understand why North Korean diplomats should enjoy what they might consider ethically undeserved diplomatic success.

Nevertheless, the North Korean media and its spokespersons have made bizarre pronouncements that on occasion appear to threaten the first-use of nuclear weapons.[16] These statements appear, however, more designed to throw adversaries off balance than to display serious intent to

---

[15] Scott Snyder, *Negotiating on the Edge: North Korean Negotiating Behavior* (Washington, DC: United States Institute of Peace Press, 1999).

[16] Sang-Hun Choe, Jake Doherty, Kim Fararo, Rick Gladstone, Andrea Kannapell, Mark Landler, Bill Marsh and David E. Sanger, 'In Focus: North Korea's Nuclear Threats', *The New York Times*, updated 16 April 2013, available at www.nytimes.com/interactive/2013/04/12/world/asia/north-korea-questions.html?_r=0, accessed 15 September 2013.

start a nuclear war, as they do not coincide with North Korea's strategic aims. The North Korean government has always been careful to distinguish between the government of South Korea and its allegedly repressed citizens. The point of North Korean strategy is to bring South Korean citizens under the 'benevolent leadership' of the North Korean government. If the DPRK dropped a nuclear bomb on Seoul, most of its eleven million inhabitants would be killed and the radiation blowback would kill many North Korean citizens, including the majority of the serving military stationed near the border. The immediate reaction would be to unite the entire globe, including China and Russia, in a military response that could result in the annihilation of large parts of the North, including in all likelihood all of Pyongyang.

Foreign interlocutors who met with Kim Il Sung and Kim Jong Il as well as the officials that acted on their behalf stressed the strategic and personal rationality of North Korean negotiating partners.[17] In recent years, the overwhelming priority of North Korean governments has been regime survival; a priority that could not be served by all-out war. The more dangerous risk is from the potential breakdown of command and control systems within the military as disaffected and poverty-stricken soldiers seek ways to make money, perhaps by the freelance smuggling and selling of military supplies, including arms, while others seek to curry favour with their commanders by launching spontaneous initiatives that risk escalation into protracted inter-Korean conflict.

Proliferation

The large claims of North Korea as a major proliferator are problematic given the flimsy evidence base, the ambiguity of some of the data and press sources that rely heavily on unnamed, anonymous intelligence officials.[18] North Korea's involvement in arms proliferation is, however, most likely at the scientific level of exchange of technical knowledge given

[17] Michishita, *North Korea's Military-Diplomatic Campaigns*; Leon V. Sigal, *Disarming Strangers: Nuclear Diplomacy with North Korea* (Princeton University Press, 1998); Joel S. Wit, Daniel B. Poneman and Robert L. Gallucci, *Going Critical: The First North Korean Nuclear Crisis* (Washington, DC: Brookings Institution Press, 2005); Yoichi Funabashi, *The Peninsula Question: A Chronicle of the Second Korean Nuclear Crisis* (Washington, DC: Brookings Institution Press, 2007).
[18] Larry A. Niksch, *North Korea's Nuclear Weapons Development and Diplomacy* (Washington, DC: Congressional Research Service, 5 January 2010), available at www.fas.org/sgp/crs/nuke/RL33590.pdf, accessed 12 September 2013.

that North Korea's scientific expertise is a sellable commodity for a cash-strapped government.[19]

United States officials periodically expressed concern about the potential proliferation of weaponry by North Korea to non-governmental actors, including terrorists, although the administration of George Bush saw such little merit in these claims that in 2008 it took North Korea off the list of state sponsors of terrorism.[20] In 2010 the discussion was revived on the basis of intelligence reports that North Korea was allegedly training Hezbollah and providing assistance to the Iranian Revolutionary Guard and the Tamil Tigers, all of which were listed by United States legislation as terrorist groups.[21]

North Korea has tried to get around arms embargoes that were implemented by the United Nations after its 2006 nuclear test, most visibly in its attempt to import obsolescent Cuban light arms, spare parts of missiles and MIG fighter jets, which were seized off a North Korean ship in Panama in 2013. In a briefing to *The New York Times*, an official party to the seizure said of the equipment that 'We're talking old ... When this stuff was new, Castro was plotting revolutions.' [22] North Korea's attempted shipping of military goods to Syria in 2013 also involved some pretty low-level material: bullets, rifles and gas masks. [23] These high-profile seizures of North Korean shipping revealed a low-tech and almost pathetic capacity given that most other countries would have been sending these goods for scrap, not for trade. The extent of actual trade in armaments was also likely significantly curtailed in the 2000s, given the vigilance of port authorities when North Korean ships and aircraft enter their territory and the scale of their surveillance by United States military.[24]

[19] Ibid.
[20] United States Department of State, *Country Reports on Terrorism 2010* (Washington, DC: United States Department of State, Office of the Coordinator for Counterterrorism, August 2011), pp. 38–9, available at www.state.gov/documents/organization/170479.pdf, accessed 15 September 2013.
[21] Mark Manyin, *North Korea: Back on the Terrorism List?* (Washington, DC: Congressional Research Service, 29 June 2010), available at www.fas.org/sgp/crs/row/RL30613.pdf, accessed 15 September 2013.
[22] Rick Gladstone and David E. Sanger, 'Panama Seizes Korean Ship, and Sugar-Coated Arms Parts', *The New York Times*, 16 July 2013, available at www.nytimes.com/2013/07/17/world/americas/panama-seizes-north-korea-flagged-ship-for-weapons.html?pagewanted=all, accessed 15 September 2013.
[23] Chad O'Carroll, 'North Korean Cargo of Gas Masks and Arms en-route to Syria', *NK*NewsPro*, 27 August 2013, available at www.nknews.org/2013/08/north-korean-arms-shipment-intercepted-en-route-to-syria, accessed 15 September 2013.
[24] Hazel Smith, 'North Korean Shipping: A Potential for WMD Proliferation?', *Asia-Pacific Issues*, No. 87, February 2009.

North Korea starves its people

A common understanding underpinning global media reports is that the North Korean government starved its people as a matter of deliberate policy.[25] There are two variations on this theme, although they are often conflated. The first version argues that during the period of the famine North Korea deliberately allowed up to three million people to starve while it could have provided food for them.[26] The second variation on this media portrayal is a more general claim that North Korean governments deliberately starved the population as a matter of policy.[27]

Media portrayals of North Korean food policy during the famine years include 'common knowledge' claims that food could have been imported during this period but the government chose not to do so; that the government impeded the activities of international humanitarian organisations by preventing them from visiting the north-east of the country where the death toll and suffering was highest; that it stopped providing or allowing food into the north-east; and that it routinely diverted food given by international humanitarian organisations for the most vulnerable to groups who were less morally deserving, such as military personnel or 'elite' groups.[28]

The North Korean government is indeed responsible for the welfare of its population. North Korea is a poor country and the government's decision to spend scarce resources on the military can well be criticised as demonstrating an immoral set of priorities. The claims that the North

---

[25] Amnesty International, *Starving North Koreans Forced to Survive on Diet of Grass and Tree Bark* (London: Amnesty International, 2010), available at www.amnesty.org/en/news-and-updates/starving-north-koreans-forced-survive-diet-grass-and-tree-bark-2010-07-14, accessed 17 July 2013; Anthony Sharwood, 'Starved of Food, Starved of the Truth: How Kim Jong Un Suppresses his People', 9 April 2013, available at www.news.com.au/world-news/starved-of-food-starved-of-the-truth-how-kim-jong-un-suppresses-his-people/story-fndir2ev-1226616134393, accessed 17 July 2013; Harry Hawkins, 'Starving North Koreans are "Forced to Eat their Children"', *The Sun*, 28 January 2013, available at www.thesun.co.uk/sol/homepage/news/4765653/north-korean-parents-eating-their-children.html, accessed 17 July 2013.

[26] A typical statement in the 'quality' press is that 'perhaps 10 per cent of the population' – that is some 2.2 million people – were killed by famine in the 1990s. See Max Fisher, 'The Cannibals of North Korea', *The Washington Post*, 5 February 2013, available at www.washingtonpost.com/blogs/worldviews/wp/2013/02/05/the-cannibals-of-north-korea, accessed 13 September 2013.

[27] For discussion see Hazel Smith, 'Crimes Against Humanity? Unpacking the North Korean Human Rights Debate', in Christine Hong and Hazel Smith (eds.), *Critical Asian Studies, Reframing North Korean Human Rights*, Vol. 46, No. 1, March 2014, pp. 127–43.

[28] Hazel Smith, 'North Korea as the Wicked Witch of the East: Social Science as Fairy Tale', *Asia Policy*, No. 5, January 2008, pp. 197–203.

Korean government has a policy of starving its people, however, go beyond the allegation of inept policy-making and allege culpability and collusion such that, if proven, would indeed constitute a crime against humanity.[29]

The famine years

The scale of fatalities and the suffering of the millions more who suffered illness, ended up with chronic disabilities and lost loved ones in the famine years of the early and mid-1990s means that there is no need to exaggerate what is bad enough already. Credible research shows that North Korea lost up to a million of its population through malnutrition-related illness and starvation.[30]

The government certainly calculated that food imports from international donors provided fungibility; according to South Korean economists the government spent $105.63 million on the import of armaments between 1995 and 2000 as the population was facing the worst of the famine years.[31] This was at the time when North Korea's import (and export) trade had collapsed – according to the same South Korean economists – from $2.76 billion in 1990 to a low of $0.88 billion in 1998 – improving slightly to $1.41 billion in 2000.[32] In the context of a security-conscious leadership whose priority was regime survival, perhaps a major surprise was the relatively low level of arms imports. Imports continued to include chemicals, fuel, spare parts and fertiliser – much of which were as important as food as they provided necessary inputs for agricultural and industrial production. The wider argument that any alternative imports to food constituted evidence of moral

[29] Human Rights Council, 'Situation of Human Rights in the Democratic People's Republic of Korea', *Twenty-second Session, Agenda Item 4, Human Rights Situations that Require the Council's Attention* (Geneva: Human Rights Council, 9 April 2013); Human Rights Council, 'Report of the Special Rapporteur on the Situation of Human Rights in the Democratic People's Republic of Korea, Marzuki Darusman, A/HRC/22/57', in Human Rights Council, *Twenty-second Session, Agenda Item 4, Human Rights Situations that Require the Council's Attention* (Geneva: Human Rights Council, 1 February 2013).

[30] Suk Lee, 'Food Shortages and Economic Institutions in the Democratic People's Republic of Korea', doctoral dissertation (Department of Economics, University of Warwick, January 2003). See also Daniel Goodkind and Loraine West, 'The North Korean Famine and its Demographic Impact', *Population and Development Review*, Vol. 27, No. 2, June 2001 pp. 219–38; Daniel Goodkind, Loraine West and Peter Johnson, 'A Reassessment of Mortality in North Korea, 1993–2008', Annual Meeting of the Population Association of America, 31 March–2 April 2011, Washington, DC, 16 March 2011. For full discussion see Chapter 8

[31] Choong-Yong Ahn, *North Korea Development Report 2003/4* (Seoul: Korea Institute for International Economic Policy, 2003/4), p. 185.

[32] Ibid., p. 31.

depravity is somewhat facile, however, given the broad needs of a complex society that requires imports for heating, shelter and manufacturing and agriculture.

A widespread claim is that the north-eastern region, whose five million or so population suffered disproportionately, compared to the rest of the country in the famine years, was 'triaged' by the government to prevent it receiving food.[33] The claim was made that the government set up a 'quarantine' of the north-east to exclude the United Nations from the region prior to 1997.[34] The assumption was that because the World Food Programme had not led UN missions to the north-east in 1995 and 1996, and because shipments of humanitarian food aid to north-eastern ports did not start until July 1997, then the region was ignored or triaged by the government and the international aid organisations.

In fact, the United Nations World Health Organisation (WHO) visited the region in October 1995 at the government's instigation.[35] International aid organisations delivered aid to both northern and southern provinces, which included North Pyongan, North Hwanghae and the northern border province of Chagang province, in 1995 and 1996.[36] The World Food Programme delivered only relatively small amounts of food aid during the first two years of the emergency operation because its North Korean operations were, initially, not well-funded.[37] More of this limited aid did not go to the north-east because food aid was targeted at the nation's five million farming families. The 1995 hailstorms and

---

[33] The claim is so pervasive that even those who do not believe it and cannot find any evidence for it find themselves having to refute it. See for example John Feffer, 'The Right to Food: North Korea and the Politics of Famine and Human Rights', in Kie-Duck Park and Sang-Jin Han, *Human Rights in North Korea* (Seoul: The Sejong Institute, 2007), pp. 88–91.

[34] Andrew S. Natsios, *The Great North Korean Famine: Famine, Politics and Foreign Policy* (Washington, DC: United States Institute of Peace Press, 2001), p. 109.

[35] The WHO visited Chagang province in the far north of the country, South Hamgyong in the north-east and North Hwanghae in the south in October 1995. For visit details see Rebecca Norton and Jane Wallace, *Refugee Nutrition Information System (RNIS), No. 22 – Supplement – Report on the Nutrition Situation in the Democratic People's Republic of Korea* (Geneva: United Nations Administrative Committee on Coordination Sub-Committee on Nutrition, 1997), Table 1, available at www.unsystem.org/scn/archives/rnis22sup_nkorea/s5115e.10.htm#Js5115e.10, accessed 8 November 2014.

[36] FAO, *Special Alert No. 267, Democratic People's Republic of Korea* (Rome, 16 May 1996), available at www.fao.org/docrep/004/w1302e/w1302e00.htm, accessed 15 September 2013.

[37] The Food and Agriculture Organisation reported that only 53,000 tonnes of food aid was delivered in the year 1996/7 [compared with one million tonnes in the year 2000/1]. FAO/WFP, *Crop and Food Supply Assessment Mission to the Democratic People's Republic of Korea, Special Alert, No. 275* (Rome: FAO/WFP, 3 June 1997).

the July 1996 rains severely damaged the nation's grain crops during the growing season. The objective was therefore to give farmers the means with which to survive and to rebuild national food supplies. After 1998, the World Food Programme was much better funded and established nationwide operations. The government and the World Food Programme then prioritised the largely non-farming north-eastern provinces of North Hamgyong, South Hamgyong, Ryanggang and Kangwon, which were targeted for international food assistance.[38]

The government's food allocation priorities in the 1990s were and are contestable but there is little evidence to show malevolence such that decisions were taken to starve whole geographical areas.[39] Another reason that a decision to 'triage' the north-east would have been unlikely is that the north-eastern provinces had provided much of Kim Il Sung's support base. The region was home to what had been a relatively privileged industrial working class and Party chiefs from North Hamgyong and South Hamgyong remained disproportionately powerful within the political system.[40]

A recurrent claim is that international food aid was diverted from the deserving poor to the undeserving such as the military and the 'elites'. Much of this argument is specious and based on ignorance of food availability, food aid allocation and distribution mechanisms in the DPRK and in other countries. The DPRK continued to grow around 80 per cent of its total food requirements throughout even the worst famine years. The military constituted one million of the twenty-three million population in the 1990s and therefore did not need 'diverted' international aid as it was stated government policy to feed the army from domestic food production.

It is very unlikely that the Kim family or the senior figures in government would need to call on World Food Programme bulk cereals to supplement their daily diet. This top level of North Korean society would no more think of relying on food aid as the foundation for their diet than any member of the elite in the United States or Europe. The Kim family sent their children to be educated in Switzerland and Moscow and they

[38] Hazel Smith, *Hungry for Peace: International Security, Humanitarian Assistance and Social Change in North Korea* (Washington, DC: United States Institute of Peace Press, 2005).
[39] Haggard and Noland resurrect these claims in 2007 while also stating that the evidence supporting such claims is 'circumstantial'. The argument is that because food aid was delivered to west coast ports the government was 'wilfully ignoring' distress in the north-east. Stephan Haggard and Marcus Noland, *Famine in North Korea: Markets, Aid and Reform* (New York: Columbia University Press, 2007), pp. 64–5.
[40] Yang, *The North and South Korean Political Systems*.

had more than sufficient funds in their bank accounts to buy high-quality food from home and abroad.

The more rational side of the 'diversion' argument is that food sent through international aid organisations was not always received by those to whom it was allocated. These were those who needed it the most – young children and pregnant and nursing women.

The food aid system in North Korea worked on the basis that the central government based in Pyongyang decided allocation priorities for the whole country, but the county-level administrations were responsible for distributing food and international assistance. It is conceivable that when food aid arrived in county warehouses that county officials would decide on different priorities for food aid allocation than those decided by the central government officials. Counties could well have decided that 'key workers' such as coal miners or power workers should receive food aid rather than pregnant and nursing women. It is also conceivable that rice aid might have been sold in markets – by food aid recipients or by county officials.

Food aid was mainly comprised of bulk grains, including wheat, wheat flour and rice. Rice was the preferred commodity as it was versatile, nutritious and relatively easy to store and cook. Rice traded at a higher price than other grains because of these attributes, so trading rice on the market could be economically rational for food aid recipient families. Rice prices could be some four times the price of the equivalent calorific value of corn or millet, so rice aid that was sold privately could return four times as much food, which could then be shared with the family or exchanged for food and other basic necessities. County officials could likewise sell the imported rice aid and buy millet, potatoes or the inferior local rice for local distribution and still have funds left for other projects.

Food aid in North Korea became 'monetised'. In other countries, monetisation of aid is very often supported by aid organisations and donors as it helps to ensure that the food ration gets to the targeted beneficiary without destroying local market mechanisms through the influx of free commodities. Food aid is delivered to central government which then sells the food to beneficiaries in order to raise funds for projects that might support food security objectives, for instance the redevelopment of farms or health facilities. The difference in the DPRK was that monetisation was not a formally agreed practice between international organisations and government, which ignored the marketisation of the economy around them and worked on the basis that there were no alternative channels for grain distribution other than the public distribution system. That *de facto* monetisation of aid constituted a breach of agreements between government and foreign donors is one thing. That these practices could be classed as evidence of crimes against humanity is somewhat of a stretch.

Starvation as a government policy

The broader claim that the North Korean government starves its population as a matter of policy does not normally reference the pre-famine years, possibly because to include this period might appear illogical. Prior to the famine, the DPRK governments had succeeded in moving the population away from the condition of potential starvation faced by most of the population all of the time for much of Korean history. It had implemented policies that had allowed the population to double in numbers between 1946 and 1993, from 9 million to 21 million.[41] By the end of the 1980s life expectancy for that massively increased population had doubled from just 38 years in 1936–1940 to a reported life expectancy of 74 years in 1986.[42] The World Bank reported a figure of 68 years in 1990 and data derived from the first North Korean census showed life expectancy at 73 in 1993.[43] Government policies must have been to feed rather than starve the population for those achievements to have been made.

The claim that the government was starving its population in the post-famine years would be more persuasive if the nutritional and health status of children had permanently worsened or even stayed static. In fact the wasting rate – a sign of acute malnutrition – decreased from the post-famine high of 15.6 per cent in 1998 to 5 per cent by 2012 – only slightly worse than the average for East Asia at 4 per cent.[44] The stunting

---

[41] On population numbers see Lee, 'Food Shortages and Economic Institutions in the Democratic People's Republic of Korea', pp. 8–9.

[42] Hwan Ju Pang, *Korean Review* (Pyongyang: Foreign Languages Publishing House, 1987), p. 188. A life expectancy for all Koreans at only 37 years between 1925 to 1930 during the colonial period is reported in Tai-Hwan Kwon, 'Population Change and Development in Korea', *The Asia Society*, available at http://asiasociety.org/countries/population-change-and-development-korea, accessed 30 May 2014.

[43] Pang, *Korean Review*, p. 188; The World Bank, 'Life Expectancy at Birth', available at http://data.worldbank.org/indicator/SP.DYN.LE00.IN/countries/KP?page=5&order=wbapi_data_value_2009%20wbapi_data_value%20wbapi_data_value-first&sort=asc&display=default, accessed 30 May 2014; Central Bureau of Statistics, '2008 Census of Population of DPRK: Key Findings', available at www.unfpa.org/webdav/site/global/shared/documents/news/2010/dprk08_censuskeyfinds.pdf, accessed 22 June 2014.

[44] Central Bureau of Statistics, *Democratic People's Republic of Korea Preliminary Report of the National Nutrition Survey, October 2012* (Pyongyang: Central Bureau of Statistics, 2012); UNICEF, *The State of the World's Children 2013: Children with Disabilities* (Geneva: UNICEF, 2013), pp. 104–7, available at www.unicef.org/sowc2013/files/SWCR2013_ENG_Lo_res_24_Apr_2013.pdf, accessed 20 April 2014.

rate – an indicator of chronic malnutrition – stood at 32 per cent in 2012, down from 62 per cent in 1998.[45] The United Nations World Food Programme and the United Nations Children's Fund (UNICEF) endorsed the findings of the 2012 nutrition survey that the food situation 'is *not* critical and does *not* suggest emergency operations'.[46]

In the post-famine years, life expectancy fell from 73 years to 69 years, according to the 2008 census, although the World Bank shows life expectancy at 70 in 2012.[47] The World Bank data give North Koreans the same life expectancy as citizens of the Russian Federation and show that in 2012 life expectancy in the DPRK was better than 69 other counties in the world and worse than 128 others. In the post-famine years, North Korean government policies certainly contributed to these falls in life expectancy but the causation of these problems was similar to that of other poor countries: skyrocketing international food prices and an underdeveloped economy.

One consequence of overgeneralisation is the lack of focus on what should be the key areas of concern regarding government food policy. Media accounts that the estimated 150,000 to 200,000 prisoners are routinely being denied food or having food allocations restricted as part of a policy of brutalisation remain of serious concern.[48] These reports are founded on the testimony of individuals who were incarcerated or employed as prison warders, and need to be treated with respect on humanitarian grounds.[49] No observer would doubt that North Korean prisons would be a terrible place but the opacity of the system has never permitted independent scrutiny of the conditions of those incarcerated in North Korea's prisons.

---

[45] EU, UNICEF and WFP in partnership with the Government of DPRK, *Nutrition Survey* (Rome/Pyongyang: WFP, 1998); UNICEF, *The State of the World's Children 2013*, p. 104.

[46] Central Bureau of Statistics, *Preliminary Report of the National Nutrition Survey October 2012*, p. 2; emphasis added.

[47] Central Bureau of Statistics, '2008 Census of Population of DPRK'; The World Bank, 'Life Expectancy at Birth'.

[48] Human Rights Council, 'Report of the Special Rapporteur on the Situation of Human Rights in the Democratic People's Republic of Korea, Marzuki Darusman, A/HRC/22/57', in Human Rights Council, *Twenty-second Session, Agenda Item 4, Human Rights Situations that Require the Council's Attention* (Geneva: Human Rights Council, 1 February 2013); Amnesty International, *North Korea: New Satellite Images show Blurring of Political Prison Camp and Villages in North Korea* (London: Amnesty International, 2013), available at www.amnesty.org/en/news/north-korea-new-images-show-blurring-prison-camps-and-villages-2013-03-07, accessed 27 July 2013.

[49] David Hawk, *The Hidden Gulag: Exposing North Korea's Prison Camps: Prisoners' Testimonies and Satellite Photographs* (Washington, DC: US Committee for Human Rights in North Korea, 2003). See also the annual White Papers on Human Rights in North Korea published by the Seoul-based Korea Institute for National Unification (KINU).

The government's refusal to allow independent scrutiny of its prisons means that the extent to which conditions in North Korean prisons and detention centres are different from those in other jurisdictions remains unknown. The lack of transparency of North Korea's penal system provides a huge cause for concern as the accusations of prisoners being denied enough food to survive are logically founded. The government conceives of the duty of all adults, including prisoners, to work and at the same time the government has not provided adequate rations to all the population since the famine years. In the absence of supplementary food sources, which are obtained by the non-prisoner population through market means, those incarcerated will continue to be some of the worst off in the country in terms of food provision. It is very plausible that prisoners, especially those incarcerated for political dissidence, are supplied with such inadequate rations that they risk death through starvation and disease on a daily basis.

Food availability for prisoners is a good example of where independent verification cannot be obtained yet where claims have a very plausible foundation. The available data does not, however, support claims that government policies are causative of deliberate violations of the right to food in terms of the overall population. In fact, if food security outcomes were used as a benchmark, one would have to argue that government policies must have contributed to improvements in the nutritional status of children over the past fifteen years. International food aid has not been of sufficient quantity or delivered in a regular enough fashion to make more than a marginal difference.

The poor nutritional status of the general population of North Korean children and women (there are few nutritional surveys of men) is sometimes cited as 'proof' that the DPRK government committed crimes against humanity. In comparison to India and Indonesia, where the wasting rate was 20 per cent and 13 per cent respectively in 2012, and the stunting rate a massive 48 per cent in India and 36 per cent in Indonesia, North Korea's child malnutrition figures were 'of "medium" public health significance according to WHO standards'.[50] Were the argument that North Korea was starving its population to hold, one would also have to argue that the democratic governments of India and Indonesia are habitually and serially committing crimes against humanity, an argument with which few would be comfortable.

---

[50] UNICEF, *The State of the World's Children 2013*, p. 105; Quote from Central Bureau of Statistics, *Preliminary Report of the National Nutrition Survey October 2012*, p. 44.

North Korea is a criminal state

North Korea is, allegedly, a criminal state.[51] It is criminal, firstly, because North Korean state representatives systematically abuse diplomatic immunity to smuggle counterfeit currency, narcotics, counterfeit cigarettes, endangered species and other illicit goods.[52] Secondly, state-owned enterprises manufacture counterfeit currency, counterfeit cigarettes and narcotics for sale abroad. Thirdly, this nefarious activity is directed by the North Korean leadership for personal pecuniary benefit. These criminal acts, it is argued, should be understood as state-sponsored as they are led by the head of the state and are managed by a shadowy Party organisation called 'Bureau 39', which in the context of the tight state–Party–governmental nexus in North Korea should be considered as an organ of the state.[53] Allegations about state criminality are confident, unqualified and, apparently, authoritative.

Most claims about North Korean criminality attempt to show some form of evidential record. The problem is that the evidentiary record is weak. United States government and international media reports, and even 'academic' analyses, derive from a small number of United States government publications that are in turn largely founded on unsubstantiated allegations from defectors and unnamed US officials, citations from global media and circular references to other government reports.[54]

---

[51] A fairly representative media article, designed for an 'informed public', is David Rose, 'North Korea's Dollar Store', *Vanity Fair*, 5 August 2009, available at www.vanityfair.com/politics/features/2009/09/office-39-200909, accessed 15 September 2013.

[52] Perhaps the most cited 'analysis' of North Korean criminality is an undergraduate dissertation which claims to collate all empirical 'sources' about North Korean criminality. These sources, however, turn out to be far from reliable; all are uncorroborated by independent evidence and cannot be checked for veracity. The dissertation for example lists fourteen 'incidents of North Korean involvement in counterfeiting' in an appendix. On investigation, none of the sources listed can be verified. See Sheena E. Chestnut, 'The "Soprano State"? North Korean Involvement in Criminal Activity and Implications for International Security', undergraduate dissertation, mimeo (Stanford University, 2005), pp. 144–5. A similar 'analysis' based on citations that turn out to be third- or fourth-hand newspaper reports, some of which have only the most tenuous relationship to the claims that they are supposed to support, is Paul Rexton Kan, Bruce E. Bechtol, Jr. and Robert M. Collins, *Criminal Sovereignty: Understanding North Korea's Illicit International Activities* (Carlisle, PA: US Army War College, 2010), available at www.strategicstudiesinstitute.army.mil/pdffiles/pub975.pdf, accessed 2 November 2014.

[53] Ibid.

[54] Perl (2005), for instance, is quoted as a main source by Chestnut (2005). Perl and Nanto (2006) then read back Chestnut's list of alleged criminal incidents involving the DPRK (derived largely from Perl 2005) as substantiation for the 2005 claims. See Raphael S. Perl, *Drug Trafficking and North Korea: Issue for US Policy* (Washington, DC: Congressional Research Service, 2005), available at http://digital.library.unt.edu/ark:/

The major source in the public arena for alleged DPRK narcotics production and smuggling is an unverified list of incidents from the Intelligence Section of the United States Drug Enforcement Agency, which was appended to a 1999 House of Representatives report to Congress.[55] This list, along with unsubstantiated press reports, is the only evidence provided in the influential Congressional Research Service reports on 'Drug trafficking and North Korea', published in 2003 and updated in 2005 and 2007.[56]

US government reports sometimes acknowledge the tentative nature of the evidence. Tucked away in the middle of a long footnote to the major United States official publication on North Korea's alleged drug trafficking is the statement: 'Given that drug trafficking is by very nature a clandestine activity and that North Korea is a closed society, any overall estimates of DPRK income from illicit drug sources are based on fragmented data and are speculative at best ... Clearly such data should be considered a "far cry" from anything that might be remotely considered as evidence in a US court of law.'[57]

North Korean production and trading of counterfeit United States dollars if demonstrated would provide a *casus belli* because if successful these activities could undermine national and international confidence in the United States currency. The reliability of counterfeiting claims is problematic, however, partly because credible international investigators have found little or no evidence of such activity.[58] There is also evidence of the deliberate dissemination of official disinformation: identical

67531/metacrs6479, accessed 14 December 2012; Raphael Perl and Dick Nanto, *North Korean Counterfeiting of US Currency* (Washington, DC: Congressional Research Service, 2006), available at www.nkeconwatch.com/nk-uploads/2006-3-22-north-korea-counterfeiting-us-currency.pdf, accessed 14 December 2012; Chestnut, 'The "Soprano State"?', pp. 144–5.

[55] North Korea Advisory Group, *Report to The Speaker, US House of Representatives* (Washington, DC: House of Representatives, 1999), available at www.fas.org/nuke/guide/dprk/nkag-report.htm, accessed 8 November 2014.

[56] There is one base report from the CRS which was reissued with minor modifications. See Raphael S. Perl, *Drug Trafficking and North Korea: Issues for US Policy* (Washington, DC: Congressional Research Service, 2003), available at http://fpc.state.gov/documents/organization/27529.pdf, accessed 14 December 2012; *Drug Trafficking and North Korea*, 2003; *Drug Trafficking and North Korea: Issues for US Policy* (Washington, DC: Congressional Research Service, 2007), available at www://fas.org/sgp/crs/row/RL32167. pdf, accessed 14 December 2014.

[57] Perl, *Drug Trafficking and North Korea*, 2007.

[58] For expert analysis that is sceptical of claims about North Korean counterfeiting of the US dollar and suggests that the CIA is printing the counterfeit dollars in question, see former foreign (business) correspondent for the respected *Frankfurter Allgemeine Zeitung* (*FAZ*), Klaus Bender, 'The Mystery of the Supernotes', 11 January 2007, reproduced on the website of the Düsseldorfer Instituts für Außen-und Sicherheitspolitik (DIAS), available at www.dias-online.org/65.0.html, accessed 14 December 2012.

claims, couched in more or less identical language, given in identical fora, were previously made about Iran (and Syria).[59]

Perhaps surprisingly, given the vehemence and 'taken-for-granted' assumption of North Korean state criminality, there are few international court cases where North Korean nationals have been charged and found guilty of producing counterfeit goods or smuggling. The alleged involvement of North Korean crew members in smuggling heroin is substantiated in official United States publications by reference to the 2003 seizure of the North Korean vessel the *Pong Su*, despite the fact that the North Korean crew were acquitted of involvement by an Australian jury in 2006.[60] The Panama case is much more concrete and involves the arrest and charging of the captain, the first officer and the political officer for breaking a United Nations arms embargo.[61] Nevertheless cases involving diplomats are few, partly because the Vienna Conventions give immunity from prosecution to diplomats; nevertheless press reports indicate that North Korean diplomats have been deported for suspected criminal activity.[62] North Korean officials would, however, be far from unique in having abused diplomatic immunity for profit. It is not uncommon for diplomats from poor and rich countries, including for example South Korea, to exploit postings abroad to enhance income.[63] The question as to the level of state involvement in such activity is again more of an open question.

Missing the point

The caricature of an omniscient state guided by a Leader sitting in an office in central Pyongyang planning on a day-to-day basis how to

[59] Kenneth R. Timmerman, 'Iran and the Supernotes', Testimony on S.277 before Congressman Spencer Bachus Chairman, Subcommittee on General Oversight and Investigations of the Committee on Banking and Financial Services, 27 February 1996, reproduced on www.iran.org/tib/krt/960227sbc.htm, accessed 8 November 2014. See also Nick Rufford, 'Iran Linked to Flood of Fake Dollars', *Sunday Times*, 17 July 1995, p. 18.

[60] Perl, *Drug Trafficking and North Korea*.

[61] BBC News, 'N Korean Ship Seized with Cuban Weapons Returns to Cuba', 15 February 2014, available at www.bbc.co.uk/news/world-latin-america-26210187, accessed 30 May 2014.

[62] Andrei Lankov, 'Narco-Capitalism Grips North Korea', *Asia Times*, 18 March 2011, available at www.atimes.com/atimes/Korea/MC18Dg02.html, accessed 13 September 2013.

[63] Kelvin S-H. Peh, 'Wildlife Protection: Seize Diplomats Smuggling Ivory', *Nature*, Vol. 500, 15 August 2013, p. 276; Christine M. Nelson, '"Opening" Pandora's Box: The Status of the Diplomatic Bag in International Relations', *Fordham International Law Journal*, Vol. 12, Issue 3, 1988, pp. 494–520.

manoeuvre 24 million people to commit criminal activity for his sole benefit misses the point. At least since the onset of marketisation in the 1990s, and probably from way before that, there *is* evidence of DPRK citizens engaging in licit and illicit activity as a means to survive and prosper, but this is *because* the central state could not provide or deliver economically and *in spite of* the state's efforts to control such activity. Thus, and yet again, the cartoon picture obscures important changes in North Korean society and therefore handicaps understanding of their political consequences.

North Koreans are different from you and me

Perhaps the most egregious myth is that North Koreans are ignorant of the world outside North Korea and believe everything the government tells them.[64] The implicit and sometimes explicit assumption is that North Koreans are educationally backward and lack sophisticated conceptual lenses to understand that world. Visual images of public behaviour at events such as the funeral of Kim Jong Il in December 2011 are presented as evidence that North Koreans are 'brainwashed', bizarre and inexplicable.[65]

Hermetic isolation

North Koreans were indeed subject to a relentless socialisation campaign that glorified the exploits of the Kim family and inflicted sanctions, including penal sanctions, on those who criticised the ruling family. Yet despite the best efforts of the North Korean government, the picture of North Korea as an absolutely hermetic society was never wholly true and is far from the truth today. North Koreans who worked and studied abroad, including diplomats and students, had access to alternative sources of information even during the days when the state was much better able to enforce its policies than it is today. Today access to non-governmentally supplied information is far from being the sole prerogative of privileged Party members. The claim of lack of knowledge about the outside world confuses government policy with actual practice in the increasingly marketised North Korean society.

[64] Kwon and Chung's work serves to provide a devastating critique of these rather stupid assumptions. See Heonik Kwon and Byung-ho Chung, *North Korea: Beyond Charismatic Politics* (Lanham: Rowman and Littlefield Publishers, 2012).
[65] Kathleen Taylor, 'Has Kim Jong-Il Brainwashed North Koreans?', *The Guardian*, 20 December 2011, available at www.theguardian.com/commentisfree/2011/dec/20/kim-jong-il-brainwashed-north-koreans, accessed 13 September 2013.

The North Korean government still works hard to prevent the free flow of information into the country. Students studying in Pyongyang have access to the major state library in Pyongyang and the university library, which contain foreign books and films, but are only permitted to access these resources if they can demonstrate a 'need' to do so. The government attempts to control telephone and postal communication with the outside world. Access to the World Wide Web is limited to those working in relevant occupations and there is no nationwide official access to foreign books and other media. A small number of students study abroad – about 500 were studying in Asia and Europe in 2002.[66] The Universities of Warwick and Cambridge in the UK have hosted North Korean students, although Chinese universities provide a more common home for North Koreans studying abroad; in 2012, ninety-six North Koran students were studying at China's Northeastern University alone.[67]

Since the 1990s official channels of information have been supplemented by unofficial information networks and sources of information that are readily available to vast swathes of North Korean society. Chinese traders and local trading networks have provided a conduit for non-state sanctioned information for nearly a quarter of a century. Many Chinese traders and visitors are of Korean ethnicity and can communicate with North Koreans in their own language. Three of North Korea's north-eastern provinces – Chagang, Ryanggang and North Hamgyong – border the Chinese prefecture of Yanbian, which is populated by ethnic Koreans of Chinese nationality.[68] The language spoken by North Koreans is familiar to Yanbian ethnic Koreans and some North Koreans also have relatives in this Korean-speaking area of China with whom they

---

[66] DPRK Government, 'Replies by the Government of the Democratic People's Republic of Korea to the List of Issues: Democratic People's Republic of Korea. 04/09/2003', *Committee on Economic, Social and Cultural Rights, Thirty-first Session Item 6 of the Provisional Agenda* (Geneva: Office of the High Commissioner for Human Rights, 10–28 November 2003), available at www.bayefsky.com/issuesresp/rokorea_hr_cescr_none_2003_1.pdf, accessed 3 November 2014.

[67] I organised the DPRK exchange with the University of Warwick that took place between 1998 and 2002 and was funded by the UK Foreign Office. DPRK students came to the UK to study for non-degree courses and UK academics visited the DPRK to teach workshops on international economics. See also *China Daily*, 'DPRK Students get in Sync with Technology', 14 July 2012, available at http://news.xinhuanet.com/english/culture/2012-07/14/c_131715635.htm, accessed 30 May 2014.

[68] Hazel Smith, 'Asymmetric Nuisance Value: The Border in China–Democratic People's Republic of Korea Relations', in Timothy Hildebrandt (ed.), *Uneasy Allies: Fifty Years of China–North Korea Relations* (Washington, DC: Woodrow Wilson Center, Asia Program Special Report, September 2003), pp. 18–25; Hazel Smith, 'North Koreans in China: Sorting Fact from Fiction', in Tsuneo Akaha and Anna Vassilieva (eds.), *Crossing National Borders: Human Migration Issues in Northeast Asia* (Tokyo: United Nations Press, 2005), pp. 165–90.

communicate through brokers who carry letters backwards and forwards and/or provide access to mobile phones that can make international calls, for a price.[69] Access to foreign media, including South Korean DVDs and CDs, is straightforward and these goods are traded throughout the country.[70] The five million of the population living in the urban northeast can communicate with relatives or acquaintances in China and South Korea through Chinese telephony networks that can be accessed in border areas.

Pyongyang's three million population come into contact with foreigners in the service sector – hotels, shops, bars – and workplaces where foreigners work side by side with North Koreans. Outside Pyongyang, the port towns of Nampo, Chongjin and Rajin are permanently host to foreigners, as have been the southern tourist development zone of Kumgangsan and the South Korea-sponsored free-trade zone of Kaesong. Short-term visitors are carefully 'minded' by accompanying North Korean officials. Long-term residents have more freedom because they are permitted to obtain North Korean driving licences, learn Korean and operate on a daily basis without permanent oversight. Over a million South Koreans visited the DPRK between 2002 and 2012.[71] South Korean visitors have been conduits of information, simply by virtue of the common language that facilitates conversation unimpeded by official interpretation.

North Koreans are anything but ignorant. They are an educated people with almost universal literacy. Despite economic deterioration, school enrolment – for girls and boys – also remains near universal.[72] About 35 per cent of high school graduates went on to receive university education in 2002. The tertiary sector, which includes universities and a

[69] The Korean language spoken in Yanbian is influenced by North Korean and by South Korean dialects. For discussion see Wenhua Jin, 'Sounds of Chinese Korean: A Variationist Approach', doctoral dissertation (University of Texas at Arlington, May 2008).

[70] Woo Young Lee and Jungmin Seo, '"Cultural Pollution" from the South?', in Kyung-Ae Park and Scott Snyder (eds.), *North Korea in Transition: Politics, Economy and Society* (Lanham: Rowman and Littlefield, 2013), pp. 195–207.

[71] The Institute for Far Eastern Studies, *A Review of the Last Five Years of People-to-People Exchanges and Inter-Korean Economic Cooperation under the Lee Myung-bak Government* (Seoul: The Institute for Far Eastern Studies, 23 January 2013), available at http://ifes. kyungnam.ac.kr/eng/FRM/FRM_0101V.aspx?code=FRM130123_0001, accessed 13 September 2013.

[72] DPRK Government, 'Second Periodic Reports of States Parties due in 1997: Democratic People's Republic of Korea, 05/11/2003, CRC/C/65/Add.24 (State Party Report)', in *Committee on the Rights of the Child, Consideration of Reports Submitted by States Parties under Article 44 of the Convention* (Geneva: Office of the High Commissioner for Human Rights, 5 November 2003), available at www.refworld.org/pdfid/403a10a44. pdf, accessed 3 November 2014.

vast array of vocational colleges, has turned out highly educated scientists, as evidenced most visibly by the development of advanced weaponry technology and engineering.[73] The skill sets manifested in different parts of the economy show a high level of creativity and problem solving given that resourcefulness was required to compensate for the absence of large capital resources and sophisticated technological devices

External impressions of North Koreans derive partly from the skewing of domestic and foreign broadcasting. The television footage of weeping crowds after Kim Jong Il's death in 2011 was not balanced by visual images of the millions more North Koreans who did not stop all their activities and rush onto the streets to engage in public mourning. Such images would have shown that almost all North Koreans continued about their daily business on the day they heard about Kim Jong Il's death.[74] Neither did the images of weeping at the funeral ceremonies necessarily demonstrate irrationality: a show of emotion may have been a question of prudent personal politics. For the rest of the population it was not a question of being brainwashed; some of the emotion was undoubtedly real even if some of the tears were clearly orchestrated.

North Koreans were brought up to revere the Kim family as the pivot of the state and society but this does not mean that North Koreans lost their critical faculties. For North Koreans, however much the current leadership was discredited by its failure to provide decent living conditions, the Kim leadership also represented an independent Korean state, which their parents and grandparents built more or less from scratch after the suffering of the Japanese colonial period and the Korean War. Like most people, North Koreans could hold different opinions at once for different reasons.

A balanced analysis might also mention that the public ceremonies were not very different from funerals elsewhere of Heads of State, which are designed to emphasise the solemnity of the occasion and a sense of collective identity. This is so even in democratic countries. Visual images of Churchill's funeral in the UK in 1965 belie the widespread antagonism towards him that caused him to lose the first post-war election in 1945 to a radical Labour Party. It is also not exceptional in Asia for a family to provide a focus for nation-building and national cohesion. In Thailand, where it is a criminal offence to criticise the royal family, the monarchy

---

[73] The Institute for Far Eastern Studies, *North Korea to Become Strong in Science and Technology by Year 2022* (Seoul: The Institute for Far Eastern Studies, 21 December 2012), available at http://ifes.kyungnam.ac.kr/eng/FRM/FRM_0101V.aspx?code=FRM 121221_0001, accessed 13 September 2013.

[74] Personal communication with international official in Pyongyang by telephone, 18 December 2011.

assumes a position in society and in law that is somewhat similar to the Kim family in the DPRK. In Japan the Emperor also assumes a position in the society that is generally accepted as beyond criticism by the press and the populace. In the United Kingdom the millions that came out on the street after Princess Diana's death in 1997, and the millions more that celebrated the Queen's Diamond Jubilee in 2012, demonstrate the deep emotional attachment that very wide sectors of society can share with those they see as representing the historical and cultural aspects of national identity.

Jettisoning the caricatures

Such is the power of the global clichés that these impoverished understandings dominate global thinking about North Korea. The impression is of a society of 24 million human beings – more or less the same size of population as Australia – as frozen in aspic. The assumption that North Korea is a homogeneous monolithic political entity rules out divisions within elites; between society and government; and within the society by fiat. A monolithic state by definition does not have divisions and an unchanging state and society does not change. These caricatures need to be jettisoned. North Korea, like every country in the world, is idiosyncratic, but it is not inexplicable. As with any other society, a useful start can be made by thinking about how history has shaped culture and society.

2   National identity

Ethnically based cultural conceptions of what it is to be Korean constituted the primary identity marker of the North Korean population in the
Kim Il Sungist period and the era of military-first politics.[1] These cultural
conceptions of national identity were partly a product of historical consciousness in the population and partly a result of the relentless promotion
by North Korean governments of ethnic identity as fundamental to
Korean political identity. North Korean governments promoted the
development of revolutionary consciousness as a normatively appropriate
aim for individuals but these ideas of what constituted the appropriate way
of life for individuals were justified through and subordinated to ethnic
conceptions of national identity.

North Korea shared with South Korea an understanding of Korean
national identity. This was underpinned by a distinctive ethnic identity
arising from a unique and special cultural patrimony constituted by a

---

[1] This chapter is not primarily a work of history. Its aim is to tell the story of what history
signifies for North Koreans in terms of their sense of national identity. It draws therefore
on synthetic historical texts, seminal historical accounts and North Korean historical
narratives. They include Carter J. Eckert, Ki-bail Lee, Young Ick Lew, Michael
Robinson and Edward Wagner, *Korea Old and New: A History* (Cambridge, MA: Korea
Institute, Harvard University/Ilchokak, 1990); Henry H. Em, *The Great Enterprise:
Sovereignty and Historiography in Modern Korea* (Durham: Duke University Press, 2013);
Kyung Moon Hwang, *Beyond Birth: Social Status in the Emergence of Modern Korea*
(Cambridge, MA: Harvard University Asia Center, 2004); Jin Wung Kim, *A History of
Korea: From 'Land of the Morning Calm' to States in Conflict* (Bloomington: Indiana
University Press, 2012); John H. Koo and Andrew Nahm (eds.), *An Introduction to
Korean Culture* (Elizabeth, NJ/Seoul: Hollym, 1997); Kirk W. Larsen, *Tradition,
Treaties, and Trade: Qing Imperialism and Chosŏn Korea, 1850–1910* (Cambridge, MA:
Harvard University Press, 2008); Andrew Nahm, *An Introduction to Korean History and
Culture* (Elizabeth, NJ/Seoul: Hollym, 1993); Andrew C. Nahm, *Korea: Tradition and
Transformation* (Elizabeth, NJ/Seoul: Hollym, 1996); Keith Pratt, *Everlasting Flower:
A History of Korea* (London: Reaktion Books, 2006). North Korean sources include
Compilation Committee of Kim Il Sung Encyclopaedia, *Kim Il Sung Encyclopaedia
Volume One* (New Delhi: Vishwanath, 1992); Hwan Ju Pang, *Korean Review*
(Pyongyang: Foreign Languages Publishing House, 1987); Hwan Ju Pang, *National
Culture of Korea* (Pyongyang: Foreign Languages Publishing House, 1988).

common history, culture, founding myths, language and homeland. North Korea also shared with South Korea a story of the constitution of modern Korea as the product of a more or less linear development traced back into ancient history, for at least five thousand years.[2] Historical Korea is understood by both states as having a recognisably common geographical heartland south of today's border with China and covering the whole of what is today understood as the 'Korean' peninsula. Also shared is the understanding of the Korean nation as having been historically vulnerable to foreign predations that threatened to eradicate core aspects of Korean identity as well as to take over the national territory.

Northern historians assert the distinctiveness of northern history in their claim that states and leaders from the northern half of the peninsula historically provided leadership to the Korean nation in the struggle for political independence. North Korean governments interpret Korean history to demonstrate northern superiority over South Korea in respect to historical, cultural and political claims to represent the Korean nation. The North Korean message to its own citizens and to all Koreans is that it was only with the advent of the Kim family onto the historical stage that the ethnically distinct Korean nation gained the opportunity to fulfil historic aspirations to political self-actualisation within a distinctively Korean state liberated from foreign domination.

'Five thousand years of history'

North Korean historians framed the story of Korea through relatively modern conceptions of national identity to fit an 'imagined community' of national antecedents.[3] For all countries, national identities provide a framing device for understanding the place of nations and states in the world. They do not have to be historically accurate and they can easily cope with an element of contradiction and a variety of interpretation providing core elements remain stable. Their function is to provide collective cement for nation-building efforts by political leaders. In most countries, deeply ingrained and shared understandings of history are based on a mix of historical events merged with myth in a complex ideational framework whose purpose is to provide a conceptualisation of what could or should be the ideal understanding of national identity.

[2] The seminal critique is Gi-Wook Shin, *Ethnic Nationalism in Korea: Genealogy, Politics, and Legacy* (Stanford University Press, 2006).
[3] Benedict Anderson, *Imagined Communities: Reflections on the Origin and Spread of Nationalism* (London: Verso, 1983).

The understanding that modern Koreans are the direct descendants of an ancient, continuous and separate Korean ethnic identity underpins popular and academic discourse in both North and South Korea.[4] Korean national identity pre-supposes a distinct, exclusive and traceable genealogy from the beginnings of humankind. The strongest interpretations suggest that all Koreans, wherever they are physically located in the world, share an ancient blood line and common racial make-up.[5] In this version Korean people are descended from distinct origins, separate if related to the rest of the human race.[6] The weaker versions focus on the unique longevity of the Korean nation and its traceable distinctiveness from other societies and peoples, in East Asia and the rest of the world. Whether the stronger or weaker version is used, the idea is that Koreans have more in common with each other through their common blood lines than they have with other members of the human race, and have a special place in world history.

The broad lines of Korean national identity conceptions are similar to those of many, perhaps most, national groups. The modern day 'exceptionalism' prized by United States politicians emphasises the special nature of the American 'way of life'. Jewish and Serbian national consciousness of historic persecution based on ethnic identity is a significant factor in explaining both a sense of distinctiveness and the fierce determination to create a nation-state. Ethnicity is still a powerful force in world politics and Korean conceptions of national identity based on ethnic heritage have much in common with self-defensive ethnic nationalisms everywhere in the world.

Popular understandings in South Korea as well as in North Korea are shaped by sometimes skewed versions of the historical record; South

[4] For critique of South Korean historiography see Hyung Il Pai, *Constructing 'Korean' Origins: A Critical Review of Archaeology, Historiography, and Racial Myth in Korean State-Formation Theories* (Cambridge, MA: Harvard University, 2000).
[5] There is a major debate as to how best to understand historical conceptions of the communal identity markers of 'nation' in respect to the Korean peninsula. I am indebted to Henry Em for introducing me to the useful summary by John. B. Duncan, '*Hyanghwain*: Migration and Assimilation in Chosŏn Korea', in *Acta Koreana*, Vol. 3, July 2000, pp. 1–15.
[6] I have been on guided tours of national museums in Seoul (2002) and Pyongyang (1990–2003 on a number of occasions). In both places, I was told outright that Koreans had different origins from other human beings. In both locations, I thought I had misheard so engaged in discussion with my Korean guides. In both cases they confirmed I had heard correctly. Both countries have sophisticated, knowledgeable and trained historians even though in the DPRK they cannot articulate anything that might contradict the official lines. The point here is that, in both countries, it was understood as fairly non-controversial and 'common knowledge' that the Korean 'race' was different from, in some primeval, historically justified manner, the rest of the 'human race'.

Korean historiography has not been immune from modern national re-readings of history that trace the past in the light of post-colonial perspectives.[7] In South Korea, however, debate took place as to the interpretation of evidence and the sometimes anachronistic foundations of accounts of Korean history. In North Korea, conceptions of national identity were developed by governmental diktat to the extent that no alternative version of cultural, political or social history was allowed to exist. North Korean historians were obliged to adopt official narratives and were not permitted to acknowledge alternatives or debate interpretations of history that contradicted state narratives.

'Proving' longevity

North Korean historians, like their South Korean counterparts, worked with an incomplete evidential record whose meaning was not clear. Understandings of historical periods thousands of years ago necessarily rely on interpretation of fragmentary archaeological evidence in lieu of written sources. Interpretations are inevitably uncertain and disputed, especially if the physical data is scarce. In the attempt to demonstrate the legitimacy of the official version of history, however, North Korean official accounts used the fragmentary historical evidence to 'prove' the longevity and continuity of the Korean race, the persistence of a distinctively Korean polity and the historical contribution of northern leadership. Northern sources pushed back historical 'founding' dates and skewed evidence to 'support' northern legitimacy claims, most specifically those of the Kim Il Sung family. These egregious political distortions served to discredit all of North Korean historiography, however well-founded the research.

North Korean historiography asserts that the ancestors of contemporary Koreans lived in the Korean peninsula from about a million years ago, in the early Palaeolithic (Old Stone) Age.[8] In so doing, North Korean historians appear to have added half a million years to the historical record. There is evidence that human beings were living on the Korean

---

[7] Pai, *Constructing 'Korean' Origins.*

[8] Clark Sorensen dates human habitation on the Korean peninsula as at least from half a million years ago, in Clark Sorensen, 'The Land, Climate, and People', in John H. Koo and Andrew Nahm (eds.), *An Introduction to Korean Culture* (Elizabeth, NJ/Seoul: Hollym, 1997), pp. 34–5. See also Eckert *et al., Korea Old and New,* pp. 1–8. Lee and de Bary suggest that human habitation can be reliably traced to between 40,000 and 30,000 BC. See Peter W. Lee and Wm. Theodore de Bary, *Sources of Korean Tradition Volume One: From Early Times Through the Sixteenth Century* (New York: Columbia University Press, 1997), p. 3. For North Korean understandings see Compilation Committee, *Kim Il Sung Encyclopaedia,* p. 7.

peninsula maybe up to a half a million years ago but the addition of another half a million years to the historical record is not widely accepted. Stone implements found near present-day Pyongyang, in Sangwon County, are also dated back to the early Palaeolithic period, supposedly demonstrating that Korea 'is one of the old cradles of mankind'.[9]

The insistence on 'proving' the homogeneity and continuity of the Korean race continues with the assertion that late Palaeolithic man demonstrated discernible features that could be understood as the 'ancient Korean type'.[10] These features were also, allegedly, characteristic of Neolithic man who, North Korean historians argue, existed from around the sixth millennium BC.[11] These Neolithic people were, they argue, the direct predecessors of Bronze Age Koreans, which they date from around the turn of the second millennium BC.[12]

The founding of Korea

The sense of special and distinct 'Korean' development is reflected in some very old stories which constitute nation-building mythology for both Koreas, not least being the foundational myth of Tangun.[13] North Korea and South Korea have promulgated the story of Tangun as the founder of 'Kojoson' or 'Old Korea', commonly translated as 'Old Choson', in 2333 BC.[14] National mythology in North and South Korea ascribes the founding of Korea to Tangun Wanggom, who was said to be born of a union between a bear, who had been transformed into a human woman, and the Lord of Heaven, Hwanung.[15] Tangun is said to have descended from heaven at Mount Thaebaek, variously located at Mount Paekdu or the Myohyang mountains, both of which are situated in present day North Korea.[16] North and South Korea trace Korean culture

[9] Compilation Committee, *Kim Il Sung Encyclopaedia*, pp. 7–9.
[10] Ibid.   [11] Ibid.   [12] Ibid.
[13] I am conscious that there is a great deal of historiographical debate about the Tangun story and how and why it was disseminated. For the purposes of this text, I only aim to show the commonalities in approach between modern North Korea and modern South Korea. I am again indebted to Henry Em, however, who has clarified that the Tangun story contains layers of different messages, not least being the intention by the thirteenth century Buddist monk, Iryŏn, from which modern understandings of the Tangun story derive, to provide some continuity between the Buddhist tradition and Korean founding mythology. See Henry Em, 'Commentary on Kim Heung-kyu's "A Community of Long Memories"', undated in private communication to the author, May 2014.
[14] Compilation Committee, *Kim Il Sung Encyclopaedia*, p. 9.
[15] Ibid.; Nahm, *Korea: Tradition and Transformation*, p. 25.
[16] DPRK Academy of Sciences, 'Information on the Disinterment of The Tomb of Tangun', *Tangun Founder-King of Korea* (Pyongyang: Foreign Languages Publishing House, 1994), p. 1.

and a continuous Korean tradition to Tangun and both celebrate Tangun as the founder of the first recognisably Korean state.

The state-sanctioned Kim Il Sung encyclopaedia does not support the idea that Tangun descended from heaven and states that 'the tale of Tangun is a myth'. Nevertheless, DPRK scholars argued that Tangun was a 'real historical person' who should be venerated as the founder of Korea.[17] North Korean historians also qualify the mythological certainty about founding dates with the argument that the historically accurate founding date of Old Choson was 'before the tenth century BC'.[18]

Old Choson was located in what is today north-east China and north-west Korea. One North Korean estimation of the territorial reach of Old Korea was that it spread from the Korean peninsula almost as far north as Harbin in modern north-east China and as far south-west as the Shandong peninsula – encompassing and including the area in China that today contains the cities of Shenyang, Beijing and Tianjin.[19] North Korean histories argue that in the third century BC Asadal, also called Wanggomsong, the legendary capital, was located on what is known today as the Liao River in present-day China.[20]

Relocation of the capital in the second century BC to the site where present-day Pyongyang stands reflected the waning of the territorial reach of Old Choson, which gradually lost military ground against its Chinese neighbour to the west.[21] Pyongyang is conventionally understood in North and South Korea as 'the oldest city in Korea'.[22] North Korean historiography further argues that Pyongyang should be understood as the cradle of the Korean nation because Tangun lived around today's capital of the DPRK.[23] In 1993, Kim Il Sung declared that the tomb of Tangun, 'the ancestral father of the Korean nation', had been found and

---

[17] *The People's Korea*, 'North, South Commemorate Accession Day of Nation's Founder', 2002, available on www1.korea-np.co.jp/pk/185th_issue/2002103113.htm, accessed 16 September 2013.

[18] Compilation Committee, *Kim Il Sung Encyclopaedia*, p. 9.

[19] For map of estimated territory of Kochosŏn see Pai, *Constructing "Korean" Origins*, Map 1, no page number, but p. xxvii if consecutive numbering is adopted.

[20] For the China location, see Compilation Committee, *Kim Il Sung Encyclopaedia*, p. 9. For the Pyongyang location, see DPRK Academy of Sciences, 'Information on the Disinterment of The Tomb of Tangun', p. 1.

[21] Nahm, *An Introduction to Korean History and Culture*, p. 16.

[22] For discussion see Pai, *Constructing 'Korean' Origins*, pp. 141–3. Quote from Soo-chang Oh, 'Economic Growth in P'yŏngan Province and the Development of Pyongyang in the Late Chosŏn Period', *Korean Studies*, Vol. 30, 2006, p. 3.

[23] Compilation Committee, *Kim Il Sung Encyclopaedia*, p. 9. For the argument that Tangun existed, see DPRK Academy of Sciences, *Tangun Founder-King of Korea* (Pyongyang: Foreign Languages Publishing House, 1994).

excavated in Kangdong county, in the Pyongyang city region.[24] There are controversies as to the authenticity of these tombs but the publicity given to this discovery, at a time when North Koreans were facing widespread hunger and dramatic deterioration in their standard of living, speaks to the importance of the mythology as a mechanism for promoting national cohesion.

The rise of Koguryo

North Korean historiography reports that Old Choson was defeated by the Han Chinese who destroyed the ancient kingdom as a political entity by 109 BC.[25] The most important successor states to Old Choson are known today in both Koreas as 'the Three Kingdoms' and include Silla and Paekje (Paekche), which occupied the southern and central parts of the Korean peninsula, and Koguryo, which encompassed the northern half of the Korean peninsula and stretched into what is today north-east China.[26] The Three Kingdoms had fluid boundaries and shifting capacities to control their inhabitants, which makes it difficult to accurately date the transformation from a political community more akin to a local clan to that of an entity with powerful state-like capacity. Conventional scholarship dates the foundation of Silla to 57 BC, Koguryo to 37 BC and Paekje to 18 BC.[27] North Korean historiography argues that Koguryo was founded as early as 277 BC.[28]

Old Choson lost its western territories to the Han invaders, who established four Chinese garrisons or 'commanderies' in what is today known as the Korean peninsula. The most important, Lelang, was located in the defeated capital city, the site of present-day Pyongyang.[29] The garrisons assumed political as well as military control over surrounding territories. Lelang was militarily defeated in 313 AD by Koguryo, the rising power in the northern Korean peninsula and Manchuria.[30] The long-lasting impact of the commanderies

---

[24] Cultural Relics Publishing House, *Tomb of King Tangun* (Pyongyang: Cultural Relics Publishing House, 1995); Hyung Il Pai, *Constructing 'Korean' Origins: A Critical Review of Archaeology, Historiography, and Racial Myth in Korean State-Formation Theories* (Cambridge MA: Harvard University, 2000), p. 60.

[25] Compilation Committee of Kim Il Sung Encyclopaedia, *Kim Il Sung Encyclopaedia Volume One* (New Delhi: Vishwanath, 1992), pp. 9–11.

[26] Pang, *National Culture of Korea*, pp. 15–28.

[27] Nahm, *An Introduction to Korean History and Culture*, pp. 25–30.

[28] Compilation Committee, *Kim Il Sung Encyclopaedia*, p. 12; Pai, *Constructing 'Korean' Origins*, p. 122.

[29] Pratt, *Everlasting Flower*, pp. 34–5.

[30] Ibid. p. 37; Pai, *Constructing 'Korean' Origins*, p. 129.

was, however, to spread knowledge and cultural practices from China into the peninsula.

The Three Kingdoms were constantly at war with each other as well as with Han China but North Korean historiography argues that Koguryo was not only the most powerful of the three, but the most important in understanding the alleged unbroken continuity of the Korean nation from Tangun to the present-day. North Korean (and other) histori-ographers argue that the continuity of Korean culture and ethnicity from Old Choson was transmitted by way of the ancient Korean state of Puyo, which was situated in present-day north-eastern China.[31] Puyo, they argue, was the direct territorial antecedent state to Koguryo. North Korean historians also argue that although the first capital of Koguryo was located in Dongu on the Yalu River that today marks the China/North Korea border, the fact that it was relocated to the site of present-day Pyongyang in 342 AD is additional confirmation of the historic legitimacy of the capital city of the DPRK.[32]

Competing claims of national continuity: Palhae versus Silla

North Korean historians argue that the northern state of Palhae (Parhae) was the direct political, cultural and social descendant of Koguryo, which was defeated by Silla in 668 AD. This is not a particularly idiosyncratic view and is shared by some distinguished non-North Korean scholars.[33] Palhae stretched from Pyongyang to the Heilong River in today's north-ern China. Two successor states to the Three Kingdoms were based in the north of the peninsula, including Palhae and what is now known as 'Later Silla', which controlled territory south of the Daedong River. Palhae inherited the territory of Koguryo and maintained control over the northern half of the peninsula, which was never ceded to Silla. Palhae was, therefore, according to the official North Korean accounts, the true successor state to Koguryo.[34]

[31] Compilation Committee, *Kim Il Sung Encyclopaedia*, p. 11; Nahm, *An Introduction to Korean History and Culture*, p. 29. For a very useful critique see Pratt, *Everlasting Flower*, pp. 32–3.

[32] Compilation Committee, *Kim Il Sung Encyclopaedia*, p. 11; Nahm, *An Introduction to Korean History and Culture*, p. 14.

[33] Henry H. Em notes that Shin Ch'ae-ho (1880–1935), one of the founders of nationalist Korean historiography, promulgated the idea that the Korean ethnic nation can be traced directly from Tangun to Old Choson, Puyo, Koguryo, Palhae, Koryo and Choson. See Henry Em, 'Nationalism, Post-Nationalism and Shin Ch'ae-ho', *Korea Journal*, summer 1999, pp. 283– 428.

[34] Compilation Committee, *Kim Il Sung Encyclopaedia*, p. 18; James Huntley Grayson, *Korea – A Religious History* (Abingdon: RoutledgeCurzon, 2002), pp. 53–76.

Southern historiography contradicts northern interpretations; it argues that it is Silla that can best be understood as expressing the continuity of the Korean nation from ancient times. The argument is that Silla's defeat of Koguryo, in alliance with the Chinese Tang dynasty, and its incorporation of Paekje in the seventh century, marks the beginnings of a politically united and specifically Korean nation.[35] The claim is not that Silla ruled over the entire peninsula but that Palhae was not a politically or culturally significant post-Koguryo state. Other scholars have argued somewhere along the middle; recognising that refugees from Koguryo lived in Palhae but arguing that Palhae was not predominately a proto-Korean state because the dominant culture was Malgal, later known as Jurchen.[36] The Jurchen later evolved as the Manchu people, eponymous inhabitants of what became known as Manchuria in territory situated today in north-east China.[37]

Koryo: the foundations of political and cultural unity

North and South Korea agree that the Kingdom of Koryo was founded in 918 AD and incorporated both Palhae and Silla.[38] The kingdom was explicitly named in homage to the defunct northern state of Koguryo and was home to a sophisticated culture shaped by Confucian teaching and Buddhist thought. Koryo succeeded in politically unifying a large part of the Korean peninsula and situated the capital city in Kaesong, at the heart of the Korean peninsula, located today in the DPRK, just north of the border with South Korea. Koryo is understood by North Korean historiographers as part of an unbroken lineage of northern political dominance on the Korean peninsula and as the first unified Korean state.[39]

[35] For the purposes of this book, there is no 'right' or 'wrong' interpretation of the significance of Silla as the progenitor of the future unified Korea. What is significant is the two different interpretations. For an account which specifically states the 'great historical significance' of Silla unification efforts and resistance to Tang China's wars of aggression see Eckert *et al.*, *Korea Old and New*, p. 43. See also, however, 'Contrary to what Most School Children in Korea [South] are Taught, Silla did not Unify the Korean Peninsula into a Single Nation', in Grayson, *Korea – A Religious History*, p. 54.

[36] Johannes Reckel Gottingen, *Korea and Manchuria: The Historical Links between Korea and the Ancestors of the Modern Manchus* (Seoul: The Royal Asiatic Society – Korea Branch, 8 November 2000), available at www.raskb.com/transactions/VOL76/VOL76.docx, accessed 18 January 2013.

[37] Ibid.

[38] For North Korean understandings of Koryo see Compilation Committee, *Kim Il Sung Encyclopaedia*, pp. 21–5. For a standard account see Nahm, *Korea: Tradition and Transformation*, pp. 59–93.

[39] Compilation Committee, *Kim Il Sung Encyclopaedia*, p. 21.

The Koryo period was dominated by a focus on the military as dynastic leaders sought to unify the peninsula and defend the territory from foreign invaders. Koryo militarily defeated the Mongolian Khitans in 1117 at Uiju (modern-day Sinuiju in North Korea) and consequently incorporated the north-west of the Korean peninsula into the polity, but it was never able to conquer the Jurchen-inhabited north-east, which had formerly been part of Koguryo.[40] A line from Wonsan to Sinuiju, both located in present-day North Korea, represented the eastern boundary of undisputed Koryo territory. Koryo did not succeed in its aim of unifying the Korean peninsula. The north-east remained unconquered.

By far the most significant intervention from abroad came from the Mongol invasions of the 1230s onwards. Hundreds of thousands of people were killed and enforced tribute was made in the form of gold, grain, women and conscripted soldiers to join attacks on Japan. The Mongol Empire forced Koryo to accept vassal status in 1259 – prior to their establishment of the Yuan dynasty in what is today known as China in 1271.[41] Koryo's military rulers also faced off Japanese pirates and 'Red Banner' (for the colour of their turbans) bandits from the west. Koryo remained in conflict with the Ming who superseded the Yuan dynasty in 1368. The Ming challenged Koryo's irredentist claims to former Koguryo territory in what is today northern China and Koryo's end came when military commander Li Song Gye (Yi Song Gye) refused to fight the Ming invaders. Li mounted a coup and assumed the throne himself, thus founding the Choson or Li (Yi) dynasty in 1392. North Korean historians have nothing but contempt for Li for his alleged betrayal of the nation – arguing that Li was 'blind with servility' to the Ming.[42]

Choson: national unity and northern distinctiveness

The Choson dynasty united the peninsula in a Korean political entity that lasted a remarkably long five hundred years, although it was regularly threatened by foreign intervention until it was finally destroyed in a territorial annexation by Japan in 1910. North Korean historiography, like southern historiography, emphasises the homogeneity of the Korean nation and the political integration of the Korean peninsula by the Choson dynasty and somewhat downplays the social and geographical fragmentation within Choson Korea. Northerners faced political and

---

[40] Gottingen, *Korea and Manchuria.*
[41] Compilation Committee, *Kim Il Sung Encyclopaedia*, p. 23.   [42] Ibid., p. 24.

social discrimination during the Choson era and were treated as backward and unsophisticated.

The continuing vulnerability of Korea as a political entity and the Korean nation as a cultural entity to foreign depredations provides a common theme in contemporary nationalist historiography in both North Korea and South Korea. An equally common trope in both Koreas is that Korean leaders frequently betrayed the nation in their anxiety to 'serve the great' – as when the founder of the Choson dynasty agreed to become a vassal of Ming China and when Korean leaders collaborated with the Japanese annexation of Korea in the early twentieth century.

Uniting the peninsula

Li Song Gye, later known as Taejo or 'Great Progenitor' of the nation, reigned from 1392 to 1398. Li established the new capital at Hanyang, later known as Seoul, in the centre of the peninsula.[43] Li accepted vassalage status to the Ming in order to secure protection from foreign invasion.

General Li came from the north-eastern part of the Korean peninsula that had not been conquered by Koryo. Li and his successors did not rely on military force to enlarge Choson territory to include the north-east but instead built on their local ties to incorporate Jurchen leaders in the Choson polity. To secure territorial gains, the Choson court built and manned military garrisons in the north. Their purpose was to defend against invasions and to maintain territorial claims over the mountainous and sparsely inhabited border regions against the perhaps equally legitimate claims of Jurchen inhabitants of the region.[44]

In the fifteenth century Choson leader King Sejong consolidated Choson rule over the north-eastern territories by resettling Koreans from the southern part of the peninsula in the north-east.[45] The Choson court pursued migration policies that forcibly resettled thousands of southerners in the north at least up until the 1560s and also encouraged voluntary migration northwards.[46] These migrating southerners were often low-born people who did not have the social or political wherewithal to maintain themselves in the south. These 'outsiders' settled in the north-east alongside Jurchens and other Koreans, including former slaves, to create a distinctive social mix that was physically and psychologically far from the aristocracy-dominated court based in the capital city in Seoul. Northern society was much less stratified than in the

---

[43] Hwang, *Beyond Birth*, pp. 248–89.   [44] Ibid., p. 252.
[45] Gottingen, *Korea and Manchuria*.   [46] Hwang, *Beyond Birth*, p. 254.

south. Slavery was less entrenched than the south where the practice persisted even after its formal abolition in the Kabo reforms of 1895 at the tail end of the dynasty.[47]

Northerners as second-class citizens[48]

The northern provinces were poorly integrated into Choson social structures that revolved around the king and court, despite the Choson dynasty having been founded by a northerner. Some benefited from the more flexible social structure away from conservative court-led machinations in Seoul. The proximity of the northern provinces of Pyongan and Hamgyong to China gave openings for commerce, and some local traders took full advantage of that proximity to get rich. Throughout the Choson dynasty, however, persons from the northern provinces were largely excluded from the *Yangban*-based patronage networks of power and status that centred on the Seoul court.[49] Northern elites had some success in achieving the lesser-regarded military appointments but less in securing the high bureaucratic offices of the state. This was not for want of trying. Northerners sat and passed the bureaucratic examinations that were necessary to be considered for state office but were discriminated against in the allocation of appointments because of their geographical and historical social origins.[50]

The Choson dynasty by and large treated northern Koreans as 'second-class citizens'. Seoul-based elites discriminated against even wealthy and well-educated northerners, who were more or less disenfranchised from bureaucratic and political power at the national level for several centuries. One result of discrimination was a northern population conscious of its national Korean heritage but also aware of geographical distinctiveness. The famous rebellion of 1811–12, led by Hong Kyongnae (Hong Gyong Rae in North Korean publications in English) in Pyongan province was as much an attempt to express the equal worth of the provincial population to Seoul-based Koreans as it was to establish a separate state centred on Pyongan. Hong accused the government of

---

[47] Ibid., p. 257; James B. Palais, 'A Search for Korean Uniqueness', *Harvard Journal of Asiatic Studies*, Vol. 55, No. 2, December 1995, p. 418.

[48] It will be clear after reading the next section that I am utterly intellectually indebted for the path-breaking scholarship of northern exclusion in the Choson dynasty to Hwang, *Beyond Birth*.

[49] Kyung Moon Hwang, 'From the Dirt to Heaven: Northern Korea in the Chosŏn and Early Modern Eras', *Harvard Journal of Asiatic Studies*, Vol. 62, No.1, June 2002, pp. 135–78; Oh, 'Economic Growth in P'yŏngan Province', pp. 1–22.

[50] Hwang, *Beyond Birth*, pp. 264–5.

treating the province with contempt, despite the population's long-suffering loyalty and sacrifices.[51] A central theme was the right to equal treatment for northerners within the Korean state and society.

Northern Korea was historically home to those whom the Choson state apparatus in Seoul found difficult to control but within northern Korea there were also important regional differences. The mountainous, hard scrabble regions of the Hamgyong north-eastern provinces were remote frontier outposts of the Choson kingdom, populated by independent farmers who had few ties to the Seoul-based state apparatus.[52] In the late nineteenth century, these independently minded Hamgyong inhabitants were joined by exiles from the Tonghak or Eastern Learning Group, some of whose members had migrated north after the defeat of the peasant revolt which it had supported in 1894.[53]

The foreign predators

Choson acceptance of Chinese vassalage meant that it had to pay homage to its western neighbour but in return it expected protection from other foreign invaders. Towards the end of the Choson dynasty as the strength of Qing China waned and Japan's expansionist vision, military capacity and ambitions waxed, Korea yet again became highly vulnerable to external predators.

Choson vassalage

Ming troops helped in the defence of Korea against Japanese assaults led by Toyotomi Hideyoshi in 1592 and 1597.[54] Hundreds of thousands of people were killed in these invasions, many abducted to Japan and the economy devastated. North Korea calls this conflict the 'Imjin Patriotic War' and although they acknowledge the help from Ming China they also boast that it was the Korean defence of their homeland that prevented the Japanese from going on to invade their powerful neighbours to the west.[55] Neither Choson's own defences nor the Ming forces, however, could save Choson from another wave of destruction wrought by foreign

---

[51] Donald N. Clark, *Living Dangerously in Korea: The Western Experience 1900–1950* (Norwalk, CT: Eastbridge, 2003), p. 223. See also Hwang, *Beyond Birth*, pp. 265–68.

[52] Charles K. Armstrong, *The North Korean Revolution 1945–1950* (Ithaca, NY: Cornell University Press, 2003), p. 14.

[53] Ibid., p. 15.

[54] Andrew C. Nahm, 'History: Pre-modern Korea', in John H. Koo and Andrew Nahm (eds.), *An Introduction to Korean Culture* (Elizabeth, NJ/Seoul: Hollym, 1997), p. 65.

[55] Compilation Committee, *Kim Il Sung Encyclopaedia*, 1992), p. 28.

invaders in the seventeenth century. The Manchu invasions of 1627 and 1637 ended with Choson Korea being forced to accept vassalage status. The Manchu defeat of the Ming in 1644 and their subsequent establishment of the Qing dynasty meant that Choson was once more formally subjected to their western neighbours. The main political dispute between vassal and suzerain was over border demarcation, which was settled in 1712 when Mount Paekdu was accepted by both countries as defining their joint frontier.[56]

The dismemberment of Choson

From the late nineteenth century onwards, Choson Korea struggled to stave off interference from industrialised states, particularly Russia, and later Japan, both of which were better organised and more economically advanced than Korea. The Choson court offered economic concessions to foreign investors – including to American companies mining for gold in Unsan, in the far north of Korea – and tried to balance the competing demands of foreign powers against each other.[57] Popular uprisings against foreign incursions included the burning of the United States vessel the USS *General Sherman* in 1866 after it sailed up the Daedong River into Pyongyang.

Choson government strategies failed to prevent Japanese aggression as other states could not or were reluctant to challenge Japanese expansionism. In 1876 the Japanese government forced Korea to accept the terms of the Kanghwa Treaty. The Treaty insisted on Korea's 'independence' and equality to Japan within the context of the law of nations.[58] The intention was to sever Choson's special relationship with the Qing so that Japan could expand its influence over Korea without the encumbrance of acknowledging Chinese authority or interest in the peninsula. Another aim was to achieve the concrete and particularistic goal of forcing Korea to accept Japanese trade and traders. The Kanghwa Treaty thus opened the port of Pusan to Japanese trade.[59] In 1883 Wonsan, which is situated in today's North Korea, and Inchon, the nearest port to Seoul, were also opened to Japanese commerce.[60]

---

[56] Nahm, 'History: Pre-modern Korea', p. 126; Daniel Gomà, 'The Chinese-Korean Border Issue', *Asian Survey*, Vol. 46, Issue 6, 2006, pp. 867–80.

[57] Clark, *Living Dangerously in Korea*, pp. 222–38.

[58] Peter Duus, *The Abacus and the Sword: The Japanese Penetration of Korea 1895–1910* (Berkeley: University of California Press, 1995), p. 48.

[59] Ibid., pp. 43–9.

[60] Duus, *The Abacus and the Sword*, pp. 43–9. On the opening of Wonsan and Inchon see Nahm, *Korea: Tradition and Transformation*, p. 152.

Japan intervened militarily in Korea in 1894 to prevent Qing China from exercising special military prerogatives in support of the Korean government, in the Sino-Japanese War of 1894–5. Japan defeated China but did not immediately attempt to colonise Korea. Indeed Japan's influence in Korea diminished after the Japanese Minister in Korea, Miura Goro, organised the assassination of Korea's independently minded Queen Min in 1895.[61] The Japanese government had not ordered Queen Min's murder and Miura was put on trial in Japan. The Court acknowledged Miura's culpability and at the same time acquitted him and his co-conspirators.[62] The verdict reflected the then ambivalence of Japanese state policy, which was aggressive but, in 1895, remained short of outright takeover.

For a short period the Russians challenged Japan for foreign supremacy in Korea. King Kojong sought Russian protection against Japan after the Queen's assassination but Russian failure to establish Korea within its 'sphere of influence' was signalled by its defeat in the Russo-Japanese war of 1904–5. Japan's victory over Russia was seen in the West through a racial lens as the shocking defeat of a European great power by a 'non-white' and hence 'naturally' inferior nation. Japan resented this inference of non-equality with other 'civilised' states but used the same racial prism in its justification for colonial expansion in East Asia.

The defeat of Russia finally allowed Japan to exercise *de facto* sovereign power over Korea and in 1905 Japan forced a protectorate status on Korea.[63] King Kojong, who declared himself Emperor in 1897, partly as an attempt to obtain recognition for the sovereignty of Korea in the modern world of nation states that were equal to each other and independent of each other in international law. Kojong appealed for support to President Theodore (Teddy) Roosevelt and to the Second Hague International Peace Conference in 1907.[64] When these appeals failed, Kojong abdicated the throne.[65] In August 1910 Japan forced Emperor Sunjong, Kojong's reputedly mentally deficient son, to abrogate the independence of Korea to Japanese direct rule.[66] Japanese power in Korea was this converted from *de facto* status to *de jure* reality.

[61] For a detailed account see F. A. McKenzie, *Korea's Fight for Freedom* (New York: Fleming H. Revell Company, 1920), pp. 42–59.
[62] Duus, *The Abacus and the Sword*, pp. 108–14.
[63] For detail on Japanese activity leading up to annexation see Ibid. For a summary see Nahm, *Korea: Tradition and Transformation*, pp. 214–19.
[64] Andre Schmid, *Korea Between Empires 1895–1919* (New York: Columbia University Press, 2002), pp. 72–8.
[65] Duus, *The Abacus and the Sword*, pp. 205–8.   [66] Ibid., p. 210.

The northern view of national identity

North Korean national identity is shaped through historically constituted social and cultural practices and an understanding of history, much of which is shared with South Korea, despite the almost hermetic sealing of one country from the other from 1945 until the 2000s. The sense of national identity is not, however, identical.

North Korean historiography argues that the continuity and political unity of the Korean ethnic nation can be traced directly via premodern Korean states that were based in the north of the peninsula. North Korean publications downplayed the distinctive ethnic, political and social heritage of the north that arose as a consequence of the region's contiguity to ancient continental empires, cultures and people that include the Han, the Manchus, the Mongols and the Slavs. Such a focus would necessarily acknowledge the genetic and cultural diversity of the origins of modern Korea. North Korea does not advertise the long-standing treatment of northerners as second-class citizens in the Choson period for similar reasons. To do so would entail acknowledgement of the reason for such treatment, which was partly because of the perceived 'foreignness' of northern Korea, many of whose inhabitants had distinctively non-'Korean' ethnic antecedents.

North Korean accounts trace the political lineage of modern Korea from Tangun through Old Choson, Puyo, Koguryo, Palhae, Koryo and Choson.[67] North Korea's version of history is at odds with standard South Korean accounts that ascribe the key foundational role of a politically united Korean nation to the defeat of Koguryo by Silla in the seventh century. What might seem fairly arcane debates about the relative significance of medieval states are meaningful in the context of contemporary competing claims of national legitimacy. The DPRK claim is that the north of the peninsula has provided thousands of years of political leadership of the Korean nation. North Korean historiography also argues that in more recent history, political leaders and protest movements based in the northern part of the peninsula provided leadership to Korean independence movements. Kim Il Sung is thus portrayed as part of a long line of a northern tradition of political leadership for Korean independence.

---

[67] Son Yong Jong, 'The Korea Nation – A Homogeneous Nation Whose Founding Father Is Tangun', in DPRK Academy of Sciences, *Tangun: Founder-King of Korea* (Pyongyang: Foreign Languages Publishing House, 1994), pp. 132–40.

The North Korean government claimed that all Kim Il Sung's ancestors had been prominent in Korean independence movements.[68] North Korean children are taught that Kim Jong Il was born on Mount Paektu, which is revered throughout Korea for its association with the Tangun myth, although his actual birthplace was Khabarovsk in the then Soviet Union.[69] These associations deliberately conflate the ancient founding myths with the Kim family in an effort to inhere the Kim family's political legitimacy in Korean tradition.

North Korea tried to eradicate and discredit aspects of cultural history that did not fit well into Kim Il Sungist politics. It also advertised to the North Korean public the idea that northern cultural and political history possessed a superior claim over the South to represent 'true' Korean identity; most notably in the assertion that the Korean language as written and spoken in the North was less influenced by foreigners than that written and spoken in the South of the peninsula.

The neutralisation of religion

The North Korean government outlawed organised religion, closed churches and persecuted religious adherents in its effort to eradicate all sources of potential opposition to Kim Il Sung. North Korean society, however, remained influenced by Korea's rich spiritual heritage that is a product of Shamanism, Confucian moral frameworks and Buddhist teachings that coexisted in Korea for at least 1,600 years and which were joined by Christian and indigenous Korean religions in the latter part of the Choson dynasty. The myths, stories, rituals and ways of behaviour ascribed by religious and spiritual influences remain embedded in folk beliefs and cultural practices and many of these are shared with the South.

Shamanism is the oldest of Korean religions and ascribes spiritual personality to places and nature. It is no longer an officially practised religion in the DPRK as it is in South Korea, as North Korean leaders understand Shamanism to be superstitious and primitive. Shamanism remains, however, incorporated in North Korean culture in folk tales and performance as well as in the popular but, strictly speaking, illegal practice of fortune-telling.

---

[68] See Chapter II 'The Lineage' in Genaro Carnero Checa, *Korea: Rice and Steel* (Pyongyang: Foreign Languages Publishing House, 1977), pp. 25–35.

[69] Ryohaengsa, *Mt. Paektu* (Pyongyang: Korea International Travel Company, undated).

Buddhism was formally recognised as the religion of Koguryo in 372 AD and Paekje in 384.[70] Originally the religion of the Korean upper classes, Buddhism was not always supported by Korean elites. During the Choson era, Buddhism was often suppressed as a challenge to the Confucian order. Nevertheless Buddhism remained an important component of Korean culture. In the DPRK, the official stance is that the Buddhist heritage should be venerated as part of Korean tradition. History texts celebrate Buddhist scriptures as a significant part of the national heritage, including one product of Korean Buddhist learning located in 'Pulguk Temple in Kyongju, North Kyongsang Province' proudly referred to as the 'oldest wood-block print in the world'.[71] That the location of the Pulguk Temple is in South Korea is not a major issue. North Korea, like South Korea, understands all of Korea as one jurisdiction, temporarily divided.

The shared literary culture of both Koreas is partly a result of the common Confucian heritage.[72] The *Yangban* class had needed a good knowledge of written Chinese to read the classic Confucian texts that would enable them to pass the examinations that were the key to high office in Choson Korea. Confucianism emphasised merit-based educational attainment as the key to promotion in society even if in practice it was mainly the *Yangban* class who were able to take advantage of the pursuit of enlightenment by way of support from the punitively taxed commoners and the rural poor who worked the land. In North Korea, the heritage of this very long-standing understanding that scholarship is useful in itself and as a means of advancement is that the classical communist symbols of the hammer and the sickle are always joined with the brush to represent the triumvirate of industrial worker, farmer and intellectual in the nation-building project.

Confucianism is not a religion but a set of moral and behavioural codes and these codes have resonated with North Korean government politics of hierarchy and collective, community-based action. The Confucian understanding of a 'harmonious', that is a well-ordered, society is based on the 'natural' social structure of relationships between inferiors and superiors – subject and sovereign; wife and husband; children and parents. Confucian thought understands the reciprocal duties and obligations that flow from these relationships as forming the foundation of societal and state stability. These ideas permeated the Korean peninsula

---

[70] Grayson, *Korea – A Religious History*, p. 25.
[71] Compilation Committee, *Kim Il Sung Encyclopaedia*, p. 19.
[72] Jahyun Kim Haboush and Martina Deuchler (eds.), *Culture and State in Late Choson Korea* (Cambridge: Harvard University Press, 1999).

from around the fourth century and became politically influential from the tenth century onwards.[73] Confucian ideas provided the framework for Korean political and social structures until very late in the Choson era when they were challenged by modernising ideologies channelled through foreign influences.

The DPRK governing philosophy is influenced by Confucian ideas in the sense of the focus on hierarchy, social harmony in which every social relationship is pre-ordained and in its respect for education. It diverges significantly from the Confucian tradition, however, in important ways. The DPRK government brooks no criticism whereas it was the duty of Confucian scholars to admonish the monarch if the common good was threatened. The DPRK government turns Confucian morality upside down in its consistent policy of prioritisation of youth over the elderly as providing the source of knowledge and practices to build a well-functioning society. Contrary philosophical influences to Confucianism are also evident in the formal institutionalisation of modern notions of legal equality of one individual with another, especially women with men, in the DPRK today. These notions of equality also emerged from a religious tradition with the advent of Christian theology, especially Protestant doctrines to Korea.

Although Catholicism had permeated Korea via China, which had been host to Jesuit missionaries since the sixteenth century, it did not receive widespread acceptance in Korea, as the Catholic religion was often viewed as an alien import that challenged Korean customs and order, including ancestry veneration.[74] Catholics were periodically persecuted and killed, as exemplified in the 'Great Persecution' of 1866–71 that resulted in the killing of 8,000 Korean Catholics, about a half of all adherents.[75] Protestant teachings were more accessible, partly because the clergy preached in the Korean language. Protestant missions trained Koreans as church leaders and clergy, thus embedding the church and Christian beliefs in indigenous culture. From the late nineteenth century, Protestant missionaries established churches, hospitals and schools that enrolled girls as well as boys.[76]

Foreign missionaries were proud of their rapid achievements in Korea, especially in the north, which were recorded in a multitude of first-hand accounts in English by participants, observers and their descendants.[77]

[73] Grayson, *Korea – A Religious History.*
[74] Ibid., pp. 140–6.   [75] Ibid., pp. 155–60.   [76] Ibid., p. 156.
[77] See for example L. H. Underwood, *Fifteen Years among the Top-Knots or Life in Korea*, second edition, revised and enlarged (Boston: American Tract Society, 1908); Clark, *Living Dangerously in Korea.*

Protestant missions were established in Korea near the China border, as well as in Sunchon and Pyongyang.[78] Pyongyang became known to foreign missionaries as the 'Jerusalem of the East'.[79] The so-called Pyongyang Great Revival of 1907 brought thousands of Christian Protestant converts.[80] It is easy to exaggerate the influence of Christianity in northern Korea because of the contemporary accessibility of missionary accounts, many of which were written in English. Nevertheless the policy of promoting indigenous leaders meant that Protestant Christianity was not seen as entirely alien. The establishment of well-regarded schools in which students could obtain a good-quality academic education increased the attraction of Christian perspectives.

The Christian influence on Korean culture was not universally understood as a positive development even prior to the installation of a communist government in the north. The indigenous 'Heavenly way' or 'Chondo' religion was founded as a reaction to foreign influence from countries including China and Japan as well as foreign religions, including Catholicism.[81] The Eastern learning supported by the Chondo religion was thus a reaction to 'western' learning. The movement emphasised the priority of indigenous Korean learning, which it associated with moral qualities of justice for all, including the rural poor.

Today, the North Korean government lauds the indigenous Korean Chondo religion as being part of the 'Tonghak' tradition.[82] By contrast, the North Korean government repressed the Christian tradition and treats the Christian heritage with contempt as an alleged tool of western imperialists. The messages conveyed in its history books and cultural artifacts are that Christian missionaries played an active part in the repression of the Korean people in the colonial period. All of these religious and spiritual traditions are, however, used for instrumental purposes when the occasion merits. The DPRK government opened Protestant, Catholic and Orthodox churches in Pyongyang as part of an effort in the 2000s to build relationships with foreign Christian non-governmental organisations (NGOs) to help encourage their participation in assisting the population and economic redevelopment.

---

[78] Grayson, *Korea – A Religious History*, p. 156.

[79] Clark, *Living Dangerously in Korea*, pp. 116–41.

[80] For a contemporaneous account by an American Christian missionary see Underwood, *Fifteen Years among the Top-Knots or Life in Korea*. For detailed numbers of converts subsequent to the Pyongyang revival see Ibid., Chapter XVIII, pp. 300–34.

[81] Eckert *et al.*, *Korea Old and New: A History*, pp. 186–222. See also Nahm, *Korea: Tradition and Transformation*, pp. 142–3.

[82] George L. Kallander, *Salvation through Dissent: Tonghak Heterodoxy and Early Modern Korea* (Honolulu: University of Hawai'i Press, 2013), pp. 147–53.

The claim of ethnic purity

The DPRK is much less accepting than South Korea of any foreign influence on the historical lineage of the Korean nation. That North Korea dates the founding of Koguryo more than three hundred years before its commonly accepted existence is not an accidental mistake. Such a reading eradicates having to acknowledge three to four hundred years of Han or 'foreign' occupation. South Korean historians, by contrast, have freely acknowledged the impact of 'Chinese language, philosophy, political concepts and system, laws, social structures, and art'.[83]

For North Korean official accounts, arguments as to the extent of what could be constituted as 'foreign' influence in Old Choson are not simply of scholarly interest. The idea that the Korean nation can trace a distinctive and discrete ancestry, largely 'uncontaminated' by 'foreign' influence, through years of history, supports national identity constructs that are useful for nationalist mythology.

The claim to linguistic superiority

The Korean language is common to North and South Korea even though there are differences in dialect and vocabulary. The fewer honorifics in northern language patterns reflect the historically less socially rigid northern social structure.[84] The common language is underpinned by a common alphabet. This is not the case for every population that speaks more or less the same language. Serbo-Croatian is basically the same language but even in the days when both formed part of the sovereign state of Yugoslavia, Serbia used the Cyrillic alphabet and Croatia the Roman script. The Korean script, known in North Korea as *Hunminjongum* and *Hangul* in South Korea, was developed in the 1440s under the instructions of King Sejong.[85] Its existence as a phonetic alphabet facilitated learning of languages and writing about subjects other than the Chinese classics, and allowed a wider range of authors to publish, especially elite Korean women, who wrote in the native Korean script.[86]

After the creation of the DPRK, Chinese characters were eradicated from everyday usage, including in newspapers and government

---

[83] Nahm, *An Introduction to Korean History and Culture*, p. 21.

[84] Oh, 'Economic Growth in P'yŏngan Province', pp. 1–22.

[85] A North Korean account is in Pang, *National Culture of Korea*, pp. 56–7; John H. Koo, 'Language', in John H. Koo and Andrew Nahm (eds.), *An Introduction to Korean Culture* (Elizabeth, NJ/Seoul: Hollym, 1997), pp. 99–117.

[86] See for example Jahyun Kim Haboush (trans. and ed.), *The Memoirs of Lady Hyegyŏng* (Berkeley: University of California Press, 1996).

publications, in a conscious effort to promote an exclusively Korean writing form. Chinese characters along with classical Chinese are taught in colleges and universities for those studying Chinese or Korean history. North Korean government sources claim nationalist credentials on the basis of a purported defence of Korean tradition. The claim is that South Korea's use of 'Chinese ideographs and other words of foreign origin' has 'adulterated' the 'purity' of the 'national language'.[87] The DPRK argues that in South Korea the Korean language 'is gradually losing its purity and degenerating into a hodgepodge of many languages'.[88] These days, however, South Koreans and North Koreans mirror each other in the inadvertent effects of globalisation. Both learn English to get by in the worlds of science, business and international transactions. Both also are re-appraising attitudes that had previously relegated Chinese to a secondary status in terms of foreign language learning because of the new-found importance of China as an economic partner.

National legitimacy claims

The DPRK claims that it is the rightful inheritor of the Korean nation's historically necessary trajectory towards independent statehood. This claim might seem absurd given the visible success of the South Korean state, its achievements at transiting from authoritarian rule to democracy and the prosperity of South Korean citizens. Yet the DPRK claims normative and political superiority over the South on nationalist grounds. North Korea routinely castigates South Korea as betrayers of the nation because of its alleged traitorous collaboration with foreign powers, especially the United States. The DPRK claims that South Korean governments have allowed too much foreign influence on Korean society. The further assertion is that it is only thanks to the Kim family that the North has prevented foreign influence and maintained Korean cultural identity on behalf of all Koreans everywhere, including those living in the South.

Northern national identity claims have persistently constituted Korean national identity around the supposed attributes of the Kim family. The naturalization of the Kim family at the heart of conceptions of national identity is one reason for the maintenance of a member of the Kim family as official Leader of the state. It would be possible to find an alternative political leader outside the Kim family but the difficulty would be in unravelling state mythologies that have argued for the Kim family as having the only legitimate claim to leadership of a liberated Korea.

[87] Pang, *Korean Review*, p. 184.   [88] Ibid.

Cultural commonality and Korean solidarity

Many publications on Korean culture from DPRK publishing houses would not be out of place in South Korea, except for perhaps a cursory reference to Kim Il Sung in the introduction. Organic expressions of common culture are visible in shared folk tales, song, musical instruments, pottery, dance, music, games and dress.[89] Common patterns in daily living range from the embedded respect for elders and family through to perhaps more mundane issues of common cuisine. The two Koreas share the same founding national mythology. Both venerate the art and textual heritage of ancient Korea.

The cultural differences between North and South Korean societies are substantive, yet the two Korean societies often seem to have an uncanny tendency to share the same perspective – sometimes about the superiority of all things Korean, from football to cuisine to historical longevity of the nation. The commonalities are not accidental and they are not entirely the result of ancient and embedded cultural habits and ideas. Korean solidarity was consolidated and entrenched by the harsh experience of Japanese colonial occupation that united Koreans because the colonial rulers treated them as if they were all the same in their 'Koreanness' and all the same in their inferiority to the Japanese.

---

[89] Hwan Ju Pang, *Korean Folk Customs* (Pyongyang: Foreign Languages Publishing House, 1990); the misleadingly titled, as it is a text not a map, Kwang Il Ju and Song Ui Jong, *Korea's Tourist Map* (Pyongyang: Korea International Travel Company, 1995). The introduction to the tourist spot of the Kumgang mountains has no reference to politics or the Kim family. See Foreign Languages Publishing House, *Mt. Kumgang* (Pyongyang: Foreign Languages Publishing House, undated, probably 1990).

Part II

The rise and fall of Kim Il Sungism

3   Colonial occupation and the rise of Kim Il Sung

The aim of Japanese colonial policy was to incorporate Korea into an expanding empire as a subordinated supplier of raw materials and labour whose inhabitants were to be stripped of national rights and aspirations. The intent was to eradicate Korean national identity and to force Koreans to assume loyalty to the Japanese state and the Emperor. The politics of colonialism brought annexation and militarised occupation enforced by a coercive police apparatus.[1] The economics of colonialism brought rapid industrialisation accompanied by mass migration that provided labour for the huge new manufacturing plants established by Japanese business in the north-east of the peninsula, in what is today the Democratic People's Republic of Korea (DPRK). The social dislocations brought about by colonial policy combined with the repression through which policy was enforced engendered the radicalisation of the population.

The denial of Korean independence and national identity and the increasingly militarised occupation, combined with the absence of outlets for moderate opposition to Japanese policies, narrowed the political options open to Korean nationalist leaders. Peaceful demonstrations failed to achieve political change, nationalist leaders were often forced into exile and some pursued guerrilla warfare from bases across the

---

[1] There is a large literature in English on the Japanese colonial occupation of Korea. Influential work includes Peter Duus, *The Abacus and the Sword: The Japanese Penetration of Korea 1895–1910* (Berkeley: University of California Press, 1995); Carter J. Eckert, *Offspring of Empire: The Koch'ang Kims and the Colonial Origins of Korean Capitalism, 1876–1945* (Seattle: University of Washington Press, 2003); Yoshihisa Tak Matsusaka, *The Making of Japanese Manchuria, 1904–1932* (Cambridge, MA: Harvard University Asia Center, 2003); Ramon H. Myers and Mark R. Peattie (eds.), *The Japanese Colonial Empire, 1895–1945* (Princeton University Press, 1984); Andre Schmid, *Korea Between Empires 1895–1919* (New York: Columbia University Press, 2002); Gi-Wook Shin and Michael Robinson (eds.), *Colonial Modernity in Korea* (Cambridge, MA: Harvard University Asia Center, 1999); Soon-Won Park, *Colonial Industrialization and Labor in Korea: The Onoda Cement Factory* (London: Harvard University Press, 1999).

contiguous Chinese border. The Japanese military ferociously hunted down and killed members of armed opposition groups, and Kim Il Sung, based first in Manchuria and then in the Soviet far east, was one of the very few survivors of Japanese retribution.[2]

Soviet troops, representing the Allied powers, entered and occupied northern Korea in August 1945. The thirty-eighth parallel almost immediately hardened into a territorial and ideological border between two political quasi state-like bodies in the northern and southern parts of the peninsula. The Soviet Union did not intend to remain in Korea but did intend to leave behind a regime friendly to the communist superpower. Soviet authorities promoted Kim Il Sung as *de facto* political Leader of the north and, in 1948, supported Kim Il Sung as the first Leader of the newly established sovereign state of the Democratic People's Republic of Korea (DPRK).

Between 1945 and 1950, Kim Il Sung implemented popular policies that included land reform, gender equality, the expansion of education and industrialisation. None of these policies were especially radical. The economy was not nationalised and elements of a private sector remained *in situ*. Kim's political methods were, from the beginning, hierarchical, authoritarian and coercive. Kim Il Sung did not situate political legitimacy claims in communist doctrine; from the outset, Kim founded legitimacy claims on nationalist credentials based on his alleged leadership of the anti-Japanese anti-colonial struggle.

Military rule

Japan imposed protectorate status on Korea in 1905 after victory over Russia and formally annexed Korea in 1910. In so doing, Japan wiped out the sovereign status of Korea as an independent state. Colonial occupation of Korea was led by the Japanese military via the Seoul-based Government-General, which was semi-autonomous from the Japanese foreign ministry and the Tokyo government. Colonial policy was aggressive and founded in a race-based perspective that understood Koreans as inferior by virtue of their ethnicity. At the inception of the occupation, military rule was enforced through outright oppression but from 1919 to the early 1930s the colonial authorities implemented the so-called 'cultural policy', in which Koreans were allowed a limited

[2] For detail on Kim Il Sung's early career see Robert A. Scalapino and Chong-Sik Lee, *Communism in Korea: The Movement* (Berkeley: University of California Press, 1972), pp. 202–30.

amount of cultural expression. The wholesale militarisation of Japanese foreign policy from the mid-1930s, however, was accompanied by an openly instrumental policy in which the function of Korea and Koreans was, more or less, only to provide rice, industrial products and labour for the Japanese war effort.

Japan justified colonial occupation as an act of altruism in bringing modernity and progress to a 'backward' country and people who were not fit for self-government. The rationalisation of self-interest and colonial policy was not very different from, for example, British policy in India, but where Japan differed with Britain, particularly in the later years of colonialism, was in the degree of cultural assimilation required. The colonial authorities expected nothing less than the adoption of Japanese 'consciousness' by their Korean subjects. Colonial authorities set out to eradicate any sense of a separate Korean ethnic identity to the extent that Koreans were expected to assume a Japanese view of the world in private as well as in public. Attempts were made to force loyalty to the Japanese Emperor and the Japanese state. Japanese colonial policy demanded of all Koreans that they worship at Shinto shrines and abjure the Korean language and family names. This was particularly offensive in a country and culture where ancestor worship and lineage status was at the core of personal, social and cultural identity.

The politics of repression

The oppression of the first phase of colonial rule was designed to wipe out Korean opposition to colonial rule. By the 1920s, members of the localised, poorly armed anti-colonial 'Righteous armies' had been mostly killed or imprisoned.[3] By the end of the first decade of Japanese annexation and occupation only a small number of groups continued the armed struggle – and these were located in the most mountainous areas of northern Korea and in Manchuria.[4]

In January 1919, the Choson king and emperor, Kojong, died. The occasion provided a platform on which the entire Korean political spectrum united to articulate Korean demands for independence. Chondogyo, Buddhist and Christian representatives combined to write a declaration of Korean independence, designed to be announced just before the funeral of King Kojong, due to be held on 4 March 1919. Thirty-three nationalist leaders signed the declaration in a Seoul restaurant on

---

[3] Andrew J. Grajdanzev, *Modern Korea* (New York: Institute of Pacific Relations/The John Day Company, 1944), pp. 43–5.
[4] Ibid., p. 45.

1 March 1919, and it was read in front of large crowds of demonstrators throughout the country, including in Seoul's Pagoda Park.[5] These intellectual and political leaders were influenced by United States President Woodrow Wilson's commitment to self-determination for all nations and colonised peoples that had been proclaimed at the post-World War One treaty negotiations in Versailles; ideas that had circulated worldwide.[6] The March First Independence Movement was not, however, confined to the salons and the educated few.

A national, cross-class independence movement brought over a million people onto the streets in nationwide mass demonstrations from March to May 1919.[7] International observers at the time commented on the large-scale involvement of girls and women in the independence movement.[8] These demonstrations were largely peaceful but the Japanese responded with wholesale force. Japanese colonial sources reported 553 'agitators' killed; 1,409 wounded; 19,054 imprisoned; and 10,592 flogged.[9] Koreans reported 7,000 killed.[10]

Japanese rulers were shaken by the scale of support for the mass demonstrations for independence. They were also embarrassed by the international condemnation that followed the repression of the demonstrators. In reaction and in attempts to prove itself a 'responsible' colonial power, Japan shifted policy to what it called 'cultural rule', whereby Koreans were permitted some self-expression in the media, education and the wider civil society. These cultural concessions remained, however, subordinated to a punitive and enhanced policing and penal regime and were often in tension with continued Japanese attempts at assimilation.[11]

Colonial policies were enforced through punitive sanctions for infractions of government policies. The criminal code penalised all activities that might challenge colonial rule, including 'thought crimes'.[12] The police force was staffed by Japanese and Koreans, the

[5] Andrew C. Nahm, *Korea: Tradition and Transformation* (Elizabeth, NJ/Seoul: Hollym, 1996), pp. 262–4.
[6] Grajdanzev, *Modern Korea*, p. 55.
[7] Nahm, *Korea: Tradition and Transformation*, pp. 262–4.
[8] F. A. McKenzie, *Korea's Fight for Freedom* (New York: Fleming H. Revell Company, 1920), pp. 290–302.
[9] Grajdanzev, *Modern Korea*, p. 55.
[10] Henry Chung, *The Case of Korea* (New York: F. H. Revell Co., 1921), p. 163, cited in ibid., p. 56.
[11] On increases in policing capacity see Carter J. Eckert, Ki-bail Lee, Young Ick Lew, Michael Robinson and Edward Wagner, *Korea Old and New: A History* (Cambridge, MA: Korea Institute, Harvard University/Ilchokak, 1990), pp. 283–4.
[12] Chulwoo Lee, 'Modernity, Legality, and Power in Korea under Japanese Rule', in Gi-Wook Shin and Michael Robinson (eds.), *Colonial Modernity in Korea* (Cambridge, MA; Harvard University Press, 1999), pp. 21–51.

latter being every bit as hated and feared as the Japanese.[13] Punishments in the first ten years of Japanese rule included flogging, imprisonment and fines. Flogging was abolished in 1920 but punishment remained brutal. A feature of the system was the virtual impossibility of being found to be innocent once arrested and accused of a crime.[14] Another feature was the ubiquity of police administration of what in other societies would be the private sphere. The police force was responsible for health surveillance, the organisation of community tasks such as road-building, support for government propaganda campaigns, agricultural direction and tax collection.[15]

From 1931, when Japan started to mobilise for expansion into China via Manchuria, until 1937, when Japan and China officially were at war, the limited cultural autonomy that Koreans had enjoyed became progressively eroded. Japanese military planners primarily viewed Korea as a forward base for expansion into China. Wartime mobilisation priorities pushed Koreans once more into their allotted position of subordinated subjects of the Empire and harshly enforced military rule again became the norm. Korean aspirations for independence were violently suppressed with the torture, killing and imprisonment of Christians, communists, nationalists and those suspected of related 'thought crimes'.

The most naked abuses occurred during the Pacific war of 1941–5 when Japan conscripted the Korean population into support for the war effort. The colonial police force rounded up hundreds of thousands of Korean men who were sent abroad to work in factories and mines or conscripted as soldiers into the Japanese army.[16] By 1944, some 4 million Koreans – out of a population of 25 million – were working in Japan or Manchuria in support of the war effort, many in mines and munitions factories.[17] Most notoriously, hundreds of thousands of Korean women – today known as the 'comfort-women', a term which hides the brutality of the experiences of these women, were sent to work as enforced prostitutes for the Japanese military.[18]

---

[13] Grajdanzev, *Modern Korea*, p. 257; Eckert *et al.*, *Korea Old and New: A History*, pp. 259–60.

[14] Grajdanzev, *Modern Korea*, p. 256.

[15] Detail from Lee, 'Modernity, Legality, and Power', p.37. See also Ching-chih Chen, 'Police and Community Control Systems in the Empire', in Ramon H. Myers and Mark R. Peattie (eds.), *The Japanese Colonial Empire, 1895–1945* (Princeton University Press, 1984), pp. 213–39.

[16] Ibid.   [17] Eckert *et al.*, *Korea Old and New: A History*, p. 322.

[18] George Hicks, *The Comfort Women: Japan's Brutal Regime of Enforced Prostitution in the Second World War* (New York: W. W. Norton and Company, 1997).

The economics of colonialism

The Government-General pursued rapid, large-scale industrialisation and set about modernising agriculture, industry, transport, government and social welfare.[19] Development projects were designed and implemented to benefit the Japanese 'motherland', although colonial authorities argued that Koreans also benefited through the provision of jobs, improvements in infrastructure and social welfare. Improved transport and communication networks facilitated the extraction of Korean resources to Japan and easier circulation of the army and the police force for the purposes of repression and control.

Rice was the most important crop in Korea and provided the basic grain of preference in the Korean diet. Colonial authorities invested in agriculture such that between 1920 and 1938 rice production in Korea increased by 150 per cent.[20] The monetary value of production increased eightfold in that same period but, between 1915 and 1938, Korean per capita rice consumption decreased by around half.[21] The reason for declining rice consumption at a time of increasing production was that the rice crop was exported to Japan. Hunger ensued as rice was not replaced by other cereals in the diet. Between 1915 and 1933, the per capita consumption of all cereals declined by 20 per cent.[22]

Japan invested in fertiliser plants, mining and metal, machine-building, chemicals, oil refining, banking, lumber, food and beverages, ceramics and textiles, among others. Japanese conglomerates like Mitsui, Mitsubishi, Sumitomo and Yasuda built huge enterprises in Korea.[23] The gross value of industrial production in Korea quadrupled between 1922 and 1938, from ¥223 million to ¥1,140 million.[24] Japan also invested in telecommunications and transport, including railroads and port development.[25]

Japanese planning envisaged a key role for northern Korea as a forward supply base for its army and its industries in its north-east Asian empire-building strategy. Industrial outputs were designed to supply the military and support expansionist plans into Manchuria and into China proper. Japanese investors expanded from gold mining, which had historically attracted foreign investors, including from the United States, into coal mining, which was a new industry to Korea. Major mines were located in what are present-day provinces of the DPRK; in North Hamgyong, South Hamgyong, South Pyongan, North

[19] For detail see Grajdanzev, *Modern Korea*.
[20] Ibid., p. 295.   [21] Ibid., p. 295 and 118.   [22] Ibid., p. 119.
[23] Ibid., p. 152.   [24] Ibid., p. 148.   [25] Ibid., pp. 185–200.

Hwanghae and South Hwanghae.[26] Japan exploited newly discovered iron ore deposits in Musan, North Hamgyong and concentrated iron and steel production plants in the northern half of the peninsula so as to be in proximity to these massive newly available mineral resources.[27]

Japanese business made major investments in heavy industry including mines, metallurgy, machine tools and chemicals. These investments were in large-scale, modern production facilities, such as the Korea Nitrogen Fertiliser Corporation factory in Hungnam, South Hamgyong, which in 1937 was the second largest fertiliser factory in the world.[28] Investment was directed to the port cities of Chongjin in North Hamgyong; Hungnam in South Hamgyong and Chinnampo – today the North Korean west coast port city of Nampo.[29] Other centres of colonial industrial development were located in Sariwon in South Hwanghae province, Pyongyang, Wonsan in Kangwon province and Songjin in North Hamgyong province.[30] Two cities on the China border were also targeted for Japanese investment. These were Sinuiju in North Pyongan province in the west and Hoiryong in North Hamgyong province in the east.[31]

The benefits of modernisation and industrialisation did not accrue proportionately to Koreans and to Japanese citizens.[32] Some, albeit a minority, made money and sent their children for education abroad, often to Japan.[33] Most Koreans, however, worked long hours for low wages. The average working day lasted between ten and thirteen hours and the two days a month nominally allocated as rest days were not always taken.[34] In real terms, wages decreased by a third between 1910 and 1940 and remained insufficient to support a family, even at subsistence levels.[35] Inequalities based on assumed Korean inferiority and Japanese superiority were embodied in the modalities of redevelopment projects. Japanese citizens were employed in the more skilled and better-paid work and Japanese workers were paid more and had better working conditions than Koreans doing the same work.

In 1938, children comprised at least 9 per cent of the workforce.[36] The prevalence of child labour was one reason that about two-thirds of primary age children did not attend school.[37] In 1939, primary schools enrolled some 1.2 million Korean children.[38] A much smaller number of

[26] Nahm, *Korea: Tradition and Transformation*, pp. 244–45.
[27] Ibid., p. 245.   [28] Grajdanzev, *Modern Korea*, p. 152.
[29] Soon-Won Park, 'Colonial Industrial Growth and the Emergence of the Korean Working Class', in Gi-Wook Shin and Michael Robinson (eds.), *Colonial Modernity in Korea* (Cambridge, MA; Harvard University Press, 1999), pp. 133 and 135.
[30] Ibid., p. 136.   [31] Ibid.   [32] Grajdanzev, *Modern Korea*.
[33] Eckert, *Offspring of Empire*.   [34] Grajdanzev, *Modern Korea*, p. 184.
[35] Ibid., pp. 179–82.   [36] Ibid., p. 183.   [37] Ibid., p. 262.   [38] Ibid.

Korean children attended school beyond primary level. In 1939 the figure was just less than 30,000.[39] Another 32,000 attended some form of further education and just 206 Koreans were university students at the Keijo Imperial University in Seoul.[40] Korean university students at the Imperial University were outnumbered by the 350 Japanese students.[41]

Schools for Korean children were not resourced to the same level as for Japanese children and the heavily skewed curriculum attempted to inculcate ideas about the inherent superiority of Japan and Japanese culture over Korea and Korean culture.[42] Teaching was carried out in Japanese. The primary aim was to provide an efficient workforce which would be socialised to accept the superiority of Japan and Japanese culture. Nevertheless some Koreans were able to access educational opportunities. A small number managed to obtain a university education and some of these graduated from prestigious Japanese and American universities.

Social change and mass migration

The colonial government promoted Korean migration as a means to supply labour for economic development and for military projects both in Korea and in Japanese-controlled Manchuria. Hundreds of thousands of northern Koreans and tens of thousands of southerners moved north to Manchuria to try to make a living, notably through the development of paddy rice farming, for which Koreans were famous for their expertise.[43] Migration was sometimes voluntary, sometimes induced by the promise of economic opportunity and sometimes propelled by the need to escape repression. These population movements were massive. The total movement of labour to staff industrial enterprises in Korea, not including labour migration to Japan and Manchuria, was nearly half a million in the ten years prior to the Japanese defeat in 1945.[44] From the late 1930s and 1940s migration was often coerced as Koreans were conscripted into mines and industrial plants throughout the empire in support of the war effort.

The northern region became host to thousands of immigrants from the south who found themselves geographically and socially dislocated from familiar patterns of life. In 1940, North Hamgyong was home to over

---

[39] Ibid.   [40] Ibid., p. 263.   [41] Ibid.

[42] For detail see Park, 'Colonial Industrial Growth', pp. 146–9.

[43] Hyun Ok Park, *Two Dreams in One Bed: Empire, Social Life and the Origins of the North Korean Revolution in Manchuria* (Durham: Duke University Press, 2005), p. 46; Adam Cathcart, 'Nationalism and Ethnic Identity in the Sino-Korean Border Region of Yanbian 1945–1950', *Korean Studies*, Vol. 34, 2010, pp. 28–9.

[44] Park, 'Colonial Industrial Growth', pp. 144–5.

100,000 non-agricultural workers – some 60 per cent of the workforce compared to the average provincial non-agricultural labour force throughout Korea of 25 per cent.[45] In the 1930s the majority of the population of North Hamgyong and South Hamgyong originated in the southern provinces (and Kangwon).[46] In 1940, of the sixteen cities in Korea with populations over 50,000, eight were located in what is today North Korea.[47] Pyongyang was the country's second biggest city – after Seoul, with nearly a million inhabitants – with a population of 286,000.[48] Chongjin was the country's fourth biggest city, with a population of just under 200,000.[49] The remaining six were Wonsan, Hamhung, Kaesong, Nampo, Haeju and Sinuiju.[50]

Girls and women were incorporated into the factory workforce so that by 1932, 45 per cent of the workforce was made up of women.[51] Everywhere in the country, women entered the industrial workforce, challenging and changing some very long-standing gendered understandings of what was right and proper in Korean society. Given that Korean women, especially middle class women, had customarily lived in a form of purdah until around the turn of the century, the entry of women into a mixed, modernised workforce reflected major and extraordinarily rapid social change in Korean society.

The bewilderingly fast transformation from Choson social rigidity to colonial modernity brought hitherto taken-for-granted social identities and relationships into question. The new industrial workforce was propelled out of agrarian, conservative social structures, which had changed only very slowly in previous centuries, into urban communities that were formed in the space of months and which were constituted around unfamiliar new ways of living and working. The repetitive rhythms of the factory work cycle marked time instead of the agrarian cycle of seasons. Discipline was enforced by foreign, Japanese supervisors, not by the community or the family.

The rise of radical consciousness

The newly displaced populations who had migrated north to take up work were receptive to well-circulated ideas of equality, liberty, fraternity

[45] Ibid., p. 137.
[46] The original reference is given as the official registration records of 'North and South Hamkyong provinces' in *Nihon Kukusei Soran* (Tokyo, 1934), vol. II p. 316. The reference is from Chungnim Choi Han, 'Social Organization of Upper Han Hamlet in Korea', doctoral dissertation (University of Michigan, June 1949), p. 26.
[47] Grajdanzev, *Modern Korea*, p. 80.   [48] Ibid.   [49] Ibid.   [50] Ibid.
[51] Park, 'Colonial Industrial Growth', p. 141. Park notes that the figure declined to 33 per cent by the end of the 1930s. See ibid., p. 141.

and independence. These radical ideas were disseminated via progressive Christianity, radical nationalism and the Chondogyo religious and political movement, as well as by clandestine communist sympathisers.[52] Not all northern communities were transformed by new ways of thinking, of course. As late as the mid-1930s, rural areas retained long-standing norms and practices that were profoundly gendered and founded in communitarian, hierarchical, Confucian practices.[53]

In 1945 the total number of northern Christians amounted to around 200,000. This was a sizeable number but still comprised just 2–3 per cent of the population.[54] Yet Christianity had a political impact disproportionate to the numerical strength of adherents, especially in the north. Many influential nationalist leaders in colonial northern Korea were Christians. The most well-known was Cho Man-Sik, a Christian leader from Pyongan province, who has been called the 'Korean Ghandi' because of his support for non-violent resistance to colonial rule.[55] Cho Man-Sik supported Korean self-help movements within the framework of Japanese rule, including the nationally popular movement to buy Korean goods.[56]

Colonial authorities tolerated Christianity, including the presence of foreign missionaries, but restrictions were placed upon the activities of the churches, which were viewed with suspicion as either providing covert or overt support for independence advocates. In fact, although foreign missionaries were critical of the Japanese occupation, most were also condemnatory of radical anti-colonial movements.[57] Foreign missionaries attempted to adapt themselves to Japanese restrictions in order to maintain a presence in Korea. According to contemporary sources, the numbers of Christians in Korea in 1920–1 were around 360,000.[58] By 1938 the number had grown to 500,000.[59] Other sources reported a total number of Korean Christians at not more than 400,000 by the time of liberation in 1945.[60] These were fairly small proportions of the total

[52] Ibid.
[53] For a detailed study of rural life in Pukchong county, South Hamgyong in the 1920s and 1930s see Han, 'Social Organization of Upper Han Hamlet in Korea'. The description of the attitudes expected from men and women as 'be gentlemanly' *chomchan-hae* and 'be ladylike' *yamchon-hae* could be used to describe the socialisation of young men and women in today's DPRK. See ibid., pp. 66–71.
[54] Charles K. Armstrong, *The North Korean Revolution 1945–1950* (Ithaca, NY: Cornell University Press, 2003), p. 119.
[55] Scalapino and Lee, *Communism in Korea*, p.314.
[56] Eckert, *Offspring of Empire*, pp. 83 and 281, note 64.
[57] Grajdanzev, *Modern Korea*, pp. 274–5.
[58] Ibid., p. 275.   [59] Ibid.
[60] Don Baker, *Korean Spirituality* (Honolulu: University of Hawai'i Press, 2008), p. 74.

peninsula population of 24 million, although the numbers in northern Korea were proportionately higher.

Northern Korea was notable for strikes and industrial action that were organised by radical workers' unions and community-based organisations.[61] Large numbers of incidences of industrial action took place throughout the north-east in the late 1920s and early 1930s – in Hamhung, Hungnam, Yonghung, Sinuiju and Pyongyang.[62] The most famous was the dock-workers' action that developed into a General Strike in Wonsan in 1929.[63] Communists and radicals of all different hues organised 'Red Peasant Unions' and associations of peasants in Hamgyong throughout the 1930s. These Leftist organising activities were savagely repressed by the colonial power, and communist and labour leaders were killed and imprisoned.[64]

From reform to revolution

In the 1920s, Korean authors and intellectuals took advantage of the opening up of cultural space to debate, within the new Korean media, the shape of a future liberated Korea. Nationalist-inspired movements encouraged the development of Korean self-consciousness and national pride. In the wake of the repression that followed the March First Independence movement, some activists moved to Shanghai where they were exposed to a melange of radical ideas. The Comintern, the Soviet Union's international organisation of communist parties, operated in Shanghai and provided one source of inspiration.[65] Soviet official political philosophy was Marxism-Leninism, which argued that the industrial proletariat would provide the leading social force in any revolution. Korean activists also absorbed ideas from Chinese communists whose experience and ideology was based on the idea that peasant-based revolutionary movements could provide the backbone of communist transformation and national liberation.

From the 1930s, after the suppression of even the most moderate expressions of Korean nationalism, the option of peaceful change and a gradual transition to Korean independence seemed remote. It began to

---

[61] Park, 'Colonial Industrial Growth', p. 155.
[62] Ibid.; Nahm, *Korea: Tradition and Transformation*, p. 281.
[63] Park, 'Colonial Industrial Growth', p. 155; Nahm, *Korea: Tradition and Transformation*, p. 281.
[64] Armstrong, *The North Korean Revolution*, pp. 16–23; Nahm, *Korea: Tradition and Transformation*, p. 281.
[65] Erik Esselstrom, *Crossing Empire's Edge: Foreign Ministry Police and Japanese Expansionism in Northeast Asia* (Honolulu: University of Hawai'i Press, 2009).

look like only the complete overthrow of Japanese rule would allow Koreans to exercise basic freedoms, including the ability to speak their own language, and only the violent overthrow of colonial rule would bring national liberation. The many who took up arms in the 1930s and 1940s included those who might not in other circumstances have turned to violence and who came from diverse ideological backgrounds, including those of liberal, nationalist and revolutionary socialist leanings.

Korean nationalists and Korean communists shifted into Manchuria in the 1930s and the 1940s, where they combined forces with Chinese and Soviet forces and engaged in armed activity against colonial outposts in Korea from bases inside China. Guerrilla forces maintained steady harassment of colonial targets but they were not able to achieve major victories. Japanese troops were numerous, well-armed, efficient and brutal, and the guerrilla forces were ravaged by internal strife.[66] Estimates vary of the numbers of Korean revolutionaries operating in the border regions between northern Korea and Manchuria in the late 1930s, with figures ranging between 2,000 and 20,000.[67]

One of the few guerrilla leaders to survive the anti-Japanese struggle was the young Kim Il Sung. Kim fought alongside Chinese comrades during the late 1930s as part of the Northeast Anti-Japanese United Army.[68] Kim was also known to the Soviet government from which he received shelter and support during the intense crackdown against anti-colonial guerrilla fighters by Japanese troops in the 1940s.

The emergence of Kim Il Sung

Kim Il Sung was born on 15 April 1912 in an outlying district of Pyongyang called Manyongdae. Kim was born Kim Song Ju and adopted the *nom de guerre* of Kim Il Sung while participating in anti-Japanese guerrilla struggle in Manchuria.[69] Some have argued that Kim Il Sung's change of name was intended as an attempt to adopt the identity of a more famous guerrilla fighter or as a means of exaggerating his achievements. There is enough evidence, however, to confirm that Kim Il Sung

---

[66] Scalapino and Lee, *Communism in Korea*, pp. 211–32.

[67] One author, writing in 1944 using Japanese sources, argued that for the year 1938 alone, over 20,000 Korean revolutionaries were operating in the border region. See Grajdanzev, *Modern Korea*, p. 257. Another author argues that by 1936, because of 'murderous suppression', numbers were reduced to 2,000. See Bruce Cumings, *The Origins of the Korean War, Vol. I: Liberation and the Emergence of Separate Regimes 1945–1947* (Seoul: Yuksabipyungsa, 2002), p. 35.

[68] Ibid.   [69] Scalapino and Lee, *Communism in Korea*, p. 203.

was indeed one and the same person as Kim Song Ju.[70] North Korean accounts do not hide the change of name and they also record that in Kim Il Sung's fighting days he was also sometimes known as Han Byol – 'the morning star' of Korea.[71]

Kim Il Sung experienced first hand both privation and family dislocation. Kim's parents, like large numbers of Koreans, went north to Manchuria for work, and both parents died there, in exile, at early ages; his father in 1926 aged 32 and his mother in 1932 aged 40.[72] Kim Il Sung must have been influenced by Christianity – although we do not know precisely how – as his father, Kim Hyong-jik, was educated at Sungsil school, established by American missionaries in Pyongyang.[73] Kim Il Sung was educated in Pyongyang and Manchuria for eight years. A lasting benefit was the future DPRK leader's fluency in Mandarin.

Kim Il Sung was well known to the Japanese as an effective and troublesome guerrilla leader. Kim's most famous exploit – celebrated in North Korea today – was the 1937 raid on Pochonbo, North Hamgyong province, in which Kim and his guerrilla force destroyed Japanese local government outposts and a police station.[74] Kim operated from Manchuria until 1941, when Japan's intensive anti-guerrilla warfare drove him into a second exile in the Soviet Union.[75] Kim Il Sung met Kim Chong-Suk, a fellow guerrilla, while in the Soviet Union, and their son, Kim Jong Il, was born in the Soviet Union, in 1942. Kim Chong-Suk was originally from Hoiryong, North Hamgyong, and like Kim Il Sung her parents had also migrated to Manchuria and had also died in exile.[76]

In North Korea, Kim's parents are portrayed as anti-colonial activists but the more tenuous claim is that Kim's distant ancestors provided leadership in the struggle for Korean independence.[77] One of these was, it is claimed, a certain Kim Gye San who as far back as in the late sixteenth century was involved in the opposition to the resistance against the Japanese invasion of Korea.[78] North Korean hagiography also claims

---

[70] Ibid., pp. 227–8.
[71] Compilation Committee of Kim Il Sung Encyclopaedia, *Kim Il Sung Encyclopaedia Volume One* (New Delhi: Vishwanath, 1992), p. 39.
[72] Dae-Sook Suh, *Kim Il Sung: The North Korean Leader* (New York: Columbia University Press, 1988), pp. 5–6.
[73] Ibid., p. 5.   [74] Ibid., pp. 34–6.   [75] Ibid., pp. 47–52.   [76] Ibid., pp. 47–52.
[77] For a North Korean authorized account of Kim Il Sung's immediate family see Bong Baik, *Kim Il Sung: Biography (1)* (Beirut: Dar Al-Talia, 1973).
[78] Bong Paek (translated in other English-language publications published in the DPRK as Bong Baek), one of Kim Il Sung's official biographers, is cited as the source of these claims by Genaro Carnero Checa, *Korea: Rice and Steel* (Pyongyang: Foreign Languages Publishing House, 1977), p.28.

that Kim's great-grandfather, Kim Ung U, led opposition to the incursion by the American vessel, the *General Sherman*, into Pyongyang in 1866.[79] South Korean accounts have, by contrast, argued that Kim Il Sung did not have credible anti-colonial credentials.[80]

The truth lies somewhere between North Korean hagiography and South Korean dismissals. Kim Il Sung was an experienced leader by the time of liberation. He had worked with both Chinese and Soviet communists and demonstrated the ability to inspire followers who were much older than himself – something quite remarkable in the context of Korean society which venerates elders and age as a source of wisdom. Kim's politics were pragmatic, opportunist and derived from guerrilla warfare in a remote, tough corner of the world that has sometimes been called the 'Wild East' because of its lawlessness.[81] Kim's politics were not a product of theoretical reflection and although they were influenced by the Soviet Union's official Marxist-Leninist ideology they were more nationalist and anti-colonial than doctrinaire communist.

The transition to Kim Il Sungism

The Soviet Union declared war on Japan on 8 August 1945. Soviet troops, representing the allied powers, advanced into the North-eastern Korean ports of Chongjn, Rajin and Unggi (now Sonbong County) on 9 August 1945 but hostilities lasted just one week. Japan announced its surrender on 15 August 1945 and the Soviet liberators marched into Pyongyang on 30 August.[82] The northern population welcomed the Soviet troops as liberators but these battle-hardened Russian soldiers – shipped into Korea straight from the fighting in Germany – committed crimes against the local population, including rape and robbery. The Soviet occupation authorities clamped down on these activities but nevertheless these crimes were widespread in 1945.[83]

The Soviet Union stopped its military at the thirty-eighth parallel and did not advance southwards into Seoul, even though American troops did not ship into Korea until 9 September 1945. The Soviet Union had

---

[79] Ibid.   [80] Scalapino and Lee, *Communism in Korea*, pp. 227–8.
[81] For an amusing and imaginative conceptualisation of the 'Wild East' whose background is the anti-Japanese activity in Manchuria see *The Good, the Bad and the Weird*, Director Kim Jee-Woon, 2008, available on DVD with English subtitles.
[82] Armstrong, *The North Korean Revolution*, pp. 38–47.
[83] Anna Louise Strong, *In North Korea: First Eye-Witness Report* (New York: Soviet Russia Today, 1949), available at www.marxists.org/reference/archive/strong-anna-louise/1949/in-north-korea/index.htm, accessed 12 October 2013.

agreed with its American ally that it would remain in the north and that American troops should occupy the south.[84] The Soviet Union's absence of interest in taking over the entire peninsula when it had the opportunity to do so was because Korea was not a priority for post-war Soviet global strategy. The Soviet Union had suffered heavy losses in the war, including over twenty million civilian deaths. Post-war priorities were domestic and military reconstruction and establishing dominance over the new communist states of eastern and central Europe.

In the immediate aftermath of liberation, northern and southern Koreans established provincial people's committees throughout Korea to fill the vacuum provided by collapsed colonial institutions.[85] Koreans were emboldened by witnessing almost half a century of annexation disappear in a matter of weeks. In the north, the Soviet Union supported the People's Committees and attempted to bring moderate nationalists into a broad governmental coalition with Korean communists.[86] Kim Il Sung was was not an automatic choice for leader. The Soviet Union only facilitated Kim Il Sung's return to Korea on a Russian ship in September 1945, a month after the Soviet army arrived in the north.[87]

In the immediate post-war period, the most prominent northern leader was Christian nationalist, Cho Man-Sik, who established the Korean Democratic Party in 1945.[88] The Party had an influential membership and was widely perceived as a potential vehicle for liberal democratic rule in northern Korea.[89] Cho Man-Sik was also the Pyongyang-based head of the South Pyongan Provincial People's Political Committee.[90] That Cho was chosen by the Soviet authorities to introduce Kim Il Sung to a mass rally in Pyongyang in October 1945 gives an indication of his standing and popularity.[91] The Soviet authorities tried to include Cho in a government of national unity but Cho fell foul of the Soviet occupation forces in his refusal to back trusteeship proposals for Korea, which had originally been proposed by President Roosevelt and accepted by the Allied Powers.

Trusteeship was not popular with Koreans, who wanted an independent Korea as soon as possible. In the south the anti-communist nationalist leader Synghman Rhee, who had been installed by the United States, refused to accept the trusteeship proposals. The Soviet Union and the

[84] Cumings, *The Origins of the Korean War, Vol. I*, pp. 120–2.
[85] John N. Washburn, 'Russia Looks at Northern Korea', *Pacific Affairs*, Vol. 20, No. 2, June 1947, pp. 152–60.
[86] Scalapino and Lee, *Communism in Korea*, pp. 314–16.
[87] Armstrong, *The North Korean Revolution*, p.55.
[88] Ibid., pp. 119–23.   [89] Ibid., pp. 119–20.
[90] Scalapino and Lee, *Communism in Korea*, pp. 314–16.
[91] Armstrong, *The North Korean Revolution*, pp. 58–9.

northern political leadership supported trusteeship but insisted on implementation modalities that the United States and Synghman Rhee argued
would be tantamount to giving the communists an inbuilt majority. The
trusteeship proposals never came to fruition as both North and South
became more and more entrenched in their opposition to each other.
Kim Il Sung used the trusteeship debate to consolidate political control
over opponents as he manoeuvred to eradicate Cho Man-Sik from Soviet
consideration for northern leadership, to shore up his political value to
the Soviet occupying authorities and his organisational prominence
within the North.

The Soviet Union had little knowledge or experience of Korea, despite
posting Soviet citizens of Korean ethnicity with the occupation army, and
within the rapidly accelerating global Cold War of the post-war era, Kim
held trump cards. Kim's formal allegiance to the communist camp and
his willingness to cooperate with the Soviet Union meant that Soviet
authorities saw Kim as reliable enough to lead a future Korea into a
dependent, allied relationship with the Soviet Union. Conversely, Kim
understood that his own political future could be best safeguarded by
Soviet support. Kim took advantage of the Soviet alliance to secure
economic and military aid. In 1948, by the time the Soviet Union
evacuated its troops, a relationship of mutual dependence was established with a Kim Il Sung-led northern Korea. A well-staffed Soviet
Embassy and civilian and military advisers continued to monitor North
Korean politics. The Kim Il Sung-led government was unequivocally
supported by the Soviet Union and embedded within the Soviet camp in
the rapidly freezing, globally polarised, Cold War.

The consolidation of power

Kim engaged in a rapid exercise in institution-building to provide organisational foundations for the exercise of power at the governmental and
the party political level. In February 1946, Kim established the North
Korean Provisional People's Committee, which oversaw and directed the
provincial people's committees.[92] As Chairman, Kim Il Sung was *de facto*
ruler of the new North Korea. Kim focused political and organisational
efforts on the creation of a mass-based and hierarchically organised
Communist Korean Workers' Party, which was formally established
in August 1946 as the North Korean Workers' Party.[93] By the end
of 1947 the North Korean Workers' Party claimed an enormous

[92] Armstrong, *The North Korean Revolution*, p.69.   [93] Ibid., p. 66.

membership of 700,000 persons out of an adult population of 4.5 million.[94] In 1949 Kim formally merged the South Korean Workers' Party with the North Korean Workers' Party to form the Workers' Party of Korea (WPK) and had himself appointed Chairman of the Party.[95]

The Soviet Union provided economic and military advisers, equipment and military materiel. By 1946 North Korea's combined military forces were assessed at between 120,000 and 150,000, with a core military of some 60,000 troops in 1948.[96] These seemingly inconsistent figures are compatible with each other as Kim's policy was to enhance the professional military with mass mobilisation that incorporated all adult members of the population between the ages of 17 and 40 in military training.[97]

Cho Man-Sik was sidelined and purged by the Soviet Union and Kim Il Sung's faction.[98] Cho was arrested in 1946 and killed in 1950 at the beginning of the Korean War.[99] Kim Il Sung replaced the leadership of the Korean Democratic Party with political allies, thus transforming the Party that Cho Man-Sik created into only a nominally independent political entity.[100] The Korean Social Democratic Party was another token political entity. Formed in 1945, in the words of a North Korean publication, to represent the interests of 'medium and small entrepreneurs, merchants, handicraftsmen [sic], petty bourgeoisie, some peasants and Christians', the Korean Social Democratic Party had no independent organisational existence.[101]

The Chondogyo Young Friends Party, established in 1923 and rooted in the popular religious Chondogyo or 'Religion of the Heavenly Way' of nineteenth-century Eastern learning, supported land reform and had substantial support from poor rural dwellers. It did not support Kim's efforts to intensify state control over the rural economy and its members clashed with the Korean Workers' Party in a number of localities.[102] Kim Il Sung piled the pressure on Chondogyo movement leaders, however, and in 1950 they agreed to subsume the Party under the leadership of the North Korean Workers' Party. The Chondogyo Party was permitted a

[94] Scalapino and Lee, *Communism in Korea*, p.374.
[95] Sung Chul Yang, *The North and South Korean Political Systems: A Comparative Analysis*, revised edition (Elizabeth, NJ: Hollym, 1999), p.270.
[96] Scalapino and Lee, *Communism in Korea*, pp. 374 and 391.
[97] Ibid., p. 391.   [98] Ibid., pp. 336–40.
[99] For detail see Armstrong, *The North Korean Revolution*, pp. 55–6 and p   116–23.
[100] Scalapino and Lee, *Communism in Korea*, p.340.
[101] Hwan Ju Pang, *Korean Review* (Pyongyang: Foreign Languages Pub 1987), p.83.
[102] Armstrong, *The North Korean Revolution*, pp. 125–33.

nominal existence so as to buttress Kim's claims that the new North Korea incorporated and represented historic Korean independence movements based on peasant rebellion but this Party, like the Korean Democratic Party and the Social Democratic Party, could not sustain an independent political existence in Kim Il Sung's post-liberation North Korea.

Mass mobilisation

Idiosyncratic to Kim's political plans was the ambition to organise the entire population within large-scale, nationwide collective organisations that could be mobilised for economic development projects.[103] These included organisations for youth, women, farmers and industrial workers, writers and artists. These were hierarchical organisations that were intended as mechanisms of control as well as for economic development. Kim anticipated combining legislative reform with mass mobilisation of a population that would enthusiastically engage in 'voluntary' nation-building activities but was disappointed to find that the population did not respond very well to exhortation alone or with the requisite revolutionary fervour. To encourage participation in economic reconstruction, the government resorted to offering extra pay, providing intensive exhortation through propaganda and using coercion through surveillance and legal sanctions.[104]

Social and economic reforms

In the months following liberation, millions of Koreans displaced by war returned home from Japan and from Manchuria; from the north to the south and from the south to the north. Also on the move were Japanese returning to Japan. The numbers are not available for all post-war movements but the scale of relocation is indicated by the nearly one million people that returned to South Korea between 1945 and 1947.[105] In the aftermath of these huge population dislocations, agricultural production plummeted and in the winter of 1945–6 food shortages were acute. Agriculture and land policy was therefore of prime importance to the new North Korean leadership. The 1946 land reform redistributed

---

[103] Scalapino and Lee, *Communism in Korea*, pp. 374–6.
[104] For detail on societal and state control mechanisms see Armstrong, *The North Korean Revolution*, pp. 191–214.
[105] For figures on population movements to the South 1945–7 see Cumings, *The Origins of the Korean War, Vol. I*, p.60.

about a million hectares of land previously owned by landlords and Japanese entities. About half of North Korea's arable land was given free of charge to 725,000 poor and landless families.[106] Land reform was relatively free from violence and coercion because the majority of the 44,000 landlords from whom land was expropriated were absentees or had fled south to escape what they understood as a communist takeover of the north.[107]

Land was left in private hands but land resale, sub-letting and mortgaging was prohibited.[108] Agricultural planning was initially implemented through state direction and administrative controls but from the late 1940s the government relied on state-led encouragement, leaving individuals to devise their own plans.[109] About three-quarters of farming households, which together comprised about 70 per cent of the country's population in 1949, were able to feed themselves without state support.[110] Food supplies in 1950 improved as government policy shifted to permit private markets and introduce rationing.[111]

The land reforms of 1946 granted women the right to own land on an equal basis with men.[112] The 1946 Sex Equality Law granted women legal equality in property inheritance, divorce and child maintenance. The 1946 Sex Equality Law outlawed forced marriages, prostitution and the buying and selling of women.[113] It also confirmed the improvements to women's legal status that had been already made by the Japanese colonial administration in 1922, including the abolition of concubinage and polygamy.[114] The 1946 Labour Law included provisions

---

[106] Ellen Brun and Jacques Hersh, *Socialist Korea: A Case Study in the Strategy of Economic Development* (London and New York: Monthly Review Press, 1976), p.131.
[107] Ibid.   [108] Ibid., p. 132.
[109] Joseph Sang-hoon Chung, *The North Korean Economy: Structure and Development* (Stanford: Hoover Institution Press, 1974), pp. 10–14; Suk Lee, 'Food Shortages and Economic Institutions in the Democratic People's Republic of Korea', doctoral dissertation (Department of Economics, University of Warwick, January 2003), pp. 69–70.
[110] Percentage of farm households able to feed themselves without state support, and percentage of farm households out of total population from ibid., p. 75 and p. 79 respectively.
[111] Ibid., pp. 59–72.
[112] Data drawn from Hazel Smith, *WFP DPRK Programmes and Activities: A Gender Perspective* (Pyongyang: WFP, December 1999); see also Armstrong, *The North Korean Revolution*, pp. 92–8.
[113] See the Appendix that transcribes 'The Law on Equality of the Sexes in North Korea', in Jon Halliday, 'Women in North Korea: An Interview with the Korean Democratic Women's Union', *Bulletin of Concerned Asian Scholars*, Vol. 17, No. 3, Jul-Sep 1985, p. 56.
[114] Yung-Chung Kim (ed.), *Women of Korea: A History from Ancient Times to 1945* (Seoul: Ewha Womans University Press, 1977), pp. 267–70.

designed to benefit women such as equal pay for equal work and the entitlement to 77 days maternity leave (later raised to 150 days). The registry system, which registered all households based around the male lineage, was abolished in 1946.[115] In 1949 legal discrimination against sons who were born of second wives or concubines was also outlawed.[116]

The new government implemented adult and child literacy projects and opened schools throughout the country. In 1949 just under two million children were reported as attending school while one million of the population were engaged in some form of adult education.[117] Just under two and a half million Koreans were taught basic literacy skills between 1945 and 1948.[118]

Post-1945 reforms, although wide-ranging and radical, were neither novel nor particularly communist. Policies reflected popular demands and were well received as the hardships of the colonial era had generated high expectations for a better future for Koreans and for Korea as a nation. Post-liberation northern Korea remained a mixed economy and in 1947 the majority of jobs, some 60 per cent, remained in the private sector.[119] These reforms echoed social and economic reforms taking place around the world at the end of the Second World War in capitalist as well as post-colonial states. In the United Kingdom the post-war socialist government sang the Red Flag in Parliament, nationalised the coal and steel industries, implemented a national health service and planned a building programme of public housing that would provide 'homes for heroes' returning from the war. North Korea's abolition of legal discrimination against women reflected post-war post-colonial political and legal emancipation of women throughout the globe, including in the capitalist countries of western Europe.

New social norms

Genuinely popular reforms and socially egalitarian policies masked Kim's increasing political authoritarianism that sought total control over politics, the military and societal organisations. The shift to authoritarian rule was also unremarkable in that it represented a familiar way of operating in society and politics. The part of the Confucian heritage that

---

[115] Suzy Kim, *Everyday Life in the North Korean Revolution 1945-1950* (Ithaca, NY: Cornell University Press, 2013), p. 200.
[116] Armstrong, *The North Korean Revolution*, on the family register see p. 98 and on the legal status of sons see p. 95.
[117] Scalapino and Lee, *Communism in Korea*, pp. 384-5.
[118] Ibid., p. 385.   [119] Armstrong, *The North Korean Revolution*, p. 156.

understood that in a good society loyalty was owed to the ruler provided they responded to the needs of the people remained embedded in Korean cultural frameworks.

Kim's policies were pragmatic in the sense that he built on the social and economic change that had taken place in the colonial period to further his political ambitions and did not promote a restoration of the Confucian heritage where this would not have been useful. Women, for instance, had become wage earners outside the home and the incorporation of women in factories and workplaces meant that women were no longer perceived as operating only in the private sphere of home and family. Kim Il Sung supported the move away from conservative notions so as to ensure that women remained able to make a contribution to economic reconstruction.

The population was receptive to Kim Il Sung's introduction of the fairly conventional mainstay of Marxism–Leninism that in socialism all must work and each able-bodied adult should only be entitled to benefits in proportion to their contribution to the society. The centrality of labour replaced Confucian norms that had stressed that a well-lived life should be one of study and reflection, but here again Kim was aided by the facts on the ground. The poor majority in post-1945 northern Korea were not the inheritors of *Yangban* privilege. These were a people who had had few educational opportunities and were used to backbreaking work patterns in the fields and the factories. A politics that suggested fair rewards for work, land reform and educational and welfare improvements was welcomed.

Korean national identity

The scale and scope of Japanese oppression fortified the idea that all Koreans shared a common national identity constituted by the sense of a common loss of political independence, a common oppression and a common opposition to colonialism. Formerly fixed personal identities and ideas of place and status had been transformed by the experience of colonialism and war. Disruption of long-standing notions of proper relationships between men and women combined with mass migration had, for example, the consequence of challenging the notion that gender and geographical provenance implied a more or less fixed identity marker in Korea.[120] Identity as constituted by ethnicity seemed much more stable than social markers once thought of as unchanging and 'natural' including class, region, gender, age and occupation.

[120] Cumings, *The Origins of the Korean War, Vol. I*, pp. 53–61; see especially chart entitled 'Interprovincial Migration, 1940', p. 58.

In the aftermath of national division both Koreas claimed that they best represented Korean national identity and that each was the true representative of an independent Korea. Both sides refused to accept the legitimacy of the other, both were highly confrontational with each other and both engaged in political manoeuvring and military skirmishes along the thirty-eighth parallel in order to try to assert their respective authority. These opposing visions of an independent Korea were not reconcilable and there was little attempt by either side at genuine compromise. The formal division of the Korean peninsula and the Korean nation into two states recognized these irreconcilable differences. The Republic of Korea (ROK), more commonly known as South Korea, declared itself an independent state on 15 August 1948, as did the Democratic People's Republic of Korea (DPRK), widely known as North Korea, on 6 September 1948.

The birth of Kim Il Sungism

North Korea, led by Kim Il Sung, was anti-colonial, sympathetic to communist ideas and nationalist. Despite the essential support that Kim received from the Soviet Union, the North Korean Leader was motivated more by a nationalist vision than an ideological commitment to communism.

Kim's policies had in common with Maoist communism the focus on restoration of the credibility and integrity of the sovereign state, but politically Kim had more in common with post-war, post-colonial leaders in Africa and Asia, including Kenyatta in Kenya, Nkrumah in Ghana, Nasser in Egypt, Ben Bella in Algeria, Sukarno in Indonesia and Nehru in India than with Stalin's Soviet Union. Kim showed initiative, ruthlessness and political skill in manipulating political support from the Soviet Union but the North Korea of the post-war period was not the fully socialised entity that it became in the 1950s and 1960s. It would take another war – that of the fratricidal conflict which began in 1950 – to provide the conditions for extreme communisation.

4   War-fighting as state-building

In June 1950 the two Koreas went to war against each other to re-unify Korea. Kim Il Sung's aim was to rid the peninsula of United States troops and establish a communist, Kim Il Sung-led polity throughout the Korean peninsula.[1] The aim of the President of South Korea, Synghman Rhee, was to unite Korea under southern leadership. China sent over a million troops and the Soviet Union provided military assistance to Kim Il Sung, while a United States-led United Nations coalition fought on the side of South Korea. Both Koreas suffered terrible physical devastation and millions died while the North suffered disproportionate loss of life and physical damage due to the bombing campaigns that targeted economic and military infrastructure, and that continued throughout the war. In July 1953 when the war ended, neither side had achieved wartime objectives. North Korea and South Korea

---

[1] There is a very large literature on the Korean War. For authoritative accounts see Bruce Cumings, *The Origins of the Korean War, Vol. I: Liberation and the Emergence of Separate Regimes 1945–1947* (Seoul: Yuksabipyungsa, 2002); Max Hastings, *The Korean War* (London: Michael Joseph, 1987); William Stueck, *The Korean War: An International History* (Princeton University Press, 1995). For a useful short and well-illustrated account see Tom McGowen, *The Korean War* (New York: Franklin Watts, 1992). For a first-hand account of the experiences of the American general captured by the North Koreans see William F. Dean as told to William L. Worden, *General Dean's Story* (New York: The Viking Press, 1954). For oral histories of American, Korean and Chinese participants see Richard Peters and Xiaobing Li, *Voices from the Korean War: Personal Stories of American, Korean and Chinese Soldiers* (Lexington: The University Press of Kentucky, 2005). For a well-written and thoughtful testimony by an American participant see James Brady, *The Coldest War: A Memoir of Korea* (New York: Thomas Dunne Books, 1990). See also the illustrated Jon Halliday and Bruce Cumings, *Korea: The Unknown War* (New York: Pantheon Books, 1988). This last book is the accompanying text for the excellent six-part Thames Television series, which has footage, interviews and commentary from all sides of the conflict and is a legacy of the short-lived window of opportunity for cooperation between old enemies opened in the immediate aftermath of the Cold War. For North Korean perspectives see Ho Jong Ho, Sok Hui Kang and Thae Ho Pak, *The US Imperialists Started the Korean War* (Pyongyang: Foreign Languages Publishing House, 1993); Democratic People's Republic of Korea Editorial Board, *Echoes of the Korean War* (Pyongyang: Foreign Languages Publishing House, 1996).

remained politically divided in more or less the same territories that each had governed prior to the war.

Kim Il Sung used the excuse of the exigencies of war to build political, economic and social systems and structures whose function was to secure Kim's personal power and to carry out his directives in every sector of politics, economy and society. Opposition figures were purged and alternative perspectives eradicated. Kim built a mass Party whose job was to function as a transmission belt for the leader's directions and as a mechanism of control over the population. Kim institutionalised the policy and practice of 'anti-bureaucratism' with the aim of preventing the opportunity for alternative political platforms or perspectives to have space to develop within the Party, the workplace and the society at large. Kim expanded mass mobilisation policies so that all of society was expected to participate in Kim-led, hierarchically organised support activities for the war effort. These organisational practices were dependent on and underpinned by the hard physical labour of the population.

Despite the terrible losses of the war and the lack of territorial gains, it was asserted that it was thanks to the 'wise' guidance of Kim Il Sung that the anti-colonial liberation struggle against Japan had been won and the United States imperialists defeated.[2] These 'wise' policies included tightly disciplined, hierarchically organised mass mobilisation, which was understood by Kim Il Sung as providing an appropriate model for nation-building in peacetime. The militarisation of society that had developed by necessity in wartime was proselytised as efficient, appropriate and legitimate in peacetime politics.

War and devastation

North Korea conventionally refers to what the rest of the world calls the Korean War as the Great Fatherland Liberation War, although occasionally it simply uses the term 'Korean War' in its English language publications.[3] North Korea insists that the South started the war while

---

[2] There are many honorifics attached to descriptions of Kim's attributes in North Korean texts including 'heroic', 'iron-willed', 'Great', 'respected' etc. Kim Il Sung is also repeatedly called 'wise' to reinforce the message that only Kim Il Sung had the ability to make correct decisions. For an example of the use of the terminology of 'wise leadership' in an approved text sold in Pyongyang see Bong Baik, *Kim Il Sung Biography (1)* (Beirut: Dar Al-Talia, 1973), p. 570.

[3] For the conventional reference see Han Gil Kim, *Modern History of Korea* (Pyongyang: Foreign Languages Publishing House, 1979). For the alternate version see Ho *et al.*, *The US Imperialists Started the Korean War*.

most of the rest of the world believes that the North did so.[4] What is undisputed is that from very soon after the liberation of Korea from Japanese occupation in 1945 and the subsequent division of the peninsula, both Synghman Rhee, the President of South Korea, and Kim Il Sung were focused on unifying Korea under their respective leaderships and both were prepared to use military force to do so. Rhee expected the Americans and the West to back him while Kim based his strategy on the premise that communists located in South Korea would lead a popular insurrection that would join with North Korean troops to overturn Rhee and unite the peninsula under Kim's leadership. Kim also anticipated that the Americans would stand aside from the conflict.

Rhee gambled correctly to a certain extent. The United States secured political backing from the fledgling United Nations for what they termed a 'police action' and authorised military action against the DPRK.[5] The leadership of the United Nations coalition remained with the Americans throughout the war and the total numbers of allied troops was small compared to the United States troop commitment. Nevertheless this was a real international coalition and a number of diverse United Nations members, including Turkey and Australia, contributed to the coalition forces.[6] Rhee's main strategic failure was that he did not envisage the later, crucial Chinese support for North Korea. On the other hand, Kim Il Sung's approach was from the outset based upon false premises as no popular insurrection took place in support of the DPRK in the south and communist sympathisers were hunted down and eradicated by Rhee's troops.

The war started after military skirmishes between North and South in June 1950. North Korean troops succeeded in taking Seoul in a matter of days and advanced rapidly until what was left in southern hands was a

[4] For discussion of the origins of the war see Halliday and Cumings, *Korea: The Unknown War*, pp. 71–94. For an account that reflects North Korean understandings see Ellen Brun and Jacques Hersh, *Socialist Korea: A Case Study in the Strategy of Economic Development* (London and New York: Monthly Review Press, 1976), pp. 88–98. See also I. F. Stone, *The Hidden History of the Korean War* (Boston: Little, Brown and Company, 1988); Ho *et al.*, *The US Imperialists Started the Korean War*.

[5] For an account that discusses the UN intervention from the perspective of a coalition partner see Callum MacDonald, *Britain and the Korean War* (Oxford: Basil Blackwell, 1990).

[6] For a list of countries that militarily supported the intervention in Korea see Andrew C. Nahm, *An Introduction to Korean History and Culture* (Elizabeth, NJ/Seoul: Hollym, 1997), p. 248.

small area around the south-east port town of Pusan. In September 1950 United States-led troops counter-attacked and by the end of the year had chased North Koreans out of the South and up towards the North Korea–China border, retaking Seoul and capturing Pyongyang in the process. General MacArthur, the United States commander in Korea, pursued a scorched earth policy in bombing attacks on North Korean border towns with China. The newly created Chinese communist state, established just one year earlier in 1949, reacted by sending 200,000 'volunteers' to support Kim Il Sung's troops, which regrouped in the countryside. The 'volunteers' – so-called because China did not wish to become an official belligerent – were crucial in saving the North Koreans from defeat and in ensuring that the DPRK remained able to defend its territory. North Korea was also assisted by the Soviet Union, which provided pilots and planes, and by eastern Europeans who provided medical and humanitarian assistance.

By the end of 1950, Chinese troop levels were increased to just less than half a million and, together with North Korean troops, they pushed the Allied coalition back to the thirty-eighth parallel. North Korean and Chinese forces retook Seoul in December 1950, although communist reoccupation of Seoul lasted only until March 1951. United Nations coalition troops pushed back up to the thirty-eighth parallel by April the same year – retaking Seoul in what was a third change of sides in just one year for the South Korean capital city. Meetings between the two sides to negotiate an end to war started in summer 1951 in the border village of Panmunjon, but brutal war-fighting continued as both sides sought battlefield victories to obtain negotiating advantage. When the Armistice was signed between the DPRK, the United States-led United Nations coalition and the Chinese 'volunteers' on 27 July 1953, little territorial advantage had been gained during the two years of simultaneous talks and combat although millions had been killed. The Armistice ended the war but the conflict between North and South Korea was not finished. South Korea was not a signatory to the Armistice and no peace treaty formally ending the war was ever signed between any of the parties to the conflict.

The end of the war left behind a geographically and politically divided Korean peninsula that was physically destroyed by battle and bombing and millions of casualties. Some families were divided out of political choice. At other times it was an accidental consequence of war. Soldiers and civilians split from families living in the territory of the opposing side because they had been conscripted or joined up in the early stages of the war when the front lines were fluid sometimes ended up on the

wrong side of the thirty-eighth parallel when the war
families ended up permanently divided because part of
been able to organise themselves to move during the war wh
not. Those who had left one side or the other hoping t
families later were to find that the border created after
become impermeable.

Casualties on both sides were very high. Of the United Na
tion forces, just over 54,000 American soldiers as well as just   _,000
non-American soldiers were killed.[7] About one million South Korean
civilians, that is, about 5 per cent of a population of about twenty million,
were killed, along with over 50,000 South Korean combatants. South
Korea was badly damaged by the war although after the stabilisation of
territorial gains and losses along the thirty-eighth parallel in summer
1951, South Korean territory remained relatively protected, as bombing
raids were not carried out by the North and its allies.[8]

In North Korea the scale of death and destruction was disproportionately high, with two million North Korean civilians and about
500,000 North Korean combatants killed, that is approximately a
quarter of the northern population of an estimated ten million.[9] Some
one million Chinese soldiers were also killed. As in South Korea, these
bare figures do not take into account the sick, injured, orphaned and
displaced casualties of war. The figures do, however, show that few
if any North Koreans escaped the impact of war.[10] United States

---

[7] Casualty figures are different in different accounts but all point to the loss of life in the
millions during the three years of war. The figures used in this paragraph and the next
are from Halliday and Cumings, *Korea: The Unknown War*, p. 200. See also Sung Chul
Yang, *The North and South Korean Political Systems: A Comparative Analysis*, revised
edition (Elizabeth, NJ: Hollym, 1999), pp. 153–4; Bruce Cumings, *The Korean War:
A History* (New York: Modern Library, 2010), p. 35.

[8] Wayne Thompson and Bernard C. Nalty, *Within Limits: The US Air Force and the
Korean War* (Washington, DC: Air Force Historical Studies Office, AF/HO,1190
Air Force Pentagon, 1996), p. 49, available at www.dtic.mil/cgi-bin/GetTRDoc?AD=
ADA440095&Location=U2&doc=GetTRDoc.pdf, accessed 8 November 2014.

[9] Halliday and Cumings, *Korea: The Unknown War*, p. 200. Sung Chul Yang identifies 1.3
million South Korean casualties and 1.5–2 million North Korean casualties. Yang uses
the term 'casualties' but the phrasing indicates that he understands casualties as fatalities,
not as fatalities plus injured persons. See Yang, *The North and South Korean Political
Systems*, pp. 153–4. Adrian Buzo states that the DPRK suffered 300,000 military
casualties and 400,000 civilian casualties and the inference here also is that casualties
means fatalities. See Adrian Buzo, *The Guerilla Dynasty: Politics and Leadership in North
Korea* (Boulder, CO: Westview, 1999), p. 23.

[10] Halliday and Cumings, *Korea: The Unknown War*, p. 172; Carter J. Eckert, Ki-bail Lee,
Young Ick Lew, Michael Robinson and Edward Wagner, *Korea Old and New: A History*
(Cambridge, MA: Korea Institute, Harvard University/Ilchokak, 1990), p. 345.

tary reports commented that the extent and duration of the bombing meant that by the end of the war all towns in the North were burned to the ground.[11]

United Nations military policy had used a broad interpretation of what constituted a legitimate military target. The deliberate targeting of civilian infrastructure was prohibited by the Geneva Conventions but military planners argued that nominally civilian infrastructure provided essential support to the North Korean war effort and should be conceived as military targets.[12] Dams and power stations were bombed by coalition forces, as were buildings that could be used to support the North Korean military.[13] Napalm was used by the United Nations forces and Kim Il Sung also accused the United States of engaging in germ warfare. Kim's allegations achieved international attention despite their disputed veracity.[14]

Normal daily activities and family and social life had been transformed by the war. Many northerners lived underground in dugout tunnels throughout the war years to escape the relentless bombing.[15] The intensity, longevity and inclusivity of wartime mobilisation entailed participation by practically all of the able-bodied population, including children and the elderly, all day, every day, over three years of war in top-down hierarchically controlled activity. Agricultural work often took place under the cover of night to avoid the continuous threat posed by bombing. Families were split up because of death and migration as refugees flowed in their millions to China, Mongolia, the Soviet Union

[11] Jon Halliday reports that at the MacArthur hearings in June 1951 'Senator Stennis asked Gen. O'Donnell: "North Korea has been virtually destroyed, hasn't it?" Gen. O'Donnell: "Oh, yes, we did it all later anyhow ... I would say that the entire, almost the entire Korean Peninsula is just a terrible mess. Everything is destroyed. There is nothing standing worthy of the name."' Halliday further reports that 'Gen. Curtis LeMay, head of Strategic Air Command during the Korean War, later recalled asking the Pentagon for permission to "burn down" five of the biggest cities in North Korea and being told "It's too horrible". But, LeMay observed, "over a period of three years or so... we burned down *every* town in North Korea ... Now, over a period of three years, that's palatable" (LeMay oral history in John Foster Dulles papers, Princeton University, cited in Bruce Cumings, 'Korea – the New Nuclear Flashpoint', *The Nation*, 7 April 1984, p. 416). See Jon Halliday, 'Anti-Communism and the Korean War (1950–1953)', *Socialist Register 1984: The Uses of Anti-Communism*, Vol. 21, pp. 130–63, available at http://socialistregister.com/index.php/srv/article/view/5509/2407, accessed 8 November 2014.
[12] Hastings, *The Korean War*, pp. 324–7.
[13] Ibid.; Halliday and Cumings, *Korea: The Unknown War*, pp. 187–9.
[14] Ibid., pp. 182–6.
[15] Ibid., p. 172; Robert A. Scalapino and Chong-Sik Lee, *Communism in Korea: The Movement* (Berkeley: University of California Press, 1972), pp. 430–2.

and eastern Europe.[16] The northern government sent large numbers of children abroad to wait out the war.[17] To live in the North throughout the war was to engage in a continuous, unremitting battle for personal, family and community survival.

The extent of the devastation in the North was widely understood around the world. In June 1951, at the United States Congressional hearings to discuss Macarthur's dismissal by President Truman for the former's insubordination in his pursuit of the war, Major General Emmet O'Donnell, Commander of the United States Air Force in Korea, informed the Public Hearing that there were no more targets in North Korea left to bomb.[18] In 1957, a South Korean government document, intended to call attention to Kim Il Sung's alleged depopulation of northern Korea, stated that between 1950 and 1951 '... the hostilities were most intense and the majority of the people [in the North] lost their settlements [homes]'.[19] In 1955, South Korea estimated that North Korea's pre-war population, which they put at just over 9 million, had been reduced to just under 4 million, while other reports cited a post-war population at a higher figure of 8.5 million.[20]

---

[16] Figures about the numbers of wartime refugees are notoriously unreliable for the Korean conflict and other conflicts. The reference to millions is not controversial, however. Yang states that there were 2.5 million refugees in total as a result of the Korean War without specifying whether from North or South. See Yang, *The North and South Korean Political Systems*, p. 154.

[17] We do not know how many children stayed behind and how many were sent to which countries. For mention of children sent to Romania and the GDR to wait out the war, see Charles K. Armstrong, '"Fraternal Socialism": The International Reconstruction of North Korea, 1953–62', *Cold War History*, Vol. 5, No. 2, May 2005, p. 164.

[18] Major General Emmett O'Donnell, Jr., testifying to the MacArthur hearings, June 25, 1951, US Congress, Senate, Committee on Armed Services and Committee on Foreign Relations, *Military Situation in the Far East: Hearings to Conduct an Inquiry into the Military Situation in the Far East and Facts Surrounding the Relief of General of the Army Douglas MacArthur from His Assignments in That Area*, 82nd Congress, 1st Session, 1951, Vol. 4, p. 3063, quoted in Halliday, 'Anti-Communism and the Korean War', pp. 145-6.

[19] The reference to 'the natural increase of the population in northern Korea between 1950 and 1951' dropping to seven per thousand of the population 'when the hostilities were most intense and the majority of the people lost their settlements' indicates an acknowledgement of the severity of the impact of war on the North. See Office of Public Information of the Republic of Korea, 'Population Survey of Korea', *Korean Survey*, Vol. 6, No. 6, Jun–Jul 1957, p. 11.

[20] Ibid. This South Korean government document argues that the 1955 population of 'northern Korea' was just 3,868,200 because '2.5 million were deported from North Korea to the former Soviet Union "according to a reliable source"'. The figures in the report seem manufactured in the context of the extreme ideological battle that continued between North and South after the war. The North Korean leadership had a policy of sending out of the country children and those who could not help in the mobilisation effort, but 'deported' might not be the most apposite term as many came back at the end of the war. For the figure of 8.5 million see Suk Lee, 'Food Shortages and Economic

Wartime Party/state-building

In spite of the calamitous and all-encompassing nature of wartime destruction, Kim accelerated the political transformation of North Korea which had begun in the immediate post-liberation period. During the war, Kim Il Sung expanded and re-organised the Korean Workers' Party as an integrated, hierarchical, command-and-obey structure. Kim worked hard to ensure that the Leader was understood as the embodiment of the Party. The Party was controlled by Kim Il Sung and the Party in its turn directed, controlled and managed what in other societies would be state functions. These were submerged into the political process so that the state as a separate bureaucratic entity ceased to exist in any meaningful manner. Military, policing, economic and social policy and planning were supervised and directed through Party structures and by Party cadres. The workplace was institutionalised as the focus of political and community life but Party direction and leadership was embedded at every level of enterprise management.

The organisational structures of the Party were designed to ensure that no alternative agendas emerged and that members were socialised into the Leader's views to the extent that alternatives became, literally, inconceivable. Ideological exhortation was used to encourage participation but Kim also emphasised throughout the war that the Party needed to insist on 'revolutionary discipline'. Kim's aims were not confined to establishing monolithic control over Party members. The idea was that the population would be trained to accept the validity of a way of life in which their primary function was to act as a national militia.

Contrary to the advice of what later North Korean historians would excoriate as 'Leftist' elements, who advocated for a vanguard Party of carefully chosen comrades, Kim Il Sung insisted on building a mass inclusive Communist Party.[21] The Party grew to a massive one million members during the war – probably at least 20 per cent of the adult population, incorporating up to 40–50 per cent of adult males.[22] The intention was to bring as wide a swathe of society as possible under the direction and discipline of the Korean Workers' Party yet at the same time to emphasise that Party membership had to be earned. It was not a right. Candidates for Party membership had to demonstrate their loyalty

---

Institutions in the Democratic People's Republic of Korea', doctoral dissertation (Department of Economics, University of Warwick, January 2003), p. 78.
[21] Kim, *Modern History of Korea*, pp. 330–4.   [22] Ibid., pp. 330–1.

to Kim Il Sung and willingness to abide by Party discipline. Their reward was potential access to higher occupational and social status as anyone in any position of authority had first to be a member of the Party. The mass nature of the Party and the underdeveloped Korean education system meant that new members were often illiterate and uneducated and, as a consequence, susceptible to propaganda that extolled the farsightedness and beneficence of the Kim Il Sung leadership. Kim Il Sung's mass Party line was thus not a strategy of political pluralism but instead a control mechanism.

Wartime practice consolidated and embedded the Party's authority as strategic decision-maker. 'Democratic centralism' or decision-making from the Leader through the Party was institutionalised in every aspect of state and society. The centralisation of Party authority and capacity was accompanied by the parallel policy of decentralisation of operational decision-making to the local level. Individual initiatives to help solve workplace or community problems were promoted and the Party encouraged technical training and the development of technical skills even during the war.[23] Technical input into enterprise and economic decisions, however, was always subordinated to political imperatives.[24]

Party organisational matters were a constant priority for Kim throughout the entire wartime period. The December 1952 Fifth Plenary Meeting of the Party Central Committee focused on how to ensure that Party members support the Party 'anywhere and in whatever conditions'.[25] Kim reminded Party members that all personal interests must be subordinated to the Party. Their function and role was to 'resolutely defend the Leader and the Party and implement his instructions and Party line and policy, their embodiment'.[26] Party strictures emphasised the necessity of strict discipline and ideological education to ensure that the Leader's orders were obeyed.

From early in the war, Party-building went hand in hand with what Kim called 'the struggle against bureaucratism'.[27] Anti-bureaucratism was a policy aim and a method of working.[28] The policy was designed

[23] Brun and Hersh, *Socialist Korea*, p. 165.   [24] Ibid.
[25] Party History Research Institute, *History of Revolutionary Activities of the Great Leader Comrade Kim Il Sung* (Pyongyang: Foreign Languages Publishing House, 1983), p. 341.
[26] Ibid.   [27] Kim, *Modern History of Korea*, p. 331.
[28] For the importance and centrality of anti-bureaucratism to Kim Il Sung's policies during the war, see Party History Research Institute, *History of Revolutionary Activities*, pp. 325–6. See also Compilation Committee of Kim Il Sung Encyclopaedia, *Kim Il Sung Encyclopaedia Volume One* (New Delhi: Vishwanath, 1992), pp. 513–14. For an extended statement see the April 1955 speech by Kim Il Sung 'on eliminating bureaucracy', reported in ibid., pp. 519–20.

to prevent the rise of a cadre of officials within the workplace and within the Party that might challenge Kim's power and authority. In the workplace, the objective was to prevent the rise of an independent (of the Party) bureaucracy, technocratic or managerial class that could eventually offer an independent point of view to Kim's policies. Within the Party, the objective was to prevent putative competitors building a power base.

Anti-bureaucratism was installed as a fundamental way of working within the Party and in every sector of society and the economy, including farms, factories, schools and offices. The population was supposed to improvise solutions to problems and to eschew 'bureaucratic' responses. The anti-bureaucratisation campaigns purposefully disavowed the use of managerial methods, which were not only discouraged but punished. Political imperatives were supposed to drive the answers and solutions to economic problems so that, for example, exhortation was preferred as a method of encouragement over material rewards and mass mobilisation was used as a method of providing productivity gains.

Authoritarian strategising and instruction from the Party was supposed to substitute for bureaucratic organisation of the state and decentralised operational problem-solving was meant to provide local answers to local problems, including those of food, welfare, shelter and economy. Individuals and organisations had therefore to manage a tricky balancing act between obedience and initiative; hierarchy and localisation. The safest option was to adopt a default option of obedience and hierarchy as an official might be reprimanded for failing to achieve policy targets but the failure to obey orders could result in much more severe penalties.

During the war Kim intensified and extended the use of mass mobilisation as a primary means of implementing political, military and economic directives. The policy subordinated the physical activity of every North Korean within military modalities in that modes of working were top-down and participation mandatory. Mass mobilisation for warfighting and for economic activities, including food production, was enforced by punitive sanctions. Kim dispatched 'great numbers of able Party and government functionaries and exemplary workers and office employees to the countryside' to help respond to food shortages.[29] In 1951 millions of adults were mobilised to help in the spring planting, which was also supported by the Chinese volunteers.[30]

---

[29] Party History Research Institute, *History of Revolutionary Activities*, p. 328.
[30] Scalapino and Lee, *Communism in Korea*, pp. 414–22.

Underpinning mass mobilisation policies was a reliance on the continuous physical effort of the entire able-bodied population. Hard physical labour substituted for technology and resource gaps in every sector of the economy, including agriculture and transport. North Koreans faced a tough life before, during and after the colonial period but the nature of the all-out war fought against them and the absence of sophisticated technology throughout the economy meant that the response could more or less only be founded on increased intensity of physical efforts.

North Korean official histories report with pride the wartime 'vigorous emulation drives for producing more goods' such as the 'drive for undertaking and over fulfilling the production quotas of two or three men'.[31] These North Korean accounts exalt the contribution of physical labour for economic purposes but downplay the hardships involved. North Korean workers no doubt performed heroically in the difficult circumstances in which they lived and worked but in official accounts North Koreans are portrayed more as troops in battle than as civilians. One account reports that when 'electricity supply failed on account of the enemy's heavy bombings, the workers turned the transmission belts by hand to cut shells and weave cloth. They even built small-sized blast furnaces in mountain recesses and smelted iron in order to secure raw and other materials for themselves, and also ensured transport of goods under gunfire.'[32]

North Korean texts portray agricultural workers as successfully growing food against all odds at the same time as fighting against enemy action. Farmers 'ploughed the fields and sowed seeds, with bomb-shelters dug at the edges of the fields and the backs of oxen camouflaged by way of precaution against the enemy's bombings and naval bombardments which continued day and night ... The peasants in the coastal areas organized "armed workteams" and did farming while mopping up enemy spies, subversive elements and saboteurs who sneaked in from the sea.'[33]

Mobilisation of all adults included women, whose lives had started to change in the colonial period and pre-war North Korea, and who were propelled even further away from conservative traditions by the exigencies of war. Women took on what were historically men's jobs such as 'operators of ploughs' as men were predominately engaged in the fighting and women were left to carry out core economic activities.[34] Some women operated as guerrilla fighters but their major role was as

---

[31] Party History Research Institute, *History of Revolutionary Activities*, p. 330.
[32] Ibid., p. 331.   [33] Ibid., p. 329.   [34] Kim, *Modern History of Korea*, p. 332.

support for combat troops. These support functions could nevertheless be arduous and highly dangerous especially where they involved reconnaissance and physical supply of troops in battle. Women were not exempt from extreme physical violence and sanctions that included death, torture, rape and imprisonment.

North Korean accounts do not acknowledge the limitations of a policy that relied so heavily on physical labour. Wartime policies failed to achieve key objectives as the country struggled to produce enough food. Farmers and their families were left with diminished food rations while being expected to work physically very hard in order to maintain agricultural production and, at the same time, they were expected to participate in fighting the war.[35] The population was exhausted and responded by using the weapons of the weak against their own leaders. They hoarded food, worked slowly so as to conserve resources and energy, appropriated common property for family and individual survival and falsified reports to Party officials.[36] The new Party cadres also falsified reports, both to curry favour and avoid punishment, while enforcing harsh penalties on local populations for failing to meet production targets.[37]

Establishing control mechanisms

While the war was being prosecuted, Kim built and established mechanisms of persuasion and coercion whose aim was nothing less than to normalise the leader's version of reality within the thought processes of the population. The two most important control mechanisms were 'ideological education' and 'revolutionary discipline', with the latter providing a pervasive threat should the former prove inadequate. The direct targets were Party members but because the Party encompassed such a large proportion of the population, mechanisms of control impacted on the population at large as well as those who held positions of responsibility.

Kim insisted that ideological education was as important as technical solutions to economic problems. The constant problems of food shortages were also subject to the mantra of ideological education as the solution to all problems. The idea was that full-time propaganda workers sent by the Party to the rural areas would 'strengthen ideological education among the peasants to raise their ideological level' and that improved ideology would encourage the farmers to produce more

---

[35] Lee, 'Food Shortages', pp. 75–6.
[36] Scalapino and Lee, *Communism in Korea*, pp. 422–6.   [37] Ibid., p. 424.

food.[38] These untrained, unskilled workers lacked knowledge about agriculture or the localities to which they were sent. Famers having to accommodate, feed and pay obeisance to interfering political officials from the cities were unlikely to be persuaded of the efficacy of Kim Il Sungist policy and, rather predictably, ideological education did not produce sufficient food for the war effort. Food was expropriated from farmers who were reluctant to surrender food stocks to the war effort and food aid was sent to North Korea from communist countries, including China and the Soviet Union.[39]

Ideological education focused on encouraging the population to accept and believe in the legitimacy, wisdom and exclusivity of Kim Il Sung's leadership. Those who did not believe were demonised as 'factionalists' and 'sectarian' and blamed for military and political setbacks.[40] Ideological education meant inculcating in the population the idea that Kim Il Sung's policies could not be challenged or opposed.

The role of Party officials was to enforce discipline and this role was consistently emphasised, even during periods of the war when military matters might have been expected to dominate strategic agendas. In December 1950 when the fighting was extremely fluid and the north faced potential defeat Kim argued that 'Intensifying Party discipline is one of the most important problems ... for defeating the enemy and winning victory'. Discipline should be 'rigid' and 'merciless' and 'strong measures should be taken even against a trifling manifestation inimical to the unity and cohesion of the Party'.[41]

When Kim Il Sung's troops retook the north from the UN Command in 1950–1, brutal retribution took place against those perceived as having collaborated with the United States and Republic of Korea (ROK) after the retreat of northern troops. Brutality was not confined to the north as killing, torture and repression was also a feature of South Korean government wartime tactics and behaviour.[42] The claim of the DPRK, however, was that it was meting out revolutionary justice. The official history of the DPRK reported that when the northern forces retook territory 'functionaries in all domains ...

[38] Party History Research Institute, *History of Revolutionary Activities*, p. 328.
[39] Scalapino and Lee, *Communism in Korea*, pp. 419–22.
[40] Party History Research Institute, *History of Revolutionary Activities*, pp. 340–4.
[41] Ibid., p. 313.
[42] For a notorious example that involved US troops see Charles J. Hanley, Sang-Hun Choe and Martha Mendoza, *The Bridge at No Gun Ri* (New York: Henry Holt and Company, 2001). For broader discussion of atrocities on both sides during the war see Halliday and Cumings, *Korea: The Unknown War*.

[were] induce[d]... to observe revolutionary discipline voluntarily' in a campaign 'against all unsound practices such as liberalism and irresponsibility'.[43] In order to carry out these campaigns, the Party instituted the practice of 'mass and people's trials' throughout the country.[44]

Purging rivals and eliminating alternatives

By the beginning of the war, Kim Il Sung had eradicated potential opposition from nationalist leaders like Cho Man-Sik. During the war, Kim used the excuse and opportunities provided by wartime exigencies to suppress and purge potential political rivals, most notably Pak Hon Yong, a founder member of the Korean Communist Party in 1925 and recognised in both halves of the peninsula as having more claims to represent indigenous Korean communism than Kim Il Sung. Anti-Kim communist cadres attempted to replace Kim Il Sung with Pak Hon Yong in 1953 but failed in the planned coup.[45]

In August 1953, within weeks of the end of the war, Kim organised show trials in which leading cadres 'confessed' to being American spies as well as to attempting to overthrow the government.[46] Kim Il Sung's line was that these cadres were traitors who had sabotaged and undermined the anticipated popular uprising in the south. Failure to achieve the unification of the peninsula under northern control was blamed on South Korean communists, whom Kim accused of working for the American 'imperialists'.[47] As with Stalin's similar show trials in the Soviet Union, the outcomes were brutal and meticulously pre-planned. Ten of the twelve accused were given the death sentence.[48] Pak Hon Yong was arrested although not arraigned until two years after the end of the war, in 1955.

Kim Il Sung used the war to eradicate alternative social and political perspectives, including the remnants of the Christian presence that had managed to survive pre-war repression. Kim had begun the suppression of Christian leaders with measures that included the confiscation of Church property and persecution of individual Christians such that many Christians had chosen to move south before the outbreak of war.[49] Kim

---

[43] Kim, *Modern History of Korea*, p. 316.   [44] Ibid., p. 317.
[45] Dae-Sook Suh, *Kim Il Sung: The North Korean Leader* (New York: Columbia University Press, 1988), pp. 126–34.
[46] Kim, *Modern History of Korea*, pp. 344–8; Buzo, *The Guerilla Dynasty*, pp. 20–1.
[47] Suh, *Kim Il Sung*, pp. 126–36.   [48] Suh, *Kim Il Sung*, p. 134.
[49] Donald N. Clark, *Living Dangerously in Korea: The Western Experience 1900–1950* (Norwalk, CT: Eastbridge, 2003), pp. 301–4.

thought that Christian communities and their leaders might potentially provide a focus for organised opposition and so continued to suppress Christian adherents who had remained in the north, many of whom were killed. By the end of the war Christian activity was virtually eradicated in North Korea.[50]

Wartime organisation as state-building template

Kim Il Sung's political thought had been shaped by the hierarchical political systems in which he had grown up and in which a single leader was represented as infallible and omnipotent. The colonial regime in Korea had done its best to inculcate in the Korean population the idea that the Japanese Emperor and his family were God-like figures. Kim was also influenced by the political practice of the Soviet leader, Joseph Stalin, who held power from 1922 until his death in 1952. Stalin had built a personality cult that was implemented through state-controlled cultural apparatus including education and the media, and Stalin also used Party institutions as an instrument of unilateral decision-making. It was the Korean War, however, that provided the conditions in which Kim could implement his own vision of monolithic politics.

By the end of the war Kim had more or less succeeded in creating a Party where the Leader was understood as more important than the organisation itself and the most important function of the Party was to act as a transmission belt for the leader's decisions. In the immediate post-war era, Kim built on these organisational practices to implement a radical and highly authoritarian conception of state-building. The North Korean post-war state was built on untrammelled leader authority, a policy of self-reliance, mass mobilisation and a commitment to national liberation of the entire Korean nation.

Kim rejected the idea that the state should be a nominally separate institution from the Party. Conventional state structures and institutions, including the government, a state bureaucracy and the military, were retained in post-war North Korea but their technical functions, with the partial exception of the military, were sublimated into the priority of permanent political campaigning.[51] In other communist countries the Party had been subordinated for long periods of time to the manipulations of individual leaders, but in North Korea the Party was constructed

---

[50] Ibid., pp. 387–96.
[51] Hazel Smith, 'The Disintegration and Reconstitution of the State in the DPRK', in Simon Chesterman, Michael Ignatieff and Ramesh Thakur (eds.), *Making States Work* (Tokyo: United Nations Press, 2005), pp. 167–92.

so that its core function was to carry out the will of Kim Il Sung. Kim Il Sung also learned from the war that in order to maintain compliance with a system that was built around the right of an individual to rule, ideological exhortation would need to be supplemented by the application of 'revolutionary discipline'.

During the war, the population learned to operate as a vast militia where individual ambitions were subordinated to an authoritarian leadership. Political and social life had been subsumed under the demands of military and economic exigency as total war required an all-encompassing response. Kim did not, however, understand these wartime practices as temporary or as an unfortunate by-product of extreme circumstances. Instead Kim's efforts were directed at institutionalising these practices as normatively acceptable and as an efficient means of organising politics, the economy and society. Wartime tactics of hierarchically controlled mass mobilisation provided the template for post-war state structures and mechanisms. Many wartime leaders have adopted wartime mobilisation policies that relied on intensive physical labour by populations who were motivated by nationalist fervour and many post-war states have relied on the physical effort of the population to kick-start economic reconstruction. Kim Il Sung had in mind, however, a more permanent policy of mass mobilisation as part of his understanding of what would necessarily be a 'self-reliant' post-war North Korea.

During the war, Kim Il Sung had been forced to rely on support from China and the Soviet Union. Chinese support had been predicated on a sense of historic obligation as well as national interest in reciprocation for the significant military contribution by Korean soldiers to the Chinese communist national liberation struggle in the 1940s. Nevertheless Kim did not consider that he could permanently rely on the two communist powers on the sole basis of 'fraternal altruism'. Kim understood that China and the Soviet Union had their own strategic objectives which might not always coincide with those of Kim's North Korea. China was engaged in its own nation-building and internal political struggles while the death of Stalin in 1953 and the relative political liberalisation that followed meant that Kim Il Sung could no longer take Soviet support for granted. Kim had also learned from wartime experience that the rivalry and divisions between China and the Soviet Union could be played to North Korea's advantage.

Kim knew he would need external assistance for national reconstruction in the post-war period. China could not offer major economic support as it was busy rebuilding its own country. The Soviet Union and communist eastern Europe indicated that they would offer economic support to post-war North Korea but such assistance would not be massive or sufficient for the rebuilding of North Korea into the modern industrial powerhouse that Kim envisaged. Kim's strategy was thus to obtain unconditional assistance from China and the Soviet Union but not to rely entirely on external support. Instead national reconstruction would be founded on the intensive political, economic and social mass mobilisation practices that had developed in wartime.

In a speech on 5 August 1953 to the Party Central Committee, just a week after the end of the war, Kim confirmed his intent to continue to rely on the mobilisation of the population to carry out hard physical labour as the basis of post-war economic reconstruction. In the words of two foreign economists who were sympathetic to Kim's approach, this meant that reconstruction would be entirely dependent on 'mass mobilisation of workers, peasants, functionaries, and army personnel ... [who] delivered the hard work'.[52]

A reliance on indigenous resources meant that China and the Soviet Union would have minimal leverage over the direction of post-war state-building, which Kim intended to develop on the basis of autonomous nationally determined priorities. In the immediate post-war period Kim thus stressed the policies of political independence, economic self-reliance, military self-defence and, underpinning all these, the taken-for-granted objective of regime survival.[53] Kim Il Sung publicly recognised the contribution of China and the Soviet Union to the war effort but also increasingly represented himself as playing the most significant leadership role during the war. This underplaying of the crucial role of external actors in saving North Korea from military defeat and Kim Il Sung from political extinction was designed to buttress Kim's position as the sole voice of authority, legitimacy and leadership in post-war North Korea.

Post-war North Korea was similar in form to other communist states in its emphasis on a one-Party state and a subordination of the population via the mechanisms of Party control to the interests of the state. In post-war North Korea Party policy and officials dominated and controlled the institutions of government, but what was idiosyncratic was the extent of the melding of Party and state structures, the degree of institutionalisation of the subordination of Party structures to the Leader's will and the extent of the attempt to eradicate the separation between the public and private lives of individuals.

---

[52] Brun and Hersh, *Socialist Korea*, p. 172.
[53] Kim, *Modern History of Korea*, pp. 389–94.

For Kim the political strategy made perfect sense. A primary lesson was that the DPRK must always be prepared to defend itself from the threat of attack.[54] A major aim of political organisation was to ensure that the population would be ever-ready to resume a war which had only been temporarily halted, and which could start again at a moment's notice. Kim's conception of political organisation was virtually synonymous with military organisation and his understanding of the primary purpose of political organisation was to constitute the entire able-bodied population as a permanently battle-prepared national militia.

The post-war window of opportunity

Kim Il Sung benefited from the immediate post-war popular readiness for images and ideas that would give meaning to the sacrifices made by North Koreans and to the extensive suffering during the colonial period and during the war. The exhortation to work hard in nation-building under Kim's leadership was not, therefore, understood as cynical or entirely met with scepticism, especially as there were no alternatives on offer. Kim's eradication of alternative voices and perspectives from the public arena closed down political debate and the organisational efforts that had produced the one-Party system also meant there were no political channels through which opposition could be pursued safely.

The burgeoning global Cold War of the 1950s meant that the strategic priority of the Soviet Union and China, the DPRK's most important allies, was to keep the DPRK in the communist camp. These communist countries were similarly politically repressive in domestic politics, making it unlikely that Kim would suffer criticism from these quarters, which also controlled their population through a mixture of fear and 'revolutionary discipline'. Kim also benefited from geographical isolation. North Korea was bordered by China and the Soviet Union in the north and separated from the Republic of Korea after the war by the militarised, mined and virtually impermeable demilitarised zone (DMZ).

The on-going battle for national legitimacy

Kim argued that North Korea had succeeded in achieving war aims as it had prevented the United States from returning all of Korea to a subordinated national status little different to that which prevailed under Japanese colonialism. The narrative was that without Kim Il Sung's leadership,

---

[54] Buzo argues that the central purpose of the North Korean state 'was to conduct effective warfare'. See Buzo, *The Guerilla Dynasty*, p. 78.

the north would be living under foreign occupation by the United States as, it was asserted, was the fate of their southern compatriots.[55] Kim portrayed the South Korean leadership as entirely subordinate to the United States and the South Korean population as being oppressed by an imperialist system controlled by the United States.

Kim positioned himself as the Leader and embodiment of the national struggle for independence of the Korean nation. Post-war claims to nationalist credentials were primarily aimed at the northern population but were meant to resonate with those in the South who opposed Syngman Rhee. Korean ethnic nationalism remained the core legitimating device for the North Korean leadership while political ideology focused on the virtues of self-reliance in ideology, politics, economy and military affairs.

The war provided an opportunity and a practical demonstration of political organisation that could implement the Kim Il Sungist vision of a mass-mobilised population controlled by an authoritarian Leader whose policies were implemented by a subservient political Party. It only remained to embed Kim's wartime template of political organisation and philosophy within the institutions of post-war politics, economy and society.

---

[55] The genre is displayed in the DPRK-approved work of a Syrian journalist who wrote hagiographies of Kim Il Sung and Kim Jong Il, both of which were translated and published by the Foreign Language Publishing House of the DPRK. See Hani Al Suma, *The Ever-Shining Star of Korea* (Pyongyang: Foreign Languages Publishing House, 1986).

5 'Socialism in our own style'

In the post-war era, Kim Il Sung's primary goal remained the national reunification of both Koreas under the leadership of the North.[1] The ambition was to build a militarily powerful state based on a monolithic society in which, as a matter of daily practice, every individual would be subordinated to the Leader's political directives. Ideological suasion was meant to socialise the population into voluntary acquiescence but, failing persuasion, enforcement mechanisms were provided by a political system that formally and organisationally subordinated state, Party and societal structures to the Leader.[2]

Political aims were explicit and formulated in the *Juche* ideology that was invented, sponsored and promulgated by the North Korean state.[3] The most important goal of *Juche* ideology was to legitimate and uphold the Leader's autonomy in domestic and foreign policy. The North

---

[1] DPRK scholarship is replete with references to this goal. See for example Compilation Committee of Kim Il Sung Encyclopaedia, *Kim Il Sung Encyclopaedia Volume One* (New Delhi: Vishwanath, 1992); Chang-gon Pak, 'Conversion from a Colonial Agricultural State into a Socialist Industrial State', in Ken'ichiro Hirano (ed.), *The State and Cultural Transformation: Perspectives from East Asia* (Tokyo: United Nations Press, 1993), 299–314.

[2] Compilation Committee, *Kim Il Sung Encyclopaedia Volume One*, pp. 332–3.

[3] Party History Research Institute, *History of Revolutionary Activities of the Great Leader Comrade Kim Il Sung* (Pyongyang: Foreign Languages Publishing House, 1983), pp. 428–40. In August 1991, I led an eight-person-strong academic delegation of UK scholars to the DPRK that was intended to research the aspects of the DPRK that were possible and to engage in dialogue with DPRK academics. One of the interviews we collectively undertook was with Hwang Yang-Yop, then a senior official in the Korea Academy of Social Science, and known as the architect of the *Juche* ideology. My contemporaneous notes show an unambiguous opposition to allowing the population access to information other than that controlled by the state in the name of 'revolutionary education', an overt contempt of 'democracy' and a dismissal of the Soviet leadership (although not by name) as making fatal mistakes abandoning revolutionary education. My notes are accompanied by my comment that 'he's absolutely mad' because of his unqualified ideological fervour. Hwang Yang-Yop went on to become the North's most high-profile defector in 1997. Whether he believed what he was saying in 1991 or was exaggerating because he was even then worried about being thought unreliable and therefore felt vulnerable, I will never know. Hwang Yang-Yop died in Seoul in 2010.

Korean state assigned exclusive authority and power to the 'monolithic' Leader and explicitly stated that it was the Kim family dynasty that provided 'continuity of leadership' that was essential to success in the building of the socialist state.[4] The *Juche* ideology trumpeted the virtues of ideological and political education over material or economic rewards as a mechanism of state-building. In foreign affairs, the remit of *Juche* was to assert a rather innocuous notion of self-reliance and commitment to the principle of national independence in international affairs.

Post-war state-building was derived partly from Soviet models. It was also a product of what Kim understood as the lessons of practical experience of wartime mobilisation. Kim Il Sung set out to create 'Socialism in our own style'. The aim was to institutionalise Kim's power and authority within an integrated state/Party/society complex in which the goals, aims and interests of the Leader were embedded and implemented.[5] Points of view that differed from those of Kim Il Sung were thus inherently traitorous to the DPRK and the entire Korean nation, according to a North Korean ideology that proclaimed the exclusive national credentials of the Kim leadership.

The institutionalisation of Kim Il Sungism

Superficially, Kim appeared to engage in conventional state-building. Kim created an army, a state bureaucracy and a governmental apparatus. In post-Korean War North Korea the military, civil service and government were not, however, envisaged as institutionally autonomous or functionally independent organisations. Technical functionality and efficiency in the management of the economy was important but secondary to the ideological goal of institutionalising Kim Il Sungism.

The Soviet Union provided the only significant revolutionary state model available to Kim Il Sung as communist China only came into being in 1949 and communist systems were only established in eastern Europe in 1945, at the end of the Second World War. Post-war Korea had in common with the classic communist model the institutionalisation of a one-party system. The Korean Social Democratic Party and the Chondoist Chongu Party maintained a nominal existence as members of the state-sponsored Democratic Front for the Reunification of the

---

[4] Compilation Committee, *Kim Il Sung Encyclopaedia Volume One*, pp. 330 and 217.
[5] For analytically and empirically sophisticated work on the differential power relations within the state see Patrick McEachern, 'Inside the Red Box: North Korea's Post-Totalitarian Politics', doctoral dissertation (Louisiana State University and Agricultural and Mechanical College, May 2009).

Fatherland but they had no independent political identity and were entirely under the control of the Korean Workers' Party.[6]

As in the Soviet Union and the east European communist countries, state institutions were subordinated to Party dictates but DPRK political philosophy was different to that of the Soviet Union. North Korea argued that the locus of institutional power should be with the leader, not with the Party. The primary function of state and Party institutions was to legitimate Kim as 'Great Leader', wise leader, fount of authority and personal saviour of North Korea. These institutions also had the responsibility to ensure that the population was prevented from being exposed to alternative ways of thinking to those of Kim Il Sung.

Kim maintained careful control over the military in that he purged generals that took too much of an independent line and promoted comrades with proven loyalty, including those who had fought with him in the anti-colonial struggle. Kim appointed generals to Party positions but on the whole Kim ruled through the Party, not the military institutions.[7] As in the classic Soviet model, the military was formally insulated from domestic politics and institutionally subordinated to Party decision-making but in North Korea the military was understood as fundamentally important to the raison d'être of Kim Il Sungist policy, which was to prepare for eventual war for Korean re-unification.

The military was important as the guarantee of *Juche* policies and Kim family leadership. Kim Jong Il consolidated his legitimacy as designate successor to Kim Il Sung in 1974 when he was appointed to the Party's Political Committee, but it was his gradual ascent to control of the military that secured dynastic control. The younger Kim insisted on a permanent campaign to imbue ideological fealty within the rank and file. At the same time, Kim Jong Il promoted the interests of Kim Il Sung's old comrades within the military institutions.[8] In 1980, Kim Jong Il became a member of the Military Affairs Committee of the Central Committee of the Party and in 1990 consolidated the succession when he became the First Vice Chairman of the National Defence Commission of the DPRK.[9]

---

[6] Hwan Ju Pang, *Korean Review* (Pyongyang: Foreign Languages Publishing House, 1987), pp. 83–4.

[7] An organagram showing the reorganised post-Korean war military–Party structures can be found in Joseph S. Bermudez, *North Korean Special Forces*, second edition (Annapolis: Naval Institute Press, 1998), p. 59.

[8] Takashi Sakai, 'The Power Base of Kim Jong Il: Focusing on its Formation Process', in Park Han S. (ed.), *North Korea: Ideology, Politics, Economy* (Englewood Cliffs: Prentice Hall, 1996), pp. 116–19.

[9] Ibid., p. 119.

The government as transmission belt for the Party

The duty of the government was to act as 'a political organisation which rallies all the members of society around the Party in disregard of their affiliation to classes or strata'.[10] The government, according to Kim Il Sung, was designed to function as 'the most comprehensive transmission belt for the working-class party'.[11] Governmental structures were explicitly designated as vehicles for Party policy. The main job of officials was to act as servants of the Party that in turn carried out the Leader's policies. It was not a function of government officials to offer independent or technically objective advice. Indeed, it would have been very risky for any official to do so; to suggest the legitimacy of views different to those of the Leader would by definition challenge the infallibility of the Leader and therefore would be a traitorous act, punishable by imprisonment and, potentially, a death sentence.

During the Kim Il Sung era, the core institution of governance was the Cabinet, renamed the Administration Council in 1972. The DPRK's first constitutional changes since the creation of the DPRK in 1948 reorganised Cabinet responsibilities so that it assumed responsibility for the coordination of economic development.[12] Cabinet members were government ministers with functional responsibilities and were directly appointed by Kim Il Sung. In de jure terms, the Cabinet was responsible to the Supreme People's Assembly, the highest legislative body of the DPRK, but the Supreme People's Assembly met only infrequently, and held no independent power.[13]

In 1972, Kim Il Sung streamlined local governmental procedures so that local people's committees were absorbed by the cooperative farm management committees.[14] Local administration operated at the provincial and county/district level. The urban district had the same status as the county in the rural areas. The function of provincial and county/district people's committee officials was to carry out central Party policy.

[10] Compilation Committee, *Kim Il Sung Encyclopaedia Volume One*, p. 331.
[11] Ibid.
[12] Dae-Kyu Yoon, 'The Constitution of North Korea: Its Changes and Implications', *Fordham International Law Journal*, Vol. 27, No. 4, 2004, pp. 1289–305, available at http://ir.lawnet.fordham.edu/cgi/viewcontent.cgi?article=1934&context=ilj, accessed 9 February 2014.
[13] Sung Chul Yang, *The North and South Korean Political Systems: A Comparative Analysis*, revised edition (Elizabeth, NJ: Hollym, 1999), pp. 287–90 and 236–7.
[14] Suzy Kim, *Everyday Life in the North Korean Revolution 1945–1950* (Ithaca, NY: Cornell University Press, 2013), p. 247.

Reporting lines were duplicated across technical and political institutions. The Party machinery dealt with disciplinary and political problems at both local and central levels and economic and functional reporting took place through the technical and economic ministries that reported, directly or indirectly, to the Cabinet. The 1972 constitutional changes created the Central People's Committee, which was assigned formal oversight powers over the provincial people's committees and their municipal equivalents at the county level, but this institutional development in practice created a third tier of reporting confusion.[15] The Central People's Committee was therefore somewhat redundant and never assumed significant authority (and did not survive Kim Jong Il's Constitutional changes in 1998).

The Party as transmission belt of the Leader's instructions

The Korean Workers' Party reportedly comprised one million members in 1955, two million by 1975 and three million by the mid-1980s.[16] In 1975, the total population was fifteen million; if half the population were adults and half of those male, given the conservatively gendered roles of women and men in North Korean society, it is likely that a very large proportion of adult males, possibly up to 50 per cent, were members of the Party by 1975. Similar proportions of the male population were likely incorporated in the Party in the 1980s, given that the same pre-conditions

[15] Dae-Sook Suh argues that 'the shift from Party to State' took place in 1972. My view is that the Constitution formalised the dominance of Kim as Leader of the state but also recognised in a post hoc manner the fact that, at least since the early 1960s, and arguably since 1948 when Kim led the first Cabinet of the new state and used the Cabinet to oversee nation-building activities. It would not be the last time in which constitutional and legal changes reflected after the fact change in North Korean society, economics and politics. The 1998 constitution and the 2002 economic reforms legalised non-state ownership of property and market relations several years after famine had brought the market to the DPRK. See Dae-Sook Suh, *Kim Il Sung: The North Korean Leader* (New York: Columbia University Press, 1988), pp. 269–76. On changes wrought by famine see Hazel Smith, *Hungry for Peace: International Security, Humanitarian Assistance and Social Change in North Korea* (Washington, DC: United States Institute of Peace Press, 2005). Yang also points to Kim's 'absolute' control of each Cabinet from 1948 onwards. See Yang, *The North and South Korean Political Systems*, p. 289.

[16] The 1955 figure was cited by Kim Il Sung and is reported in Robert A. Scalapino and Chong-Sik Lee, *Communism in Korea: The Movement* (Berkeley: University of California Press, 1972), p. 469. The 1975 figure is in Chong-Sik Lee, *The Korean Workers' Party: A Short History* (Stanford, CA: Hoover Institution Press, 1978), p. 114. The figure of three million is cited in Pang, *Korean Review*, p. 82. One analyst calculated 1990 Party membership at about 17 per cent of the total population. See Yang, *The North and South Korean Political Systems*, p. 278.

applied. Most families therefore had some family member belonging to the Party – making almost the entire population subject to Party discipline, demands and strictures.

Lacking space for debate or dissent, the Party could not and did not provide a framework for debate or policy development. Instead the Party became institutionalised as a mechanism of societal control and as a transmission belt for Kim's directives. The Party was supposed to 'move as one man in accordance with his [Kim's] orders and instructions'.[17]

Kim Il Sung constantly complained that the reason that policies did not produce hoped-for results was because officials were more interested in providing 'administrative, technical and business-like' solutions than they were in promoting the Leader's policies.[18] In the early years, most of Kim's dissatisfaction was directed at rural policies as although the farming population decreased from 74.1 per cent in 1946 to 56.6 per cent in 1958, its influence went beyond the numbers employed.[19] Relatives that had migrated to the new urban areas came back to the farms every year to help at the transplanting and harvest seasons and maintained family links in rural areas.[20]

Between 1953 and 1958, the percentage of farming households organised in cooperatives grew from 1.2 per cent to 100 per cent.[21] Cooperative farms were formed from amalgamations of pre-existing farming communities and cooperativeisation did not by and large rely on coercion.[22] Nevertheless, up until all farms were incorporated into the cooperatives, farmers had largely directed their own activities and had not been keen to abandon their autonomy. These reluctant cooperative members and their families were of primary concern for Kim as he sought to build and consolidate political power and to achieve the important post-Korean War goal of food self-sufficiency.[23] Kim argued that failures in agricultural production were due to political 'shortcomings'.[24] Party functionaries were to blame for operating in 'an administrative and

---

[17] Party History Research Institute, *History of Revolutionary Activities*, p. 430.
[18] Ibid.
[19] Ellen Brun and Jacques Hersh, *Socialist Korea: A Case Study in the Strategy of Economic Development* (London and New York: Monthly Review Press, 1976), p. 204.
[20] Ibid., pp. 212–14.   [21] Ibid., p. 201.
[22] UNDP and DPRK government, *Report of the First Thematic Roundtable on Agricultural Recovery and Environmental Protection in DPR Korea* (Geneva UNDP, 28–9 May 1998), p. 12.
[23] Ellen Brun and Jacques Hersh, Western economists sympathetic to the Kim Il Sung project, acknowledged that farmers were 'reluctant' to enter the cooperatives. See Brun and Hersh, *Socialist Korea*, p. 201.
[24] Party History Research Institute, *History of Revolutionary Activities*, p. 433.

business-like manner'.[25] Kim therefore chose the farming sector as the springboard for the re-organisation of Party modalities that was designed to ensure that unhappy rural dwellers could not hinder or – worse – sabotage the achievement of food production goals.

In a February 1960 visit by Kim Il Sung to Chongsan village, known in Korean as *Chongsan-ri*, Kim proposed that Party functionaries should work directly with the people.[26] Party committees would take the leading role in workplaces, including farms.[27]

Technical advice from farmers was integrated into the new '*Chongsan-ri* spirit' but decisions would be made according to the direction of the Party. The *Chongsan-ri* method did not only apply to the agricultural sector. The message was that Party institutions should assume political control in every workplace. *Chongsan-ri* modalities established beyond doubt the norm of political direction over technical matters and political methods as, ultimately, more important than technical or professional mechanisms, as a means of economic development.

The Party controlled decision-making in every workplace and in so doing controlled the population's social lives as well as their working lives. All welfare services, including the provision of food and accommodation, remained the responsibility of the enterprise which, under the *Chongsan-ri* method, was controlled by the Party. The Party controlled all aspects of individual's lives. All able-bodied adults except the sick, the disabled and pensioners were expected to work in the waged labour force and those who did not register for work were not entitled to food rations. All adults were guaranteed employment but the corollary of the system was a constraint on social and geographical mobility as jobs were allocated by Party authorities.

The *Chongsan-ri* method valorised the authority of the Party but only as a transmission belt for the leader's authority. Kim Il Sung implemented continuous 'anti-bureaucratisation' campaigns that kept a check on independent thinking by Party officials.[28] Group criticism sessions, which every member of the workplace had to attend, were held in every workplace on a regular basis, from once a week to once a day. Workers had to learn parts of the works of Kim Il Sung, which they also had to recite in these sessions. Ordinary members of the population and Party members were encouraged to criticise each other and Party functionaries, although in practice the system evolved so that admissions of minor infraction

---

[25] Ibid., p. 429.   [26] Ibid., p. 433.   [27] Ibid., pp. 428–40.

[28] The origins of the anti-bureaucratic model are described in Lee, *The Korean Workers' Party*, p. 101. For a North Korean official perspective see Compilation Committee, *Kim Il Sung Encyclopaedia Volume One*, 1992), p. 254.

became the norm so as to avoid accusations of non-participation, and criticism of senior Party officials remained a dangerous activity.[29] These organisational arrangements encouraged exaggerated protestations of loyalty and reinforced the power of the leadership. They helped root out those who might take an independent policy line and made it extremely difficult and dangerous to express alternative points of view.

These continuous anti-bureaucratism campaigns were designed to prevent the rise of any source of authority other than from the directives of Kim Il Sung. The idea of independent professional advice was politically suspect and individuals who were seen to prize technical efficiencies or impartiality over and above the political directions of the Leader were castigated as 'bureaucratic'. The continuing 'anti-bureaucratisation' campaigns that glorified *ad hoc* solutions to technical problems by heroic individuals and local communities were supposed to counter what were proclaimed as unhelpful bureaucratic tendencies.

The *Chongsan-ri* method embedded the authority of Kim Il Sung within and over the Party machinery as Party policy was theorised as the 'embodiment' of the Leader's instructions.[30] The Party provided a mechanism of control and supervision of the state machinery and of the workplace but only as an instrument of the 'Great Leader'. The aim of the Party was to uphold 'the lofty will of the Great Leader'.[31] The 'basic line of Party-building and the main task of Party work' were to strengthen and 'actively' promote 'unitary leadership' and the 'monolithic ideological system'.[32] Explicit pronouncements reinforced over and over again that the function of the Party was to implement the Leader's policy and that the Leader's thoughts, and his alone, were to provide direction to the Party and hence the entire state and society in North Korea.

Party members were categorised in terms of their political loyalty and alleged historic ties to class and colonial enemies.[33] These could be family relationships or connections through association or employment. The results of investigations into actual or perceived political reliability were written into Party records.[34] The Party developed, therefore, as a mechanism of surveillance over its millions of members. In 1967 Kim elaborated on the necessity of monolithic ideological leadership to the

[29] Scalapino and Lee, *Communism in Korea*, pp. 467–71.
[30] Party History Research Institute, *History of Revolutionary Activities*, pp. 435–6.
[31] Ibid., p. 615.   [32] Ibid.
[33] Kim Il Sung, *On Improving and Strengthening the Training of Party Cadres* (Pyongyang: Foreign Languages Publishing House, 1975), pp. 23–32.
[34] Balázs Szalontai, 'The Four Horsemen of the Apocalypse in North Korea', in Chris Springer (ed.), *North Korea Caught in Time: Images of War and Reconstruction* (Reading: Garnet Publishing, 2010), pp. xxiv–xxv.

Party Central Committee.[35] He confirmed that monolithic leadership explicitly entailed subordination of Party and society to the 'Leader as hub' of the Party.[36] Monolithic leadership was not Party leadership but was exclusive leadership by a specific leader. The duty of the entire Party was to ensure 'the predominance of only the leader's ideology in the Party'.[37] In 1974, Kim again took pains to emphasise the monolithic ideology of the Party and the necessity for Party cadres, members and organisations to 'act as one under the unitary leadership of the Party Centre'.[38] In the 1974 speech the 'Party Centre' refers to Kim Il Sung although the term was increasingly used to refer to his son and putative political heir, Kim Jong Il.[39] These were not contradictory usages as, by the 1970s, the continuity of leadership was theorised in North Korean ideology as constituted through the notion of dynastic legitimacy of the Kim family in which resided the locus of power, authority, legitimacy and omnipotence.[40]

Mass mobilisation and the militarisation of society

Kim Il Sung's idea was that the new state should be constituted by the permanent mobilisation of the population, mediated by the Party, which would in turn be controlled by the absolute authority of the Leader. The mass organisations were expected to act as transmission belts for the Leader's policies. The masses have 'responsibilities' to become organised but it is 'only' the Leader who provides direction, 'guidance' and cohesion.[41] A further aim was to integrate the population into a vast campaigning force within which private and civic life were to be constituted as public affairs and in which the entire population would 'voluntarily' subordinate their individual well-being to the goal of making North Korea a major power. Kim justified the methods of enforced participation and controls over civic life with rhetoric in which he talked of creating a new type of society in the future that would be a 'communist paradise'.[42] The promise was that sacrifices in the present would bring rewards for future generations.

In December 1993, less than a year before he died, Kim Il Sung reported proudly that 'everyone in our country belongs to a particular political organisation and leads an organisational life'.[43] Literally all the

---

[35] Ibid., p. 519.   [36] Ibid., p. 521.   [37] Ibid.   [38] Ibid., pp. 612–13.

[39] Suh, *Kim Il Sung*, pp. 276–86.

[40] Party History Research Institute, *History of Revolutionary Activities*, pp. 612–13.

[41] Compilation Committee, *Kim Il Sung Encyclopaedia Volume One*, p. 90.

[42] Kim Il Sung, *Tasks of the People's Government in Modelling the Whole of Society on the Juche Idea* (Pyongyang: Foreign Languages Publishing House, 1982).

[43] Speech by Kim Il Sung to the 21st Plenary Meeting of the Sixth Central Committee of the Workers' Party. See Kim Il Sung, 'On the Direction of Socialist Economic

population, not just able-bodied adults but children and the elderly, were incorporated into hierarchically organised mass organisations.[44] The most important politically were the youth organisation, the Democratic Women's Union, the Union of the Agricultural Working People and the General Federation of Trade Unions. Mass organisations acted as mechanisms of economic development, civil defence and social control but all their activities incorporated reiteration and reinforcement of Kim Il Sungist ideology.

Workplace and education commitments took second priority to mass mobilisation activities that included self-defence drills, national immunisation campaigns, mass sporting events and cleaning neighbourhoods. Those participating carried out their normal role in the workplace or in school and at the same time engaged in activities that were often highly physically demanding and could be more or less popular.

The members of the mass organisations were not always members of the Party but their leaders were always Party officials. The mass organisations were affiliated to the Party, whose role was organisational and ideological. The Party's role was to organise activities and to exhort the members of mass organisations to carry out the tasks set by the Leader. The practice of the reading of and referral to the writings and idealised activities of Kim Il Sung and Kim Jong Il at each and every mass activity was deliberately designed to reinforce the hegemony of the leadership. Mass organisation activity was always accompanied by slogans, flags, music and study sessions whose function was to embed the idea that the leadership in the form of Kim Il Sung was personally responsible for any benefits that might accrue to the population and outside forces such as 'imperialists' or domestic forces such as unreconstructed domestic 'factionalists' were responsible for the suffering of the population.

Mass mobilisation was institutionalised in a quasi-militarised pattern such that the population became used to taking orders, however apparently illogical. Militarised ways of working encouraged innovation to get things done but at the same time discouraged strategic initiatives. The population avoided placing themselves in potential danger and played safe. Inefficiencies and illogical processes and outcomes were unchallenged because to do so was to risk punitive sanctions for implied criticism of the Great Leader. Questioning of strategic decisions could

Construction for the Immediate Period Ahead', in Kim Il Sung, *Works, Vol. 44* (Pyongyang: Foreign Languages Publishing House, 1999), p. 251.
[44] Ibid.

be interpreted as anti-nationalist and anti-patriotic. The effect was to reinforce the culture of administration by hierarchy.[45]

Decision-making took place through vertical authority channels with a simultaneous lack of horizontal communication between and across societal units, such as workplaces or neighbourhoods, except at the most trivial or informal level.[46] Practices developed out of the guerrilla warfare tradition of operating on a 'need to know' basis in order to protect the physical security of combatants became part of the way that both the Party and the mass organisations operated.[47] The population became socialised within a culture of secrecy as the norm, as 'common-sense'.

Ideological education

Kim's view was that the capacity of the state/Party apparatus to inculcate revolutionary ideology in the population was fundamental to political success.[48] The aim was to socialise the population such that individuals would be prepared to sacrifice individual expectations for a long time in the interests of state-building. The means chosen was the development, promulgation and embedding of *Juche*, a neologism – from *ju* as master or ruler and *che* as body or entity – and often translated into English as 'self-reliance'. The doctrine sought to incorporate and convey that it is the Leader who is 'master' of the 'body' of the population and the Party.[49]

Kim mooted the *Juche* idea in 1955 as a means to distance North Korea from the Soviet Union and China and to stress the necessity for the DPRK to develop independently of big power sponsors. The idea was barely mentioned again until 1965 when Kim expanded on *Juche* in a

---

[45] The information in this paragraph comes out of direct observation through visiting the DPRK regularly since 1990 but most specifically working with North Koreans in the DPRK between 1998 to 2001. It is also the product of indirect observation from hundreds of conversations with other international residents in the DPRK and with North Koreans throughout the country.

[46] This was an explicit policy. See Chang-sik Sok, 'Experiences of State-building in the Democratic People's Republic of Korea', in Ken'ichiro Hirano (ed.), *The State and Cultural Transformation: Perspectives from East Asia* (Tokyo: United Nations Press, 1993), p. 340.

[47] Adrian Buzo's account of the development of the Kim Il Sung dynasty stresses the formative impact of the guerrilla heritage on methods of political operation. My view is that what is also important is how this process happened. This heritage, in other words, is constitutive of state and societal patterns of organisation in very specific and historically constituted ways. Adrian Buzo, *The Guerrilla Dynasty: Politics and Leadership in North Korea* (Boulder, CO: Westview Press, 1999).

[48] Han Gil Kim, *Modern History of Korea* (Pyongyang: Foreign Languages Publishing House, 1979), pp. 389–91.

[49] Suh, *Kim Il Sung*, p. 301.

speech in Indonesia designed to rally support for the DPRK from the non-aligned nations.[50] In this manifestation, *Juche* is not much more than a vague policy of self-reliance, much akin to what many of the non-aligned countries were arguing for at the time.[51] As developed by North Korean ideologists, *Juche* iterates how and why domestic politics, the economy and society should be built exclusively around Leader-dominated, Party-centric, mass mobilisation strategies.[52] *Juche* asserts that 'man is the master of his own destiny' but that the Leader is the repository of the peoples' demands and 'is the top brain of the popular masses' and the 'brain of [the] socio-political organism'.[53] In turn, the Party functioned as the pivot 'in rallying the popular masses into one socio-political organism around the leader'.[54] The role of the Party is to inculcate the people with the central idea that the Leader is omnipotent and must be obeyed. The role and duty of the population is to mobilise around the leader's will.

Juche formalised and justified national autonomy in international politics and proclaimed North Korea's right to make decisions based on discrete national interests even as the leadership solicited aid, trade and military support from alliance partners, China and the Soviet Union. Underpinning the contrivances of the *Juche* doctrine was Kim's recognition that North Korea had few good choices if it were to develop economically and maintain itself as a sovereign state. China and the Soviet Union might not always be able or willing to offer substantial economic support. In that case, Kim would need to make compromises in international politics to obtain capital and technology from capitalist countries or would need to rely on the physical labour of the population as a substitute. The more or less mutual lack of interest in ameliorating relationships with the West therefore contributed to continued efforts to systematise and institutionalise 'Kim Il Sungism' or *Juche* as a theory of rule. The aim was to convince the population that Kim's policies were both correct and that there were no alternatives.

Some of the rhetoric drew on Korean cultural tropes; the most obvious being that Kim was the 'father' to whom, in Confucian thought, obedience was owed. North Korean ideologues, however, also argued that the

---

[50] Ibid., p. 308.
[51] A. W. Singham and Shirley Hune, *Non-alignment in an Age of Alignments* (London: Zed, 1986).
[52] Kim Jong Il, *On the Juche Idea of our Party* (Pyongyang: Foreign Languages Publishing House, 1985).
[53] Compilation Committee, *Kim Il Sung Encyclopaedia Volume One*, pp. 332–3 and p. 109.
[54] Compilation Committee of Kim Il Sung Encyclopaedia, 'Revolutionary Outlook on the Organisation', in ibid., p. 112.

Juche ideology was scientific and rational. They paid homage to Marxism-Leninism but argued that *Juche* was distinct from and more advanced than other communist doctrines.[55] North Korean publications argued that, although the Juche ideology was formulated in North Korea, it had universal application.[56]

The means of ideological transmission

Social and cultural life were saturated with the message that Kim Il Sung and his family were the natural rulers of Korea because of historically derived legitimacy gained from patriotic contributions to furthering the independence of the nation. These messages were conveyed in the nurseries, kindergartens, schools and universities; the health and social services sectors; in the wider cultural arenas of literature, dance, music, painting and film; and in each and every workplace. Education and cultural policy were explicitly designed to instil state ideology into the thinking of the population.[57] Children learned to sing songs that celebrated North Korean achievements as the result of Kim Il Sung's policies. Every media – including movies, television, posters, newspapers, songs, dance, opera, novels, textbooks, and even health messages – glorified Kim and his family as the creators of an independent Korea. The duty of cultural production was to convey ideological messages, although the production of non-ideological culture was not prohibited as long as those products were devoid of messages that might challenge state ideology. Movies and music production provided entertainment as well as propaganda for a wider audience.

Education delivered technical skills as well as socialisation into the goals and ideas of Kim Il Sungism.[58] Educational curricula were developed so as to inculcate obedience and respect for the Kim family and the Kim Il Sungist political system. In kindergartens children gained literacy and numeracy skills through material based on the Kim family mythology. 'Morality' classes, which were essentially ways of conveying civic duty in the context of Kim Il Sungist ideology, started in kindergarten and continued through primary and secondary education.[59] Primary

[55] For example see Party History Research Institute, *History of Revolutionary Activities*.
[56] Ibid., pp. 29–34 and 372–83.
[57] Jiangcheng He, 'Educational Reforms', in Han S. Park (ed.), *North Korea: Ideology, Politics, Economy* (Englewood Cliffs: Prentice Hall, 1996), pp. 33–50; Pang, *Korean Review*, pp. 159–92.
[58] Compilation Committee, *Kim Il Sung Encyclopaedia Volume One*, pp. 277–302.
[59] National EFA 2000 Assessment Group, Democratic People's Republic of Korea, National EFA Assessment Report: The Implementation of the 'World Declaration on

school students followed courses on 'The Childhood and Youth of Kim
Il Sung' and 'The Childhood and Youth of Kim Jong Il'.[60] In schools,
about 10 per cent of the children's time was allocated to studying the life
and works of Kim Il Sung and his family, but other parts of the curriculum, for example, Korean language, history and geography, also used as
textbook examples the life and work of Kim Il Sung.[61]

Politicised education took place through the mobilisation of children
aged between 7 and 13 out of school hours in the Children's Union.[62]
Children's Union activities reinforced the responsibility of all members
of the community to act in an unselfish manner for the benefit of the
community as a whole. Activities included helping to kill pests, looking
after roadside trees and plants, helping with growing vegetables and
looking after small livestock like rabbits.[63] By themselves these activities
were innocuous and for the children sometimes fun events, as children
were not expected to work physically hard. The point of these activities,
though, was the socialisation messages that accompanied them. Children
learned to operate as a group, under the guidance of their teachers and
volunteers who were also Party officials. The messages accompanying
these activities contained explicit homage to the wise leadership of the
Kim family.

In the Kim Il Sung period, when North Korea was closed to most
outside influences except from other communist countries that were
also authoritarian and whose official media equally stifling, for the
overwhelming majority of children this ideologically suffused curriculum
was the only source of information about the world in which they lived.
Children could not avoid being influenced by state ideology as the curriculum was saturated with political messages and most young children
attended educational institutions, including the nurseries, from a few
months of age.[64] Teachers were trained in pedagogy, student–teacher
ratios were low and government policy encouraged child enrolment in
nurseries – although attendance was not mandatory –so that women with

Education for All' (Pyongyang: National EFA 2000 Assessment Group, 1999), p. 26 and
28; He, 'Educational Reforms', p. 40.
[60] Ibid., pp. 42–3.   [61] Ibid., pp. 33–50.
[62] Yong-Bok Li, *Education in the Democratic People's Republic of Korea* (Pyongyang: Foreign
Languages Publishing House, 1986), p. 74; Soon-Hee Lim, *Value Changes of the North
Korean New Generation and Prospects* (Seoul: Korea Institute for National Unification,
2007), p. 5; Jiangcheng He, 'Educational Reforms', in Han S. Park (ed.), *North Korea:
Ideology, Politics, Economy* (Englewood Cliffs: Prentice Hall, 1996), p. 43.
[63] Yong-Bok Li, *Education in the Democratic People's Republic of Korea* (Pyongyang: Foreign
Languages Publishing House, 1986), p. 75.
[64] UNICEF, *Draft Situation Analysis DPR Korea 1997*, revised and edited (Pyongyang:
UNICEF, 1997), p. 23.

young children could participate in the paid workforce.[65] Attendance was, however, mandatory in kindergartens and schools where children were again subject to the Kim Il Sungist curricula.

The younger Kim was well known for his personal involvement in the movie industry but perhaps less well understood was the impact Kim Jong Il had on wide swathes of cultural production including literature, architecture and music.[66] Arts and culture were placed under the control of Kim Jong Il after he was appointed to senior positions in the Party's propaganda divisions in 1964.[67] He ensured that revolutionary histories were written, monuments to his father erected and popular light operas, music and films created that sang the praises of the anti-Japanese guerrilla struggle. Kim Jong Il borrowed techniques from the Soviet Union in literature, the arts and musical form and cinematic techniques from Europe and colonial Japan, although *avant garde* approaches were not permitted.[68]

Many cultural productions were overbearingly didactic but, equally, many were not. Children and adults had access to a fairly varied cultural production – from fairy stories to folk tales, romantic films to historical epics. Not all children's media contained direct references to the Kim family, although fairy tales, depictions of historic events and interpretations of folk stories carried standard moral messages of fables everywhere, for example, doing good, helping the elderly and working hard. These messages chimed with the *Juche* message – of respect for the community and submerging individual ambition.

Significant attempts were made to appeal to audiences in a way that emulated Hollywood blockbusters and that copied techniques used in South Korean movies made for a mass audience.[69] North Korea's very large cinema-going public watched popular films containing elements of romance, spectacle, martial arts and horror genres.[70] The state emphasised that movies, music and song should carry a revolutionary message but there was quite an amount of latitude as to what counted as

[65] Ibid., p. 13.
[66] Sakai, 'The Power Base of Kim Jong Il, pp. 105–22.
[67] Sung Chull Kim, *North Korea under Kim Jong Il: From Consolidation to Systemic Dissonance* (Albany: State University of New York Press, 2006), pp. 39–40.
[68] Keith Howard, '*Juche* and Culture: What's New?', in Hazel Smith, Chris Rhodes, Diana Pritchard and Kevin Magill (eds.), *North Korea in the New World Order* (London: Macmillan Press, 1996), pp. 169–95.
[69] Steven Chung, 'The Split Screen: Sin Sang-ok in North Korea', in Sonia Ryang (ed.), *North Korea: Toward a Better Understanding* (Lanham: Lexington Books, 2009), pp. 85–107.
[70] Steven Chung states that 'North Koreans were likely watching more films than any other people in the world'. See ibid., p. 87.

'revolutionary'. Romance and fable were permitted as the focus of artistic production as well as more obviously political themes such as the anti-Japanese struggle or incidents in the life of the 'Great Leader'.

Music, song and dance was introduced at a very early age into the nursery, kindergarten and school curriculum and continues to inform popular culture. Adults commonly end formal as well as informal social occasions with impromptu songs and have access to a wide repertoire. English-speaking foreigners are often startled to hear Korean versions of 'Danny Boy', a North Korean standard, sung as emotionally as it might be in the song's native Ireland.[71] Folk songs such as the popular 'Arirang' – equally popular in South Korea – were therefore as likely to be heard as the 'Song of Kim Il Sung'. Karaoke is popular in North Korea and tunes belted out in bars and restaurants include local 'classics' such as 'Bang gap suumnihda' (Pleased to meet you) but can also include Elvis's 'Love me Tender' (another favourite) or perhaps Michael Jackson's 'Heal the World'. Kim Jong Il's *Juche* messages were therefore mixed with a dose of populism that permitted non-political entertainment.

Political criticism could not of course be conveyed in any part of the arts and strict censorship as to theme and content was the absolute rule. All cultural production was state-censored and there was no possibility of producing cultural artifacts that were potentially critical or oppositional to the state. Serious literature written by foreigners could only be found in libraries and translations of foreign 'classics' were not produced for the general public.[72] Nevertheless, foreign films from Russia were occasionally broadcast on television and classical and pop music from Europe and the United States was sometimes available in restaurants and bars. North Korean state socialisation did not also limit itself to political censorship. State cultural dictates had a rather puritanical streak; abstract works of art and the depiction of nudity were not permitted in North Korea.[73]

All media, including newspapers, journals, magazines, radio and television broadcasts were state-controlled and the messages were relentlessly focused on the population's duty to glorify the Kim family, to engage in national reconstruction and to be prepared for war. The news media stressed the inhuman nature of North Korea's historic enemies, particularly the United States, which, it repeatedly stated, had used

[71] Author's observations, 1990–2011.
[72] Vladimir Pucek, 'The Impact of *Juche* upon Literature and Arts', in Han S. Park (ed.), *North Korea: Ideology, Politics, Economy* (Englewood Cliffs: Prentice Hall, 1996), pp. 51–70.
[73] For a representative sample of permitted subjects and styles see Foreign Languages Publishing House, *Korean Paintings of Today* (Pyongyang: Foreign Languages Publishing House, 1980).

'bestial methods' against the population in the Korean War.[74] Kim Il Sung painted all atrocities as only having been committed by US forces and the south. Every generation of North Koreans was told that Americans were bloodthirsty monsters incapable of normal human feelings and interaction. The message was that unless the population remained ever vigilant they might face these self-same predations once more. DPRK propaganda made a distinction between the people and government of South Korea in that it argued that the regime in the south was a puppet of the United States, which mistreated the people of South Korea because they were constantly struggling to overturn their government.

The failure to achieve monolithic unity of state and society

The absence of alternative political perspectives supported the naturalisation and acceptance of the Kim Il Sung model of Leader-controlled mass mobilisation. Ideological education was reinforced by government control over alternative information sources. No foreign newspapers, books, films, music or foreign cultural artifacts could be bought or sold in the country. The government maintained tight control of audio-visual equipment such that radios and televisions were restricted to government channels. A trusted few had access to material produced and published abroad through their jobs or as university students studying in foreign countries and university students had access to foreign publications in university libraries, but the government limited contact with visiting foreigners so as to suppress the possibilities of unauthorised access to non-sanctioned sources of information.

Kim benefited from the vestiges of community solidarity organically and historically derived from family and social ties. Communities worked together to achieve objectives, for example construction of homes and workplaces and, initially, the population saw rewards for these efforts.[75] Houses were built, agriculture was revived and a new heavy industrial sector developed. Never having experienced political freedom, the tangible advances offered by rapid economic growth, the provision of improved health, housing and education and the national pride engendered because of what was understood as a successful battle for national independence may have seemed at first worth the price.

Party discipline outside the big cities was ameliorated by the *de facto* accountability of Party officials and Party members to local communities.

---

[74] Kim, *Modern History of Korea*, pp. 334–40.
[75] Brun and Hersh, *Socialist Korea*, pp. 165 and 167.

Most of the millions of Party members and many of the hundreds of thousands of officials shared the same living conditions with the citizens with whom they interacted on a day-to-day basis. This did not mean that Party officials were at liberty to disobey political instructions from Pyongyang but it did mean that they faced constant local pressure, including from their own families, to improve lives and livelihoods. These pressures resulted in a less than stringent application of the rules on occasion and when disciplinary retribution could be avoided.

The persistent focus on improving Party adherence to Kim's instructions of itself indicates that Kim was not entirely successful at achieving 'monolithic unity'. As late as 1969, after the Party had established undisputed political control over the country, Kim Il Sung complained that the Party had very poor personnel records and lacked systematically organised and reliable data about its own members.[76] Kim regularly and bitterly criticised officials for not doing their jobs properly. In 1971 he accused some officials of employing the 'motorcar-style work method' because 'he meets his subordinates and workers while driving, he stops his car and asks them a few questions and then drives on'.[77] These regular harangues of officials for not doing their jobs properly illustrates the limitations of state capacity, perhaps even more than the use of prison camps, to punish political dissidents.

In 1986 Kim Il Sung admitted that the struggle to maintain disciplined Party cadres was on-going.[78] He complained that cadres needed to study more and warned Party members that they needed to adhere to Party rules. Party members needed 'to improve their attitude ... and acquire the habit of leading their Party life willingly ... with enthusiasm as required by the regulations of Party life.'[79]

Revolutionary discipline

Ultimately, Kim Il Sung enforced policy through the implementation of 'revolutionary discipline'. Pak Hon Yong, the former communist leader from South Korea, was given a death sentence in December

---

[76] Kim Il Sung, 'On Some Problems in Party Work and Economic Affairs', in Kim Il Sung, *Works, Vol. 23, October 1968–May 1969* (Pyongyang: Foreign Languages Publishing House, 1985), pp. 257–62.

[77] In 1980 Kim Il Sung stated that agricultural problems arose because 'our officials lack a sense of responsibility'. Kim, *On Improving and Strengthening the training of Party Cadres*, pp. 20–1; Kim Il Sung, *Works, Vol. 35* (Pyongyang: Foreign Languages Publishing House, 1990), p. 239.

[78] Kim Il Sung, *Historical Experience of Building the Workers' Party of Korea* (Pyongyang: Foreign Languages Publishing House, 1986), pp. 27–53.

[79] Ibid., p. 42.

1955.[80] Korean revolutionaries with ties with the Soviet Union or the Chinese communists as well as the 'domestic communists' – mainly those who had a history of political activity in South Korea – were systematically eradicated.[81] By the late 1950s Kim had decimated potential rivals but continued to fear potential opposition to his leadership. Kim removed and replaced senior Party officials and prominent generals on a regular basis from the 1960s onwards.[82] Kim Il Sung continued to purge opposing voices as he concentrated on ensuring a smooth political succession for Kim Jong Il.[83]

For most of the population, the sheer physical time necessary to engage in work, school and Party-directed activities meant that there was little opportunity or incentive for political activity that in any way might challenge the government. All households were placed into small neighbourhood groups, or *inminban*, whose responsibility was both to monitor the activities of their neighbours for politically suspicious activities as well as to engage in more innocuous tasks that included preventive health care and keeping local areas clean and tidy.[84]

When the vast ideological apparatus failed, the pervasive institutions of coercion, including the military, police force and security services, were used to enforce Kim Il Sungist policies.[85] The legal and penal system punished political dissenters as well as criminal and civil offenders.[86] Practices derived from the Japanese colonial system, including punishing 'thought crimes' and collective sanctions against entire families as retribution for individual law-breaking, were retained in the Kim Il Sungist polity.[87] Kim Il Sung retained the idea of hereditary family responsibility

---

[80] Scalapino and Lee, *Communism in Korea*, p. 440.
[81] Suh, *Kim Il Sung*, pp. 123–57.
[82] Ibid., pp. 191, 228–32 and 238–42.   [83] Ibid., pp. 295–6.
[84] Vasily Mikheev, 'Politics and Ideology in the post-Cold war era', in Han S. Park (ed.), *North Korea: Ideology, Politics, Economy* (Englewood Cliffs: Prentice Hall, 1996), pp. 94–5.
[85] For numbers see the very useful annual *The Military Balance*, a publication of the International Institute of Strategic Studies (IISS). See for example IISS, *The Military Balance 2001–2002* (Oxford University Press, 2001), pp. 196–7.
[86] It is impossible to obtain independent accounts of the North Korean criminal and penal systems. The main source is North Korean defectors. Some of their testimony must be treated with caution but the weight of the evidence very heavily suggests a sometimes arbitrary system of punishments and, unquestionably, penal sanctions used as a mechanism to enforce political control. For one report based on defector accounts see David R. Hawk, *The Hidden Gulag: Exposing North Korea's Prison Camps: Prisoners' Testimonies and Satellite Photographs* (Washington, DC: US Committee for Human Rights in North Korea, 2003).
[87] There is a discussion in the literature about the nature of the North Korean legal system: sometimes characterised as a system of 'rule by law', as differentiated from 'rule of law'. For this distinction see Marion P. Spina, Jr., 'Brushes with the Law: North Korea and

in the construction of 'revolutionary discipline' such that loss of political status could have extraordinary negative consequences for both the individual and their family. In the worst-case scenario, individuals judged as criminals were forced to relocate with their families to 'the countryside', a euphemism used in North Korea to describe varying degrees of punitive banishment to remote areas.[88] In less severe circumstances an individual might be forced to accept a low-status job, leading to less pay and tougher living conditions.

The management and operations of the penal system remained opaque. Defector accounts portrayed a picture of vast labour camps, established throughout the country, whose purpose was to incarcerate political prisoners and their families in degrading and abusive conditions.[89] One of the most well-known was thought to be in Yodok, a county in South Hamgyong which in 1993 had a population of 37,000 spread out over a sparsely populated area, as indicated by its very low population density of twenty-six persons per square kilometre.

Stories of extreme abuses including infanticide and chemical experiments on human guinea pigs who lived in concentration camps were part of the discourse on North Korean human rights abuses. Some defectors recounted inhuman horror stories of systematic torture and Nazi-like behaviour by prison and security officials. As the North Korean government refused to allow access to its penal facilities to independent, external observers, suspicions remained that the government must indeed have something to hide.

At best, prison conditions likely remained on a par with the poorest parts of North Korean society, implying that prisoners faced extremely tough living with the ever-present risk of malnutrition and disease. The difference between political camps and other places of incarceration was not that they entailed compulsory labour camps; all adults except the sick and the elderly were supposed to work, including those imprisoned. The important difference was that the release of political prisoners was a matter for political and therefore arbitrary official decision-making.[90]

---

the Rule of Law', *Academic Series Papers on Korea* (Washington, DC: Korea Economic Institute, 2008), pp. 75–97, available at www.keia.org/Publications/OnKorea/2008/08Spina.pdf., accessed 9 February 2014.

[88] Kook-shin Kim, Hyun-joon Cho, Keum-soon Lee, Soon-hee Lim, Kyu-chang Lee and Woo-taek Hong, *White Paper on Human Rights in North Korea 2011* (Seoul: Korea Institute for National Unification, 2011), pp. 134–44.

[89] Hawk, *The Hidden Gulag*; for an account by an inhabitant of one of these labour camps see Chol Hwan Kang and Pierre Rigolout, translated by Yair Reiner, *Aquariums of Pyongyang: Ten Years in the North Korean Gulag* (New York: Basic Books, 2001).

[90] Human Rights Watch, 'The Invisible Exodus: North Koreans in the People's Republic of China', *North Korea*, Vol. 145, No. 8, November 2002. For discussion see Kie-Duck

The DPRK modelled its prison system on that employed by a number of other countries, including the Soviet Union, which sent prisoners to work in mines and on farms. There are no reliable figures as to the numbers sent to work, but those exiled away from their homes would have found the conditions almost unbearable. Even for local inhabitants used to the work, living and working conditions in mines and poor farming areas were extraordinarily tough; the hard labour and privations required would have been devastating for anyone used to city life.

Juche in foreign policy: the myth of the hermit nation

Juche in foreign policy for Kim meant something akin to the international norm of state sovereignty that constitutes states in international law as formally equal to and independent of each other, even as states are unequal to each other in terms of their power capacities.[91] *Juche* did not mean abandoning alliances or ignoring international power relations but rather overlay a rather pragmatic understanding about North Korea's relative power in the world. North Korea 'sheltered' under the Soviet Union's nuclear umbrella, which protected North Korea, as many small countries allied to the two Cold War superpowers, from international intervention.[92] Kim did not only, however, rely on alliances for protection. From the early 1960s, Kim Il Sung built a large army in the effort to enhance self-defence capacity and military self-reliance.

In 1961 North Korea signed defence treaties with China and the former Soviet Union that committed the two communist superpowers to come to the aid of the DPRK if it was attacked. North Korea never had to call in that guarantee and, given that the relationship between the DPRK and its major allies was by no means harmonious, Kim Il Sung did not know for sure if those guarantees would have been honoured.

Park and Sang-Jin Han (eds.), *Human Rights in North Korea* (Seoul: The Sejong Institute, 2007).

[91] For discussion on North Korean conceptions of independence and equality in relationship to sovereignty in foreign affairs see Hazel Smith, 'North Korean Foreign Policy in the 1990s: The Realist Approach', in Hazel Smith, Chris Rhodes, Diana Pritchard and Kevin Magill (eds.), *North Korea in the New World Order* (London: Macmillan, 1996), pp. 93–113.

[92] Fred Halliday, *The Making of the Second Cold War*, second edition (London: Verso, 1986); See also Chae-Jin Lee, *A Troubled Peace: US Policy and the Two Koreas* (Baltimore, MD: The Johns Hopkins University Press, 2006). For detail on how Kim Il Sung maximised opportunities from the Soviet–US rivalry see Georgy Bulychev, 'Korean Security Dilemmas: A Russian Perspective', in Hazel Smith (ed.), *Reconstituting Korean Security: A Policy Primer* (Tokyo: United Nations Press, 2007), pp. 182–212.

North Korea relied, however, on the political support of both states, especially the Soviet Union, which until 1973 when the Chinese communist government was recognised as the legitimate holder of the China Security Council seat, was the only communist power holding veto power in the United Nations Security Council.

Juche policies meant balancing diplomatic relations to remain on reasonable terms with both China and the Soviet Union in the conflict between the two communist powers during the Cold War.[93] Kim veered towards China during the early 1960s, as he believed that the Soviet Union had 'betrayed' Cuba in the Cuban Missile Crisis of 1962 and worried that the Soviet Union might not be a trustworthy ally.[94] In the late 1960s, Kim Il Sung leaned more towards the Soviet Union, especially during the Cultural Revolution when contingents of Chinese Red Guards paraded through the streets with posters calling Kim Il Sung a 'fat revisionist' in the late 1960s.[95]

North Korea was not as isolated from the non-communist world as the Western imagination portrayed. During the Kim Il Sungist years, North Korea had few diplomatic contacts with western Europe and the United States but it had a broad network of diplomatic relations with other states worldwide. North Korean diplomats interacted with a wide gamut of communist states but they also developed active contacts with member states of the ideologically diverse Non-Aligned Movement, of which the DPRK was a member from the 1970s onwards. The DPRK established diplomatic links with African, Asian and Latin American states.[96] It established diplomatic relations with the small social democratic state of Malta in 1971, Sweden, Norway, Finland and Iceland in 1973, Austria in 1974 and Portugal in 1975.[97] North Korea also had a permanent diplomatic presence at

[93] Jian Chen, 'Limits of the "Lips and Teeth" Alliance: An Historical Review of Chinese–North Korean Relations', in Timothy Hildebrandt (ed.), *Uneasy Allies: Fifty Years of China–North Korea Relations* (Washington, DC: Woodrow Wilson Center Asia Program Special Report, September 2003), p. 7; Bulychev, 'Korean Security Dilemmas', p. 185.

[94] James F. Person (ed.), *The Cuban Missile Crisis and the Origins of North Korea's Policy of Self-Reliance in National Defense, E-Dossier #12* (Washington, DC: Woodrow Wilson International Center for Scholars, 2012), p. 2, available at www.wilsoncenter.org/sites/default/files/NKIDP_eDossier_12_North_Korea_and_the_Cuban_Missile_Crisis_0.pdf, accessed 29 December 2013.

[95] Scalapino and Lee, *Communism in Korea*, p. 641.

[96] Kim Il Sung, *The Non-Aligned Movement is a Mighty Anti-imperialist Revolutionary Force of our Times* (Pyongyang: Foreign Languages Publishing House, 1986); Kim Il Sung, *The Non-Aligned Movement and South–South Cooperation* (Pyongyang: Foreign Languages Publishing House, 1987).

[97] See www.ncnk.org/resources/briefing-papers/all-briefing-papers/dprk-diplomatic-relations, accessed 7 June 2012.

its missions to the International Maritime Organisation in London and UNESCO in Paris.

Diplomatic engagement outside the communist bloc was often superficial but not always so. North Korea was an aid donor to states in Africa up until the end of the Cold War; providing technical assistance to Guinea, Tanzania, Ethiopia and Mozambique, among others, on projects in the agricultural and industrial sectors into the early 1990s.[98] North Korea had, however, negligible diplomatic contact with the United States and South Korea and only very limited dealings with the non-Scandinavian states of western Europe.

The global Cold War stalemate did not prevent low-level insurgency by principals and satellites on both sides of the Cold War divide.[99] Both superpowers tolerated unpleasant and recalcitrant regimes in support of Cold War balancing.[100] Kim Il Sung used the autonomy available to him and the military forces he had built up to engage in belligerent activity abroad. North Korea's military adventures were opportunistic and designed to humiliate the enemy; most notoriously the capture of the United States spy ship, the USS Pueblo, in 1968 and imprisonment of the crew for a year.[101] These adventures deepened the hostility between the United States and the DPRK but they did not precipitate full-scale war.

North Korea's Special Forces abducted Japanese civilians from Japan at least as late as the 1970s and 1980s, in criminal acts that were only admitted in the 2000s.[102] These illegal acts were symptomatic of the continuing, unresolved regional conflict but were not confined to Pyongyang. In the late 1960s, South Korean secret services abducted South Koreans from Berlin to stand trial in Seoul on the basis of allegations of being North Korean sympathisers.[103] In 1973, South Korean opposition leader Kim Dae-Jung, later elected president, was

[98] 'South–South Cooperation: Cause for Optimism', The Pyongyang Times, 11 November 1995, p. 8

[99] Halliday, The Making of the Second Cold War; Fred Halliday, Cold War, Third World: An Essay on Soviet–American Relations (London: Hutchinson Radius, 1989).

[100] Ibid.

[101] Mitchell B. Lerner, The Pueblo Incident: A Spy Ship and the Failure of American Foreign Policy (Lawrence, KS: University Press of Kansas, 2002).

[102] When Kim Jong Il met with Japanese Prime Minister Junichiro Koizumi in Pyongyang in 2002, he apologised for the abduction of thirteen Japanese citizens, blaming these crimes on rogue intelligence agents. In turn Prime Minister Koizumi apologised for the suffering perpetrated by colonial Japan on the Korean people. For discussion see Gavan McCormack, 'Japan and North Korea – The Quest for Normalcy', in Hazel Smith (ed.), Reconstituting Korean Security: A Policy Primer (Tokyo: United Nations Press, 2007), pp. 162–81.

[103] Scalapino and Lee, Communism in Korea, pp. 651–2.

kidnapped in a Tokyo hotel room by the South Korean Central Intelligence Agency and only escaped being killed because of United States diplomatic protests.[104]

Unification strategy

North Korea's official unification policy was to establish a confederation of the two Koreas.[105] In 1972 Kim Il Sung told South Korean officials, at one of the first of post-Korean War diplomatic negotiations, that 'We have declared on many occasions that we have no intention to "invade the south"... As for "communization", neither do we intend to "communize" south Korea nor would it be "communized" even if we tried to.'[106] Given that from the late 1960s Kim's unification strategy was based on the hope that the assassination of unpopular South Korean military dictators might provide a political space for the South Korean masses to rise up, overthrow their governments and join in a unified Korea led by Kim Il Sung, this declaration of non-intent to invade was therefore at least partially sincere.[107]

In 1968 North Korean commandos attempted to assassinate Park Chung-Hee, the South Korean President in Seoul: North Korea was also alleged to be behind a second attempted assassination of President Park Chung-Hee by a Korean resident of Japan in 1974.[108] In October 1983, North Koreans failed in an attempt to kill South Korean President Chun Doo-hwan in Rangoon, Myanmar, but the bombing of the South Korean high-level political delegation resulted in the killing of seventeen South Koreans, including the foreign minister, Lee Beom-seok, two other senior ministers and four Burmese.[109] A North Korean national admitted to planting the bomb on board (South) Korean Air Flight 858 in November 1987 that exploded in mid-air, killing all 115 people on board.[110]

[104] Carter J. Eckert, Ki-bail Lee, Young Ick Lew, Michael Robinson and Edward Wagner, *Korea Old and New: A History* (Cambridge, MA: Korea Institute, Harvard University/ Ilchokak, 1990), p. 370; Lee, *A Troubled Peace*, p. 108.
[105] Loszek Cyrzyk, 'Pyongyang's Reunification Policy', in Han S. Park (ed.), *North Korea: Ideology, Politics, Economy* (Englewood Cliffs: Prentice Hall, 1996), pp. 205–19.
[106] Kim Il Sung, *On the Three Principles of National Reunification* (Pyongyang: Foreign Languages Publishing House, 1982), p. 11. The North Korean confederation proposal is in Kim Il Sung, *On the Proposal for Founding a Democratic Confederal Republic of Koryo* (Pyongyang: Foreign Languages Publishing House, 1990).
[107] See chapter entitled 'National Salvation Struggle of the South Korean People', in Kim, *Modern History of Korea*, pp. 458–99.
[108] Eckert *et al.*, *Korea Old and New*, p. 367.
[109] Lee, *A Troubled Peace*, pp. 119–20.
[110] The North Korean woman that admitted responsibility for the bombing of the airliner also admitted to being a North Korean agent. The DPRK government continues to deny it had anything to do with the bombing. See Natalya Bazhanova, 'North Korea's

The 1972 détente between communist China and the Republican administration of Richard Nixon provided the occasion for the first diplomatic foray between North and South Korea, as both feared abandonment by their superpower sponsors.[111] The brief and superficial rapprochement between the two states resulted in the 1972 Joint Communiqué, which established a North–South Coordination Commission. The Commission was supposed to pave the way for re-unification and it continued to meet until 1975.[112]

From the 1970s, North Korean unification policy combined belligerent hostility towards the South aimed at the violent overthrow of South Korean governments with intermittent diplomatic overtures. There is little indication that North Korea understood that the struggles against dictatorship by South Korean activists and the population were struggles for democracy – not for a re-imposition of dictatorship from the North.

Socialism 'in our own style' ... to an extent

In formal institutional terms state and Party relations were similarly constructed to that of the Soviet Union and other communist states. What was different about Kim Il Sungism was the huge, sustained political effort made to eradicate any space in which the population could build a civic sphere separate from public life. Conventional communist practice insisted on Party dominance of the state institutions and the society but not on the obliteration of the civic sphere altogether.

Other communist states had been dominated by dictatorial leaders but none had so integrated the leadership as a political institution in the constitution of the state. In the Soviet Union, Joseph Stalin had taken key decisions and the role of the Party's central machinery was to implement the leader's strategic directions but the position of Leader had never been formalised as an essential and necessary state institution. This meant that when Stalin died, subsequent Soviet leaders could denounce the cult of personality without also

Decision to Develop an Independent Nuclear Program', in James Clay Moltz and Alexandre Y. Mansourov (eds.), *The North Korean Nuclear Program: Security, Strategy and New Perspectives from Russia* (London: Routledge, 2000), p. 131.
[111] Charles K. Armstrong, 'North Korea's South Korea Policy: Tactical Change, Strategic Consistency', in Sung Chull Kim and David C. Kang (eds.), *Engagement with North Korea: A Viable Alternative* (Albany: SUNY Press, 2009), pp. 228–9.
[112] Smith, 'North Korean Foreign Policy in the 1990s, pp. 98–9.

denouncing the Soviet state. In North Korea, the Kim family was constitutive of the state. To attack Kim was to attack the state. Logically, the fundamental failure of the state to prevent economic collapse and starvation for nearly a million in the early 1990s also implied therefore a direct challenge to the rationality, legitimacy and authority of Kim family rule.

6   Sisyphus as economic model

In the early 1960s, policy changed from the rapid reconstruction of the civilian infrastructure that had characterised the immediate post-Korean War period to that of prioritising 'economic and defence construction simultaneously'.[1] The objective of economic policy was to secure regime survival by building a self-sufficient, modern military capability to act as a deterrent against foreign intervention and to use as an offensive force if required.[2] Self-sufficiency meant minimising external dependence and maximising the use of internal resources. The major internal resource was the physical labour of the population organised by way of the 'mass line' that was constituted by a top-down command structure and a political system that did not permit opt-outs by individuals. The model was not entirely self-sufficient as it relied on allies and supporters to fill crucial resource gaps, including advanced technology and oil, but it was autarkic in that external players did not have much of an impact on Kim Il Sung's strategy and policies.

Initial results were stunning. The economy grew rapidly and the population benefited from improved social welfare provision. The problem was that the model did not bring self-sustaining growth and it suffered from intrinsic flaws including the skewing of investment to the military sector. Economic strategy never fundamentally changed during the Kim Il Sung years and structural problems were not resolved. The worst of these was the inability to produce sufficient quality and quantity of consumer goods. The most serious weakness was that economic strategy never delivered food security for the population.

---

[1] Un Hong Song, *Economic Development in the Democratic People's Republic of Korea, 18 April 1978* (Pyongyang: Foreign Languages Publishing House, 1990), p. 26. In 1962 Kim Il Sung had proposed that equal weight be allocated to military 'preparedness' and the civilian economy. See Robert A. Scalapino and Chong-Sik Lee, *Communism in Korea: The Movement* (Berkeley: University of California Press, 1972), p. 594.

[2] Song, *Economic Development*.

Self-reliance: the military imperatives

Economic policy aimed to establish national self-sufficiency in industry and agriculture so the DPRK would not become a dependency of either the Soviet Union or China.[3] The intention was that an indigenous heavy industrial capacity would provide the motor-force of an integrated industrial, agricultural, consumer goods and, most importantly, an armaments and military materièl manufacturing sector.[4] The absolute centrality of heavy industry to state-building was overt and visible in the symbol of a power station at the heart of the national emblem, although the government in 1961 announced that it would seek a balanced economic policy, developing the light industrial sector and agriculture in parallel with the development of heavy industry.[5] In 1962, fearing a similar disregard of North Korea's interests after what he saw as the abandonment of communist Cuba by the Soviet Union in the 1962 Cuban Missile Crisis, Kim re-aligned economic policy towards support for military-related investment.[6]

Military-led inward industrialisation meant that heavy industry remained the overwhelming priority in economic planning. Much of the country's heavy engineering capacity was physically located in the north-east and comprised of redeveloped manufacturing plants and mining operations from the colonial period. Important port cities included Chongjin in North Hamgyong province and Hamhung in South Hamgyong, the country's second largest city after Pyongyang.

The industrial sector significantly increased its share in national production – from 57.1 per cent in 1960 to 66 per cent in 1983, while the share of agriculture in production fell from 23.6 per cent to 20 per cent in

[3] In 1993, Kim told Party officials that he had refused an offer from Khrushchev of electricity supply from Lake Baikal in the then Soviet Union as 'if we had accepted his offer, the Soviet people might have cut off the electric supply whenever they deemed it necessary'. Kim Il Sung, 'On the Direction of Socialist Economic Construction for the Immediate Period Ahead', in Kim Il Sung, *Works, Vol. 44* (Pyongyang: Foreign Languages Publishing House, 1999), p. 252.
[4] For a DPRK scholar's perspective see Chang-gon Pak, 'Conversion from a Colonial Agricultural State into a Socialist Industrial State', in Ken'ichiro Hirano (ed.), *The State and Cultural Transformation: Perspectives from East Asia* (Tokyo: United Nations Press, 1993), pp. 299–314.
[5] On the national emblem see Foreign Languages Publishing House, *100 Questions and Answers: Do you Know about Korea?* (Pyongyang: Foreign Languages Publishing House, 1989).
[6] James F. Person (ed.), *The Cuban Missile Crisis and the Origins of North Korea's Policy of Self-Reliance in National Defense, E-Dossier #12* (Washington, DC: Woodrow Wilson International Center for Scholars, 2012), available at www.wilsoncenter.org/sites/default/files/NKIDP_eDossier_12_North_Korea_and_the_Cuban_Missile_Crisis_0.pdf, accessed 29 December 2013.

the same years.[7] Heavy industry amounted to 55 per cent of the entire
industrial sector in 1960, dipping to 51.2 per cent in 1965, but rising to a
preponderant share of 62 to 65 per cent between 1970 to 1983.[8] The
policy of building a self-reliant military capacity meant investment in
industries of direct use to the military, that is, in the machinery and
metals industries, including the steel industry. In 1980, some 45.7 per
cent of all industrial output came from these sectors and in 1989 these
industries still comprised 37.5 per cent of all industrial output.[9] These
large industrial enterprises were designed to produce intermediate or
capital goods such as machine tools. Capital goods would furnish mines
and factories with the heavy equipment that would allow North Korea to
exploit its plentiful natural resources, produce finished industrial goods
and provide inputs for other important economic sectors, especially
agriculture, but also energy, transport and construction.[10]

The government supplemented indirect investment in military-
related industries with direct investment in increasingly sophisticated
munitions industries. In the 1960s, North Korea produced basic weaponry, small torpedo speedboats and high-speed patrol ships, with help
from the Soviet Union and China.[11] By the 1970s, North Korea had
developed a more or less autonomous military industrial sector that
could mass-produce weapons.[12] In the 1980s, North Korea expanded
the munitions industry to develop and produce modern precision
weapons.[13]

The remit of research and development in technology was narrowed
to the support of industrial production processes. North Korea did
not pursue research and development in information technology and
computer industries in a sustained manner during the Kim Il Sung era.
The Korea Computer Centre, the first dedicated informatics research
centre, only opened in 1990.[14] Nevertheless technology policy had
some successes, most notably in the development of techniques that
produced an artificial material called Vinylon from chemical products.[15] Other indigenous outputs included steel-making processes using
anthracite coal from North Korean mineral deposits.[16] North Korea
'reverse engineered' imported technology. The aim was to replicate

[7] Soo-Young Choi, A Study on the Structure of Industry in North Korea (Seoul: Korea
Institute of National Unification, 2006), p. 13.
[8] Ibid., p. 9.   [9] Ibid., p. 12.   [10] Ibid.
[11] Choong-Yong Ahn, North Korea Development Report 2003/2004 (Seoul: Korea Institute
for International Economic Policy, 2003/4), pp. 172–3.
[12] Ibid., p. 173.   [13] Ibid.   [14] Ibid., p. 271.
[15] Ibid., pp. 266–8.   [16] Ibid., p. 267.

foreign technology so that the country would not have to use scarce hard currency for foreign imports.[17]

Agro-industry and food-self sufficiency

The goal of autarky relied on food self-sufficiency at national and local levels. In peacetime the country should produce sufficient grain to cover the basic requirements of the population. In case of war and the potential cutting of supply and communication lines, the plan was that the entire population should operate as a vast but decentralised fighting force capable of being locally self-sufficient in terms of daily subsistence.

To achieve food self-sufficiency, intensive agriculture was required of the nation's limited productive land. The south-western provinces of South Hwanghae and North Hwanghae are the bread-basket of the nation because of their relative abundance of agriculturally productive land, but even these provinces suffer from natural handicaps, most notably the extremes of temperatures that can fall to minus forty degrees centigrade, with January averages regularly below twenty degrees centigrade. Summer brings the humid, muggy rainy season, in which temperatures of forty degrees centigrade are common and which also brings flooding. The north-eastern provinces of North Hamgyong, South Hamgyong, Kangwon, Chagang and Ryanggang are part of the 80 per cent of the country that is mountainous; they have a relatively scarce supply of arable land.[18]

Intensive crop production requires industrial inputs in the shape of fertiliser, chemicals including pesticides, sophisticated irrigation technology, mechanisation and efficient and reliable infrastructure including water and electricity supplies. North Korea's relatively poor agricultural endowment militated against the expansion of agricultural production through simply farming more land with the same techniques and technology. North Korean economic planning therefore envisaged a key role for agro-industry in the provision of chemicals, pesticides, fertiliser, equipment and spare parts for the agricultural sector.

The government engaged in 'nature remaking' to expand land resources for agricultural production. Land was reclaimed from the sea, reservoirs built, forest land cleared and terraced fields carved out of steep

---

[17] Hy-Sang Lee, *North Korea: A Strange Socialist Fortress* (London: Praeger, 2001), pp. 82–4.

[18] Sung Ung Kim (ed.), *Panorama of Korea* (Pyongyang: Foreign Languages Publishing House, 1999), p. 1.

slopes.[19] Much of this activity was carried out by tens of thousands of workers whose contribution was confined to physical movement of inputs. The economic model was reduced to emulating Sisyphus. Lack of quality control procedures and shoddy materials resulted in badly constructed economic infrastructure, including dams, dykes, irrigation facilities and flood barriers. These literally started to fall apart as soon as construction works ended or as soon as they confronted even a moderate weather event such as a storm.[20]

Grain was transferred from agriculturally productive provinces to the less well endowed; although local self-sufficiency policies were never abandoned, even in places where it was very difficult for farmers to grow crops, including the mountainous regions of the north-east. Kim Il Sung's wartime experiences of how difficult it had been to secure food supplies informed a policy designed to achieve combat preparedness. It was not economically rational to grow basic grains like maize in areas that had little or no comparative advantage in agricultural production but in political terms it was an absolutely logical policy.

Light industry

Government policy was that county administrations were responsible for the supply and administration of light industry, which included consumer goods production of processed foods like noodles and basics like utensils, lamps, matches and soap. Light industry was integrated into national planning but the central state did not provide large investment in this economic sector. The government decreed that light industry should rely on the waste products of heavy industry and agriculture and local resources. Investment in light industry, excluding food processing industries, accounted for only 15 per cent of investment in the industrial sector in 1980 and 15.9 per cent in

---

[19] Lee, *North Korea*, p. 94; Tae-Jin Kwon, Young-Hoon Kim, Chung-Gil Chung and Hyoung-Jin Jeon, 'Research on North Korean Agriculture Development Planning: Executive Summary', undated but probably 2002.

[20] This depressing method of operation remained the *modus operandi* as at 2014. When I was supervising large food for work projects between 2000 and 2001 in the DPRK for the United Nations World Food Programme (WFP), the most common complaint of visiting technicians and evaluators was that the end product created through mass physical labour (absent technology) could not survive what in Korea, North and South, are normal weather events such as the heavy rains that characterise the summer climate in Korea. These activities were justified by international organisations as temporary measures but for North Korean authorities they provided a key method of land use management.

1989.[21] The analogous figures for the food industry were 10 per cent in 1980 and 9.7 per cent in 1989.[22]

Basic consumer goods were produced and sold locally. Agricultural waste products were recycled into cooperative farm production of, for example, farming tools. Local authorities made imaginative use of available resources but, without substantial investment and with minimal technology, end-products remained of poor quality. Overall shortages were compounded by the absence of effective domestic trade mechanisms between different localities. Economically, light industrial policy did not deliver results but politically, government aims were met. To the extent that local communities were self-sufficient in basic goods, they would be better prepared for war.

Self-reliance from above

The North Korean government followed a nominal policy of decentralisation of operational decision-making. The province was adopted as the unit of planning for heavy industry. The county, or its urban equivalent, the district, was given the same status for light industrial planning.[23] The government argued that the province was the rational level for agricultural planning but at the same time called on each county to be self-sufficient in food production.[24] From 1959 to 1961 the government formally decentralised economic planning and administration from the ministry level to the twelve provinces and to the 213 rural counties and urban districts, which comprised the lowest level of local government administration.[25] In 1959 county-level economic commissions were established. They reported to the Provincial Economic Commissions and had responsibilities for industrial planning. In 1961 the equivalent

[21] Choi, *A Study on the Structure of Industry*, p. 12.
[22] Ibid.
[23] Lee, *North Korea*, p. 154.
[24] Suk Lee, 'Food Shortages and Economic Institutions in the Democratic People's Republic of Korea', doctoral dissertation (Department of Economics, University of Warwick, January 2003), pp. 114–15.
[25] Strictly speaking there were nine provinces and three Cities under Central Authority (CCAs) which were Pyongyang, Kaesong and Nampo. In terms of local government administration the CCAs were treated by North Korea as more or less synonymous with the provinces. Local government reorganisation took place in 2004 that reduced the number of provinces to ten. There have been a number of county reorganisations so that county numbers have changed periodically but not significantly. The county number cited here is from UNICEF, *DPRK Social Statistics* (Pyongyang: UNICEF, 1998). Lee reports the existence of 209 counties. See Lee, *North Korea*, p. 155.

institutional reforms took place in agriculture with the establishment of Provincial Rural Economic Commissions.[26]

County Cooperative Economic Commissions were given ownership of all county-based farming-related industries, which in a predominantly agricultural county, meant effectively taking over economic direction of the whole county.[27] Provided the county did not have to call in central government or the provincial authority too often, the agriculturally productive counties could develop a degree of real autonomy. This type of autonomy was not, however, conducive to productivity gains. Counties were not permitted to engage in trade outside the national plan and the limited availability of consumer goods meant that there were few rewards available for increased productivity. These constraints discouraged expansion outside the county and encouraged an insular and survivalist mode of activity.

The predominantly agricultural provinces of South Hwanghae and North Hwanghae contained urban districts (the urban equivalent of the county) that could not achieve food self-sufficiency through agricultural production. Mixed industrial-agricultural provinces, like South Pyongyan, were home to counties where local food self-sufficiency was always difficult to achieve. If the province was responsible for grain redistribution then farmers in agriculturally productive counties within the province would need to give up surpluses or even to reduce their own basic rations to secure equality of distribution when times were hard. If the county was the unit of self-sufficiency then farmers in agriculturally productive counties could argue to retain more of their own production, particularly when they were not producing much more than enough for subsistence and basic investment purposes. The lack of clarity contributed to tensions between localities and provided a disincentive to agriculturally productive counties to produce more.

Strategic industries, including steel, chemicals, fertilisers and machine production, fell under a system of overlapping jurisdiction. The heavy industrial sector was intimately integrated into defence planning and remained a high priority for military authorities and the Cabinet. Provincial Economic Commissions, which had nominal responsibilities for industrial planning in their localities, retained reporting functions. The military was a particularly important economic force in Chagang, a 'garrison province', located in a mountainous and remote inland region bordering China.[28] Chagang was home to large numbers of the country's

[26] Lee, 'Food Shortages', pp. 110–11.   [27] Ibid., p. 112.
[28] For details of military industries in Chagang see Ahn, *North Korea Development Report*, pp. 173–7.

military forces and munitions industries as its physical location meant that, in case of war, it would be difficult to access from South Korea and relatively easy to supply from China.[29]

Provincial Economic Commissions and Provincial Rural Economic Commissions were not accountable to the local administrative bodies – the Provincial People's Committees – but reported directly to the Cabinet.[30] Nominal decentralisation from the central ministries to local planning commissions therefore resulted in tighter state-controlled centralisation in practice, as local administrations were cut out of the decision-making loop. Central authorities regularly intervened in operational decisions, such as which seeds to plant or products to produce. Local authorities had no choice other than to implement central directives, even if these were inappropriate for local conditions.

Local authorities were inhibited from developing effective institutions because the fundamentals of state organisation decried principles of economic rationality, technical efficiency or division of labour as 'bureaucratic' and antithetical to the *Juche* method of putting politics first in the guidance and management of the economy. Economic institutions were not permitted to embed learning processes, rules and regularised norms in a process of formal institution-building. Productivity initiatives, in terms of encouraging entrepreneurship, individual profit-seeking behaviour and competition were thus not only considered unnecessary but as threatening to state ideology and practice that insisted on political control, ideological exhortation and state direction of every aspect of the economy and society. The primary role of local authorities was to act as transmission belts for centralised and politically determined economic directives. This was a policy of 'self-reliance from above'.

The mass line: work hard, stay disciplined and obey the Leader

Shortages of capital and technology persisted such that physical labour, organised around the principle of the mass line, provided a crucial factor of production for industry and agriculture, which still employed around three-quarters of the non-military workforce by 1993. The lack of success in achieving mechanisation of agriculture meant that the urban workforce was mobilised for several weeks at a time, every year, to assist in

---

[29] Lee, *North Korea*, p. 155.   [30] Lee, 'Food Shortages', pp. 108–9.

144 Sisyphus as economic model

spring transplanting and summer harvest.[31] Agricultural production was dependent on these mass mobilisations of urban labour, which became routinised as a standard way of operating.

The mass line was built around physical activity, organised and disciplined by the Party. The labour force was supposed to work hard in the workplace in return for non-material rewards such as the political satisfaction of acting as a new type of unselfish individual who was contributing to nation-building. Able-bodied adults were also expected to participate in unpaid economic activity via their membership of the mass organisations which, along with the workplaces, provided 'volunteers' for mass line activity.[32] This 'voluntary' work was in addition to their eight hours of daily work every day, excluding Sunday.[33] The work involved more or less strenuous physical activity, including keeping the streets clean, contributing to harvesting and building roads. These activities could be very physically demanding, involving heavy lifting and kilometres of walking onsite and to workplaces. Unskilled workers were also vulnerable to workplace accidents.

State propagandists glorified the use of hard physical labour as justified, necessary and appropriate as it represented the self-reliant activity of the mass of the people who, by their collective labour, had become 'masters' of their own destiny as idealised by *Juche* ideology. Kim Il Sung never lost faith in mass mobilisation although mechanisms were fine-tuned in the *Chollima* system, the *Taean* work-team system and the 'Three Revolutions' Movement. These manifestations of mass mobilisation policy emphasised the three key principles of Kim Il Sungism which were, respectively, 'work hard, stay disciplined, and obey the Leader'.

Mass campaigns provided continuous ideological surveillance of the population but each incarnation of the mass line failed to achieve economic goals. The economy did not achieve self-sustaining growth and productivity did not increase. Nevertheless the lesson drawn was not that the methods themselves were unhelpful or incorrect but that they needed

---

[31] In a 1980 speech, Kim Il Sung referenced the spring mobilisation of local industry workers. See Kim Il Sung, 'Let us Further Develop Local Industry', in Kim Il Sung, *Works, Vol. 35* (Pyongyang: Foreign Languages Publishing House, 1989), p. 161. Kim referenced the practice as standard in Kim Il Sung, 'On This Year's Experience in Farming and Next Year's Direction of Agricultural Work', in Kim Il Sung, *Works, Vol. 35* (Pyongyang: Foreign Languages Publishing House, 1989), pp. 256–7.

[32] For a DPRK scholar's perspective see Chang-sik Sok, 'Experiences of State-building in the Democratic People's Republic of Korea', in Ken'ichiro Hirano (ed.), *The State and Cultural Transformation: Perspectives from East Asia* (Tokyo: United Nations Press, 1993), pp. 328–43.

[33] UNICEF, *An Analysis of the Situation of Children and Women in the Democratic People's Republic of Korea 2000* (Pyongyang: UNICEF, 1999), p. 28.

to be applied more correctly and more rigorously. Kim Il Sung blamed officials for economic failure and repeatedly accused officials of not maintaining 'ideological standards' and not having up-to-date 'practical qualifications'.[34] As late as 1989–90, the DPRK was soliciting support for economic development in order to 'complement and not undermine the *Juche* policy'.[35]

Work hard

The *Chollima* system was initiated in the late 1950s and was named for the mythical winged horse of Korean tradition that, according to legend, could travel at great speed over long distances.[36] To compensate for technology deficits, the government exhorted *Chollima* work-teams to expend superhuman levels of physical energy to beat production targets and encouraged individual workers to improvise solutions to technical problems.[37] *Chollima* echoed the Stakhanovism of Soviet Russia but in North Korea the emphasis was less on the individual and more on the work-team, although individual contributions were recognised with the status of 'Labour Hero'. The rewards were the satisfaction of carrying out patriotic nation-building tasks. The *Chollima* campaign contributed to the early quantitative achievements of the North Korean economy. It also instituted the primacy of political methods in response to economic problems and the reliance on mass mobilised labour as the mechanism for economic activity.

Stay disciplined

From the 1960s onwards, the government subordinated industrial and agricultural economic management to Party management. In 1960, the government introduced the *Taean* work-team system to the industrial

---

[34] Compilation Committee of Kim Il Sung Encyclopaedia, *Kim Il Sung Encyclopaedia Volume One* (New Delhi: Vishwanath, 1992), pp. 55–6.

[35] Frederick Nixson and Paul Collins, 'Economic Reform in North Korea', in Hazel Smith, Chris Rhodes, Diana Pritchard and Kevin Magill (eds.), *North Korea in the New World Order* (London: Macmillan, 1996), p. 167.

[36] Brun and Hersh date the start of the *Chollima* movement to December 1956; Chung to 1959. The 1959 date would suggest an emulation of the Chinese 'Great Leap Forward'. The 1956 date may imply a policy of independent origin. Ellen Brun and Jacques Hersh, *Socialist Korea: A Case Study in the Strategy of Economic Development* (London and New York: Monthly Review Press, 1976), pp. 186–9; Joseph Sang-hoon Chung, *The North Korean Economy: Structure and Development* (Stanford: Hoover Institution Press, 1974), p. 96.

[37] Han Gil Kim, *Modern History of Korea* (Pyongyang: Foreign Languages Publishing House, 1979), pp. 394–405.

sector. The aim was to institutionalise Party discipline and Party leadership over workplace planning and management and the focus of policy was to establish the system in the heavy industrial enterprises.[38] The *Taean* system entrenched the workplace as the fundamental unit of societal organisation, responsible for welfare functions that included food allocation and supply.[39]

The *Taean* system explicitly subordinated engineers and technical experts to the Party workplace committees and subordinated workplace Party committees to 'the higher bodies' in the Cabinet, most specifically to the authority of the leader.[40] Kim Il Sung's interventions were significant in that a single instruction from the centre could alter operational practices at a stroke, throughout the country. At a day-to-day level, however, Kim's influence was less than might have been expected. North Korea was a complex economy, employing millions, with hundreds of thousands of enterprises and economic processes. One individual simply could not micro-manage the operation of millions of discrete processes. The Party was responsible for implementing Kim Il Sung's directives but there were many areas over which detailed guidance was not specified; leaving some room for manoeuvre in local workplaces.

The pernicious aspect of the *Taean* system was that it produced ongoing tensions which encouraged stasis rather than growth. On the one hand the model encouraged the creation of a skilled workforce and concentrated on applied science and engineering to respond to the technical problems of building the economy.[41] On the other hand innovation and improvisation were only encouraged within certain limits that were not always clearly defined and could change for political rationales. Technicians and enterprise managers therefore learned to favour caution in case they were accused of bureaucratism or of not following the mass Party line.

The *Taean* system of direct Party management was never adapted for the farming sector.[42] The Party was not given the same direct levels of managerial authority over farm production as existed in industry.[43] At the micro level, the organisation of agriculture functioned around specialist work-teams, which were often constituted around family

---

[38] Ibid., pp. 413–15.

[39] Compilation Committee of Kim Il Sung Encyclopaedia, 'On Improving the Guidance and Management of Industry to Fit the New Circumstances', in Compilation Committee, *Kim Il Sung Encyclopaedia Volume One*, pp. 538–9.

[40] Kim, *Modern History of Korea*, pp. 413–15; Chung, *The North Korean Economy*, pp. 62–4.

[41] Foreign Languages Publishing House, *Do you Know about Korea? Questions and Answers* (Pyongyang: Foreign Languages Publishing House, 1989), pp. 48–58.

[42] Lee, 'Food Shortages', pp. 92–119.

[43] Chung, *The North Korean Economy*, p. 15.

relationships.[44] As cooperatives had been formed around existing villages, community bonds and family ties provided the foundation for a degree of genuine local solidarity. Farm managers reported to the county cooperative farm management commission, and then upwards through the Agricultural Commission to the Cabinet.[45] These bodies were staffed by professionals and agricultural experts who were also of course likely to be Party members but their primary reason for employment was as farming experts.

Nevertheless, cooperative farms did not escape Party controls because of their strategic importance, given that they were responsible for 90 per cent of the country's agricultural production. Kim Il Sung blamed the grain shortages of the early 1970s on farmers for not following central state directives closely enough.[46] In 1973, Kim introduced the 'unified and detailed planning' system in agriculture that was intended to minimise the latitude available to farmers.[47] The aim was to shift farm management towards central control and direction, and the effect was to displace local knowledge and experience from the farm planning cycle.

Obey the Leader

From the 1970s onwards thousands of young people were mobilised in a nationwide movement of exhortation called the 'Three Revolutions Movement' as a response to what Kim Il Sung identified as the incompetence, inefficiency and 'bureaucratism' of local officials who were blamed for failing to follow the Leadership's directives and therefore culpable for the decline of the economy.[48] The focus was redirection of the older generation by young people.[49]

The Three Revolutions Movement drew on the heritage of *Chollima* and *Taean* but the Movement was different to the earlier campaigns in the specific focus on youth.[50] Teams of young university graduates were sent around the country to industrial enterprises and farms to try to inculcate the Leader's thoughts within local Parties as well as in

---

[44] UNDP and DPRK government, *Report of the Thematic Roundtable on Agricultural Recovery and Environmental Protection in DPR Korea* (Geneva: UNDP, 28–9 May 1998).
[45] Diagrams illustrating the agricultural management system from the late 1950s onwards can be found in Foreign Languages Publishing House, *Do you Know about Korea?*, p. 44; and 'Chart VI', in Brun and Hersh, *Socialist Korea*, p. 410.
[46] Compilation Committee, *Kim Il Sung Encyclopaedia Volume One*, p. 56.
[47] Lee, 'Food Shortages', pp. 120–38.
[48] Ibid., p. 125.
[49] Foreign Languages Publishing House, *Do you Know about Korea?*, pp. 20–1.
[50] Adrian Buzo, *The Guerilla Dynasty: Politics and Leadership in North Korea* (Boulder, CO: Westview, 1999), p. 109.

enterprises.[51] Young students were supposed to politically educate the older generation so that improvements in economy would follow.[52] Techniques copied from the Chinese Cultural Revolution were used to induce compliance with central state economic and ideological directives. The Movement bypassed provincial and local Party leaderships under the banner of forestalling 'bureaucratism'. The raison d'être was to support economic growth through encouraging ideological, cultural and technological transformation in every sector of the economy.

These young people lacked professional experience in industry and agriculture and often, much idea of how to work in complex work environments. Paradoxically, the result of these policies reinforced the population's respect for experience over revolutionary voluntarism. The Three Revolutions Movement did not bring productivity gains but the policy brought political benefits for the leadership. The influx of highly ideologically motivated youths helped to inhibit criticisms from disaffected older members of the population, who had not seen the improvements in living conditions they had been promised since the end of the Korean War.

Living standards

The 1993 census reported with some pride that as a product of the success of 'socialist industrialization' in the 1950s and 1960s, urbanisation took place at 'unparalleled rapid speed' such that by 1993 some 61 per cent of the population lived in urban areas.[53] Urbanisation was understood as a sign of modernity as the idea was that families moving to urban settlements from rural areas could access new homes that would have the advantage of piped water supplies, sanitation facilities, heating and electricity. The extensive bombing of the Korean War had also left a need for new homes. Multi-storey residences were constructed in urban and small rural communities comprised of just a few households so that urban and rural settlements could be efficiently provided with services like electricity and potable water, and these were built as quickly as possible. These multi-storey dwellings remain a common feature of rural landscapes along with traditional low-rise structures.[54]

---

[51] Compilation Committee, *Kim Il Sung Encyclopaedia Volume One*, p. 56.
[52] Foreign Languages Publishing House, *Do you Know about Korea?*, pp. 20–1.
[53] Sun Won Hong, *Analysis of 1993 Population Census Data DPR Korea* (Pyongyang: Population Center, 1996), pp. 91–2.
[54] Author's observations, 1990–2011.

The proliferation of welfare services provided free at the point of use compensated to a certain extent for low incomes and the lack of access to variety and quality of consumption goods. The government provided universal free housing, health, social and education services and for the first time in Korean history, the vast majority of the population had access to healthcare, educational opportunities and social services. Improvements in public services resulted in visible and sometimes extraordinary improvements to standards of living. Average life expectancy improved from 38 years between 1936 and 1940, to 60 years by 1964, to 74.5 years in 1991.[55]

An extensive nationwide curative system of hospitals and clinics was established and thousands of medical workers trained such that the DPRK boasted of 27 doctors per 10,000 of the population in 1986 compared to 0.5 doctors per 10,000 of the population between 1936 and 1940.[56] Preventable diseases such as polio were sharply reduced after successful nationwide vaccination campaigns, while public health measures assisted in the prevention of disease. Public health and preventive health priorities were enshrined in law.[57] Increases in life expectancy resulted from the state's emphasis on preventive care given that medicines and chemicals were always in short supply and the government continued to rely on 'natural' or 'Koryo' medicines.[58]

Concrete policies eradicated the illiteracy and innumeracy that had been endemic throughout Korean society until Liberation in 1945.[59] Transformed from a nation of 80 per cent adult illiteracy in 1945 to one of 100 per cent literacy by the 1990s, the DPRK had plenty to boast about in its basic educational achievements.[60] The DPRK became a nation that was numerate and literate. Schools and clinics were

---

[55] Economic and Social Council, 'Implementation of the International Covenant on Economic, Social and Cultural Rights, Second Periodic Report submitted by State Parties under Articles 16 and 17 of the Covenant: Addendum, Democratic People's Republic of Korea, E/1990/6/Add.35', mimeo, 15 May 2002, p. 25. See also Hwan Ju Pang, *Korean Review* (Pyongyang: Foreign Languages Publishing House, 1987), pp. 187–90; UNDP and DPRK government, *Thematic Roundtable*, p. 8.

[56] Pang, *Korean Review*, p. 188.

[57] Kim Il Sung, 'Let us Implement the Public Health Law to the Letter', in Kim Il Sung, *Works, Vol. 35* (Pyongyang: Foreign Languages Publishing House, 1989), pp. 91–103.

[58] Foreign Languages Publishing House, *Korea Guidebook* (Pyongyang: Foreign Languages Publishing House, 1989), p. 129; Pang, *Korean Review*, p. 190.

[59] The DPRK pointed out in its 1999 submission to the international review on how well states were meeting their educational commitments that in 1945 more than 65 per cent of school age children did not go to school. See National EFA 2000 Assessment Group, *National EFA Assessment Report: The Implementation of the 'World Declaration on Education for All'* (Pyongyang: National EFA 2000 Assessment Group, 1999), p. 4.

[60] See National EFA 2000 Assessment Group, *National EFA Assessment Report*.

established in even the most remote islands and mountain regions.[61] All children from the age of three months to four years old had access to a nursery place and many of these were situated in the parents' workplace as were some kindergartens.[62] Children started formal education at age four in kindergartens where they stayed for two years before moving on to primary and middle school education (in the same school), and then to high school at age 14.[63] By 1972 all children aged between 5 and 16 experienced eleven years of free universal compulsory education.[64] Over 300 tertiary education institutions were also established.[65] A nationwide system of what was termed 'part work part study' was established so that workers could continue their education while employed.[66] The system of life-long learning was expressed in the slogan of 'work eight hours, study eight hours and rest for eight hours'.

Generous and paid time off work was made available to pregnant women and mothers, and pensions provided to women and men.[67] Mothers were targeted for extra support through food rations, regular health checks, generous maternity leave provisions and nationwide nursery and kindergarten provision.[68] Housing and utilities were provided for free, and personal taxation was eradicated. Child labour was outlawed and it was mandatory for all girls and boys to attend school. Student–staff ratios were high with reported average pupil–teacher ratios in the primary education system of 27:1 and 23:1; either would represent a very high level of teacher involvement with school students.[69]

Post-war housing policy generated large quantities of homes and for much of the population post-war housing provision was an improvement on pre-war conditions, but scarcity of resources combined with the

---

[61] UNICEF, *Situation Analysis of Women and Children in the DPRK* (Pyongyang: UNICEF, 1999); Hazel Smith, *Hungry for Peace: International Security, Humanitarian Assistance and Social Change in North Korea* (Washington, DC: United States Institute of Peace Press, 2005).

[62] UNICEF, *Situation Analysis of Women and Children*, p. 49.

[63] National EFA 2000 Assessment Group, *National EFA Assessment Report*, p. 17.

[64] Ibid., pp. 12–14.   [65] Ibid., p. 4.

[66] Jiangcheng He, 'Educational Reforms', in Han S. Park (ed.), *North Korea: Ideology, Politics, Economy* (Englewood Cliffs: Prentice Hall, 1996), pp. 47–8.

[67] Economic and Social Council, 'Implementation of the International Covenant on Economic, Social and Cultural Rights', p. 5.

[68] Foreign Languages Publishing House, *The Public Health Law of the Democratic People's Republic of Korea, 3 April 1980* (Pyongyang: Foreign Languages Publishing House, 1988).

[69] These figures were published in 1998 but they represent the figures for the Kim Il Sung era. The 27:1 figure is cited in UNICEF, 'An Analysis of the Situation of Children and Women in The Democratic People's Republic of Korea', draft, Pyongyang, May 1998, p. 43. The 23:1 figure is cited in National EFA 2000 Assessment Group, 'National EFA Assessment Report, p. 17.

laudable aim of housing a population that had hitherto never been able to envisage living in their own homes resulted in poor-quality structures. The speed of the build and construction by self-help meant that these newly constructed apartments lacked reliably functioning services from the beginning. The urban landscape was characterised by small towns full of uniform-looking, concrete, characterless, five storey or more apartment buildings.[70] Urban settlements lacked amenities apart from a few restaurants, maybe a movie theatre and the local children's palace, as the children's community centres were known. The large city conurbations, including Pyongyang, had more amenities, but the condition of most of the housing and infrastructure was also poor.

The grouping together of households in multi-storey dwellings was efficient but economic shortages meant that living in apartment blocks was physically arduous. Lack of state investment in these jerry-built buildings meant that residents had to make do without functioning lifts, plumbing, sewage, potable water, electricity and heating. They were cold in winter and hot in summer. Inside space was at a premium. Families lived in overcrowded homes as the social norm was that families should provide homes for children whose parents had died or who could not look after their own children and elderly dependants and others, including sometimes non-family members, rather than expect the state to provide residential accommodation or to allow individuals to live on the streets. Families thus assumed primary responsibility for social care, although state residential homes for the elderly and those with disabilities existed.

Consumer shortages and chronic food insecurity

Kim Il Sung's speeches demonstrated an awareness of the inadequacies of the consumer goods sector.[71] Kim repeatedly pointed out that provision was poor and did not respond to the needs of the population. Kim acknowledged the extent of the failure to deliver consumer goods and the extent of shortages, even in Pyongyang. In 1980 Kim reported that the population of the capital did not have access to adequate clothing and other consumer goods.[72]

---

[70] Between 1998 and 2001 I worked and travelled in every province in the DPRK except Chagang and travelled around the country on a regular basis by car. These comments on the urban landscape are a result of my observations in these years and also from other visits to the DPRK between 1990 and 2011.

[71] Kim, 'Let us Further Develop Local Industry', pp. 159–69.

[72] Kim Il Sung, 'Let us Increase the Standard of Living of the People Through the Development of the Textile, Food and Consumer Goods Industries', in Kim Il Sung, *Works, Vol. 35* (Pyongyang: Foreign Languages Publishing House, 1989), pp. 77–8.

Central state policy response to inadequacies in production and supply of consumer goods was to control demand and allow for equity in distribution by extending the scope of goods covered by the household ration system. The major policy response, however, was political. Instead of attributing failures to lack of investment, the leadership argued that the failings of the sector were due to insufficient revolutionary ardour in those local officials responsible for the production of consumer goods. Kim Il Sung argued that 'a more intensive ideological struggle should be conducted among officials in order to improve the quality of products.'[73] The argument was that county administrations and local enterprises should work harder to use 'untapped local resources'.[74]

The most significant failing in the consumer goods sector was the structural incapacity to generate an adequate and sufficient supply of food.[75] Food supplies were never munificent, even in times of relatively good grain production, as surpluses were stockpiled for national emergencies, including the possibility of war.[76] Food shortages were chronic but were acute between 1954 and 1955, and between 1970 and 1973.[77] In 1973 food rations were cut for the first time since the Korean War and cuts in food rations continued throughout the 1970s.[78] In an effort to drive down demand, a birth control policy was introduced in the 1970s.[79] Women's jobs were reclassified such that their ration allocation could be reduced.[80]

Poor farms in difficult growing regions relied on annual grain transfers from agriculturally productive cooperative farms, which also supplied the state's food distribution system that, by the late 1950s, was virtually the only source of food supply for non-farmers, including the military. 'Farmers Markets' provided an alternative source of food supply for urban workers outside the public distribution system but they were so

---

[73] Kim Il Sung, 'Let us Further Develop Local Industry', in Kim Il Sung, *Works Vol. 35* (Pyongyang: Foreign Languages Publishing House, 1989), p. 165.

[74] Ibid., p. 168.

[75] Kim Il Sung was still arguing for modernisation of agriculture in 1992 in a speech in which he recognised that there was a 'problem of food', but in which he seemed unaware of the scale of the food shortages of that year and was oblivious to the profound structural problems in the food economy. Kim Il Sung, 'Officials Must Become True Servants of the People', in Kim Il Sung, *Works, Vol. 44* (Pyongyang: Foreign Languages Publishing House, 1999), p. 24.

[76] Lee, *North Korea*, p. 101.   [77] Lee, 'Food Shortages'.

[78] Ibid., p. 122; Bong Dae Choi and Kab Woo Koo, 'The Development of Farmers' Markets in North Korean Cities', in Phillip H. Park (ed.), *The Dynamics of Change in North Korea: An Institutionalist Perspective* (Seoul: IFES Kyungnam University Press, 2009), p. 97.

[79] Lee, 'Food Shortages', p. 122.

[80] Choi and Koo, 'The Development of Farmers' Markets', p. 110.

constrained by the government that they only played a very marginal role in the food economy. From 1957, basic grains could not be sold in these markets. Only the products of small private plots could be sold, for example vegetables and maybe a chicken or eggs.[81] These farmers' markets were only allowed to open on certain days and were located in urban areas that were difficult to access.[82]

Government-controlled farmers' markets were not permitted to expand in order to act as alternative supply mechanisms to the public distribution system. In the 1980s, these restrictions were sometimes ignored because chronic shortages of food and consumer goods encouraged the population to seek alternative sources of supply to state provision.[83] Illegal consumer goods markets emerged that sold imported manufactured goods from China as well as locally produced consumer goods that were diverted from the state distribution system.[84] Some farmers sold produce that was intended for government procurement although such activity by farmers was very marginal.[85] Apart from anything else, it was very risky as individuals who engaged in illegal selling of produce, faced severe punishment if caught. Illegal markets were not a major source of supply because of government sanctions on their operations, goods cost more than many could afford, most individuals had little cash money and the general normative environment was such that as long as the basics were supplied by the public distribution system, it was 'unthinkable' to use non-state provision.[86]

Learning to cope

Inequality between those who had access to modern, relatively advanced technological goods, such as cars, refrigerators and washing machines, and those who did not was not a visible feature of the economy. This was because only the very top elite in the Kim Il Sungist era had access to these high-quality consumer goods and the lifestyles of these people were

---

[81] Ibid., pp. 75–134.

[82] Ibid.; UNDP and DPRK government, 'Thematic Roundtable Meeting on Agricultural Recovery', p. 20.

[83] Hyung-Min Joo, 'Visualizing the Invisible Hands: The Shadow Economy in North Korea', *Economy and Society*, Vol. 39, No. 1, February 2010, pp. 110–45. For discussion of the prevalence of the market in the early 1990s see Anthony R. Michell, 'The Current North Korean Economy', in Marcus Noland (ed.), *Economic Integration of the Korean Peninsula* (Washington, DC: Institute for International Economics, 1998), pp. 137–63.

[84] Choi and Koo, 'The Development of Farmers' Markets', pp. 75–134.

[85] Ibid., pp. 111–13.   [86] Ibid., pp. 122–4.

not accessible to the majority of the population. The leadership discouraged displays of conspicuous consumption by the privileged elite.

Differentials between standards of living did not vary very much across the country although there were differences because the availability of consumer goods depended on local resources, local ingenuity and local purchasing power. Nominal wages were not subject explicitly to regional adjustment but geographical variations occurred because of the nature of the industry. A farmer living on an agriculturally productive farm in a southern province, for example, was likely to be better off than a northern farmer because the state geared farmers' remuneration to productivity. More productive farms meant more income for farming families but also more investment in local social infrastructure including schools and clinics. An industrial worker in a big chemicals factory in the north would similarly receive higher wages, more food and goods than someone located in a small engineering works in a small county town in the south of the country. This was because the output of large industrial plants was highly valued as a national priority; wages for workers in heavy industry reflected these priorities and heavy industry was concentrated in the north.

The population developed coping mechanisms to deal with the requirements of the system that demanded continuous 'voluntary' labour but at the same time did not provide a sufficient food supply. The practice whereby one individual could substitute for another providing the overall quota from the responsible organisation was fulfilled, developed and was accepted as a working norm.[87] Nevertheless, labour conditions remained tough and individuals were not motivated to work harder for few or no material rewards.

The intrinsic flaws

In the 1950s and early 1960s Kim's policies appeared remarkably successful and growth took place in every sector of the economy.[88] The overall thrust of available economic indicators show that initial aggregate

---

[87] Part of my work in the DPRK in 2000/1 for the WFP was the development and monitoring of food for work projects that could employ up to 10,000 urban workers in physically hard work in extreme winter and summer temperatures in rural settings. Monitoring ration cards and discussions with supervisory engineers on site indicated the widespread taken-for-grantedness of household responsibility so that one family member could substitute for another in the workplace assignment.

[88] Useful sources on the North Korean economy are Chung, *The North Korean Economy*; Sung Chul Yang, *The North and South Korean Political Systems: A Comparative Analysis*, revised edition (Elizabeth, NJ: Hollym, 1999); Lee, *North Korea*; Marina Ye Trigubenko, 'Economic Characteristics and Prospect for Development: With

growth rates were very high indeed. North Korea outpaced South Korea in the rate of economic growth every year during the 1950s and 1960s – a much trumpeted indicator of economic success.[89] One reason for high growth figures was because the base economic level was so low, but this was also true for South Korea.

One problem in assessing the North Korean economy for the Kim Il Sung period is that the data is not robust. The DPRK did not as a matter of course produce reliable statistical data. Other communist states had access to North Korean data but these were also closed societies and did not consider it necessary or appropriate to disseminate statistical analysis for consumption by those it considered its adversaries in the then Cold War. To make matters more complicated, available data was constituted on a different basis than that of capitalist countries, making it difficult to engage in meaningful comparative analysis of the North Korea economy with other economies.[90] Foreign analysts also used different kinds of statistical comparators to assess the North Korean economy.[91] Nevertheless, accounts from economists from the former Soviet Union who well understood planned economies and had some access to the DPRK provide a reasonable base of understanding and they reported that the economy grew by an annual average of 16.6 per cent between 1954 and 1967.[92] Growth probably continued into the 1970s and 1980s, although there is a fairly wide variance in the figures. North Korea reported growth as high as 17 per cent in 1978 while external analysts calculated results that ranged from negative growth to a growth of around the 10 per cent mark.[93]

DPRK economic planners regularly pointed out that the capitalist economies had not brought an end to poverty and homelessness in their

Emphasis on Agriculture', in Han S. Park (ed.), *North Korea: Ideology, Politics, Economy* (Englewood Cliffs: Prentice Hall, 1996) pp. 141–59.

[89] Yang, *The North and South Korean Political Systems*, p. 642.

[90] Chung, *The North Korean Economy*, p. 144; Yang, *The North and South Korean Political Systems*, p. 610.

[91] Chung and Yang, for example, are both useful sources on the North Korean economy but use different measures. Chung uses a measure of national income derived from North Korea's own understanding to measure growth. See Chung, *The North Korean Economy*, p. 144; Yang derives a measure of GNP so that comparisons can be made with South Korea. See Yang, *The North and South Korean Political Systems*, pp. 642–3.

[92] Chung, *The North Korean Economy*, p. 145. Yang, by contrast, calculates that from 1963 to 1970, North Korea's GNP growth rates ranged between a high of 36.7 per cent in 1966 and a low of 13.3 per cent in 1968. In the same period, he calculates that South Korea's GNP growth rates ranged between a high of 13.8 per cent in 1969 and a low of 5.8 per cent in 1965. See Yang, *The North and South Korean Political Systems*, pp. 642–3.

[93] Ibid.

own countries whereas North Korea delivered considerable social, educational and welfare benefits to its population and produced improvements in life chances for many millions. Kim blamed slow progress in achieving improved living standards on inadequate political work by Party officials and United States sanctions which had first been imposed on the DPRK in 1950, despite the fact that, during the Kim Il Sungist era, North Korea was not prevented from trading with other countries, including western Europe.[94] Kim condemned communist states that did eventually adopt capitalist economic methods, principally Gorbachev's Soviet Union, as traitors. There was no recognition that North Korea's economic model largely depended on the back-breaking work of the population and an underlying dependence on the rest of the communist world, most notably in their willingness to forgive debt and to provide cheap fuel.[95]

Economic policy achieved the political aim of building a powerful military capacity but in doing so it under-invested in agriculture and light industry and consequently generated an economy in which basic consumer goods were limited in quality and quantity. Economic weaknesses included diminishing returns from exhausted individuals, poor productivity, bottlenecks in production and distribution and poor-quality outputs.[96] The absence of quality inputs, professional quality controls and modern technology resulted in the building of an economic infrastructure that was unfit for purpose. North Korean economic planners recognised these difficulties yet never questioned the credibility or efficacy of the goals or methods of the basic development model.

---

[94] Dianne E. Rennack, *North Korea: Legislative Basis for US Economic Sanctions* (Washington, DC: Congressional Research Service, 2010).

[95] Referring to the late 1960s and early 1970s, Gordon White argued that aid was 'not ... a crucial factor in North Korean economic development over the past decade'. This conclusion is arrived at by conceptually limiting the understanding of foreign aid to direct financial transfers. Dependence, including trade dependence, is understood by White as a conceptually separate category of relationship, which, he argues, could be understood as characterising relations between the DPRK and its major economic partners of the Soviet Union and China. Gordon White, 'North Korean *Chuch'e:* The Political Economy of Independence', *Bulletin of Concerned Asian Scholars*, Vol. 7, No. 2, p. 50. For the entire discussion see ibid., pp. 44–54. Charles Armstrong also argues that 'fraternal assistance' from Communist countries diminished sharply after 1962. Armstrong, similarly to White, focuses on direct transfers of technological assistance and capital. See Charles Armstrong, '"Fraternal Socialism": The International Reconstruction of North Korea, 1953–62', *Cold War History*, Vol. 5, No. 2, May 2005, p. 162. That the North Korean economy was able to sustain itself at all after 1962, however, was helped considerably by the protected markets and subsidised trade system in which it participated as an observer member of the Communist trading bloc, Comecon.

[96] Chung, *The North Korean Economy*, p. 96.

The priority of heavy industry trumped investment in consumer industries because of national security priorities.

Other communist countries, including the Soviet Union and the relatively liberal former Yugoslavia, had incorporated large numbers of adults and young people in intensive 'voluntary' and state-directed nation-building activities such as road-building, construction and agricultural work in peacetime. They had used mass mobilisation techniques for short periods of time to encourage young people to consider themselves part of a selfless collective and as an economic expedient when technological resources were scarce. No other communist state, however, apart from perhaps the Pol Pot regime in its short-lived existence, had understood mass mobilisation as a means of sustainable economic development. Nevertheless, in North Korea, the method of the mass line was maintained because it allowed for political control of the population.

Increased aggregate growth and improvements in social welfare masked declining growth rates while failure to reach economic targets provided evidence of stagnant productivity. The three-year plan (1954–6) and the following five-year plan (1957–61) marked a period of rapid economic recovery, but between 1961 and 1993 the state failed to achieve economic targets by substantial margins in each of the four planning cycles.[97] The growth target over the period of the first seven-year plan of 1961 to 1967 was 14.6 per cent but the actual achievement was 8.6 per cent.[98] The subsequent six-year plan of 1971 to 1976 had a goal of 10.3 per cent growth; actual achievement was 6 per cent.[99] The second seven-year plan of 1978 to 1984 achieved 4.5 per cent growth compared to a target of 9.6 per cent.[100] The third seven-year plan of 1987 to 1993 achieved 3 per cent growth against a target of 7.9 per cent.[101]

Local self-sufficiency policies and political exhortation encouraged improvisation of low-tech solutions in farms and enterprises but these policies could not generate the scale of productivity gains required to modernise the economy or sustain the growth figures of the immediate post-Korean War economy. The total share of industry, including mining, manufacturing, fuel and light industries, doubled as a percentage of gross output, from just under 31 per cent in 1953 to 66 per cent in 1983 but by 1990 mining, manufacturing and construction as a share of

---

[97] Trigubenko, 'Economic Characteristics', p. 148.
[98] Chung reports that growth in the 1960s halved from the previous decade, to 8.9 per cent between 1961 and 1967. Chung, The North Korean Economy', p. 96.
[99] Ibid.   [100] Ibid.   [101] Ibid.

gross national product (GNP) had decreased to 56 per cent, while the share of agriculture in national product was just under 27 per cent.[102]

A shrinking industrial sector need not necessarily have indicated economic failure if the economy was growing and industrial output was sufficient for domestic and export requirements, or if there had been diversification to a services sector in which North Korea could have earned income, perhaps in the expansion of tourism, or if agriculture had been modernised, thus perhaps creating surpluses for export. After all, Vietnam, 'a comparable-sized economy and [with] a similar history of development' to North Korea, developed a successful growth strategy on the foundation of rice exports and became the world's second largest rice exporter after its communist leadership promoted economic reform.[103] South Korea also suffers from a disproportionally low amount of arable land and poor climatic conditions yet it managed to produce agricultural surpluses, some of which were donated as aid to North Korea in the 2000s. The decrease in output in the 1980s did not, however, demonstrate a healthy restructuring process but instead indicated a savage economic decline.

The defence burden

In some countries spending in the defence sectors contributes to economic growth as research and development spinoffs have applications that are used to generate export earnings and make productivity gains in the civilian economy. Advances in mobile telephony and aircraft design provide good examples of where military budgets have helped to pump-prime technological and economic development worldwide. In North Korea, however, the defence budget, which some estimates indicated was

---

[102] Yang, *The North and South Korean Political Systems*, p. 659. These figures are derived from different sources than in Choi, *A Study on the Structure of Industry*, which provides 1953–83 figures. The composition of industry in Choi is delineated in more detail than that in Yang and thus it is possible that there may be some marginal difference in the composition of categories in the two sources. The overall economic composition figures for both authors, however, are similar enough to provide a useful base for comparative analysis.

[103] Georgy Toloraya, *The Economic Future of North Korea: Will the Market Rule?* Academic Paper Series on North Korea: Vol. 2, No. 10 (Korea Economic Institute, 2008), p. 35, available at www.keia.org/sites/default/files/publications/toloraya.pdf, accessed 8 November 2014. On Vietnam, economic growth and the rice trade see IFAD, *Enabling Poor Rural People to Overcome Poverty in Vietnam* (Rome: IFAD, 2010), available at www.ifad.org/operations/projects/regions/Pi/factsheets/vn.pdf, accessed 8 November 2014. See also Danny M. Leipziger, 'Thinking about the World Bank and North Korea', in Marcus Noland (ed.), *Economic Integration of the Korean Peninsula* (Washington, DC: Institute for International Economics, 1998), pp. 201–19.

running at 15 to 20 per cent of GNP in the 1960s rising to 25 to 30 per cent of GNP in the 1970s, placed a huge strain on the economy.[104]

The military occasionally helped with construction and seasonal agricultural activities but the leadership did not permit military involvement in the civilian economy on a regular basis, as Kim Il Sung argued that soldiers should be engaged in 'political and combat training' not 'farm work'.[105] Military spending did not stimulate productivity gains in other sectors of the economy as the military sector, including heavy industry, was organised separately from consumer-related industries, which made it difficult to generate spillover from one to the other. In addition, the military sector consumed civilian basic goods, including food, clothing and shelter, for the two-thirds of a million military personnel and the hundreds of thousands in the part-time militias.

Organising self-defence activities around the mass line transferred nearly a million potentially economically active young people every year into non-economically productive activities such as guarding borders, beaches and bridges. Towards the end of the Kim Il Sung era, signs of change emerged as the DPRK government reported that between 1986 and 1987 it voluntarily reduced its armed forces by 250,000 'and sent them to the peaceful construction sites'.[106] These policy changes showed a recognition of the drain on the economy of defence spending but did not alter the absolute priority of the defence sector within economic planning. Military priorities always trumped economic rationality and crowded out the possibilities of efficient economic planning. In a kind of Kim Il Sungist vicious circle, the decline in the economy partly caused by the skewing of resources towards the military threatened the most fundamental Kim Il Sungist goal of building a strong military power.

Labour shortages

North Korea remained chronically short of the physical labour on which it was dependent yet the state employed large numbers in occupations that were not directly economically productive. The 1993 census classified those working in industry at 4,118,332 people or 37.42 per cent of

---

[104] Yang, *The North and South Korean Political Systems*, p. 709.
[105] Kim referenced the practice as standard in Kim, 'On This Year's Experience', pp. 256–7.
[106] Délégation générale de la RPD de Corée en France, 'On the Measures Taken by the Government of the DPRK to Implement the Articles VI and VII of the Nuclear Non-Proliferation Treaty', *Bulletin d'information*, No. 11/591 (Paris: Délégation générale de la RPD de Corée en France, 28 May 1991), p. 2.

the working population.[107] The 1993 census records a total of 3,381,930 people working in agriculture, that is, 30.73 per cent of the total workforce.[108] The industrial sector and the agricultural sector took, respectively first and second largest share in employment in 1993. Yet in 1993, public service workers, officials and military comprised about three million people, just less than a quarter of the workforce, and nearly as many as the numbers employed in agriculture. Along with the three-quarters of a million people in the military, there were 843,647 people working in education, culture and health, the third largest employment sector at 7.67 per cent of the workforce.[109] Educators and health workers contributed indirectly to the economy through the creation and development of an educated and healthy labour force but many of this public sector workforce were employed primarily to supervise the political outlook of the population.

Unacknowledged dependencies

Standard industrial policies, even of the most powerful states, allow for a measure of trade interdependence with other countries but in North Korea the default foreign trade policy was to minimise import and export interdependence. Resource gaps that could not be filled from domestic sources were primarily addressed by the solicitation of free and/or subsidised economic assistance from allies and sympathisers. The option of expanding export earnings to pay for necessary imports was less-favoured.

North Korea developed economic links with the 'General Association of Korean Residents in Japan' or *Chongryon*, which organised the 700,000 strong Korean community in Japan.[110] *Chongryon* was organisationally well developed, relatively prosperous and to all intents and purposes acted as an overseas outpost of the DPRK. Until the 1990s, its educational system and media replicated those of the DPRK. North Korea imported $2 billion worth of capital goods, that is, those goods that are primarily useful for industry, from Japan between 1972 and

---

[107] Hong, *Analysis of 1993 Population Census Data*, pp. 69–70.
[108] Ibid.   [109] Ibid.
[110] The DPRK financially assisted the establishment of *Chongryun* schools in Japan but it did not fund *Chongryun*. The economic links ran the other way although no detailed accounts are available of the amount of subvention from Koreans in Japan to the North Korean government. Sonia Ryang's account of the General Association of Korean Residents in Japan alludes to the 'many joint management firms' established with the North Korean government. *Chongryun* had its own trading and financial businesses and a major activity of the organisation was to raise funds. For quote see Sonia Ryang, *North Koreans in Japan: Language, Ideology and Entity* (Boulder, CO: Westview, 1997), p. 4.

1995.[111] This was a very large share of North Korea's global import bill for capital goods; it was only second to the Soviet Union/Russian trade volume of $2.26 billion in the same period.[112] Given that North Korea ran a persistent trade deficit in those same years, *Chongryon* contributions likely contributed to meeting the cost of these imports.[113] Kim Il Sung acknowledged economic support from *Chongryon* which he argued had 'the greatest honour to support and defend the socialist homeland and [it] has made every effort for... [North Korea's] prosperity and development'.[114] *Chongryon*, in other words, was fulfilling a nationalist duty to the homeland by supporting the DPRK.

North Korea used its plentiful coal and hydro resources to generate electricity for the military, industrial, domestic and transport sectors, including the railways that provided its major mode of freight and passenger transport, but it relied on imported oil for key economic sectors.[115] Oil-based imports were needed to produce essential agricultural products, including fertiliser and pesticide. Oil was also required to supply two oil-fired power stations and as fuel for vehicles.[116] Despite periodic attempts to negotiate oil deliveries from friendly countries including Iraq, Iran and Algeria, the Soviet Union remained the main supplier of oil, which was delivered at highly concessionary rates.[117] North Korea also received free and concessional transfers of capital goods and technology from a number of socialist states, including the Soviet Union, China and the central and east European states, East Germany, Poland, Hungary, Romania, Czechoslovakia and Bulgaria.[118]

[111] Nicholas Eberstadt, 'International Trade in Capital Goods, 1970–1995: Indications from "Mirror Statistics"', in Nicholas Eberstadt, *The North Korean Economy: Between Crisis and Catastrophe* (New Brunswick: Transaction Publishers, 2007), p. 75.

[112] Ibid.

[113] Data on trade gap in Ahn, *North Korea Development Report*, p. 31.

[114] Kim Il Sung, 'On the Occasion of the 25th Anniversary of the Formation of the General Association of Korean Residents in Japan', in Kim Il Sung, *Works, Vol. 35* (Pyongyang: Foreign Languages Publishing House, 1989), p. 137.

[115] Anthony R. Michell, 'The Current North Korean Economy', in Marcus Noland (ed.), *Economic Integration of the Korean Peninsula* (Washington, DC: Institute for International Economics, 1998), p. 147; David F. Von Hippel and Peter Hayes, 'North Korean Energy Sector: Current Status and Scenarios from 2000 and 2005', in Marcus Noland (ed.), *Economic Integration of the Korean Peninsula* (Washington, DC: Institute for International Economics, 1998), pp. 77–117.

[116] Ibid.

[117] Brun and Hersh, *Socialist Korea*, p. 287.

[118] Joseph Chung's analysis of DPRK foreign trade between 1946 and 1969 shows that over 85 per cent of the DPRK's trade was with Communist nations until 1967, decreasing to just less than 73 per cent in 1969. See Chung, *The North Korean Economy*, pp. 110–11. A detailed appendix of individual socialist country aid to the DPRK between 1953 and 1963 is in Karoly Fendler, 'Economic Assistance from

Non-repayable assistance from the socialist countries funded the heavy industrial sector, paying for projects that included steel works, chemical production facilities, cement plants, port facilities, paper mills, battery plants and machinery production.[119]

North Korea aimed to increase export earnings in order to earn cash or to swap North Korean exports for imports but in the 1980s, barter trade with the Soviet Union and the socialist countries amounted to some 60 per cent of North Korea's trade.[120] North Korea could never produce quality manufactured goods to attract sustained interest in its manufactured exports, even from within Comecon, the closed communist trading bloc, in which its observer status gave it preferential trading benefits.[121] North Korea amended its trade strategy to export raw materials and primary products, including anthracite, iron ore and magnesite.[122] Nevertheless North Korea remained short of capital and borrowed from communist allies and, like many other non-oil producing countries, North Korea also borrowed from Western banks, gambling on commodity price inflation to increase export earnings.[123] This seemed a logical strategy after 1974 when the success of oil producer countries forced Western countries to quadruple the price they paid for oil, making some formerly poor countries very rich indeed.

When non-oil world commodity prices collapsed in the 1970s, North Korea, again like many other countries, could not pay its debts but, unlike other countries, it did not successfully renegotiate its debts but simply stopped payments to its creditors.[124] North Korea became an international debt defaulter and unable to borrow from the global credit

Socialist Countries to North Korea in the Postwar Years: 1953–1963', in Han S. Park (ed.), *North Korea: Ideology, Politics, Economy* (Englewood Cliffs: Prentice Hall, 1996), pp. 161–73. For Chinese assistance see Robert Scalapino, 'China and Korean Reunification – A Neighbour's Concerns', in Nicholas Eberstadt and Richard J. Ellings (eds.), *Korea's Future and the Great Powers* (Seattle: University of Washington Press, 2001), pp. 107–24. For Russian perspectives on Russian relations with the DPRK see the excellent compilation James Clay Moltz and Alexandre Y. Mansourov (eds.), *The North Korean Nuclear Program: Security, Strategy and New Perspectives from Russia* (New York: Routledge, 2000).

[119] Fendler, 'Economic Assistance', pp. 161–73.
[120] Nixson and Collins, 'Economic Reform in North Korea', p. 157.
[121] On the DPRK's capital goods trade see Eberstadt, 'International Trade', pp. 61–97. On Comecon benefits see Hazel Smith, 'North Korean Foreign Policy in the 1990s: The Realist approach', in Hazel Smith, Chris Rhodes, Diana Pritchard and Kevin Magill (eds.), *North Korea in the New World Order* (London: Macmillan, 1996), pp. 97–8.
[122] Trigubenko, 'Economic Characteristics', p. 149.
[123] Smith, 'North Korean Foreign Policy in the 1990s', pp. 97–8.
[124] Iuli Banchev, 'Prerogatives of the New Foreign Economic Policy Making', in Han S. Park (ed.), *North Korea: Ideology, Politics, Economy* (Englewood Cliffs: Prentice Hall, 1996), pp. 198–9.

markets or from its allies.[125] Most of the debt was owed to the Soviet Union and China. In 1989, the Soviet Union accounted for 46 per cent of North Korea's debt liabilities and China 13 per cent.[126] In 1990, the Soviet Union refused to make further loans to North Korea and would only sell its exports for payment in hard currency at market prices.[127] The 1989 debt burden of $6.78 billion rose to $10.66 billion by the time of Kim Il Sung's death in 1994.[128]

Economic collapse

Kim Il Sung never accepted that the end of command economic systems in the Soviet Union and communist Europe was inevitable or necessary. The country was not prepared for the abrupt end of subsidies from the Soviet Union and other communist countries in 1989/90 and the economy collapsed. In 1989 growth rates fell by 5.3 per cent.[129] North Korea was not unique. Non-oil producing former communist countries, including Romania, Albania and Bulgaria, none of which spent heavily on defence, also suffered rapid economic deterioration because of their similar dependence on support from the wealthier states in the communist bloc. North Korea was, however, much more dependent on cheap oil imports and concessionary trade than its leadership had been prepared to admit. The already precarious food system collapsed and the population, which had learned to rely on the government for every aspect of their existence, including food rations, could not initially find alternatives. The worst of times was imminent.

[125] Callum MacDonald, 'The Democratic People's Republic of Korea: An Historical Survey', in Hazel Smith, Chris Rhodes, Diana Pritchard and Kevin Magill (eds.), *North Korea in the New World Order* (London: Macmillan Press, 1996), p. 12; for details of external debt at 1989 see Soogil Young, Chang-Jae Lee and Hyoungsoo Zang, 'Preparing for the Economic Integration of Two Koreas: Policy Challenges to South Korea', in Marcus Noland (ed.), *Economic Integration of the Korean Peninsula* (Washington, DC: Institute for International Economics, 1998), pp. 254–7.

[126] Ibid., p. 257.

[127] Georgy Bulychev, 'Korean Security Dilemmas: A Russian Perspective', in Hazel Smith (ed.), *Reconstituting Korean Security: A Policy Primer* (Tokyo: United Nations Press, 2007), p. 186.

[128] Young *et al.*, 'Preparing for the Economic Integration of Two Koreas', p. 256.

[129] Trigubenko, 'Economic Characteristics', p. 149. Based on Bank of Korea reporting, Michell reports growth rates starting to fall in 1990 by 3.7 per cent and reports 1989 as the last year of economic growth at 2.4 per cent, until 1997. I have used the 1989 date as the Soviet experts were generally better informed than others and because the use of the date 1989 or 1990 makes little difference to the thrust of the argument of the chapter and the book, that the cut-off in external aid at the end of the Cold War is a crucial variable in understanding North Korea's economic decline and collapse. See Michell, 'The Current North Korean Economy', p. 139.

7   Social stratification in the workers' state

Kim Il Sung's North Korea is conventionally understood as if there were few social cleavages other than those founded around political fault lines.[1] Kim Il Sung attempted to create a monolithic society in which social differentiation was always a function of the political system, but to think of Kim Il Sung as having been uniquely successful in achieving the absolute subordination of the society to the state is misleading. Kim Il Sungist society was also shaped by multiple identity markers including occupation, geographical provenance, gender and generation.

Kim Il Sung set out to create a society where loyalty to the Leader provided the most important qualification for social status and privilege. Occupational status also followed political allegiance as the best jobs were reserved for Party members and officials. To the extent that Kim Il Sungist politics created a new social structure it was through reinforcing the power and privilege of Party members over and above the broader society. North Korean society was not, however, a historical and social tabula rasa. Regional differences, especially between the

---

[1] Much more attention has been given to the aims and mechanisms of DPRK state social policy than to analysing the outcomes of these policies. For the former see Ellen Brun and Jacques Hersh, *Socialist Korea: A Case Study in the Strategy of Economic Development* (London and New York: Monthly Review Press, 1976); Kongdan Oh and Ralph C. Hassig, *North Korea Through the Looking Glass* (Washington, DC: Brookings Institution Press, 2000); Han S. Park (ed.), *North Korea: Ideology, Politics, Economy* (Englewood Cliffs: Prentice Hall, 1996). A substantial effort to analyse Kim Il Sungist North Korean society is handicapped because of its lack of referencing, uncritical reliance on defectors and overtly political bias (it was originally written as a CIA briefing). See Helen-Louise Hunter, *Kim Il Song's North Korea* (Westport: Praeger, 1999). Glimpses into North Korean society as a mix of tight governmental control and quotidian humanity are visible in the accounts of foreigners who have lived in the country. See Michael Harrold, *Comrades and Strangers: Behind the Closed Doors of North Korea* (Chichester: John Wiley and Sons, 2004); Charles Robert Jenkins with Jim Frederick, *The Reluctant Communist: My Desertion, Court-martial and Forty-year Imprisonment in North Korea* (Berkeley: University of California Press, 2008). An example of scholarship that attempted to interrogate the relationship between state social policy and societal outcomes is Sung Chull Kim, *North Korea under Kim Jong Il: From Consolidation to Systemic Dissonance* (Albany: State University of New York Press, 2006).

164

north-eastern Hamgyong provinces and the south-western Pyongyan provinces, remained salient even as they were attenuated by proactive regional redistributive policies.

Despite the social dislocation caused by colonial policies and the Korean War, Kim Il Sungist North Korea retained and embedded some very long-standing social conceptions, including a view of women as natural home-makers. Kim Il Sungist policy was to valorise women as mothers although not all of Kim Il Sungist social policy resonated with conservative, historically constituted social norms. Kim Il Sung was resolutely anti-Confucian in that he consciously implemented policies that sought to overturn social relations that had prioritised age and experience over youth. The mix of modernity and tradition in Kim Il Sungist social policy was demonstrated in the recognition of the family as the core unit of the national society but in Kim Il Sungist society the family was important as a micro-unit of Kim Il Sungist politics whose main function was to educate future generations of revolutionary cadres. The family was not primarily meant to provide private space for relationships between kin whose loyalties might be to each other more than to the state.

Social class and social differentiation

In North Korea life chances depended on social class and occupation as much as anywhere else in the world and, as everywhere in the world, North Korea's elites had better life opportunities than most of the population. Privilege came from and was manifest in, among other things, high status and powerful family connections, inherited wealth and access to elite schools. In North Korea, as in a number of other post-Second World War communist states, the basis of social stratification was loyalty and obedience to the Leader and the new regime. Party members were privileged, although not all to the same extent. Other social groups benefiting from relatively high social status in the Kim Il Sung era were demobilised military and workers in heavy industry.

In post-Korean War North Korea, the privileged class were the Kim family and those who assumed senior positions in the Party. The apex of the social pyramid in the Kim Il Sung era was constituted by a fairly small number of people, comprised of the extended Kim family and half a dozen other families.[2] Individuals came and went in the struggle for

---

[2] Alexandre Y. Mansourov, 'Inside North Korea's Black Box: Reversing the Optics', in Kongdan Oh and Ralph Hassig (eds.), *North Korean Policy Elites* (Alexandria, VA: Institute for Defense Analyses, 2004), unpaginated but pp. 159–226 on pdf, available at www.nkeconwatch.com/nk-uploads/dprkpolicyelites.pdf, accessed 2 November 2014.

patronage and power but political and familial proximity to the Kim family provided some guarantee of longevity in the country's upper echelons.[3] Only the Kim family had unfettered privileges, including the ability to more or less freely travel abroad. The upper echelons of North Korean society had high social status, but their lives were constrained by the strictures of the state that controlled and monitored all those that had the potential to oppose Kim Il Sung.

The North Korean class system was reportedly formalised within a bureaucratic classification system that divided the entire population into a complex system of fifty-one different sub-classes founded on the basis of political loyalty and hereditary social position.[4] The reported categories included 'landlords' and 'wealthy capitalists', although these social groups did not exist by the late 1960s.[5] Another reported version of the bureaucratic classification scheme is that the North Korean govern- ment delineated three broad groups according to political loyalty and these were understood as the core, complex (or wavering) and hostile classes.[6]

The government denied that it divided the population into social categories based on loyalty to the regime and such categorisations were not identified in the Constitution or legal system.[7] Nevertheless, irrespective of whether or not a finely tuned, bureaucratic and legalistic categorisation of the population existed or for how long it was in exist- ence, assessments of political loyalty were certainly extremely important for the authoritarian North Korean state.[8] The state distrusted those

---

[3] For details on who was who in the political firmament between 1946 and 1980 see Sung Chul Yang, *The North and South Korean Political Systems: A Comparative Analysis*, revised edition (Elizabeth, NJ: Hollym, 1999), pp. 325–58.

[4] Richard Kagan, Matthew Oh and David Weissbrodt, *Human Rights in the Democratic People's Republic of Korea* (Minneapolis/Washington, DC: Minnesota Lawyers International Human Rights Committee/Asia Watch, 1988), pp. 34–9 and Appendix 2, pp. 1–12.

[5] Ibid.

[6] Kook-shin Kim, Hyun-joon Chon, Keum-soon Lee, Soon-hee Lim, Kyu-chang Lee and Woo-taek Hong, *White Paper on Human Rights in North Korea 2011* (Seoul: Korea Institute for National Unification, 2011), pp. 219–25.

[7] See for example Standing Committee of the Supreme People's Assembly, *The Criminal Law of the Democratic People's Republic of Korea* (Pyongyang: Foreign Languages Publishing House, 1992); Standing Committee of the Supreme People's Assembly, *The Civil Law of the Democratic People's Republic of Korea* (Pyongyang: Foreign Languages Publishing House, 1994).

[8] Charles K. Armstrong, *The North Korean Revolution 1945–1950* (London: Cornell University Press, 2003), Note 4, p. 73. A detailed account that both shows the complications facing one family in 1962 in respect to marriage because of social background, and indicates that social background was investigated but not automatically recorded on citizen registration cards (at that time), is given in Mun Woong Lee, 'Appendix 1: A Case Study of a Marriage', in Mun Woong Lee, 'Rural North Korea

whom it thought had any reason to be dissatisfied with the regime and discriminated against them. It was also suspicious of those it judged to be politically disloyal or potentially disloyal because of family background. These included a wide range of people ranging from descendants of Christians and religious adherents through to family members of uprooted former owners of land and wealth.[9] Conversely, the family members of those judged loyal to the regime – from revolutionary leaders to Party officials – were trusted and privileged.

Political loyalty and political connections were a necessary but not sufficient condition for advancement. The Korean Workers' Party was a mass Party, not a vanguard cadre Party.[10] Most could never hope to achieve much more than a low to mid-ranking supervisory post and the occasional perk such as access to seats at prestige entertainments like the mass games or the state circus performances and perhaps occasional travel to Pyongyang. A Party member in a non-supervisory job – perhaps a middle-rank teacher or doctor – would only receive a fairly basic income. Party members had, however, a higher social status than non-Party members as, by definition, with their acceptance into the Party, they had proved that they were more loyal and more trusted servants of the state than those who had not yet made the grade.

Party members had access to jobs that might allow for opportunities to travel, perhaps to engage in some discreet private trade. At minimum these might provide a bit of spare cash to spend in the constrained markets that existed in the Kim Il Sung period.[11] Party membership was not a formal prerequisite for access to coupons that entitled the recipient to eat at restaurants at a very low cost and for tickets to leisure activities including the cinema, but with Party membership the likelihood of obtaining these perks was enhanced.[12] Without Party membership, an individual and their family remained without hope of advancing through the occupational and social hierarchy. As in other communist countries, avenues for career

under Communism: A Study of Sociocultural Change', doctoral dissertation (Houston: Rice University, 1975), pp. 208–9.

[9] Ibid., pp. 144–7.
[10] Jon Halliday, 'The North Korean Enigma', in Gordon White, Robin Murray and Christine White (eds.), *Revolutionary Socialist Development in the Third World* (Lexington: University Press of Kentucky, 1983), p. 137.
[11] Lee, 'Rural North Korea Under Communism', pp. 79–80.
[12] Lola Nathanail, *Food and Nutrition Assessment Democratic People's Republic of Korea, 16 March–24 April 1996* (Pyongyang: World Food Programme, 1996), p. 24.

advancement were closed off to those considered politically unreliable.[13] By virtue of unavailability of good jobs and a higher education, government policy directly discriminated against those who were perceived to be disloyal or potentially disloyal.

The government gave rewards to soldiers who enlisted and families viewed 'selection for military service [as] a great honor, since the regime carefully selects its soldiers'.[14] Those who did well in the military could access preferential educational and employment opportunities on completion of their service.[15] Workers in heavy industry benefited from core state policy that aimed to transform the country into a major industrial power.[16] They received relatively good incomes, decent food rations and access to well-provisioned social, educational and health services provided by and through the workplace. Workers in heavy industry were also encouraged to become Party cadres, reinforcing the centrality of heavy industry to national development and, in the process, consolidating the position of skilled industrial workers as a somewhat privileged social class.[17]

---

[13] Some definitive allegations have been made about the use of social classification schemes in the DPRK. The problem is that corroboration of many of the strongest claims is not available. It is very plausible, however, given the pervasive nature of the security-centred state and the well-documented history of social surveillance in Communist states like East Germany that all citizens would be monitored and categorised in 'loyalty' terms. The primary source for secondary accounts referring to social classification of the North Korean people is Kagan et al., Human Rights, pp. 32–40. This report relies on only three sources, respectively, a 'former agent', 'former spy' and 'former pilot'. The report uses qualifiers like 'appeared', 'seemed' and 'apparently' throughout. Large numbers of human rights reports have since repeated these claims but have withheld the qualifiers. Often quoted sources for social classification claims are the annual White Papers on North Korean human rights published by the South Korean government-funded Korea Institute for National Unification. Again, claims are not sourced or are sourced to unnamed defectors. See for example Korea Institute for National Unification, White Papers on Human Rights in North Korea 2007 (Seoul: Korea Institute for National Unification, 2007), pp. 116–23.

[14] Lee, 'Rural North Korea under Communism', p. 111.

[15] Ibid.

[16] Un Hong Song, Economic Development in the Democratic People's Republic of Korea, 18 April 1978 (Pyongyang: Foreign Languages Publishing House, 1990), pp. 16–17.

[17] See comment by a visiting Hungarian delegation in 1954 to the DPRK about the Hungnam [in South Hamgyong] chemical factory providing a 'main source of cadres'. Quoted by Balázs Szalontai, 'The Four Horsemen of the Apocalypse in North Korea', in Chris Springer (ed.), North Korea Caught in Time: Images of War and Reconstruction (Reading: Garnet Publishing, 2010), p. xxii. The political importance of industrial workers, mostly congregated in the industrial cities of the north-east, correlates with the preponderance of individuals originating from the Hamgyong provinces in central Party (Central Committee) and government (Supreme People's Assembly) structures. See Yang, The North and South Korean Political Systems, pp. 278–86.

The social structure remained rigid but it was not a caste system.[18] Upward social mobility could and did occur, sometimes through the army and the education system or through recognition of meritorious contributions to the state. Those from 'impure' family backgrounds could progress from associate membership of cooperative farms to the status of full members through participation in farming and community activities.[19] Equally, loss of privilege and status could take place if an individual failed to show sufficient zeal or in the worst-case scenario, if they fell out of favour with the government to the extent that they were charged with 'political' crimes.[20]

The workers' state

In Kim Il Sung's North Korea, as in all societies, occupation reflected and contributed to social status and, in turn, access to well-paid and prestigious occupations was easier for those with a privileged social background. As in other communist states, occupation was determined by local Parties who allocated jobs to individuals that were supposed to be commensurate with their training and aptitudes. Also as in other communist states, the workplace provided the nodal point of political and social life as well as providing employment.[21]

The North Korean state extolled participation in the waged workforce as a political, legal, moral and social responsibility for all adults of working age. The state classified the working age as aged 16 to 59 for men and 16 to 54 for women, that is, from the end of mandatory schooling to the

---

[18] I agree with the direction of travel of Hwang's comments that North Korea's social structure resembled that of Choson hierarchies but disagree with the inference that North Korean society, even in the Kim Il Sung era at the height of the state's capacity to enforce its will, could be understood as a caste system. There was always some social mobility and the rhetoric of the state, including from Kim Il Sung, was contradictory, sometimes condoning hereditary responsibility and sometimes warning about the dangers of overzealousness on this issue. In the post-Kim Il Sung era as is shown in this chapter social hierarchies became much more fluid. See Kyung Moon Hwang, 'Nation, State and the Modern Transformation of Korean Social Structure in the Early Twentieth Century', *History Compass*, Vol. 5, No. 2, 2007, pp. 330–46.

[19] Lee, 'Rural North Korea under Communism', p. 65.   [20] Ibid.

[21] Details of how the factory managers in large enterprises worked with local authorities to deliver social welfare functions can be found in Brun and Hersh, *Socialist Korea*, pp. 356–7.

beginning of the legal retirement age.[22] All able-bodied adults below the pension age, including those incarcerated in prisons, were required by law to participate in the workforce.[23] Absence from the workforce was generally only permitted for reasons of participation in higher education, disability, sickness or maternity.[24] The labour laws prohibited children under the age of 16 from working and by and large children did not participate in the workforce as it was compulsory for them to attend school until they were 16.[25]

Unemployment did not officially exist in North Korea in the sense that any individual was out of work and seeking a job, but this did not mean that all adults were in waged work. In 1993, the total working age population was 12,011,000 but 1,259,212 individuals were categorised as 'non-working'.[26] Most of the non-working were involved in alternative activities that were legitimated by the state as contributing to nation-building – including the 686,809 attending university and the 49,308 participating in other forms of adult education.[27] Just 57,833 were classed as non-working by virtue of disability.[28]

The main anomaly in Kim Il Sung's occupational structures were the 465,262 individuals, all female, classed as non-working 'by choice'

---

[22] Sun Won Hong, *Analysis of 1993 Population Census Data DPR Korea* (Pyongyang: Population Center, 1996), p. 60.

[23] Foreign Languages Publishing House, *The Socialist Labour Law of the Democratic People's Republic of Korea, 18 April 1978* (Pyongyang: Foreign Languages Publishing House, 1986).

[24] DPRK Government, 'Replies by the Government of the Democratic People's Republic of Korea to the List of Issues: Democratic People's Republic of Korea, 04/09/03', *Committee on Economic, Social and Cultural Rights, Thirty-first Session Item 6 of the Provisional Agenda* (Geneva: Office of the High Commissioner for Human Rights, 10–28 November 2003), available at www.bayefsky.com/issuesresp/rokorea_hr_cescr_none_2003_1.pdf, accessed 3 November 2014.

[25] Foreign Languages Publishing House, *The Socialist Labour Law of the Democratic People's Republic of Korea, 18 April 1978* (Pyongyang: Foreign Languages Publishing House, 1986). School enrolment was reportedly nearly 100 per cent. See UNICEF, *An Analysis of the Situation of Children and Women in the Democratic People's Republic of Korea 2000* (Pyongyang: UNICEF, 1999), p. 78. A DPRK report stated that there are 'no drop-out pupils due to heavy burdens of tuition fees and family economical reasons'. See National EFA 2000 Assessment Group, Democratic People's Republic of Korea, *National EFA Assessment Report: The Implementation of the 'World Declaration on Education for All'* (Pyongyang: National EFA 2000 Assessment Group, 1999), p. 18. Attendance rates were undoubtedly very high during the Kim Il Sung period as it was state policy for children to attend school; children were prohibited from working; schools provided the key socialisation space for the government and effective state sanctions were in place to enforce the law.

[26] Hong, *Analysis of 1993 Population Census Data*, p. 75.   [27] Ibid.   [28] Ibid.

in 1993.[29] The 1993 figures probably represented pre-1989 arrangements or what were understood as 'normal' social status as the census was undertaken when famine was underway and many families still hoped that the economy would recover quickly and things would go back to pre-economic collapse days. These figures imply that even when Kim Il Sungist ideological control was most effective many women and their families openly evaded the strict letter of the law on labour participation. By virtue of their choice not to work, these half a million women and their families were rejecting an important foundation of the philosophy and practice of the Kim Il Sungist state, which was that all adults who could, should participate in the waged workforce. The reporting of almost half a million 'housewives' as non-employed in the waged workforce also indicated that, prior to economic collapse, a considerable number of households had been well-off enough to feed and support at least one non-earning adult in the home.

The government tolerated this gender 'anomaly' because non-working 'housewives' tended to be aged over 50 and more likely than their younger colleagues to be non-working due to sickness. The tacit approach by local authorities was that as long as the household was fulfilling its social and economic responsibilities to the community and state, the family would not be sanctioned. Most importantly, both government and society considered it natural that women would stay at home if the family could manage without the state-provided food rations that they would forego if the woman was not participating in the waged workforce.

Occupation as social status

The social status of families was directly related to occupational status and the population was categorised as farming families; workers and their families; and officials and their families.[30] In Kim Il Sungist terminology, the category of 'farmer' only included cooperative farmers and did not include waged workers on the 500 or so state farms, who were classed as 'workers' for planning purposes.[31] The social category of 'workers families' comprised all non-cooperative farming families, except for those classified as 'officials and their families'.

[29] Ibid.   [30] Ibid., p. 70.
[31] Roberto Christen and Gamal M. Ahmed, *Agriculture in DPRK* (Pyongyang: FAO, undated but probably 2001), p. 1.

In the country's first ever census in 1993, of the 11,004,842 persons active in the workforce; 6,944,058 persons were socially categorised as workers, 2,588,925 as farmers and 1,471,859 classified as 'officers' – the last category being a mistranslation of 'officials'.[32] The numbers did not include all adults as the census separately categorised the 691,000 predominantly young men living in military camps.[33] The 'worker' population included those working in heavy industry and other sectors including building and geology; transport and communication; land and urban management; commerce; education, culture and health; and what the 1993 census labelled as 'other' occupations.[34] The relatively small group of officials included all those employed full-time by the state on Party and security duties – much less than the total of Party members, which amounted to around three million in 1993.

The government recognised a cross-cutting category of worker, which it called the 'intellectuals'. These included scientists, educators, technicians and all those with tertiary education. The state had a schizophrenic attitude to those working as intellectuals. On the one hand they were valued as necessary for economic development.[35] On the other hand they were viewed with suspicion as independent thinkers and potentially therefore a challenge to the omnipotent wisdom of the Leader.[36]

In Kim Il Sung's North Korea intellectuals as they are normally conceived of in the rest of the world – as people engaged in independent analysis – were eradicated both physically and conceptually.[37] In the early post-war years, intellectuals were a target for physical elimination as they were considered to constitute potentially dangerous opposition to Kim's authority. Kim Il Sung advertised policies aimed at producing large numbers of intellectuals, but what he meant by this was the production of obedient, technically skilled people who would

---

[32] Hong, *Analysis of 1993 Population Census Data*, p. 71.

[33] On numbers of military see Central Bureau of Statistics/UNDP, *Thematic Roundtable Meeting on Agricultural Recovery and Environmental Protection for the DPRK* (Pyongyang: UNDP, 1998). On the exclusion of the military see Hong, *Analysis of 1993 Population Census Data*, p. 64.

[34] Ibid., p. 70.

[35] Kim Il Sung, 'The Role of Intellectuals in Building an Independent New Society', in Kim Il Sung, *Works, Vol. 35* (Pyongyang: Foreign Languages Publishing House, 1990), pp. 222–31.

[36] Foreign Languages Publishing House, *Intellectuals should Become Fighters True to the Party and the Socialist Cause: Report to the Conference of Korean Intellectuals* (Pyongyang: Foreign Languages Publishing House, 1992).

[37] Kim, *North Korea under Kim Jong Il*, pp. 165–91.

not engage in critical or independent thinking that would in any way challenge state policy.[38] Innovative workers were required to provide indigenous economic development but at the same time these workers were penalised if they expressed views that could in any way be interpreted as being contrary to the state's policies. Individuals tended to be cautious about generating new ideas for which they could suffer penalties and so the quality of scientifically grounded knowledge diminished as creativity was coerced out of the system.

State policy and practice tried hard to produce intellectuals who were unquestioningly obedient to Kim Il Sung. The contradiction of trying to produce creative and intelligent people who could contribute to economic development and at the same time operate as unthinking perpetuators of Kim Il Sungism was never resolved and intellectuals were constantly admonished for not being better revolutionaries. The state's continuing need for castigation of the educated suggests, however, that even within the confines of very closely monitored intellectual production, university-educated young people were not entirely indoctrinated into uncritical acceptance of Kim Il Sungism.[39]

Income and food rations

The rationing system was directly linked to occupational status in that basic goods, including food, were allocated around a set of criteria determined by a matrix of occupation, gender and age, and the ration coupon was distributed by the enterprise.[40] Income and food allocations were not determined directly by social status, social class or Party membership but, because occupation was determined by political as well as technical criteria, the indirect impact of the system was to exclude non-Party members from some jobs that could attract higher food rations, such as managerial positions. Individuals in low-paid jobs would inevitably fare worse when times were tight and be relatively more vulnerable to malnutrition when food shortages occurred. Not all higher-rated jobs for food allocation purposes were, however, occupied by Party members. Miners and heavy industrial workers, not all of whom were Party members, were allocated the top rate of food ration.

---

[38] Foreign Languages Publishing House, *Intellectuals should Become Fighters.*   [39] Ibid.
[40] For details of the occupation-based food rationing system prior to the breakdown of the system in the 1990s, see Nathanail, *Food and Nutrition Assessment.*

The ration system was introduced in 1946 and expanded such that by the 1970s, the non-farming population was dependent on the public distribution system for food as well as for non-food basic goods, including fuel.[41] The scope, scale and longevity of the rationing system were unusual even for communist countries. In the Soviet Union food ration systems had been used only three times, in cases of national emergency, and the last time had been during the Second World War.[42] In Kim Il Sungist North Korea, all but the very rich and the very privileged relied on the basic ration that was allocated and managed directly by the state and which was channelled to the population through two separate allocation and distribution mechanisms. One was designed to meet the needs of workers and officials and their families and is known in English as the public distribution system or PDS. The other mechanism was designed to meet the requirements of cooperative famers and their families.

For non-farmers, the workplace provided the ration card through which the worker obtained a minimum entitlement to basic food supplies.[43] The workplace determined housing allocations and provided the gateway to other social benefits such as the right to travel.[44] Workers and officials physically received their food entitlements from the nearest of the 3,600 public distribution centres, where they collected basic rations once every fortnight for themselves and their families.[45] Individual allocations depended on work points determined by occupation, gender and the age and gender of dependents.[46] A miner or worker in heavy industry could expect a ration of 900 grams of cereal a day – commonly in the form of maize or rice – while a young child might be allocated between 50 to 200 grams of grain per day.[47]

[41] Bong Dae Choi and Kab Woo Koo, 'The Development of Farmers' Markets in North Korean Cities', in Phillip H. Park (ed.), *The Dynamics of Change in North Korea: An Institutionalist Perspective* (Seoul: IFES Kyungnam University Press, 2009), pp. 90 and 98.

[42] Hyung-min Joo, 'Visualizing the Invisible Hands: The Shadow Economy in North Korea', *Economy and Society*, Vol. 39, No 1, February 2010, p. 112.

[43] On historic food shortages see Suk Lee, 'Food Shortages and Economic Institutions in the Democratic People's Republic of Korea', doctoral dissertation (Department of Economics, University of Warwick, January 2003).

[44] Nathanail, *Food and Nutrition Assessment*.

[45] FAO/WFP, *Crop and Food Supply Assessment Mission to the Democratic People's Republic of Korea, Special Report* (Pyongyang, FAO/WFP, 6 December 1996), pp. 10–11; United Nations, *DPR Korea Common Country Assessment 2002* (Pyongyang: UNOCHA, February 2003), p. 16.

[46] Nathanail, *Food and Nutrition Assessment*, p. 24.

[47] There is agreement in the literature on the maximum entitlement of 900g per day. See Tae-Jin Kwon and Woon-Keun Kim, 'Assessment of Food Supply in North Korea', *Journal of Rural Development*, Vol. 22, Winter 1999, p. 51; Central Bureau of Statistics/ UNDP, *Thematic Roundtable Meeting*, p. 19. The former source, however, cites the 100g

Food and other goods like clothes and school books that were also provided through the PDS were not free but they were sold at very low, government-subsidised prices.[48]

Farmers and their families received entitlement to food and social benefits via the cooperative farm of which they were a member, but the distribution mechanism differed from that applicable to workers and officials. Farming families received a proportion of the harvest once a year and were also permitted small private plots for non-grain production. The annual allocation of grain was based on the agricultural productivity of the cooperative farm. A complicated points system based on occupation as well as productivity of individual work-teams provided the means to allocate grain to individual families within the cooperative farm.[49]

Cooperative farms were supposed to produce enough food and/or generate enough income to cover food, housing, energy, education and cultural life for all farm workers and their families.[50] The farm was responsible for providing and maintaining social welfare facilities including nurseries, kindergartens and clinics. Cooperative farms were also supposed to generate enough surplus to pay for farm investment, including the purchase of seed, fertiliser and equipment.[51] In practice, however, only the most productive farms were able to produce a surplus. Many poorer farms in less agriculturally productive regions never even achieved self-sufficiency in food. Consequently these farmers and their families relied on grain transfers from other farms and subsidies from the government.[52]

Regional loyalties

North Korea is not a large country – with a land area of 123,000 square kilometres it is about the size of Pennsylvania or Mississippi – but it has, like South Korea, distinct regional characteristics.[53] These regional

---

figure for 'kindergarten' age children while UNDP cites the 300g figure for 'babies'. There appears to be a dual mistake here. A better source is the report written by a nutritionist who reports a graduated grain allocation from 50g a day for infants aged 3 to 7 months, to kindergarten age children (5–6 years) being allocated a ration of 150g per day, and primary school age children 200g per day. See Nathanail, *Food and Nutrition Assessment*, p. 26.

[48] Ibid., pp. 24–5.   [49] Lee, 'Rural North Korea under Communism', pp. 95–8.
[50] Christen and Ahmed, *Agriculture in DPRK*.
[51] Nathanail, *Food and Nutrition Assessment*, pp. 10–12.   [52] Ibid., p. 25.
[53] Sung Ung Kim (ed.), *Panorama of Korea* (Pyongyang: Foreign Languages Publishing House, 1999), p. 1.

characteristics are evidenced in linguistic differences, the most well-known perhaps being the dialects of the Hamgyong provinces in the north-east and the Pyongan provinces in the south-west.[54] Poor transport infrastructure had historically consolidated regional identification because of the natural constraints on mobility provided by the mountainous topography and inhospitable climate.[55]

Regional loyalties were understood by the state as providing a potential source of dangerous political division and a threat to what state propaganda idealised as 'monolithic unity'.[56] Regional policy was designed to ensure that citizens identify themselves primarily by reference to national political ideas rather than to geographical origin. The goal was that geographical location should only provide an informational category for planning purposes and should not support historic notions of regional demarcation and identity. The 1993 census delineated three official administrative regions; these were the western coastal area, the inland area and the east coastal area.[57]

In the effort to eradicate grounds for complaint about regional disparities, social and economic policy attempted to ameliorate economic and social inequalities between urban and rural areas; coast, plains and mountains; and between the north-eastern industrial cities and the agricultural heartlands of the south. Security priorities constrained travel, thus compounding the consolidation of regional identity formation, but at the same time policy was implemented that was designed to minimise regional inequality as a source of grievance. Food was redistributed from southern food surplus provinces to the grain deficit provinces of the north-east. Regional loyalties were also diffused by the geographical mobility that became a feature of the system of military service. The state permanently relocated demobilised soldiers away from their natal homes

[54] Sun Joo Kim (ed.), *The Northern Region of Korea: History, Identity and Culture* (Seattle: University of Washington Press, 2010). For detailed discussion of Korean dialects see Ross King, 'Dialectical Variation in Korean', in Ho-Min Sohn (ed.), *Korean Language in Culture and Society* (Honolulu: University of Hawai'i Press, 2006), pp. 264–80.

[55] Central Bureau of Statistics, *Democratic People's Republic of Korea Preliminary Report of the National Nutrition Survey October 2012* (Pyongyang: Central Bureau of Statistics Pyongyang, 2012), p. 5.

[56] For discussion of different understandings of what historically constituted a region in Korea, see Shannon McCune, 'Geographic Regions in Korea', *Geographical Review*, Vol. 39, No. 4, 1949, pp. 658–60.

[57] Hong, *Analysis of 1993 Population Census Data DPR Korea* (Pyongyang: Population Center, 1996).

to where the state deemed them most needed for post-military service employment.[58]

The Kim Il Sungist state discarded the family lineage system that classified individuals by family name, geographical origin and male head of household (and which prevailed in South Korea until its formal abolition in 2005) when it abolished the family register system in 1947.[59] The replacement of the household register with a citizenship registration card did not, however, mean that families stopped considering geographical origin as an important part of their social identity or that gendered hierarchies disappeared.[60]

Women: formal equality and separate functions

Kim Il Sungist policy was to treat women as equal to men in legal status and intellectual capacities but to argue that women and men had naturally different functions in the society, based on the biological role of women in reproduction. Kim Il Sung argued that women and men were like two wheels of a wagon in the work of nation-building. He stated that 'a society cannot develop on a sound basis when only men fulfil their duties'.[61] In the Kim Il Sungist state, the adult male population was primarily valued for its contribution to economic development while the female population was valued for its maternal role in bringing up new generations of revolutionaries.

Public ideology consecrated women as mothers and care-takers but this did not mean that women were confined to the home. Adult women were expected to engage in paid work, to participate in mass mobilisations and at the same time were responsible for taking care of domestic tasks within the family.[62] In 1993, an astounding 89 per cent of adult women of working age (16–54) were reported as employed in the paid workforce, compared to 94 per cent of men of working age (16–59).[63]

---

[58] Lee, 'Rural North Korea under Communism', p. 141.
[59] Ibid., pp. 142–4; Suzy Kim, 'Revolutionary Mothers: Women in the North Korean Revolution, 1945–1950', *Comparative Studies in Society and History*, Vol. 52, No. 4, p. 763.
[60] Lee, 'Rural North Korea under Communism', p. 142.
[61] Compilation Committee of Kim Il Sung Encyclopaedia, *Kim Il Sung Encyclopaedia Volume One* (New Delhi: Vishwanath, 1992), p. 577.
[62] Hazel Smith, *WFP DPRK Programmes and Activities: A Gender Perspective* (Pyongyang: WFP, 1999), p. 38
[63] UNDP and DPRK government, *Report of the Thematic Roundtable Meeting on Agricultural Recovery and Environmental Protection* (Geneva: UNDP, 28–9 May 1998), Table #8: Labour Force and Employment (no page number given).

According to the United Nations Development Programme (UNDP) the 1995 census showed that the DPRK had probably the highest female participation rate in the labour force in the world.[64] Young women aged 16–19 were least likely to be engaged in the labour force, with a participation rate of 66 per cent, while the highest participation rate was for women aged 20 to 24, at 93 per cent.[65] From age 25 to 34, the female participation rate was 87 per cent.[66]

Women were not formally excluded from jobs that were conventionally understood as male preserves. There were no legal barriers to women becoming pilots, engineers, heavy industrial workers and senior politicians, but relatively few women entered these professions. In 1993 women made up slightly less than half of the total workforce at just over 5.4 million, compared to just under 5.7 million men.[67] Women comprised just over half of the workforce in industry and just under half the workforce in agriculture.[68] As industry and agriculture together employed just under two-thirds of the workforce, these figures superficially indicated an even spread of men and women in the workforce. The 1993 census also reported, however, that female employees were employed disproportionately in different sectors of the economy. The North Korean report on the census returns, written in English and published in 1996, states that the number of females in the workforce 'was over ... half, but it was related with high female proportion in the light industry sections'.[69] Women were employed in 'commodity circulation ... and purchasing and food administration bodies, the female proportion of which was 68.3 per cent ... And then [the] next [economic sectors] ... with high proportion [of females] are education, culture and art, and medical fields, in which 60 per cent of the female[s] worked.'[70]

Women predominated in the retail sector and service sectors, including childcare, nursing and education. Similarly to many other countries, this work was rhetorically valued, but in practice these 'women's jobs' were paid less and had less social status than 'men's jobs'.[71]

[64] Ibid., p. 8.
[65] Ibid., Table #8: Labour Force and Employment (no page number given).   [66] Ibid.
[67] Hong, *Analysis of 1993 Population Census Data*, p. 69. The document is written in English and has probably been translated into English from Korean. There are some infelicities in language, but these do not affect meaning and intelligibility.
[68] Ibid.   [69] Ibid.   [70] Ibid.
[71] Young-Hee Shim, 'Human Rights of Women in North Korea: Factors and Present State', in Kie-Duck Park and Sang-Jin Han (eds.), *Human Rights in North Korea: Toward a Comprehensive Understanding* (Sungnam: The Sejong Institute, 2007), pp. 182–3.

The 1993 census further reports that 'the sections with the lowest proportion of ... female[s] are ... building, geological prospecting and transportation, [and the] communication service. These sections are hard for female[s] to work because of the characteristics of the job, so three-fourths of the population working here were males.'

Kim Il Sung argued that North Korea encouraged women's participation in the workforce to revolutionise women so that they could become more supportive wives and mothers to their husbands and children, who were building the new socialist North Korea.[72] The policy was not, he argued, pursued for economic reasons, as the policy was expensive, presumably because of the cost of state provision of childcare and social services.[73] Kim's argument was that participation in the organised workplace would allow women to obtain political, economic and social experiences that would make her a socialist mother, capable of inculcating socialist values within the family. These arguments were somewhat disingenuous given North Korea's perennial labour shortages but they reflected a deep-seated notion that women were important primarily as mothers.

Women who grew up in the Kim Il Sung period were literate and numerate but socialised to understand their 'natural' role as domestic worker within the family. Naturalised distinctions were reflected in education. All girls were enrolled in school, as were boys, but girls studied domestic science while boys studied basic mechanics.[74]

Kim Il Sung promoted an active, interventionist social policy towards women to provide support for women's domestic work. Policies were not designed to encourage change in gendered norms so that, for example, men might share in housework and childcare. Nevertheless, these social support programmes brought real benefits and entailed significant improvements to living standards for many women and men. For the first time in Korean history, women were given access to healthcare, educational opportunities and welfare services, such as the generous and paid time off work made available to pregnant women and mothers and the provision of pensions.[75] Given that domestic responsibilities were the domain of women, government social reforms that introduced

---

[72] Compilation Committee, *Kim Il Sung Encyclopaedia Volume One*, p. 578.
[73] Ibid.   [74] National EFA 2000 Assessment Group, *Assessment Report*.
[75] Economic and Social Council, 'Implementation of the International Covenant on Economic, Social and Cultural Rights, Second Periodic Reports submitted by State Parties under Articles 16 and 17 of the Covenant: Addendum, Democratic People's Republic of Korea, E/1990/6/Add.35', mimeo, 15 May 2002, p. 5.

free housing and provided utilities to homes went a considerable way to improve women's quality of life.

The state aimed to 'socialise' housework with the intention of giving women more time to participate in activities outside the home.[76] The food production industry was geared towards providing 'instant' noodles and food that would require little preparation.[77] The public distribution centres delivered food to households if women could not collect food because they were at work. Public laundries were established so that women would not have to spend time on cleaning clothes. There is little data about the scale and scope of 'take-out food' provision although, if it at all parallels the development of nationwide childcare facilities, it is likely to have been extensive and comprehensive. In addition women's domestic responsibilities within the home were recognised such that one of the explicit aims of state policy was to 'reduce their [women's] house burdens'.[78] Policy focused on providing labour-saving devices, more public transport and better water supplies but it was still expected that women, not men, supply domestic labour.[79]

As women in the DPRK did not normally have their first child until after the age of 25, high female labour participation figures meant that pregnant women and mothers of young children in the DPRK were very likely to be engaged in employment out of the home. Working mothers were helped by five months' paid maternity leave and provision.[80] They also benefited from reduced hours of work on full pay if they had three or more children.[81] Working women depended heavily on the children's institutions – including pre-school nurseries and the schools. Many women sent their children to residential nurseries and only saw their children at weekends, such was the emphasis on ensuring women participated in the paid workforce.[82]

[76] Kyung Ae Park, 'Ideology and Women in North Korea', in Han S. Park (ed.), *North Korea: Ideology, Politics, Economy* (Englewood Cliffs: Prentice Hall, 1996), pp. 76–7.

[77] This paragraph draws on Smith, *WFP DPRK Programmes and Activities*, p. 38.

[78] Kim Il Sung, 'Let us Further Develop Local Industry', in Kim Il Sung, *Works*, Vol. 35 (Pyongyang: Foreign Languages Publishing House, 1989), p. 166; Compilation Committee, *Kim Il Sung Encyclopaedia Volume One*; Hwan Ju Pang, *Korean Review* (Pyongyang: Foreign Languages Publishing House, 1987), pp. 156–7.

[79] Song, *Economic Development in the DPRK*, pp. 41 and 49.

[80] Foreign Languages Publishing House, *Korea Guidebook* (Pyongyang: Foreign Languages Publishing House, 1989), p. 128.

[81] Masood Hyder, 'The Status of Women in the DPRK' (Pyongyang: UNOCHA, 5 September 2003), available at http://reliefweb.int/report/democratic-peoples-republic-korea-status-women-dprk, accessed 8 November 2014.

[82] UNICEF, *Situation Analysis of Women and Children in the DPRK* (Pyongyang: UNICEF, 1999).

Moulding the youth

The function of the League of Socialist Working Youth of Korea, renamed the Kim Il Sung Socialist Youth League in 1996, was to reproduce generations of North Koreans as disciplined, obedient to the Leader and ready to sacrifice themselves for the nation, whether in the economic arena or in the military. The aim was to enrol all young people from the age of 14 to 29.[83] Young people joined in high school, and membership included university and college students.[84] In 1987, towards the end of the Kim Il Sung era, membership was reported to be over 3.8 million.[85] The primary function of the youth organisation was to inculcate political fervour in young people while they were in 'their ideological and mental adolescence' so that 'they can be moulded into a revolutionary generation'.[86]

The primary responsibility of young people was to study hard and attend school until at least aged 16, but young people also had other obligations. They were expected to participate in civil defence exercises through school and the youth organisation. Young people were expected to contribute to tasks such as the building of roads and power stations.[87] Students and youth were mobilised every year to help with the hugely labour-intensive tasks of transplanting seedlings and harvesting. The primary goal of youth mobilisation, however, was not economic but political. The rationale was to inculcate in young people that they must always put the interests of the state before their own.

Young people were subject to constant ideological socialisation in the youth organisation as well as in schools and workplaces. Kim Il Sung warned that: 'One does not become a revolutionary of one's own accord just because one's father is a revolutionary. Those youngsters who are brought up under [the] socialist system do not automatically adopt the communist creed. The historical experience and lessons of the international communist movement show that if the ideological education

---

[83] *Democratic People's Republic of Korea* Editorial Board, *Kim Jong Il: Short Biography* (Pyongyang: Foreign Languages Publishing House, 2001), p. 190

[84] Yong-Bok Li, *Education in the Democratic People's Republic of Korea* (Pyongyang: Foreign Languages Publishing House, 1986), p. 74; Soon-Hee Lim, *Value Changes of the North Korean New Generation and Prospects* (Seoul: Korea Institute for National Unification, 2007), p. 5.

[85] Pang, *Korean Review*, p. 85.

[86] Kim Jong Il, *Let us Exalt the Brilliance of Comrade Kim Il Sung's Idea of the Youth Movement and the Achievements Made under his Leadership* (Pyongyang: Foreign Languages Publishing House, 1996), p. 3.

[87] Li, *Education in the Democratic People's Republic of Korea*.

of youth and students is neglected, they will not work sincerely but live in indolence, loafing away their time.'[88]

All young people participated in some form of mobilisation as part of the routine of daily life. Young people might be enthusiastic about participating in high-profile events arranged for visiting dignitaries but less happy about having to migrate to the countryside, where physical conditions were tough, to help with transplanting rice or maize. Duties, such as the regular civil defence drills, could be irksome, but participation in state-funded and organised activities brought rewards, including organised vacations, trips to the seaside and the mountains, access to entertainment and participation in sporting activities. These benefits partially compensated for the ideological framework in which youth activities were set and the sheer effort of engaging in physical labour for which many of the urban youth were not well suited. Prescribed activities could be arduous and boring but they could also be fun and exciting. Young people socialised with each other as they participated in mass gymnastics, sports and trips to national landmarks such as Kumgansan (the Diamond Mountains) and the national park at Mount Myohyang.

Young people were not involved in organised activity all of the time. Young people, as anywhere in the world, found ways to hang out together, in parks, by the rivers, in sports venues as players and spectators, at the movies and in each other's homes. In the Kim Il Sungist period, young people did not frequent restaurants, because coupons issued by the workplace were required and these were not available to everyone. Restaurants tended to be the domain of older men and women, either families or older men out on their own after work (much like Japan), with the ubiquitous karaoke rooms well-used and popular (again like Japan). In Pyongyang, the most popular 'hanging out' venue for young people was the open space at the traffic intersection in front of the railway station where, in clement weather, young people met their friends, strolled around, squatted, sometimes playing guitars.

Family life

Kim Il Sungist society retained a conservative view of family life founded on marriage between a man and a woman that was constituted by hierarchical patterns in which husband and wife, parents and children

---

[88] Compilation Committee, *Kim Il Sung Encyclopaedia Volume One.*

had clearly defined social roles.[89] Government policy proclaimed the family as providing 'the basic unit of society' and the government translated a somewhat idealised understanding of the family into law.[90] The family was recognised in law as possessing rights and duties over and above the individual and was, unusually for communist societies, given ownership rights.[91] The family was seen as the natural framework in which the most vulnerable should live so that state policy promoted adoption for children without parental support and encouraged families to shelter and care for the elderly who did not have assistance from their own relatives.

It is perhaps not surprising that the family unit remained so important in North Korea, as long-standing Korean cultural norms highly valorised the family, which was envisioned as comprising ancestors as well as current living members.[92] The North Korean dictionary stipulated that 'a household is a family of one livelihood' and it remained the norm for households to be composed of the nuclear family comprised of parents, children, sometimes grandparents and, more rarely, extended family.[93] In law, a household could include individuals not related to each other by birth as long as they were sharing the same occupation and living together.[94] The congruence between household and livelihood represented a continuation of social norms that pre-dated Kim Il Sungism by several hundred years. It remained common for family members to work in similar occupations, especially in the rural areas.[95] It was also common for one family member to substitute for another in the workplace when required, especially in non-skilled work.

The government's promulgation of a conservative and idealised notion of family life helped Kim Il Sung to portray himself as restoring the national identity of an authentic Korea. Another spin-off for Kim Il Sung was that he was able to justify the institutional prerogatives of his own family by arguing that the Kim family provided the natural embodiment of Korean values.

[89] Foreign Languages Publishing House, *The Family Law of the Democratic People's Republic of Korea, 24 October 1990* (Pyongyang: Foreign Languages Publishing House, 1994), p. 2.

[90] Ibid., p. 1.

[91] Eun-Jung Lee, 'Family Law and Inheritance Law in North Korea', *Journal of Korean Law*, Vol. 5, No. 1, 2005, pp. 172–93.

[92] Kyung Moon Hwang, 'Citizenship, Social Equality and Government Reform: Changes in the Household Registration System in Korea, 1894–1910', *Modern Asian Studies*, Vol. 38, No. 2, 2004, pp. 355–87.

[93] Hong, *Analysis of 1993 Population Census Data*, p. 119.

[94] The DPRK Population Center offers a detailed discussion on what constituted a household in the DPRK. See Hong, *Analysis of 1993 Population Census Data DPR*, pp. 119–222.

[95] Ibid.

In practice, because of the huge commitment required by adults and children to the activities sponsored by the various collective organisations, the time available for family life was severely truncated.[96] The continuing demands for activity in the workplace and the community curtailed the time and energy available for personal lives.[97] As Party institutions always kept a watchful eye on signs of dissent, family life was hampered by the constant need for caution in private conversation. It could be dangerous if children and youth schooled in the idealism of state ideology overheard scepticism or disillusion expressed by older family members and repeated those conversations in the hearing of the many Party functionaries that populated all societal organisations including schools and workplaces.[98]

On the other hand it would be a mistake to think of North Koreans as lacking family, personal and private lives separate from their political and public lives. Young people chose their own marriage partners whom they met in a wide variety of venues – in the local community, through the family, at school, at college, in the military, at work or at play – although, like China until recently, they needed the permission of the workplace to marry. The family also provided a vehicle for the transmission of Korean customs that pre-dated Kim Il Sungism and remained a significant part of the culture. These included the norm that the eldest son take on the responsibility of looking after parents in old age and that the daughter-in-law should be obedient to her husband's parents.

The family was the only place within North Korean society where trust-based relationships could thrive – especially within and between adult members. It was the only social location in which non-state-controlled communication and relationships based on private not political relationships were considered legitimate and therefore authorised by the state. Indeed, the state justified the coercive practices of punishing entire families for the alleged crimes of individuals precisely because of the knowledge that it was only within the family that any discussion of anti-state or non-state-approved activity or ideas could take place.

A monolithic society ... in some respects

Kim Il Sung was successful in building a social structure based on political loyalty in that political status determined social status, but the aim of creating a monolithic society in which state policy dictated every

---

[96] UNICEF, *An Analysis of the Situation of Children and Women.*   [97] Ibid.

[98] Vasily Mikheev, 'Politics and Ideology in the Post-Cold War Era', in Han S. Park (ed.), *North Korea: Ideology, Politics, Economy* (Englewood Cliffs: Prentice Hall, 1996), pp. 87–104.

aspect of daily life was not achieved. The workers' state was an institution in which good jobs and a decent standard of living were accessed through political criteria but the society in which people lived out their daily lives was not entirely a product of social policy and political intention.

The failure to convince families of the benefits of women entering the waged workforce provides an example of embedded cultural ideas trumping communist exhortation. Social policy that prioritised the youth did not succeed in overturning age hierarchies in North Korean society. The ideal of the family as the core unit of society that possessed hereditary rights, duties and responsibilities demonstrated the longevity and strength of pre-Kim Il Sungist ideas. In the 1990s, when the population confronted starvation and the state failed, many were saved from catastrophe only because of these norms and social practices that had pre-dated and survived Kim Il Sungism, most notably the society-wide expectation that women had primary responsibility for food provision.

The Kim family leadership perceived the end of the Cold War in Europe as providing the opportunity for the exercise of untrammelled power by the United States and feared military intervention from abroad to secure regime change. The government attempted diplomatic engagement with South Korea but also engaged in a nuclear development programme so as to provide the option of building a North Korean nuclear weapon. Kim's policies were challenged by the United States administration of President Clinton to the point that both sides understood the outbreak of war as imminent in mid-1994.[1] Only a last-minute intervention by former United States President Jimmy Carter de-escalated the conflict and allowed for bilateral negotiations that continued after Kim Il Sung's death, in July 1994 aged 82. The North Korean political establishment continued to negotiate with the United States to produce the 'Agreed Framework', sometimes known as the Geneva Agreement for the location in which it was signed, in October 1994.

The diplomatic crisis of the early 1990s consumed government attention to the extent that the economic crisis, triggered by the decision of the Soviet Union and China to end subsidies to the DPRK, was initially treated by the North Korean government as similar in scale to crises of previous eras. The population was urged to do more with less and muddle through. The government made defence cuts but these were not substantial enough to have much of an impact on the expanding economic crisis that developed into a national food emergency.

Kim Il Sung and Kim Jong Il initially appeared paralysed by the scale and scope of what turned into a catastrophe for North Korea's population, as both continued to prioritise regime security over economic

---

[1] For the North Korean perspective see Chol Nam Jon, *A Duel of Reason between Korea and US: Nuke, Missile and Artificial Satellite* (Pyongyang: Foreign Languages Publishing House, 2000). For analysis of the United States perspective see Leon D. Sigal, *Disarming Strangers: Nuclear Diplomacy with North Korea* (Princeton University Press, 1998); Joel S. Wit, Daniel B. Poneman and Robert L. Gallucci, *Going Critical: The First North Korean Nuclear Crisis* (Washington, DC: Brookings Institution Press, 2005).

policy. Industrial and agricultural production plummeted. Most of the population had few alternatives to state provision as private production was minimal and markets were undeveloped. When the state's food distribution system finally collapsed in the mid-1990s, starvation ensued and the resulting famine killed up to a million people between 1993 and 1998.[2]

In the face of continuing acute food shortages and state ineffectiveness, families and communities were left to look after themselves. The 21 million or so who survived the famine did so because they engaged in self-help. These self-reliant activities owed little to government ideology and were a product of initiatives 'from below' – often in the face of government policy. These survival initiatives included swapping, selling and producing food and goods for private consumption and for private trade. To survive, individuals and communities created a marketised society 'by default'.

Regime vulnerability

The end of the Cold War in Europe brought an end to the more or less unwavering diplomatic support from the Soviet Union and the communist states of eastern and central Europe that the DPRK had relied on since the Korean War. Kim Il Sung could no longer rely on the nuclear weapons of the former Soviet Union to provide strategic defence. At the same time, China's policies that focused on developing economic capacity through integration in globalised capitalist markets entailed an effort to develop better relations with North Korea's adversaries, including South Korea and the United States. The Soviet Union

[2] The most rigorous analysis of the causation and context of the famine can be found in Suk Lee, 'Food Shortages and Economic Institutions in the Democratic People's Republic of Korea', doctoral dissertation (Department of Economics, University of Warwick, January 2003). See also Daniel Goodkind and Loraine West, 'The North Korean Famine and its Demographic Impact', *Population and Development Review*, Vol. 27, No. 2, June 2001; Hazel Smith, *Hungry for Peace: International Security, Humanitarian Assistance and Social Change in North Korea* (Washington, DC: United States Institute of Peace Press, 2005); Hazel Smith, 'The Disintegration and Reconstitution of the State in the DPRK', in Simon Chesterman, Michael Ignatieff and Ramesh Thakur (eds.), *Making States Work* (Tokyo: United Nations Press, 2005), pp. 167–92; W. Courtland Robinson, Myung Ken Lee, Kenneth Hill and Gilbert M. Burnham, 'Mortality in North Korean Migrant Households: A Retrospective Study', *The Lancet*, Vol. 354, No. 9175, Saturday 24 July 1999. For American scholarship that argues for the moral culpability of the government as the most important causational factor see Andrew S. Natsios, *The Great North Korean Famine: Famine, Politics and Foreign Policy* (Washington, DC: United States Institute of Peace Press, 2001) and Stephan Haggard and Marcus Noland, *Famine in North Korea: Markets, Aid and Reform* (New York: Columbia University Press, 2007).

and China established diplomatic relations with South Korea, in 1990 and 1992 respectively.[3]

In June 1990, the North Korean media denounced President Gorbachev's negotiations with South Korean president Roh Tae-Woo as 'criminal dealings'.[4] In September 1990, Gorbachev's foreign minister, Eduard Shevardnadze, visited Pyongyang to discuss the Soviet Union's realignment in international politics. North Korean officials told Shevardnadze that in the absence of strategic protection by the Soviet Union's nuclear umbrella they would have to consider all other options.[5] The implied threat was that North Korea would build its own nuclear weapons. North Korean officials did not hide their anger at what they considered a betrayal. Shevardnadze was treated so disrespectfully that on his return to Moscow he brought forward the schedule for diplomatic recognition of South Korea.

Boris Yeltsin, who led the post-communist government of the Russian Federation, created in December 1991 until 1999, had nothing but contempt for Kim Il Sung and when the Soviet Union's 1961 defence treaty with the DPRK was renegotiated in 1992 the commitment to support North Korea in time of war was much diluted. In the initial years of the new democratic Russia, no domestic constituency was prepared to argue for a continued commitment to North Korea on strategic or any other grounds.[6] The new Russia stopped providing loans, cheap oil and subsidised technology and both the Russian state and Russia's new capitalist consumers were not willing to buy poor-quality North Korean exports, given their new-found ability to access Western markets.[7] Economic relationships between the two states were

---

[3] Georgy Bulychev, 'Korean Security Dilemmas: A Russian Perspective', in Hazel Smith (ed.), *Reconstituting Korean Security: A Policy Primer* (Tokyo: United Nations Press, 2007), p. 187; Xiao Ren, 'Korean Security Dilemmas: Chinese Policies', in Hazel Smith (ed.), *Reconstituting Korean Security: A Policy Primer* (Tokyo: United Nations Press, 2007), p. 147.

[4] Quote from *Rodong Shinmun*, Pyongyang, 12 June 1990, p. 2, cited in Natalya Bazhanova, 'North Korea's Decision to Develop an Independent Nuclear Program', in James Clay Moltz and Alexandre Y. Mansourov (eds.), *The North Korean Nuclear Program: Security, Strategy and New Perspectives from Russia* (2000), p. 130.

[5] Bulychev, 'Korean Security Dilemmas'. On Shevardnadze's visit to Pyongyang in September 1990 in the context of deteriorating DPRK–Soviet relationships at the end of the Cold War, see also Jane Shapiro Zacek, 'Russia in North Korean Foreign Policy', in Samuel S. Kim, *North Korean Foreign Relations in the Post-Cold War Era* (Oxford University Press, 1998), pp. 80–3.

[6] Evgeniy P. Bazhanov, 'Russian Views of the Agreed Framework and the Four-Party Talks', in James Clay Moltz and Alexandre Y. Mansourov (eds.), *The North Korean Nuclear Program: Security, Strategy and New Perspectives from Russia* (London: Routledge, 2000), p. 197.

[7] Ibid., p. 219.

transformed as bilateral trade between the two states fell from $3.5 billion in 1988 to a tiny $100 million in 1995.[8]

Diplomatic relations degenerated into public name-calling. In December 1995, without mentioning Yeltsin by name, Kim Jong Il made a written denunciation of 'modern revisionists and renegade socialists ... [who] have driven socialism to degeneration and collapse'. Kim wrote that the blame for the demise of the communist states lies with 'traitors [who] claimed that they are carrying out "reform" and "restructuring" for "democracy" and "economic welfare"' and who no longer respect 'Marx, Engels, Lenin and Stalin as the leaders of the working class'.[9]

The DPRK's growing diplomatic isolation was compounded by a sense of increased military vulnerability. In February 1991, the large but low-tech Iraqi army disintegrated in the face of the United States-led Operation Desert Storm and was wiped out in days. The Iraqi army, like the North Korean army, had been understood worldwide as being imbued by nationalist fervour that would sustain the million-strong armed forces in combat. The rapid collapse of the Iraqi forces was also unexpected because, unlike the Korean People's Army, military commanders had experience of battle from the brutal Iran–Iraq conflict that had been fought through the 1980s. The message for DPRK political and military leaders was that confidence in the capacity of their conventional forces to withstand foreign intervention might be misplaced. This was particularly so given that the DPRK's famed million-man army, like the population as a whole, was increasingly tired, hungry and demoralised.

North Korea's leaders responded to increasing diplomatic isolation and military vulnerability by trying to reduce the risk of North–South armed conflict. North Korea re-engaged diplomatically with the South after an interregnum of nearly twenty years, and in September 1990 the North Korean premier of the Administration Council (in effect the Cabinet), Yon Hyong Muk, led a delegation of civilian and military officials to meet with counterparts in Seoul.[10] The subsequent North–South talks resulted in two diplomatic agreements; the 1991 'Basic Agreement on

---

[8] Figures from Russian language source, quoted with full citation in James Clay Moltz, 'The Renewal of Russian-North Korean Relations', in James Clay Moltz and Alexandre Y. Mansourov (eds.), *The North Korean Nuclear Program: Security, Strategy and New Perspectives from Russia* (London: Routledge, 2000), pp. 219–20.

[9] Kim Jong Il, 'Respecting Seniors in the Revolution is a Noble Moral Obligation of Revolutionaries', in Délégation générale de la RPD de Corée en France, *Bulletin d'information, Special Issue* (Paris: Délégation générale de la RPD de Corée en France, 27 December 1995), pp. 1–4.

[10] Délégation générale de la RPD de Corée en France, 'First-day Sitting of First North-South High-Level Talks', in *Bulletin d'information, No. 11/990* (Paris: Délégation générale de la RPD de Corée en France, 7 September 1990), pp. 1–2.

reconciliation and non-aggression', and the 1992 North–South agreement on 'the denuclearisation of the Korean Peninsula'.[11] The talks between the two sets of officials did not, however, result in a substantive rapprochement and were characterised by mistrust throughout. North Korean officials complained throughout that South negotiating behaviour was disingenuous. In a sideswipe at South Korea's attempts to secure support from the Soviet Union, Yon Hyong Muk told South Korean counterparts that '... far from trying to settle national problems between fellow countrymen at the talks, you [sic] entreating foreign countries for intervention and interference in an effort to force your will upon the other side ... In accordance with the "northern policy" your high-level authorities visit different countries and ask them to help you in "guiding" us towards "openness". It cannot but be considered as an extremely insidious and provocative act of attempting to force us to change our system with the help of others.'[12]

The DPRK government reduced defence spending in the early 1990s, cutting the defence budget from 12 per cent of planned national expenditure in 1990 to 11.4 per cent in 1994.[13] The Korean People's Army (KPA) reported in 1991 that it had made troop reductions of 100,000 and mobilised the armed forces for civilian construction.[14] These cuts were likely taken as a result of reduced economic support from former allies but they did not imply radical reduction in military expenditure. Even in the face of growing economic crisis, defence expenditures remained protected and still consumed a large share of national resources. DPRK military spending was also likely underestimated given that almost all able-bodied adults were allocated civil defence functions

---

[11] Nada Takashi, *Korea in Kim Jong Il's Era* (Pyongyang: Foreign Languages Publishing House, 2000), pp. 85–6; Charles K. Armstrong, 'North Korea's South Korea Policy: Tactical Change, Strategic Consistency', in Sung Chull Kim and David C. Kang (eds.), *Engagement with North Korea: A Viable Alternative* (Albany: SUNY Press, 2009), pp. 231–2.

[12] Délégation générale de la RPD de Corée en France, 'Keynote Speech of the Premier of the Administration Council of the DPRK at Third Inter-Korean High Talks', in *Bulletin d'information, Special Issue* (Paris: Délégation générale de la RPD de Corée en France, 14 December 1990), p. 9.

[13] Chung-in Moon and Sangkeun Lee, 'Military Spending and the Arms Race on the Korean Peninsula', *Asian Perspective*, Vol. 33, No. 4, 2009, p. 81.

[14] Délégation générale de la RPD de Corée en France, *Communiqué of the Supreme Command of the Korean People's Army* (Paris: Délégation générale de la RPD de Corée en France, 26 February 1991). A government statement issued on 28 May 1991 reported that 250,000 'officers and men' of the KPA had been sent to work at 'peaceful construction sites'. It is not clear if the 250,000 were demobilised or on temporary duties. See Délégation générale de la RPD de Corée en France, *Bulletin d'information, No. 11/591* (Paris: Délégation générale de la RPD de Corée en France, 28 May 1991), p. 2.

in a nationwide structure of reservists. Actual expenditure on the military could have been as high as 30 per cent of the budget in the first half of the 1990s.[15]

The 'first nuclear crisis'

The KPA was uneasy about diplomatic engagement with the South. In 1991 it issued a public statement arguing that a military imbalance existed on the Korean peninsula because of North Korea's unilateral troop reductions.[16] The KPA would have been aware of increases in the South Korean defence budget, which doubled between 1984 and 1990 to a figure that in absolute terms was eighteen times that of the DPRK defence budget.[17] In 1991 the KPA stalled moves to reduce the numbers of troops and civilians mobilised for defence activities when it announced that 'no one can vouch that the "Team Spirit 91" … exercises may not go over to a real war', and it ordered national mobilisation of all the armed forces and militias.[18]

North Korea argued that South Korea had linked the 1990/1 Gulf War (the first Iraq war) to a 'fictitious threat from the north … spreading rumours that the north would invade the south' thus providing an excuse for 'reckless military exercises'.[19] The North Korean government and the KPA made frequent statements as to the alleged threat from the 50,000 American troops stationed in South Korea, South Korea's rising military expenditure and the annual joint military exercises by the United States and South Korea known as 'Team Spirit' that had taken place since 1976, as well as the alleged presence of United States tactical nuclear weapons in the South.

The sense of military vulnerability underpinned the DPRK intent to develop a nuclear capacity. Under Article III of the Nuclear Non-Proliferation Treaty (NPT) that North Korea had joined in 1985 as a quid pro quo of receiving Soviet assistance to establish an experimental nuclear energy facility, the DPRK was mandated to sign a Safeguards

---

[15] Moon and Lee, 'Military Spending', p. 82.
[16] Délégation générale de la RPD de Corée en France, *Communiqué of the Supreme Command*.
[17] Moon and Lee, 'Military Spending', pp. 74–81. A truncated version of this article, omitting some of the figures in the original, is reproduced at www.japanfocus.org/-Sangkeun-Lee/3333, accessed 5 January 2014.
[18] Délégation générale de la RPD de Corée en France, *Communiqué of the Supreme Command*.
[19] Délégation générale de la RPD de Corée en France, 'Statement of DPRK Foreign Ministry on the "Team Spirit 91"', in *Bulletin d'information, No. 2/191* (Paris: Délégation générale de la RPD de Corée en France, 28 January 1991), p. 3.

Agreement with the International Atomic Energy Agency (IAEA). Membership of the Nuclear Non-Proliferation Treaty (NPT) was meant to ensure that only the recognised nuclear powers – the United States, the UK, the former Soviet Union, and later Russia, China and France – had nuclear weaponry capacity. NPT membership implied recognition by the international community of North Korea's nuclear energy programme but it also committed North Korea to implementing safeguards designed to prevent the country from using its nuclear energy programme to develop nuclear weapons.[20]

The DPRK delayed signing the Safeguards Agreement as it argued that the United States should first eradicate the nuclear weapons it had stationed in South Korea.[21] In 1991, however, President George H. W. Bush gave assurances that no tactical nuclear weapons would be stationed on the Korean peninsula and in January 1992 the DPRK signed the agreement, which came into force in April 1992.[22] For North Korea the United States President's announcement 'removed its [the United States'] nuclear threat'.[23] North Korea was also reassured by the suspension in 1992 of the joint United States and South Korea military and naval 'Team Spirit' exercise; a measure explicitly undertaken by the Bush administration in order to ease tensions on the peninsula. Relations between the KPA and the United States military, which had previously been confined to resolving border incursions along the demilitarised zone – commonly known as the DMZ – also became more substantive. From 1990 the two armies engaged in joint activities to recover the remains of American soldiers 'missing in action' (MIA) in the Korean War.[24]

[20] Joel S. Wit, Daniel B. Poneman and Robert L. Gallucci, *Going Critical: The First North Korean Nuclear Crisis* (Washington, DC: Brookings Institution Press, 2005); Sigal, *Disarming Strangers*.
[21] DPRK Ministry of Foreign Affairs, 'Statement of the Ministry of Foreign Affairs of the DPR of Korea on the Question of Signing the Nuclear Safeguards Accord', in Délégation générale de la RPD de Corée en France, *Bulletin d'information, Special Issue No. 26/1191* (Paris: Délégation générale de la RPD de Corée en France, 26 November 1991), pp. 1–2.
[22] Délégation générale de la RPD de Corée en France, 'DPRK Welcomed President Bush's Announcement', in *Bulletin d'information, Special Issue No. 22/1091* (Paris: Délégation générale de la RPD de Corée en France, 1 October 1991), pp. 5–6. For treaty dates see also DPRK Ministry of Foreign Affairs, 'On the Truth of Nuclear Inspection by IAEA in DPRK', in Délégation générale de la RPD de Corée en France, *Bulletin d'information, No. 11/0393* (Paris: Délégation générale de la RPD de Corée en France, 5 March 1993), p. 1.
[23] Takashi, *Korea in Kim Jong Il's Era*, p. 29. As a publication from the Foreign Languages Publishing House, the text is, effectively, a government position.
[24] Ibid., p. 97.

From 1992, as a consequence of signing the Safeguards Agreement, North Korea was legally committed to allowing regular inspections of its nuclear facilities by officials from the IAEA. IAEA officials first visited North Korea in May 1992 and conducted six inspections of North Korea's nuclear facilities between May 1992 and January 1993.[25] IAEA inspectors, who had been criticised for their seeming absence of alacrity in Iraq, were assiduous and remained critical of the DPRK's nuclear reporting, which they argued contained 'inconsistencies'.

North Korea did not deny discrepancies but argued that these could be explained because of North Korean lack of experience in the development of nuclear technology, which had resulted in operational problems. The DPRK argued that although work had started on the nuclear facility in 1986 'it took us four to five years to grasp its technology'.[26] During that period, because 'we had no other possibility of learning the experience of other countries than the data introduced in public magazines' experimental work was undertaken before any further nuclear facilities were built.[27] North Korean officials also argued that the IAEA inspectors were assessing the DPRK as if it had already constructed fully operational nuclear facilities.

From North Korea's perspective, the country had offered full cooperation with the IAEA yet every concession resulted in further demands. In February 1993, in a detailed defence of their nuclear programme, a North Korean statement complained that the Director-General of the IAEA 'proposed a "special inspection" to us on February 9 even before the sixth inspection team recalculated the result after flying back to Vienna on February 8'.[28] North Korea's view was that repeated inspections were unjustified and entirely a product of United States pressure on the IAEA.[29] North Korea argued that the United States was systematically spreading false information that the DPRK had undeclared nuclear

[25] Ministry of Atomic Energy of the Democratic People's Republic of Korea, 'Detailed Report of the Ministry of Atomic Energy of the Democratic People's Republic of Korea on Problems in Implementation of Safeguards Agreement, Pyongyang, 21 February 1993', in Délégation générale de la RPD de Corée en France, *Bulletin d'information, No. 05/0293* (Paris: Délégation générale de la RPD de Corée en France, 22 February 1993), p. 3.

[26] Ministry of Atomic Energy of the Democratic People's Republic of Korea, 'Detailed Report of the Ministry of Atomic Energy of the Democratic People's Republic of Korea on Problems in Implementation of Safeguards Agreement, Pyongyang, 21 February 1993', in Délégation générale de la RPD de Corée en France, *Bulletin d'information, No. 05/0293* (Paris: Délégation générale de la RPD de Corée en France, 22 February 1993), p. 4.

[27] Ibid.   [28] Ibid., pp. 2–9. Quote is ibid., p. 5.   [29] Ibid., pp. 2–9.

development sites and that the United States had attempted to influence the composition of the IAEA inspection team.[30]

Within this general atmosphere of mistrust and fear of military vulnerability, North Korea viewed the 1993 resumption of the joint United States–South Korea 'Team Spirit' military exercises as constituting a warlike escalation of hostilities.[31] The reaction was to put the entire country on a 'semi-war' footing in March 1993.[32] North Korea also announced its 'decision to withdraw unavoidably from the Nuclear Non-Proliferation Treaty'.[33] One aim of the threat to withdraw from the NPT was to end the legal right of foreign inspectors to access DPRK nuclear facilities which the DPRK government understood as bringing unacceptable pressures designed to undermine the regime.[34] North Korea knew that the threat of NPT withdrawal was a highly risky diplomatic manoeuvre; officially sanctioned publications referred to 'do-or-die tactics'.[35]

Globally, North Korea's statements were understood as dangerous and provocative. No state had ever previously withdrawn from the NPT and the United States' view was that North Korea's threatened withdrawal from the Nuclear Non-Proliferation Treaty (NPT) was a declaration of intent to develop nuclear weapons, and for the Clinton administration, this was a *casus belli*. Initially, the DPRK and the United States attempted to resolve differences through bilateral diplomacy and, in a historic first diplomatic agreement between the two states, issued a joint statement on 11 June 1993 in which the DPRK agreed to 'suspend' its withdrawal from the NPT.[36] On 10 June, however, the Board of Governors of the IAEA had passed a resolution cutting off technical assistance to North Korea, because of 'non-compliance' with its

---

[30] Ibid., pp. 7–9.

[31] Takashi, *Korea in Kim Jong Il's Era*, pp. 26–34; Sigal, *Disarming Strangers*, pp. 17–51.

[32] Kim Jong Il, 'Order of the Supreme Commander of the Korean People's Army', in Délégation générale de la RPD de Corée en France, *Bulletin d'information, No. 09/0393* (Paris: Délégation générale de la RPD de Corée en France, 8 March 1993).

[33] DPRK Government, 'Statement of DPRK Government on Withdrawal from NPT', in Délégation générale de la RPD de Corée en France, *Bulletin d'information, No. 10/0393* (Paris: Délégation générale de la RPD de Corée en France, 12 March 1993). See also the excellent analysis in Robert Carlin and John W. Lewis, *Negotiating with North Korea: 1993–2007* (Stanford: Center for International Security and Cooperation, January 2008).

[34] Jon, *A Duel of Reason*; Sigal, *Disarming Strangers*; Wit *et al.*, *Going Critical*.

[35] Jon, *A Duel of Reason*, p. 113; Takashi, *Korea in Kim Jong Il's Era*, p. 93.

[36] The text of the 11 June 1993 joint agreement is reproduced in Carlin and Lewis, *Negotiating with North Korea*, pp. 26–7.

safeguards commitments.[37] When North Korea was informed of the IAEA decision, it reacted by announcing its withdrawal from the IAEA, of which it had been a member since 1974.

Both sides anticipated the outbreak of war in what has become known as the 'first nuclear crisis', as United States war planners met to consider the use of force to eradicate North Korea's nuclear facilities.[38] A last-minute intervention by former United States President Jimmy Carter, who visited Pyongyang to meet with Kim Il Sung on 15 June 1994, defused the crisis and led North Korea into substantive negotiations with the United States.[39] The first nuclear crisis of 1993–4 was concluded through bilateral negotiations that ended in a security deal in the guise of the 'Agreed Framework', signed between the United States and the DPRK on 21 October 1994.[40]

The Agreed Framework brought a cessation of North Korean nuclear development and the establishment of the Korea Peninsula Energy Development Organization (KEDO), the key members of which were the United States, South Korea and Japan.[41] The objectives of KEDO were to build light water nuclear reactors that would eventually bring nuclear energy to North Korea and to provide mechanisms to prevent nuclear weapons development.[42] Part of the KEDO mandate was to fund and build two light water reactor nuclear power plants in North Korea. In return for the provision of light water reactors, North Korea agreed to close its graphite-moderated nuclear reactors that had the potential to facilitate the development of nuclear weaponry. The DPRK agreed to remain in the Nuclear Non-Proliferation Treaty (NPT) and to permit IAEA monitoring of the freezing of its nuclear programme.

---

[37] IAEA, *Fact Sheet on DPRK Nuclear Safeguards* (Vienna: IAEA, undated), available at www.iaea.org/newscenter/focus/iaeadprk/fact_sheet_may2003.shtml, accessed 4 January 2014.

[38] Wit *et al.*, *Going Critical*; Sigal, *Disarming Strangers*.

[39] Marion Creekmore, Jr., *A Moment of Crisis: Jimmy Carter, The Power of a Peacemaker, and North Korea's Nuclear Ambitions* (New York: Public Affairs, 2006); Sigal, *Disarming Strangers*, pp. 150–62; Wit *et al.*, *Going Critical*, pp. 192–246.

[40] Sigal, *Disarming Strangers*; Wit *et al.*, *Going Critical*; Gary L. Jones, *Nuclear Nonproliferation: Heavy Fuel Oil Delivered to North Korea under the Agreed Framework*, *GAO/T-RCED-00-20* (Washington, DC: General Accounting Office, 1999), available at http://gao.gov/assets/110/108176.pdf, accessed 24 September 2012. The text of the Geneva Agreement is reproduced in Carlin and Lewis, *Negotiating with North Korea*, pp. 27–9.

[41] For details on KEDO structure, membership and financing see Korea Peninsula Energy Development Organization, *Annual Report 2001* (New York: KEDO, 2001).

[42] Sigal, *Disarming Strangers*; Wit *et al.*, *Going Critical*.

North Korea's nuclear diplomacy achieved a long-standing aim of persuading the United States to treat North Korea as a sovereign, equal state. The concrete commitment in the Agreed Framework that both states would aim for 'full normalisation of political and economic relations' seemed to signal the achievement of another core goal of North Korean foreign policy.[43] The DPRK hoped that if normalisation of relations between the United States and the DPRK took place then one consequence would be that the United States would no longer oppose DPRK membership in the international multilateral banks. Continuing United States sanctions policies effectively precluded the DPRK from International Monetary Fund (IMF) membership and thus the DPRK was not eligible for funds from other multilateral banks, including the World Bank and the Asian Development Bank (ADB).[44] Were normalisation to happen, the DPRK might be able to access substantial concessional loans for economic redevelopment.

North Korea was hopeful that normalisation could be achieved because the Geneva Agreement was 'an official document signed for the first time between [North] Korea and the United States and Clinton assured its implementation by the authority of the President'.[45] North Korean policy-makers seemed confident of the capacity and intent of the United States president to implement the Agreed Framework. North Korean negotiators were aware of the hostility to the deal from powerful critics within the United States, who warned that the by-product of any permitted nuclear energy programme enabled the development of materials and technological capacity that could eventually be used as part of a North Korean weapons programme, but the North Korean view was that if 'the promise [Geneva Agreement] is revoked, the national prestige of the United States will be shattered, and this will lead the two countries to go back to the state before the [North] Korea–US talks i.e. mistrust and confrontation'.[46]

The collapse of the economy and the failure of government

In the early 1990s, North Korea lost subsidies from Russia, China and the former communist states of eastern and central Europe. One of the

---

[43] Ibid., p. 423.
[44] Thomas F. McCarthy, 'Managing Development Assistance in the DPRK', in E. Kwan Choi, E. Han Kim and Yesook Merrill (eds.), *North Korea in the World Economy* (London: RoutledegeCurzon, 2003), pp. 74–9.
[45] Jon, *A Duel of Reason*, p. 171.
[46] Ibid.

reasons that China and Russia were unwilling to offer economic assistance to the North Korean government was because they did not support North Korean policies, which both understood as economically anachronistic and leading to dangerous political instability in north-east Asia. Another reason was that in the early 1990s both China and Russia were fully engaged in resolving their own domestic economic problems. In 1995, China itself became a large grain importer as it had not produced sufficient grain to feed its own population.[47] North Korea had few other sources of foreign assistance to fill the resource gap generated by Russian and Chinese economic disengagement. The 1994 nuclear deal with the United States was not accompanied by significant economic assistance and bilateral relations with the United States remained conflictual.[48]

The UNDP calculated that between 1992 and 1996 per capita income fell from $1,005 to $481.[49] Between 1993 and 1996, production in the heavy industrial and construction sectors all but collapsed, with 70 per cent of workers in these sectors made unemployed.[50] Fuel for transport, electricity generation and heating to combat the average winter temperatures of minus 5.5 degrees centigrade became scarce.[51] Absent necessary oil and oil-product imports, industrial and agricultural productivity declined abruptly. Agricultural production depended on the heavy use of agro-industrial products such as fertilisers, chemicals and pesticides and these were increasingly unavailable.[52]

The economic crisis that was marked by drastic reductions in economic output was compounded by the devastating floods that the UN reported 'were unprecedented in their intensity and impact', which occurred in the middle of the crop-growing seasons in 1995 and 1996.[53]

---

[47] FAO/WFP, *Crop and Food Supply Assessment Mission to the Democratic People's Republic of Korea, Special Report* (Rome: FAO/WFP, 22 December 1995), available at www.fao.org/docrep/004/w0051e/w0051e00.htm, accessed 12 January 2014.

[48] Wit *et al.*, *Going Critical*.

[49] UNDP and DPRK government, *Report of the Thematic Roundtable Meeting on Agricultural Recovery and Environmental Protection* (Geneva: UNDP, 28–9 May 1998), Table M: Gross Domestic Product 1992–6.

[50] Jinwook Choi, 'The North Korean Domestic Situation and its Impact on the Nuclear Crisis', *Ritsumeikan Annual Review of International Studies*, Vol. 5, 2006, pp. 11 and 4, available at www.ritsumei.ac.jp/acd/cg/ir/college/bulletin/e-vol.5/CHOI.pdf, accessed 5 January 2014.

[51] World Food Programme, *Full Report of the Evaluation of DPRK EMOPs 5959.00 and 5959.01 'Emergency Assistance to Vulnerable Groups' 20 March–10 April 2000* (Rome: WFP, 2000), p. 4.

[52] On the necessity for intensive exploitation of land in the DPRK see Roberto Christen and Gamal M. Ahmed, *Agriculture in DPRK* (Pyongyang: FAO, undated but probably 2001).

[53] UNDP and DPRK government, *Thematic Roundtable Meeting*, p. 6.

Harvests were destroyed as were emergency grain reserves that had been stored in tunnels.[54] Floods destroyed buildings, bridges and irrigation facilities. Coal mines were flooded. The country's electricity supply, necessary for agriculture, industry and railway transport as well as residential lighting, depended substantially on coal, which also provided the most important fuel for domestic heating. Crop production relied on electricity-fed irrigation because of the difficult topography that militated against gravity-fed irrigation, so power shortages contributed to the dramatic reduction in industrial and agricultural production. The following year brought no let-up in natural catastrophes as 1997 saw drought that the World Food Programme (WFP) estimated caused grain losses of between 1.6 and 1.9 million tonnes – up to 40 per cent of what was necessary to feed the population at subsistence level.[55] A country that was already in emergency mode simply had no safety net upon which to fall – either domestic or external.

In 1997, the DPRK Agricultural Commission reported that, between 1990 and 1997, basic grain production had fallen from over 8 million tonnes to 2.6 million tonnes.[56] It reported 1994 grain production totals of 7 million tonnes; which dropped to 3.5 million tonnes in 1995 and 2.5 million tonnes in 1996.[57] South Korean agronomists reported a decline in agricultural production between 1995 and 1996 from 4 million tonnes to 3 million tonnes.[58] Both of these estimates confirmed a precipitous drop in production of basic grains such that from 1995 production did not reach the threshold of 5 million tonnes that was required to meet the survival needs of the 22 million or so population.

The stove-piped central state machinery remained focused on the 1993/4 nuclear crisis and appeared oblivious to the extent of the domestic crisis.[59] Old methods that had been used to deal with previous food crises were revived and, in 1990 and 1991, the government attempted to

---

[54] For information on flood damage see ibid. The FAO and WFP reported that grain stocks were already depleted by 1995 and at a 'negligible' level. See FAO/WFP, *Crop and Food Supply Assessment Mission*, p. 4.

[55] WFP/FAO/UNICEF/Save the Children Fund UK, *Nutritional Assessment Mission to the Democratic People's Republic of Korea* (Pyongyang/Rome: WFP, November 1997), p. 22.

[56] Agricultural Commission figures were reported to WFP and published in WFP, *Full Report of the Evaluation of DPRK EMOPs*, p. 5.

[57] Ibid.

[58] Young-Hoon Kim, 'AREP Program and Inter-Korean Agricultural Cooperation', in *East Asian Review*, Vol. 13, No. 4, Winter 2001, pp. 93–4, available at www.ieas.or.kr/vol13_4/13_4_6.pdf., accessed 6 January 2014.

[59] The official news source of the DPRK reported that on 6 April 1993 Kim Il Sung 'guided the work in different domains of the national economy'. This short report did not indicate anything other than the standard imprecations to do better but it did contain an implied reference to agricultural problems. The KCNA report stated that Kim Il

compensate for decreases in agricultural output by a combination of tighter rationing and use of food stocks. In 1990 and 1991 slogans appeared urging the population to 'eat two meals a day' so as to save food.[60]

The leadership carried on with business as usual as Kim Il Sung maintained his routine visits to workplaces to offer 'on-the-spot' guidance. In September 1993 Kim Il Sung visited farms in Onchon County, South Pyongan province, where he expressed 'great satisfaction with the fact that the agricultural working people have brought about an epochal change in farming on tideland-turned fields by doing farm work assiduously'.[61] It remains an open question as to how much the ageing Kim Il Sung knew about the agricultural crisis given that farm visits were highly orchestrated. At a time when the agricultural sector was largely without mechanisation, Kim Il Sung was shown mechanised farms. Kim's recorded comments were largely platitudes, including reminding farmers to provide fruit trees with adequate water.[62]

From 1993, Kim Jong Il was *de facto* head of state even though Kim Il Sung was still alive and held the position of President.[63] In 1992, a constitutional amendment established that the KPA report directly to the National Defence Commission (NDC) and not to the President, so Kim Jong Il's election as Chairman of the NDC in April 1993 gave him control over the armed forces and, effectively, the state.[64] Kim Jong Il's view was that 'socialism in some countries ... failed ... [because] they had not

Sung 'instructed that it is necessary to direct efforts to a [*sic*] successful farming in South Hwanghae Province, a granary of our country, in particular'. See Korea Central New Agency (KCNA), 'On-the-spot Guidance of President Kim Il Sung', in Délégation générale de la RPD de Corée en France, *Bulletin d'information, No. 15/0493* (Paris: Délégation générale de la RPD de Corée en France, 7 April 1993), p. 4.

[60] Hazel Smith, *Hungry for Peace: International Security, Humanitarian Assistance and Social Change in North Korea* (Washington, DC: United States Institute of Peace Press, 2005), p. 66.

[61] Délégation générale de la RPD de Corée en France, 'President Kim Il Sung Gives On-the-spot Guidance to Farms', in *Bulletin d'information, No. 15/0493* (Paris: Délégation générale de la RPD de Corée en France, 27 September 1993), p. 1.

[62] Ibid.

[63] Dae-Kyu Yoon, 'The Constitution of North Korea: Its Changes and Implications', *Fordham International Law Journal*, Vol. 27, No. 4, April 2004, p. 1299, available at http://ir.lawnet.fordham.edu/cgi/viewcontent.cgi?article=1934&context=ilj, accessed 9 February 2014.

[64] Foreign Languages Publishing House, *Socialist Constitution of The Democratic People's Republic of Korea* (Pyongyang: Foreign Languages Publishing House, 1993); Alexandre Y. Mansourov, 'Inside North Korea's Black Box: Reversing the Optics', in Kongdan Oh Hassig (ed.), *North Korean Policy Elites* (Alexandria, VA: Institute for Defense Analyses, 2004), unpaginated but 159–226 on pdf, available at www.nkeconwatch.com/nk-uploads/dprkpolicyelites.pdf, accessed 2 November 2014.

adhered consistently to the fundamental principles of socialism'.[65] Other communist states, unlike the DPRK, had not been careful enough to imbue their populations with correct ideology.[66] The argument was that existing methods should not be abandoned but implemented more effectively.

Critics and potential critics who might be sympathetic to political change that was taking place in other communist states were dealt with by way of 'revolutionary discipline'. Choe Ju-hwal, a high-ranking military defector from the DPRK to South Korea, reported that from '1992 to 1994, many senior military figures who had studied in USSR military academies were purged or executed en masse'.[67]

As late as September 1995, after a second year of major flood damage, the government refused to admit the scale of the economic catastrophe and food crisis, referring only to 'minor and temporary' problems.[68] Some cost-cutting of government expenditure took place and in 1995 twelve foreign diplomatic missions were closed to save money.[69] These policy adjustments did not prevent the precipitous slide of the economy. A substantive decision was therefore taken to put the armed forces to work in key industries, including farming and the mining, power and transport industries.[70]

The government remained fixated on regime security as the economy imploded. Vast numbers of the newly unemployed and underemployed were mobilised in make-work projects. The objective was to avoid the risk of organised protest from workers who no longer held jobs that paid a living wage or guaranteed adequate food rations. Between 1994 and 1995, at the same time that the scale of the crisis was generating worldwide alarm, the government organised thousands to build the Monument to the Party Foundation in Pyongyang. The government reported that the

[65] Kim Jong Il, 'Historical Lesson in Building Socialism and the General Line of our Party', in Délégation générale de la RPD de Corée en France, *Bulletin d'information, No. 02/ 0292* (Paris: Délégation générale de la RPD de Corée en France, 4 February 1992), p. 2.
[66] Kim Jong Il, 'Our Socialism for the People will not Perish', in Délégation générale de la RPD de Corée en France, *Bulletin d'information, No. 10/591* (Paris: Délégation générale de la RPD de Corée en France, 27 May 1991), pp. 1–17.
[67] New Focus International, 'Exclusive: in Conversation with North Korea's Highest-ranking Military Defector', *New Focus International*, 4 January 2014, available at http:// newfocusintl.com/exclusive-conversation-north-koreas-highest-ranking-military-defector, accessed 23 January 2014.
[68] Reuters, 'BC-Korea-Rice', 27 September 1995.
[69] Associated Press (AP), 'North-Korea-Diplomacy', 19 September 1995.
[70] North Korean literature refers to the involvement of the Korean People's Army in farming in 1997 and traces the involvement of the KPA in economic reconstruction in 'key industries' including 'coal-mining, power and rail transport' from this period. Chol U Kim, *Songun Politics of Kim Jong Il* (Pyongyang: Foreign Languages Publishing House, 2008), pp. 66–70.

monument was built in one year through the 'dynamic endeavours of the members of the Party Shock-Brigade and active support of workers, peasants, soldiers, intellectuals, youths and students'.[71]

The government maintained control over the apparatus of repression. Agence France-Presse (AFP) reported in September 1995 that 'travellers [presumably from China] said public grievances are running high in the North because of unprecedented economic difficulties'.[72] Dissatisfaction with the government reportedly resulted in attempted coups in 1992 and 1996, but these were repressed by Kim Jong Il via military action.[73]

In 1995 reinforcing the sense that it had run out of ideas, the government made an unprecedented worldwide appeal for food assistance to those countries it considered as enemies – the United States, Japan and South Korea.[74] The government requested aid from United Nations humanitarian organisations including the United Nations Children's Fund (UNICEF), the World Food Programme and the Red Cross and Red Crescent movement, as well as from non-governmental organisations (NGOs).[75] Humanitarian agencies provided over a million tonnes of food aid between 1995 and 1998, averting an even larger disaster.[76] Japan gave a very large donation of 500,000 metric tonnes of rice (enough to feed 20 per cent of North Korea's then 22 million population for one year) in 1995. DPRK officials consistently pursued the objective of obtaining food assistance during negotiations within the Four Party Talks between the DPRK, South Korea, the

---

[71] Délégation générale de la RPD de Corée en France, 'Monument to Party Foundation completed', in *Bulletin d'information, No. 12/1195* (Paris: Délégation générale de la RPD de Corée en France, 17 November 1995), pp. 3–4.

[72] AFP, 'North Korea Resumes Massive Military Drills', Tuesday 19 September 1995.

[73] McEachearn dates a coup attempt against Kim Jong Il to 1992. Choi reports an attempted coup by 'dozens of generals' in 1996. Mansourov reports serious criticism of Kim Jong Il by senior officials in 1998. See Patrick McEachearn, 'Inside the Red Box: North Korea's Post-Totalitarian Politics', doctoral dissertation (Louisiana State University and Agricultural and Mechanical College, May 2009), p. 57; For detail on the purges of the mid-1990s see Choi, 'The North Korean Domestic Situation', p. 11; Mansourov, 'Inside North Korea's Black Box', pp. 28–9. For disaffection after the famine see Young-Tai Jeung, *Internal and External Perceptions of the North Korean Army* (Seoul: Korea Institute for National Unification, 2008), pp. 2–4.

[74] Hazel Smith, '"Opening up" by Default: North Korea, the Humanitarian Community and the Crisis', *Pacific Review*, Vol. 12, No. 3, 1999, pp. 453–78; Hazel Smith, *Overcoming Humanitarian Dilemmas in the DPRK, Special Report No. 90* (Washington, DC: United States Institute of Peace, July 2002).

[75] I discuss early contact with international humanitarian agencies in Smith, '"Opening up" by Default', pp. 453–78.

[76] UNDP and DPRK government, *Report of the First Thematic Round Table Conference for the Democratic People's Republic of Korea* (Geneva: UNDP, 28–9 May 1998), p. 3.

United States and China, which followed the Agreed Framework of October 1994.[77]

In 1996, for the first time, the government acknowledged the scale of the economic crisis, which had 'a serious impact on the livelihood of the people and the development of the national economy and, especially, cause[d] a temporary food problem', but also reported that the reason was 'unprecedented natural disasters which have been repeated in recent years'.[78] The official position was that economic difficulties were a result of 'natural disasters', including flooding, exemplified by the government decision to name the coordinating structure for international aid the Flood Damage Rehabilitation Commission (FDRC). The government denied that 'temporary difficulties' were because of a 'structural mistake' and denounced those wishing to force North Korea to change its system.[79]

The government argued that 'American imperialism' was to blame for the economic crisis and encouraged the population to consider themselves as taking part in a struggle for national survival akin to that fought against Japanese colonialism, and to overcome economic obstacles as they had during post-Korean War reconstruction.[80] The government expressed gratitude for international assistance but insisted that the ideology of *Juche* would prevail as the 'the [North] Korean people are surmounting ... hardships in the spirit of "Arduous March"'.[81]

Famine[82]

The population of the DPRK had grown used to living with recurrent food shortages but the food crisis of the mid-1990s was on a different scale in that it was transformed into nationwide famine that lasted, from around 1995 to 1998.[83] The United Nations World Food Programme reported a 'famine in slow motion' as consecutive years of insufficient

[77] Don Oberdorfer, *The Two Koreas: A Contemporary History* (London: Warner Books, 1997), p. 397.
[78] Délégation générale de la RPD de Corée en France, 'Foreign Ministry Spokesman on Flood Damage in DPRK', in *Bulletin d'information, No. 22/0896* (Paris: Délégation générale de la RPD de Corée en France, 16 August 1996), pp. 1–2.
[79] Ibid.
[80] For DPRK official comment on the 'arduous march' and the 'forced march' see 'Editor's Note', in Sung Un Kim (ed.), *Panorama of Korea* (Pyongyang: Foreign Languages Publishing House, 1999), no page number given; and ibid., pp. 43–8.
[81] Délégation générale de la RPD de Corée en France, 'Foreign Ministry Spokesman on Flood Damage', pp. 1–2.
[82] I provide a book-length treatment of the famine in Hazel Smith, *Hungry for Peace*.
[83] Lee, 'Food Shortages'.

food meant that 'people try to cope year after year, but probably many of them do not manage'.[84] People died of starvation everywhere in the country. Rural and city dwellers died as did Pyongyang residents, who were better off than those who lived in the rest of the country, but not exempt from malnutrition and hunger.[85]

The government could not supply the public distribution system with enough food to guarantee minimum rations, nor provide basic health supplies to respond to the inevitable increase in ill-health.[86] There were no significant alternative food allocation and distribution mechanisms to those provided by government. Neither indigenous private sector nor independent civic organisations existed that could mobilise food relief. Few people could feed themselves from growing their own food or had access to cash or enough goods to sell or swap for food. Many North Koreans were forced into destitution.

Rural communities in the breadbasket areas were badly affected. In 1997 the Food and Agriculture Organisation (FAO) of the United Nations reported that 'The situation is ... desperate for some five million collective farm workers and their families ... contrary to earlier expectations that cereal allocations would help sustain farm families up to June/July, the beginning of the lean season, observations indicate that some households had already depleted stocks by as early as March. As a result, some families were ... subsisting on an assortment of alternative "foods", such [as] grasses and roots. Additionally, the consumption of meat and dairy products is negligible since the majority of livestock have been culled due to the lack of feed over the last two years.'[87]

Industrial workers living in the densely populated cities of Chongjin, Kimchaek and Hamhung, in the north-eastern provinces of North and South Hamgyong, no longer received grain transfers from the

---

[84] World Food Programme (WFP), *Report on the Nutrition Survey of the DPRK* (Pyongyang: WFP, 1999), p. 8.

[85] Pyongyang institutions were regularly visited by resident international humanitarian organisations, as they were logistically easier to organise than visits to more remote areas. A WFP report records that in 2001 it carried out 592 visits to beneficiaries in Pyongyang. International agency visits to children's institutions, homes and hospitals in the Pyongyang province recorded persistently widespread chronic malnutrition, although there is no specific data on province-wide malnutrition figures in Pyongyang until the 2002 nutrition survey, which showed that 4 per cent of Pyongyang's children were severely malnourished. See WFP, *Pyongyang Province* (Pyongyang: WFP, 2001).

[86] WFP, 'Emergency Operation DPR Korea No. 5710.00: Emergency Food Assistance for Flood Victims', in WFP, *WFP Operations in DPR Korea as of 14 July 1999* (Rome: WFP, undated but 1999).

[87] FAO/WFP, *Crop and Food Supply Assessment Mission to the Democratic People's Republic of Korea, Special Alert No. 275* (Rome: FAO/WFP, 3 June 1997)

breadbasket provinces after national agricultural production plummeted.[88] These city dwellers lacked gardens and often lived miles away
from land that could be used to grow survival rations. Within the space of
a few years, as factories closed and state-supplied provisions were all
but cut off, these formerly relatively privileged industrial workers
became some of the worst-off people in the country. The population of
the two Hamgyong provinces was disproportionately affected by famine
and death rates were high.[89] Some turned to petty trade, bartering
and selling assets they had accumulated from more prosperous times.
Not surprisingly, those living in the north-east, near the China border,
where heavy industry was concentrated, provided a disproportionate
share of the clandestine emigration to China that began in the wake
of famine.[90]

North Korea's inhabitants were ill-equipped to adapt to the new
reality. The theory, practice and norms of the society had penalised even
the idea of non-state-directed or -approved economic transactions. Professionals had grown up in a society where the state had supplied income
and food and was relatively free of money-based corruption. It was not
easy for many doctors, nurses and teachers to organise their lives so as to
expect 'gifts' from patients and parents as a substitute for a living wage.
Others were reluctant to participate in non-state-sanctioned economic
transactions because they remained hopeful that things might get better.
The continuing capacity of state security services prevented some
of the population from participating in grey area economic activity.
Community solidarity gave life-saving help to some but also came under
major strain as the famine reached its peak and families did not have the
wherewithal to look after even their nearest relatives. Individuals less able
or willing to participate in non-state-sanctioned activities, and those with
least ability to find individual solutions to food shortages and resources
for healthcare, including babies and children, the sick and the disabled,
the elderly and the unemployed, were most vulnerable to malnutrition
and starvation.

In 1997, a survey by the United Nations World Food Programme of
3,965 children in five of the DPRK's twelve provinces found that 'global

---

[88] FAO/WFP, *Crop and Food Supply Assessment Mission to the Democratic People's Republic of Korea, Special Report* (Rome: FAO/WFP, 29 June 1999), p. 10.

[89] Robinson *et al.*, 'Mortality in North Korean Migrant Households'.

[90] Hazel Smith, 'North Koreans in China: Sorting Fact from Fiction', in Tsuneo Akaha and Anna Vassilieva (eds.), *Crossing National Borders: Human Migration Issues in Northeast Asia* (Tokyo: United Nations Press, 2005), pp. 175–8.

malnutrition' in the form of severe 'wasting', or low weight for height, was recorded at over 15 per cent in over a third of the forty-two nurseries and kindergartens they visited.[91] The same nutritional survey found that in these children's institutions, stunting or low height for age, a sign of chronic malnutrition, ranged from 0.6 per cent to 74 per cent of children.[92] The WFP reported that there were areas within North Korea where children faced the risk of dying from malnutrition.[93] Given widespread chronic malnutrition and the limitation of the non-randomised methodology in this survey, the WFP concluded that 'nearly all children must be considered similarly vulnerable [to risk of death], although to a lesser degree'.[94] In 1998, a further international nutritional survey found that indications of famine persisted with 60 per cent of children suffering from chronic malnutrition and 15 percent of children from severe malnutrition.[95] UNICEF ascribed the proximate causes of mortality in children who had been weakened by malnutrition to respiratory infections and diarrhoeal diseases.[96]

The 1998 nutrition survey found that male toddlers aged 12 months to 24 months were more at risk of acute malnutrition than females of the same age.[97] The working hypothesis within the international aid agencies was that this was probably not so much a question of differential food access as to different gendered expectations of boys and girls.[98] In times of extreme food stress, even if girls and boys were allocated the same amount of survival rations, little boys may have been treated as if they were less vulnerable, for example by encouraging them to play outside in cold weather while girls were more likely to have been kept inside in the warm.[99]

---

[91] This survey was 'non-random' and therefore had less scientific validity than later surveys that were underpinned by more rigorous methodology. Nevertheless the findings of the survey informed government policy and international humanitarian organisations, and its conclusions were considered valid given the observations of in-country international nutritionists. WFP/FAO/UNICEF and Save the Children Fund UK, *Nutritional Assessment*, p. 2.

[92] Ibid.   [93] Ibid., p. 3.   [94] Ibid.

[95] EU, UNICEF and WFP in partnership with the Government of DPRK, *Nutrition Survey of the Democratic People's Republic of Korea* (Rome/Pyongyang: WFP, 1998).

[96] UNICEF, *UNICEF Revised Funding Requirements: United Nations Consolidated Inter-Agency Appeal for the Democratic People's Republic of Korea: April 1997–March 1998* (Pyongyang: UNICEF, undated but 1998).

[97] EU, UNICEF and WFP in partnership with the Government of DPRK, *Nutrition Survey*.

[98] Hazel Smith, *WFP DPRK Programmes and Activities: A Gender Perspective* (Pyongyang: WFP, 1999).

[99] WFP, *Nutrition Survey*, p. 5.

Marketisation 'by default'

Despite the terrible hardship suffered by so many, North Korean society
did not implode. In the continuing absence of state response to economic
crisis, the population organised to help themselves.[100] Not all succeeded,
as is evidenced by the brutally high death toll, but those that found a way
to find food and income did so through non-state-sanctioned and non-
state-directed initiatives. North Koreans swapped, bartered and traded
goods outside the state system and, in so doing, created a primitive
market economy. In the absence of alternatives, the government more
or less tolerated the expansion of market activity that allowed farmers to
sell more of their own produce and allowed expansion of market activity,
although only as temporary expedients.[101]

Family members, usually the women, scavenged for food.[102] Men had
to participate in military and militia service and were mobilised to
respond to floods, infrastructure collapse and for construction. The
government permitted women to roam the country because women's
self-help initiatives on behalf of their families were not understood as
politically threatening and because it was normatively accepted that it
was the woman's job to provide food for the family. The entire society
considered it legitimate that women should leave their workplaces to
search for food and goods to support their families, as women were
understood as 'naturally' responsible for domestic duties, including food
provision, caring for children, the elderly and the sick and maintaining
the household.[103] Women's participation in market activities was understood as a 'temporary measure' to deal with 'temporary difficulties'.[104]

Women, who in the Korean tradition eat last, ate tree bark, a wholly
non-nutritious commodity, sometimes resulting in death or permanent
chronic digestive problems.[105] Women looked after sick and dying children who could no longer be cared for very well in hospitals that had run
out of medicines, fuel and spare parts. Elderly and often frail women

---

[100] FAO/WFP, *Crop and Food Supply Assessment Mission*, 25 June 1998), p. 2.

[101] Choi, 'The North Korean Domestic Situation', p. 8.

[102] FAO/WFP, *Crop and Food Supply Assessment Mission to the Democratic People's Republic of
Korea* (Pyongyang: FAO/WFP, 6 December 1996), p. 10.

[103] One draft document, probably written by a North Korean national officer for UNDP/
UNIFEM, remarked that 'The diligence of women in managing a wholesome family life
through dedicated household management is a good indication that woment [*sic*] can
also channel similar diligence on part time management participation and decision-
making in community affairs, business and government activities'. See No author,
'Phase II DRK/92/WO1/A, Rationalizing Cottage Industry in Pyongyang', mimeo,
undated but probably 2000.

[104] Smith, *WFP DPRK Programmes and Activities*.   [105] Ibid.

foraged for firewood and food. In the absence of functioning transport systems, women walked very long distances, from county to county, without government authorisation, to seek help from relatives and to search for food.[106]

In some localities, enterprises mobilised to feed their employees through local initiatives that included expanding crop production to urban areas and selling off scrap on the emerging private markets. Farmers and urban dwellers walked miles to forest and mountain areas to search for edible vegetation. Nursery school staff collected 'wild foods', such as seaweed and edible grasses, to feed those for whom they were responsible.[107] The DPRK became a country of individual entrepreneurship, with a population physically and constantly on the move.

Local officials responded to economic problems by supporting coping solutions about which central government and Party officials were much more ambivalent. Provincial and county officials condoned and sometimes encouraged short-term population movement in-country and across the China border, developed unofficial swapping mechanisms with other counties, farms and enterprises and, most importantly, tolerated and encouraged the development and expansion of market activities.[108] Local officials refrained from implementing legal penalties against cultivating forest land for growing crops and ignored non-state-sanctioned marketplaces. It was a logical step for Party officials at the provincial, county, village and workplace level to look to the market to help their constituents and themselves.[109] Officials could appeal to decades of government propaganda which had insisted on local 'self-reliance' to provide justification for the adoption of what they could also argue were 'temporary measures'.[110]

The disassociation of local authorities from central government was reinforced by way of day-to-day decision-making necessities. Given an absence of food, county officials were forced to decide between hungry children, the hungry elderly or hungry key workers whenever food supplies were available for public distribution. Coal miners, for instance, engaged in arduous physical activity without real income other than the

[106] Ibid.
[107] WFP/FAO/UNICEF and Save the Children Fund UK, *Nutritional Assessment Mission*, p. 22.
[108] Varieties of coping mechanisms are discussed in ibid.
[109] Hyung-Min Joo, 'Visualizing the Invisible Hands: The Shadow Economy in North Korea', *Economy and Society*, Vol. 39, No. 1, February 2010, pp. 110–45.
[110] Discussion of attempts at local food self-sufficiency at county and provincial level can be found in Hy-Sang Lee, *North Korea: A Strange Socialist Fortress* (London: Praeger, 2001).

more or less worthless *won* and needed food in order to physically be able to mine coal for community and national electricity supplies. Deciding who should be provided with limited resources was a common dilemma for local officials.

Individuals, families, communities and local authorities learned that they could not rely on the central government, as they had grown used to throughout the Kim Il Sung era, but that to survive they needed to depend on their own efforts.[111] Some rural communities found ways to survive by calling on communal solidarity mechanisms that were founded on social practices of long duration. Others were so short of food that they could neither help themselves nor others. All who could engaged in private domestic and cross-border China trade.[112] Thousands migrated to China – many for recurrent short-term visits to obtain food and goods before going back when supplies ran out.[113]

The end of Kim Il Sungism

In the 1990s, successive North Korean governments focused all efforts on regime security goals as defined by the ability to prevent and deter foreign invasion. The government was incapable of dealing with the loss of economic support from abroad and the result was economic collapse and starvation. The population who survived did so through the creation of a marketised society that emerged as a product of the spontaneous self-help activity of millions of individuals and thousands of workplaces. The government never admitted that it had failed or contemplated a change in political philosophy and practice. Instead, the state retrenched around the priority of regime survival in a new era of marketisation and military rule.

---

[111] On the innovative coping strategies of households see FAO/WFP, *Crop and Food Supply Assessment Mission to the Democratic People's Republic of Korea, Special Report* (Rome: FAO/WFP, 12 November 1998), p. 16.

[112] Trade with China as a coping mechanism is reported in FAO/WFP, *Crop and Food Supply Assessment Mission to the Democratic People's Republic of Korea, Special Alert, No. 267* (Rome: FAO/WFP, 16 May 1996). Coping mechanisms are discussed in detail in FAO/WFP, *Crop and Food Supply Assessment Mission*, 6 December 1996, p. 10.

[113] Robinson *et al.*, 'Mortality in North Korean Migrant Households', 24 July 1999.

Part III

Marketisation and military rule

9   Marketisation from below

In reaction to what became a permanent loss of reliable provision of food and basic goods from the state, the reiteration of coping reactions of the population reconstituted the economic system from the bottom up.[1] In military-first era North Korea, markets became the primary source of supply of goods, including food, for most of the population.[2]

---

[1] I discuss the beginnings of marketisation in the DPRK in detail in Hazel Smith, 'La Corée du Nord vers l'économie de marché: faux et vrais dilemmas', *Critique Internationale*, No. 15, April 2002, pp. 6–14. See also Hazel Smith, *Hungry for Peace: International Security, Humanitarian Assistance and Social Change in North Korea* (Washington, DC: United States Institute of Peace Press, 2005); Hazel Smith, 'Crime and Economic Instability: The Real Security Threat from North Korea and What to Do about it', *International Relations of the Asia Pacific*, Vol. 5, No. 2, 2005, pp. 235–49; Hazel Smith, 'North Korea: Market Opportunity, Poverty and the Provinces', *New Political Economy*, Vol. 14, No. 3, June 2009, pp. 231–56; Anthony R. Michell, 'The Current North Korean Economy', in Marcus Noland (ed.), *Economic Integration of the Korean Peninsula* (Washington, DC: Institute for International Economics, 1998), pp. 137–63; Hyung-Min Joo, 'Visualizing the Invisible Hands: The Shadow Economy in North Korea', in *Economy and Society*, Vol. 39, No. 1, February 2010, pp. 110–45; Phillip H. Park (ed.), *The Dynamics of Change in North Korea: An Institutionalist Perspective* (Boulder, CO: Lynne Rienner Publishers, 2009). Useful studies of aspects of North Korean marketisation are available from the Seoul-based Korea Institute for National Unification. See for example Jeong-Ah Cho, *The Changes of Everyday Life in North Korea in the Aftermath of their Economic Difficulties* (Seoul: Korea Institute for National Unification, 2007); Soo-Young Choi, *North Korea's Agricultural Reforms and Challenges in the Wake of the July 1 Measures* (Seoul: Korea Institute for National Unification, 2007); Young-Yoon Kim, *A Study on the Reality and Prospect of Economic Reform in North Korea* (Seoul: Korea Institute for National Unification, 2007); Jae-Jean Suh, *Economic Hardship and Regime Sustainability in North Korea* (Seoul: Korea Institute for National Unification, 2008). A useful short summary of the causation of bottom-up marketisation can be found in Geir Helgeson and Nis Høyrup, *North Korea 2007: Assisting Development and Change* (Copenhagen: Nordic Institute of Asian Affairs, 2007), pp. 36–8.

[2] For surveys of North Korean refugees on the prevalence of markets as the major source of food supply for most of the population in the 1990s and the 2000s, see Byung-Yeon Kim and Dongho Song, 'The Participation of North Korean Households in the Informal Economy: Size, Determinants, and Effect', *Seoul Journal of Economics*, Vol. 21, No. 2, Summer 2008, pp. 361–85; Stephan Haggard and Marcus Noland, *Witness to Transformation: Refugee Insights into North Korea* (Washington, DC: Peterson Institute for International Economics, 2011).

Marketisation was an uneven and unpredictable process as not all had access to market opportunities and those that did were not always able to take advantage of them, yet market transformation in North Korea was notable for its visible feminisation.[3] Women's participation in market activities was not viewed as primarily commercially motivated but as providing for the family. In the face of a government that remained fundamentally hostile to liberal capitalism, women's participation in markets was not undertstood as a direct challenge to the economic organisation of the DPRK.[4]

Marketisation was a social phenomenon and an economic process and also had political consequences. The daily practices of local Party officials promoted, legitimised and valorised market dynamics and had the unintended effect of contradicting central state messages, all of which were founded on the pretence that the state could control and direct economic and political life as it had in the Kim Il Sung era. Marketisation generated incentives for poorly paid officials to waive and reduce penalties such that the legal system became more porous and less of an absolute bulwark of state repression. The Party became the driver and *de facto* legitimator of marketisation and in so doing ceased to act as a well-functioning, reliable transmission belt for ideological education and revolutionary discipline. Marketisation brought new ideas along with goods imported from abroad. The continued

---

[3] Andrei Lankov and Seok-hyang Kim, 'North Korean Market Vendors: The Rise of Grassroots Capitalists in a Post-Stalinist Society', *Pacific Affairs*, Vol. 81, No. 1, Spring 2008, pp. 53–72.

[4] For discussion of women's gendered roles in North Korea, see Kyungja Jung and Bronwen Dalton, 'Rhetoric versus Reality for the Women of North Korea: Mothers of the Revolution', *Asian Survey*, Vol. 46, No. 5, September/October 2006, pp. 741–60; Soon-Hee Lim, *The Food Crisis and Life of Women in North Korea* (Seoul: Korea Institute for National Unification, 2005); Jin Woong Kang, 'The Patriarchal State and Women's Status in Socialist North Korea', *Graduate Journal of Asia-Pacific Studies*, Vol. 6, No. 2, 2008, pp. 55–70 available at https://cdn.auckland.ac.nz/asserts/arts/Departments/asian-studies/gjaps/docs-vol6-no2/Kang-vol6.pdf, accessed 8 November 2014; Kyung Ae Park, 'Ideology and Women in North Korea', in Han S. Park (ed.), *North Korea: Ideology, Politics, Economy* (Englewood Cliffs: Prentice Hall, 1996), pp. 71–85; Kyung Ae Park, 'Economic Crisis, Women's Changing Economic Roles, and their Implications for Women's Status in North Korea', *The Pacific Review*, Vol. 24, No. 2, May 2011, pp. 159–77; Sonia Ryang, 'Gender in Oblivion: Women in the Democratic People's Republic of Korea (North Korea)', *Journal of African and Asian Studies*, Vol. 35, No. 3, August 2000, pp. 323–49; Young-Hee Shim, 'Human Rights of Women in North Korea: Factors and Present State', in Kie-Duck Park and Sang-Jin Han (eds.), *Human Rights in North Korea: Toward a Comprehensive Understanding* (Sungnam: The Sejong Institute, 2007), pp. 171–208; Eun-young Shin, 'Ideology and Gender Equality: Women's Policies of North Korea and China', *East Asian Review*, Vol. 13, No. 3, Autumn 2001, pp. 81–104, available at www.ieas.or.kr/vol13_3/13_3_5.pdf, accessed 8 November 2014.

inability of the government to deliver decent consumer goods and to provide a decent standard of living contrasted with what the population knew about the living standards of their neighbours in China and South Korea. The result was to diminish the authority and legitimacy of the leadership.

One unanticipated affect of marketisation was the rise of the family as the nexus of economic and associational life and the gradual displacement of collectivist, state-led priorities from private life. As state services deteriorated the family stepped in to cover the gap and in turn the family cohered around a mission to look after itself. The family, always an important institution in North Korea, supplanted Party and mass organisation structures as the most important focus of loyalty for most of the population. Marketisation forced private life to assume priority over public duties.

Marketisation by default

The self-help system that had started as a reaction to crisis became institutionalised from the 2000s onwards as the state was never again able to provide a reliable supply of food and goods. In military-first era North Korea, the population operated in an economic system whose fundamental dynamic was that the price of goods was determined by the relationship between supply and demand.[5] Needless to say these were not uniform prices across the country. Poor transport facilities and the vagaries of irregular and unreliable supply meant that there was local variation in the price of goods, including basic foods like rice and vegetables.

Petty trading and commerce were not seen as 'men's jobs' in North Korea and the opportunities for engaging in non-state-directed private economic activity were more readily allowed to women.[6] It remained mandatory for women and men to register and to turn up to workplaces throughout the military-first era, even when there was no economically productive work available, but men were given much less latitude than women to ignore these obligations.[7] The aim was both to ensure that

---

[5] Soo-Young Choi, *A Study on the Structure of Industry in North Korea* (Seoul: Korea Institute for National Unification, 2007), p. 33; Smith, 'La Corée du Nord vers l'économie de marché', pp. 6–14.

[6] Park, 'Economic Crisis', p. 165.

[7] It was technically illegal for both women and men not to attend the workplace even if the workplace was not operating. Lim reports that these rules were strictly enforced for men. See Lim, *The Food Crisis*, p. 38.

unemployed and underemployed men were left with as little free time as possible in which they might have the opportunity to express dissatisfaction at their increasing immiseration and to use these men as a pool of labour for large-scale construction projects.

Gendered norms that women's market activity was 'natural' meant that come the intermittent state crackdowns on market dynamics, it was still socially acceptable for women to carry on trading wherever they could. When the large, formal marketplaces such as the showpiece Tongil market in Pyongyang were closed down for a few weeks in 2009, the only source of food for most people was the informal trading activities that were dominated by women pedlars.[8] One South Korean report stated that by the end of the 1990s, over 70 per cent of women participated in trading activities.[9] Irrespective of the accuracy of the detail, there is no doubt that all who could do so engaged in trade, and that women were the primary 'face' of trade.[10]

Private production and commercial trade

Individuals used whatever resources they could find from their natural, social and political environment to make money. Families grew food for their own consumption and to sell on markets.[11] Those rural families lucky enough to own private plots expanded them as far as possible. Others cultivated marginal land, including steep hill-slopes and scrubland.[12] Families and workplaces cleared forest land to grow crops and, even though illegal, most local authorities permitted the practice.

Individuals, households and enterprises developed production capacities designed specifically for market outlets.[13] Households engaged in

---

[8] Lankov and Kim, 'North Korean Market Vendors', pp. 53–72; John Everard, 'The Markets of Pyongyang', *Korea Economic Institute: Academic Paper Series*, Vol. 6, No. 1, January 2011, pp. 1–7, available at www.keia.org/Communications/Programs/Everard/Everard.pdf, accessed 8 November 2014.

[9] Hyeon-Sun Park, 'A study on the Family System of Modern North Korea', doctoral dissertation (Ewha Womans University, 1999), p. 148, cited in Soon-Hee Lim, 'The Food Crisis and Life of Women in North Korea', mimeo, no page numbers, revised version published, without this reference, as Lim, *The Food Crisis*.

[10] Ibid.; Lankov and Kim, 'North Korean Market Vendors', pp. 53–72.

[11] Kim and Song, 'The Participation of North Korean Households', pp. 361–85.

[12] Smith, 'North Korea: Market Opportunity', pp. 231–56.

[13] Dae-Kyu Yoon, 'Economic Reform and Institutional Transformation', in Phillip H. Park (ed.), *The Dynamics of Change in North Korea* (Seoul: Institute for Far Eastern Studies, 2009), p. 57.

small-scale production of handicrafts and basic goods like noodles or liquor. Some of these small-scale enterprises were based at home and some in non-functioning or partially functioning workplaces.[14] These makeshift production facilities were innovative in their use of scrap and out-of-date equipment no longer used by the decrepit and non-functioning state-owned factories, but their operations and output remained at a fairly primitive level.[15] These small-scale operations did not attract serious investment but they did enable the development of a new private or semi-private production sector to a level that could generate basic household goods.

Professionals like doctors and teachers accepted gifts from patients and parents to supplement wages that literally could not support survival.[16] Wages remained miserably low so patients and parents would also often feel obliged to offer some food or money as additional remuneration to those working in the health and education services. Those responsible for admission to good schools became susceptible to bribery.[17] Private tutoring became commonplace as students competed to obtain places at prestigious universities like Kimchaek University and Kim Il Sung University.[18] Individuals made money by selling personal services through the establishment of small private businesses including hairdressing salons, photoshops and restaurants.[19]

A wide variety of goods was available in North Korea's markets from the mid-2000s, provided the consumer had the money to pay. In the Kim Il Sung era a private market in medicines had not existed but in the era of marketisation and military rule, if the family could afford to pay, they obtained medicines and supplies from market sources. Markets were supplied by trade goods from China, goods that leaked out of what remained of the state enterprises and local private producers.[20]

Markets varied in physical size, location, permanence and degree of tolerance and control by the government. Some were little more than

[14] Joo, 'Visualizing the Invisible Hands', p. 129.

[15] Suh, *Economic Hardship*, pp. 23–6.

[16] Jasmine Barrett, 'The North Korean Healthcare System: On the Fine Line Between Resilience and Vulnerability', *Resilience: Interdisciplinary Perspectives on Science and Humanitarianism*, Vol. 2, March 2011, pp. 59–60.

[17] New Focus International, 'Education in North Korea is a Lucrative Industry', *New Focus International*, 7 June 2013, available at http://newfocusintl.com/education-in-north-korea, accessed 7 February 2014.

[18] *Chosun Ilbo*, 'N. Korea's Underground Economy Booming', *Chosun Ilbo*, 8 February 2014, available at http://english.chosun.com/site/data/html_dir/2011/09/21/2011092101133.html, accessed 7 February 2014.

[19] Yoon, 'Economic Reform', p. 57.

[20] On products from China see Joo, 'Visualizing the Invisible Hands', p. 124.

petty trade in, for example, cigarettes and fruit and vegetables, which operated on street corners and were unlicensed. These operations could be easily dismantled if police or security officials decided to harass these mostly poor, mostly women, street traders. At the other end of the spectrum were what by the 2010s had become large, permanent, state-surveilled city establishments, most notably the Tongil market in Pyongyang.[21]

The population of Pyongyang had the advantage of access to more opportunities to buy, sell and to make money than most people living in the rest of the country, although not all the capital's inhabitants were well off. The city comprises a large number of residential neighbourhoods, split by two rivers, the Daedong and the Potong, and spread over a 2,500 square kilometre area. The population was reliant on a much over-stretched metro, trolley car and bus transportation system with a lucky few owning bicycles, although many simply walked as a means of trans-port. By 2014, Pyongyang's streets were filled with privately owned automobiles, a multitude of government- and enterprise-owned cars and trucks and even a few modern container lorries, but these transport options were only available to a tiny proportion of the three million plus population.

Markets required means of transport and bicycles supplemented the physical carrying of goods by individuals, the creation of homemade wheelbarrows and the historically familiar A-frame device used in urban and rural areas. These makeshift devices were limited in the distances that could be covered and were only useful for local exchanges of goods and services. Individuals used workplace vehicles to transport goods for private purposes where they could but this was a risky process as it depended on the connivance of officials and col-leagues in getting round the law. Even with the advent of personally owned vehicles in the military-first era, road transport remained fraught with difficulties due to the general shortage of vehicles, the scarcity and expense of fuel and poor road conditions. The main arterial road between west and east that connects Pyongyang with the port city of Wonsan was kept in reasonable repair but it could be impassable in the winter, especially when any of the many road tunnels were closed for maintenance. The journey from Pyongyang to Chong-jin via Wonsan could take three days as travel at night was dangerous and not normally authorised by security forces. Market responses to poor inter-regional transport included the conversion of trucks into

---

[21] Choi, *North Korea's Agricultural Reforms*, p. 20.

passenger-carrying vehicles. Truck drivers picked up hitchhikers who signalled they needed a lift by waving currency notes at passing drivers. In the late 2010s semi-privatised long-distance bus services were established by newly launched trading companies.

Goods were sold at prices analogous to those prevailing in China, in other words at world prices. The local currency, the North Korean *won*, was used for market transactions but only as a currency of last resort as it was subject to mega inflation. The population sought to acquire hard currency, and by the 2000s foreign currencies including the US dollar, the Chinese renminbi, the Japanese yen and the euro were in wide use.[22] Prior to the mid-1990s, the security apparatus would have arrested poor lower social class individuals caught handling dollars, but by the late 1990s the entire population, including Party members and members of the security forces, was trying to obtain hard currency, by definition through illegal means as only the *won* was legal tender in the DPRK. Hard currency was obtained through contact with foreigners in Pyongyang, and port towns such as Nampo and Wonsan, and through contact with Chinese traders in the north-east.

Border crossings into China were undertaken on a relatively frequent basis, the vast majority involving individuals making recurrent trips over the border to obtain food and income and then returning home to the DPRK.[23] The north-eastern stretch of the North Korean border where the Tumen River narrows provides a relatively easy crossing point for those who need or want to make the trip over the border to Yanbian. In winter, North Koreans hoping to trade in China could walk over the frozen river if they could escape detection by border guards, or if they could pay off the right people so that the crossing could take place unimpeded. Both the Chinese and the North Korean government periodically cracked down on the many hundreds who repeatedly crossed illegally, but this did not prevent continuing border crossings, which were increasingly mediated by the Chinese brokers who facilitated

---

[22] Discussion on dollarisation of the economy in Smith, 'La Corée du Nord vers l'économie de marché', pp. 6–14; see also John Ruwitch and Ju-min Park, 'Insight: North Korean Economy Surrenders to Foreign Currency Invasion', *Reuters*, 2 June 2013, available at www.reuters.com/article/2013/06/03/us-korea-north-money-idUSBRE9510E720130603, accessed 7 February 2013.

[23] Jinwook Choi, 'The North Korean Domestic Situation and its Impact on the Nuclear Crisis', *Ritsumeikan Annual Review of International Studies*, Vol. 5, 2006. p. 5, available at www.ritsumei.ac.jp/acd/cg/ir/college/bulletin/e-vol.5/CHOI.pdf, accessed 5 January 2014.

transfers of people, goods, food and money between the two countries.[24] This was a lucrative trade as brokers earned 30 per cent on money transfers from Koreans abroad to North Koreans and charged 10,000 dollars and more to arrange a transfer of a North Korean to Seoul.

The population participated in markets as sellers as well as buyers.[25] Market participation remained uneven partly because of government practices that differentially applied state controls to different occupational sectors. The government tolerated market participation by waged workers, including those employed in functioning workplaces, as enterprises could not provide a living wage to employees. Non-farming families obtained all or the vast majority of the food from markets, for the simple reason that they had no alternative if they were not to starve.[26] Where they could, farmers under-declared yields and sold produce privately but the government was punitive towards farmers who attempted to avoid the law, especially those who worked in the agriculturally productive areas.[27] Farmers located in poorly producing arable land were not expected by the government to do much more than feed themselves and their families.[28] These poor farmers were less surveilled than those in more productive farms.

State enterprises developed as crucial players in market activities. Initial aims were to provide food for employees and to find the means to purchase goods, including fuel and spare parts, to keep enterprises functioning.[29] Officials and workers sold metal and building components from decaying factories for scrap to Chinese traders and transferred

---

[24] Hazel Smith, 'North Koreans in China: Sorting Fact from Fiction', in Tsuneo Akaha and Anna Vassilieva (eds.), *Crossing National Borders: Human Migration Issues in Northeast Asia* (Tokyo: United Nations Press, 2005), pp. 165–90; Hazel Smith, 'Brownback's Bill will not help North Koreans', *Jane's Intelligence Review*, February 2004, pp. 42–5; Hazel Smith, 'Intelligence Matters: Improving Intelligence on North Korea', *Jane's Intelligence Review*, April 2004, pp. 48–51.

[25] Hazel Smith, 'North Korean Migrants pose Long-term Challenge for China', *Jane's Intelligence Review*, June 2005, p. 35; Choi, *North Korea's Agricultural Reforms*, p. 29; Soon-Hee Lim, *Value Changes of the North Korean New Generation and Prospects* (Seoul: Korea Institute for National Unification, 2007), pp. 43–4; Suh, *Economic Hardship*, pp. 33–6; Joo, 'Visualizing the Invisible Hands'; Kim and Song 'The Participation of North Korean Households', pp. 361–85; Haggard and Noland, *Witness to Transformation*, pp. 58–62.

[26] Cho, *The Changes of Everyday Life*, Note 26, pp. 23–4.

[27] FAO/WFP, *Crop and Food Supply Assessment Mission to the Democratic People's Republic of Korea*, Special Alert, No. 275 (Rome: FAO/WFP, 3 June 1997), p. 4.

[28] The variety in the farming sector is attested by the continuing involvement by humanitarian non-governmental organisations in agricultural assistance to poor and middle-income farms. See Caritas, *Caritas and the DPRK – Building on 10 Years of Experience* (Hong Kong and Rome: Caritas Hong Kong, 2006).

[29] Smith, 'Crime and Economic Instability'; Suh, *Economic Hardship*; Joo, 'Visualizing the Invisible Hands'.

materials to home industrial production.[30] Enterprises with access to vehicles and fuel swapped transportation capability for the supply of food from farming households and cooperatives. As military-first era shortages continued, these innovative and often extra-legal activities, originally designed as an emergency response to temporary difficulties, became routinised.

The Party and the military, at both central and local level, established businesses whose raison d'être was to make money from trade. The government permitted the growth of these companies to the extent that this hybrid private/Party sector evolved as the motor force of the institutionalisation of marketisation in the DPRK. Military units invoked the propaganda of both 'military-first' and 'self-reliance' to justify entrepreneurial activity and were allowed to set up trading companies whose initial function was to earn foreign exchange to buy food for military personnel. The Party owned the Daesung General Enterprise, the largest North Korean company; while the military owned the Kangsung General Enterprise Company.[31] Military companies controlled strategically important although nominally civilian enterprises such as the container port at Nampo, which was the target of major investment in the 2000s.[32]

The system worked by government grants of a licence to trade to an enterprise or public body, for example a Ministry or a university. The organisation was then permitted to hire entrepreneurs to carry out trade through a joint venture that was owned by the originating body. The commodities traded did not have to be linked to the originating organisation in any way. The system merely provided a licence to trade and therefore a way that the government could tax and to some extent monitor commercial activity. These semi-private/semi-public trading companies had a large amount of leeway to make private profit for those responsible for running these companies.[33] These joint ventures fulfilled the persistent demand for imported goods as local production was insufficient and of poor quality. Imports ranged from the basics, such as food, soap, hammers and nails, to the sophisticated, including

---

[30] Suh, *Economic Hardship*, pp. 23–6.
[31] Choi, 'The North Korean Domestic Situation', p. 6.
[32] Information on Nampo port from author's interviews, WFP logistics personnel, Pyongyang, 2000–1.
[33] Information in this paragraph is from author interviews with North Korean defectors in Seoul, August 2011. See also John S. Park, *North Korea, Inc.*, working paper (Washington, DC: United States Institute of Peace, 2009), available at www.usip.org/files/resources/North%20Korea,%20Inc.PDF, accessed 15 February 2013; Suh, *Economic Hardship*, p. 33.

everything from computers to vehicles. These trading companies developed as a core mechanism for the supply of goods to individuals and government agencies.[34]

The marketisation of the Party

The unanticipated outcome of self-help market activities by thousands of Party officials was that the Party was transformed into the major vehicle for the marketisation of North Korea. Participation by public officials in market activity legitimised and normalised the market as a framework for day-to-day living for North Koreans. The Party remained organisationally intact and its authority did not disintegrate but it became less feared as an instrument of state control as officials had little motivation in enforcing laws that threatened their own economic interests. The Party was less able to carry out its historic functions of inculcating Kim Il Sungism by way of ideological education and revolutionary discipline as officials were not rewarded for these activities and had less time to carry out these duties. Party membership remained important, not least because it could provide a means to private gains as officials and Party members leveraged political connections to supplement the insufficient income they earned from the state.[35] The intrinsic involvement of public officials in marketisation meant that central government attempts to control and curtail market dynamics were never successful.

Unlike officials and Party members in Mao's China, who had been more or less protected from food shortages during the 'Great Leap Forward', the majority of North Korea's vast army of officials were as much at risk of poverty and hunger as the rest of the population.[36] Senior officials in the Provincial Party Committees were nationally important political figures but for the most part the on-going economic troubles affected local Party and state officials and their families as much as their neighbours.[37] The demand for opportunities to buy and sell through non-state channels came therefore from Party officials and Party

---

[34] *North Korea, Inc.*

[35] Kyo-Duk Lee, Soon-Hee Lim, Jeong-Ah Cho, Gee-Dong Lee and Young-Hoon Lee, *Changes in North Korea as Revealed in the Testimonies of Saetomins* (Seoul: Korea Institute for National Unification, 2008), pp. 41–55; Joo, 'Visualizing the Invisible Hands'; Suh, *Economic Hardship.*

[36] Frank Dikötter, *Mao's Great Famine* (London: Bloomsbury, 2011).

[37] Alexandre Y. Mansourov, 'Inside North Korea's Black Box: Reversing the Optics', in Kongdan Oh Hassig (ed.), *North Korean Policy Elites* (Alexandria, VA: Institute for Defense Analyses, 2004), p. 31.

members as much as from the rest of the population.[38] It was not in the interests of those tens of thousands of Party and government officials who were supposed to enforce state controls over private economic activity to close down or restrict market operations.[39] Neither was it in their interests to rigidly enforce government prohibitions on the non-state sale of rice, maize, corn and potatoes, which is why these basic grains never disappeared from private markets.[40]

With the partial recovery of the economy from the mid-2000s, Party officials were again guaranteed access to a basic ration but officials had to pay near market prices even for rationed goods. For most officials this meant that someone in the family had to continue to engage in private, quasi-legal, economic transactions in order to supplement family income. Nominal Party membership remained necessary and useful as a sign of formal belonging to the state system, but it was not sufficient to protect against deprivation and hunger or to secure prosperity.[41] Far more important was the ability of individuals to use contacts and creativity to make money through engagement in trade and business.

Party and government officials at the mid and lower level used their positions to broker partnerships with entrepreneurs and traders.[42] Some of this business activity was lawful after the economic reforms of 2002 that legalised the pursuit of profit.[43] Some of this was more 'grey-area' activity and some was downright illegal. Officials participated in small irregular transactions, from perhaps selling food obtained from relations in the country in their homes and at work, to more systematic operations where the law was systematically ignored.[44] Officials earned monies from facilitating all sorts of activities that had been impossible and illegal and in some instances remained so.[45] Personal travel both within North Korea and across the border into China became relatively straightforward, given a mutually agreeable economic arrangement between the traveller and the

[38] Choi, *North Korea's Agricultural Reforms*, pp. 19–20.
[39] Hazel Smith, 'The Disintegration and Reconstitution of the State in the DPRK', in Simon Chesterman, Michael Ignatieff and Ramesh Thakur (eds.), *Making States Work* (Tokyo: United Nations Press, 2005), pp. 167–92.
[40] Joo, 'Visualizing the Invisible Hands'.
[41] Lee et al., *Changes in North Korea*, p. 55.
[42] Joo, 'Visualizing the Invisible Hands'; Suh, *Economic Hardship*.
[43] Jinwook Choi and Meredith Shaw, 'The Rise of Kim Jong Eun and the Return of the Party', *International Journal of Korean Unification Studies*, Vol. 19, No. 2, 2010, p. 179.
[44] Suh, *Economic Hardship*, pp. 33–7.
[45] A well-researched and theoretically framed study on the prevalence and reasons for bribe-taking by Party officials is Byung-Yeon Kim, 'Markets, Bribery, and Regime Stability in North Korea', working paper (Seoul: East Asia Institute Asia, April 2004), available at www.eai.or.kr/data/bbs/eng_report/2010040811122565.pdf, accessed 8 November 2014.

appropriate official.[46] Officials earned kick-backs and also received gifts in kind of food, medicine or other goods. Not every Party member or government official was corrupt but all had to use their connections and resources to earn money for themselves and their families and there was a tacit recognition by all levels of government that they could only survive by doing so.

Poorly paid officials could do well if they were able to sustain alliances that allowed them to access and utilise market opportunities but they were also vulnerable to criticism, purges and legal sanctions should their activities fall foul of more well-connected and assiduous officials or those who had a personal or professional reason to inform on their colleagues. Every member of the population that bought or sold grain in the markets and every official who took a payment in kind or money in return for tolerance of unlicensed market activities became a *de jure* law breaker. Participation in market activity was tolerated by the central state because it had no alternatives, although it would periodically try to enforce tough controls against what it called 'speculators'. As practically all of the population, including officials, were heavily involved in market trading – buying and selling – and so could at any time be accused of 'speculation', government and Party officials led a much more insecure life than in the previous era.

Managing the contradictory aspects of their jobs became fundamental to the daily life of local officials. On the one hand officials were supposed to ensure that farmers and workers turned up for state employment no matter how little they were paid and to keep control over the unofficial economy to maximise state revenues and central state political controls. On the other hand officials had the experience of famine, knew the state would not provide *in extremis* and were propelled by survival motives of their own to circumvent the rules.

The end of ideology

Party and security officials became less stringent in their application of formal state edicts to the control of markets, trade and travel as they themselves became dependent on those self-same markets and trade networks.[47] One consequence was the diminishing capacity of the Party to act as the transmission belt for ideological education. Party officials

---

[46] Hyeong-Jung Park and Kyo-Duk Lee, *Continuities and Changes in the Power Structure and the Role of Party Organizations under Kim Jong Il's Reign* (Seoul: Korea Institute for National Unification, 2005), pp. 18–19.

[47] Joo, 'Visualizing the Invisible Hands', pp. 132–3.

saw no reason or profit in enforcing what had become useless and out-of-date models of surveillance and restrictions on personal decision-making. Officials simply did not have the time to spend all their waking hours on ideological education.[48]

Party publications and media continued to operate as the mouthpiece for official pronouncements, recording of state visitors and as a vehicle for messages that the leadership wished to transmit to the population and abroad, but the state employed fewer officials to carry out propaganda activities.[49] In 2002, government legislation reduced Party activity in the workplace and sanctioned a drastic reduction in the number of workplace Party functionaries.[50] The reduced number of officials combined with the diminished ability of the Party to enforce economic sanctions and offer inducements meant that self-criticism sessions in which individuals had been forced to criticise their own behaviour and that of others lost their force and were transformed from effective means of discipline into rote activities.[51] Compulsory study sessions remained part of workplace routines but their performance was cursory and understood by the population as a systemic necessity, devoid of much meaning other than an acknowledgement that the Kim family still ruled the country.[52]

The disintegration of Party mechanisms and activities designed to keep the population fully occupied outside the workplace, the closing or partial shutdown of many workplaces and the growth of market activities gave individuals more time away from intrusive state controls. At the community level, the Party-directed local neighbourhood associations, or *inminban*, no longer functioned as effective political surveillance organisations. The stay-at-home women that had formerly been their mainstay were propelled into market activities as these formerly authoritative community leadership positions no longer gave status, income or guaranteed food rations.[53] Some of these women entered the market as traders and others benefited from 'sideline' payments as an inducement to ignore semi-legal trading activity that took place in the communal eras of apartment blocks. The women's organisation, the National Democratic

---

[48] World Food Programme (WFP), *Nutritional Survey of the DPRK* (Rome: WFP, January 1999), p. 8.

[49] See, for example, the official webpage of The Democratic People's Republic of Korea (DPRK), www.korea-dpr.com, accessed 14 December 2014.

[50] Mansourov, 'Inside North Korea's Black Box', p. 11.

[51] Choi, 'The North Korean Domestic Situation', p. 7.

[52] An example of Kim family hagiography is *Democratic People's Republic of Korea* Editorial Board, *Kim Jong Il: Short Biography* (Pyongyang: Foreign Languages Publishing House, 2001).

[53] Park and Lee, *Continuities and Changes*, pp. 52–4.

Women's Union, remained active at the formal level, but as its major constituency of 'housewives' were busy in market activity it, like the Party, also had less capacity to act as a conduit of ideological education.[54]

Information about the outside world leaked into the society through Chinese traders and the various foreigners that regularly visited North Korea from all over the world. All brought in information on a day-to-day basis in the form of conversation, magazines, books, DVDs and CDs.[55] The spread of ideas was as much a part of the reach of the market as the transborder buying and selling of food, fuel and basic consumer goods. By 2011 when Kim Jong Un became Leader of the state, China had been transformed into a modern global economic power. In 1994 when Kim Jong Il ascended to power, China had been at an early stage of economic revival but as the military-first era progressed, the North Korean population learned more about the increasing prosperity of their neighbours. The population knew that Chinese people had experienced a very similar recent political history and yet their economic opportunities and standards of living were significantly better than those of North Koreans. Each and every individual, to a greater or lesser extent, knew that far from the DPRK being a great country surrounded by less fortunate neighbours, the opposite was true. The juxtaposition of an increasingly wealthy China side-by-side a poverty-stricken North Korea of itself raised questions of governmental legitimacy and capacity.

The dissonance between government pronouncements and edicts and day-to-day reality increased the tendency of the population to treat the government as irrelevant except as an obstacle around which everyday economic life needed to be constantly negotiated. The population learned to circumvent the regular attempts by government to prevent growth in market activity such that all the population almost all of the time were effectively acting outside the law and in defiance of government dictates, even though these activities continued to carry risk. The population was forced into pretending to each other that they were operating under state direction whereas each and every member of the population knew that none of the state political rhetoric was true. Neither did the population believe continued government pronouncements of one state success after another in the revival of industry, agriculture and

---

[54] For history of the women's organisation see Kang, 'The Patriarchal State', pp. 55–70. Information on the disintegration of local organising capacity of the women's organisation from author's interview with North Korean female Party official, Pyongyang, 2001.

[55] Lee et al., *Changes in North Korea*, p. 48.

the economy.[56] The result was the embedding of a culture of cynicism about government and the degradation of the Party as an institutional power and political authority.[57]

The marketisation of law and order

The involvement of Party officials in the market and diminished ideological capacity did not result in political liberalisation. Military-first politics continued to demand obedience and state security services continued to function in a repressive manner.[58] Dissent was not tolerated and executions for political reasons continued.[59] The freedom to criticise the state and the Leader and to mobilise alternatives against the government remained non-existent. The security apparatus continued to provide revolutionary discipline when it was required by the government. Nevertheless, the ability of the Party to enforce the intensity of 'revolutionary discipline' that had prevailed in the Kim Il Sungist era diminished as marketisation provided powerful incentives for legal officials to accept bribes.[60]

Public security officials (the police) were authorised to make 'on the spot' decisions about whether an individual had broken the law and whether to send malefactors for labour training. Judicial officials were also permitted flexibility in application of the law, for instance, in terms of deciding the type of penalty or length of detention. This relative autonomy of officials and the arbitrary nature of the legal system facilitated the marketisation of law and order as officials could be 'persuaded' not to pursue a case by a judicious offer of food, goods and money.

[56] One North Korean official told me in Pyongyang in May 2011 that 'the government told us the glass covering of the pyramid-shaped Rugyong Hotel was made in our country'. He went on to say: 'I don't think that's true. It must have been imported from China.'
[57] A discussion of the inability of Party cadres to implement state policy and the open distrust of the population of Party officials is Jae-Jean Suh, 'The Transformation of Class Structure and Class Conflict in North Korea', *International Journal of Korean Unification Studies*, Vol. 14, No. 2, 2005, pp. 53–84.
[58] A useful discussion of the security services is in Patrick McEachern, *Inside the Red Box: North Korea's Post Totalitarian Politics* (New York: Columbia University Press, 2010), pp. 93–7.
[59] The North Korean state does not report who is punished and how. Accounts of executions come from those North Koreans who have left the country and whose accounts for perfectly understandable reasons cannot be verified. The normally well-informed Alexander Mansourov details individuals executed for political 'crimes' in the Kim Jong Il period. See Mansourov, 'Inside North Korea's Black Box'.
[60] Soo-Am Kim, Keum-Soon Lee, Kook-Shin Kim and Min Hong, *Relations between Corruption and Human Rights in North Korea* (Seoul: Korea Institute for National Unification, 2013).

De facto civic freedoms to buy, sell, travel and assemble emerged as a by-product of market activity. In everyday life individuals were less surveilled than during the Kim Il Sungist period and daily economic life was de-coupled from political life. The separation of economic and political spheres allowed for muted criticism of the government on issues that could be understood as non-political. These criticisms were very loud indeed when the government's November 2009 currency reform left the population with worthless savings and facing starvation as the official markets closed down for some weeks.[61]

The marketisation of the armed forces

All young men over the age of 17 were expected to participate in military service, although the government reported in 2003 that '[E]nlistment is on a voluntary basis and there is no system of forced conscription'.[62] As military-first norms were propagandised as the highest good, it would have been very difficult for any young person to refuse to 'volunteer' for military service during the constant rallies that the youth were obliged to attend.[63] The government commented that '[T]hose who are healthy,

---

[61] Choi and Shaw, 'The Rise of Kim Jong Eun', p. 184.

[62] DPRK Government, 'Second Periodic Reports of States Parties due in 1997: Democratic People's Republic of Korea, 05/11/2003, CRC/C/65/Add.24 (State Party Report)', *Committee on the Rights of the Child, Consideration of Reports Submitted by States Parties under Article 44 of the Convention* (Geneva: Office of the High Commissioner for Human Rights, 5 November 2003), p. 15, available at www.refworld.org/pdfid/403a10a44.pdf, accessed 3 November 2014.

[63] There is confusion in the literature as to the nature of military conscription in North Korea. Young-Tai Jeung reports a conscription law being enacted at the Tenth Supreme People's Assembly, which took place in 1998. As at 2003 the North Korean government reported that there was no forced conscription into the military. Some of the confusion arises from semantics. All young people were – in the Kim Il Sung era – and are – in the military-first era – expected to participate in some form of defence and nation-building activity, some of which takes place in the military after young people 'enlist'. In Kim Il Sung's time there were more rewards for military service and in the post-Kim Il Sung era much fewer. In Kim Il Sung's day, there was more pressure from families for young people to join the army to secure their future, and therefore in this sense the government had less need to coerce young people into the military. In the military-first era, given the lack of rewards and the high costs paid by individuals in terms of absence from families for sometimes many years, combined with living in difficult and demoralising conditions, it is logical that enlistment to the very large standing army must take place in the form of coercion, to the extent that we can understand the practice as conscription. It is also likely that 'voluntary' enlistment is very difficult to avoid. Young-Tai Jeung, *Internal and External Perceptions of the North Korean Army* (Seoul: Korea Institute for National Unification, 2008), pp. 35 and 40; United Nations, *Committee on the Rights of the Child Consideration of Reports Submitted by States Parties under Article 44 of the Convention, Second Periodic Reports of States Parties due in 1997 Addendum Democratic People's Republic of Korea, 16 May 2003, CRC/C/65/Add.24*

able-bodied, sane and have no family problems are selected from among the volunteers and are educated in full-time military or technical educational institutes for one to two years before being posted to units as servicemen on active duty'.[64] In practice, this meant that young men who did not go on to university and whose families were not understood as politically problematic would enter military service.

The 2008 census showed that some 700,000 military personnel were living in camps, a number similar to the 1993 level, although not all young people fulfilled their military obligations by serving long stretches in camps.[65] Women benefited from gendered social conventions that deemed it inappropriate or necessary for young women to live away from home. Army service of seven to ten years meant that it was common for young male soldiers not to see their families for years. Leave was not frequent and few could afford transport back to their homes. Unskilled and poorer men, who could not find a way to avoid military service, might find themselves sent to a military camp for years on end, without home leave, living in poor conditions and with insufficient food throughout their period of service.[66] Military personnel were supposed to be guaranteed food rations, but the majority of personnel were not noticeably better off or better fed than their compatriots. Rations were very basic, composed of potatoes, millet, barley and sometimes rice, and with meat, eggs, vegetables and fruit rarely available.

Military camps were instructed to be self-sufficient in agricultural production and, where possible, to earn foreign exchange.[67] Without sufficient fertilisers, chemicals, functioning irrigation equipment and spare parts, and with many of these young people lacking agricultural know-how or experience, it was not easy to meet self-sufficiency targets. The work

(United Nations: New York, 5 November 2003), p. 15, available at www.unhcr.org/refworld/country,,,STATEPARTIESREP, PRK,4562d8cf2,403a10a44,0.html, accessed 27 January 2012; Coalition to Stop the Use of Child Soldiers, *Child Soldiers Global Report 2008* (London: Coalition to Stop the Use of Child Soldiers, 2008), pp. 198–9, available at www.childsoldiersglobalreport.org/files/country_pdfs/FINAL_2008_Global_Report.pdf, accessed 27 January 2012.

[64] DPRK Government, 'Second Periodic Reports', p. 15.

[65] The 2008 census gives a number for the total DPRK population including all those 'individuals living in private households, institutional living quarters and military camps'. It also gives a lesser number for the population including 'all individuals living in private households and institutional living quarters'. The inference is that the number of those living in military camps can be deduced by subtracting the smaller number from the total. Chang Su Kim, *DPR Korea 2008 Population Census National Report* (Pyongyang: Central Bureau of Statistics Pyongyang, 2009), pp. 14–22.

[66] There were reports of starvation and malnutrition in the military. Lee *et al.*, *Changes in North Korea*, pp. 54–5.

[67] Suh, *Economic Hardship*, p. 21.

was arduous as military camps were predominantly situated in the remote and mountainous northern regions that were difficult to farm because growing seasons were short due to extreme climates and inhospitable terrain. Soldiers, just the same as Party officials, therefore used their positions and contacts to earn money through trade or, if they were posted to the China border, by taking money and gifts in return for permitting North Koreans to cross into China without papers.[68] Army units collaborated with local authorities to buy and sell food outside the state sector for the purpose of survival and in order to obtain goods and services no longer provided reliably by the state.

The marketisation of the family

Daily social and economic practices reinforced the vitality and agency of the family compared to the moribund nature of state institutions as marketisation generated pressures on the family to compensate for the lack of state resources for the most vulnerable. The government admitted in its reporting on the condition of the elderly that most relied on family support.[69] Young children were less institutionalised and had more contact with their families, especially their mothers, than had been the case in the previous era.[70]

The Kim Il Sungist state had never been entirely successful in constituting the family unit as a means of ideological education and as an instrument of politics but it had succeeded in forcing individuals into public activities to the extent that the family was marginalised in everyday life. In the military-first era, the family reconstituted itself much more explicitly into a socio-economic unit in which private, trust-based and non-state-directed social relations could flourish. At the same time, the family unit developed as the key social institution in and through which marketised relations were organised and directed.[71]

---

[68] Choi, 'The North Korean Domestic Situation', p. 6.

[69] UNESCAP, 'Report by the Delegation of the Democratic People's Republic of Korea', in Economic and Social Commission for Asia and the Pacific, High-level Meeting on the Regional Review of the Madrid International Plan of Action on Ageing (MIPAA), 9–11 October 2007, p. 6, available at http://globalaging.org/agingwatch/desa/aging/mipaa/Korea.pdf, accessed 8 November 2014.

[70] I visited the DPRK in May 2011 after an eight-year absence, having lived and worked in the country for two years. The most astounding difference was the obvious diminution of regimentation of children, hundreds of whom could be observed playing and moving freely, with and without families, on the streets in Pyongyang. Between 1990 to 2003 it was rare to see unaccompanied children on the streets.

[71] A useful discussion of, inter alia, the changing role of the family in North Korea is Kang, 'The Patriarchal State'.

The family remained constituted by quite conservative gender roles even as women became breadwinners within marketised North Korea. Women's new-found commercial freedoms did not translate into increased economic, social and political status. Many women, especially young mothers, remained poor and lived on the margins of hunger, but the consequence of allowing women to engage in informal economic activity meant that women travelled, assembled in small groups, engaged in non-state-directed bargaining and learned how to navigate state structures that otherwise put obstacles in the way of individual economic activity. In the absence of the state's ability to provide, women took on more responsibilities but also gained a limited increase in personal freedom. Women's participation in market activities thus translated into increased flexibility in personal decision-making and diminished state control of family life.

In other authoritarian societies, churches and civic groups have provided civic and social support mechanisms, but in North Korea, where non-state organisational life was not permitted, individuals turned to the family as the primary social organisation within which they could mobilise economically and socially. Non-state-organisational activity of any sort risked very heavy penalties, but the informal politics of private family-directed economic and social networking was conceived of by the state as 'non-political' and, hence, permissible. The state rhetoric that legitimised and praised the ethical value of family allowed the family unit to develop as a relatively safe space around and in which economic and social activity could be organised.[72]

The family was naturalised in North Korean society to the extent that in 2008 the incidence of non-married adults was more or less confined to the widowed and those not yet married.[73] Marriage was legal for men at age 18 and women at age 17 but few young people married until they were over 25 years old.[74] In 2008 the median age for marriage was 28 for men and 26 for women.[75] The main constraint on marriage remained the necessity to complete national service, whether performed as an enlisted soldier or as a member of quasi-military civil defence units.[76]

---

[72] The state's categorisation of political loyalties by family is discussed in Suh, 'The Transformation of Class Structure', pp. 63–5.

[73] Central Bureau of Statistics, '2008 Census of Population of DPRK: Key Findings', available at www.unfpa.org/webdav/site/global/shared/documents/news/2010/dprk08_censuskeyfinds.pdf, accessed 22 June 2014; 1996 figures from UNICEF, *Situation Analysis of Women and Children in the DPRK* (Pyongyang: UNICEF, 1999).

[74] Ibid.

[75] Central Bureau of Statistics, '2008 Census of Population of DPRK', p. 2.

[76] Sun Won Hong, *Analysis of 1993 Population Census Data DPR Korea* (Pyongyang: Population Center, DPRK, 1996), p. 39.

The government supported delayed marriage – explaining that 'women tend to marry later in order to devote their early young period of life to the work for the benefit of the society'.[77]

Women's breadwinner role in the era of marketisation did not mean that women's and men's social relationships changed substantially.[78] Women acknowledged the man as the head of the family even as it became more common for men to contribute to domestic labour in the home.[79] Pragmatic changes to everyday life did not undermine the profound understandings in North Korean society that the family and private sphere were more naturally the domain of the woman and the public domain more naturally that of the man.[80] Social attitudes that subordinated women to their husbands, even if women had become the main income earner, remained prevalent. These same social expectations left women to shoulder the burden of poor state services when the state could no longer provide a functioning social safety net. Ironically, one of the reasons for poor state services was under-staffing caused by the exodus of women into the marketplace.

Family goals were not synonymous with state goals and could be understood in some ways as directly antithetical to those goals. Families survived by getting around state prohibitions on daily activities, especially the myriad trading activities in which all families engaged. Military-first era policies were therefore understood by most as inimical to the core economic interest of most families. It did not necessarily follow that families supported regime change but it did follow that families had few stakes in the continuation of regime policy.

Market values

Marketisation was a social and an economic process. The individual was forced into taking daily economic decisions for themselves and to stop relying on the state. Continued food shortages forced the population to ignore and circumvent state regulations such that everyday practices embedded a disregard for state authority and at the same time institutionalised market values of private property and individual self-interest. The pursuit of trade and profits and the change from top-down economic control to bottom-up marketisation did not eradicate Kim Il Sungist norms, but it significantly eroded them. Widespread awareness that

[77] Ibid.   [78] Kang, 'The Patriarchal State'.
[79] Hazel Smith, *WFP DPRK Programmes and Activities: A Gender Perspective* (Pyongyang: WFP, 1999); Lim, *The Food Crisis*.
[80] Ibid., pp. 32–6.

survival meant self-help called into question the legitimacy of sacrifice for
the good of the community and the state. It became taken for granted
that those that could leverage advantages through self-help would survive
and might even prosper but those who were less adept confronted
impoverishment, poor health and, sometimes, premature death.

Instead of largely accepting of the right to rule by centralised decision-
making, twenty-first century North Koreans valued the right to make
individual, self-interested decisions that involved circumventing government policy as a matter of daily practice. The population found themselves income, began saving individually (in hard currency where
possible), engaged in personal budget planning, and bought and sold
goods within a whole variety of both legal and semi-legal market
arenas.[81] Economic rewards and penalties assumed a much greater
importance than the system of political rewards and political penalties
hitherto provided by Party dictates. Value hierarchies were transformed
from an emphasis on the collective to the self-interested pursuit of
making money.[82]

The lives of young people growing up in the Kim Jong Il era were less
privileged but also less intellectually sealed from outside influence than
previous generations.[83] They were bounded since birth by poor living
standards and a marketised economy in which the survival of the fittest
was a reality. At the same time North Korean youth had increasingly easy
access to South Korean DVDs and music that showed an alternative, yet
Korean, way of life. North Korean youth knew that South Korean youth
did not spend their time breaking up rocks with the most primitive tools
to build roads in below freezing temperatures, without proper sanitation,
warm clothes or adequate food.[84]

Indications of social change can partially be detected through the
reported data on teenage pregnancies. The 1996 Family Law prohibited
conjugal relations outside marriage, although it guaranteed equal rights
for any child born outside legal marriage, thus recognising that the law
could not prevent extra-marital relationships.[85] There is no information

[81] Helgeson and Høyrup, *North Korea 2007*, pp. 36–8.
[82] Suh, *Economic Hardship*, pp. 30–7.   [83] Lim, *Value Changes.*
[84] Jae-Jean Suh, *North Korea's Market Economy Society from Below* (Seoul: Korea Institute
for National Unification, 2005), p. 55; Suh, *Economic Hardship*, p. 11; Lee et al., *Changes
in North Korea*, pp. 48–51.
[85] Foreign Languages Publishing House, *The Family Law of the Democratic People's Republic
of Korea* (Pyongyang: Foreign Languages Publishing House, 1996), p. 2; Committee on
Economic, Social and Cultural Rights, Thirty-first Session, Item 6 of the Provisional
Agenda, Implementation of the International Covenant on Economic, Social and
Cultural Rights: Replies by the Government of the Democratic Republic of Korea
(E/1990/6/Add. 35), HR/CESCR/NONE/2003/1 (Geneva: Committee on Economic,

on births outside marriage even today and there were no recorded births for any teenage woman in the 1993 census.[86] In the 2008 census, however, 303 women in the age group of 15–19 years were reported as giving birth in the year preceding the census.[87] These were very small numbers, less than 0.2 per cent of the total numbers of 169,231 live births, but the figures were significant.[88] The fact that the data was reported at all demonstrates an increasing acceptance of teenage pregnancies and acknowledgement of a changing society.[89] Teenage pregnancies were twice as common in rural areas and although the numbers are too low to draw definitive conclusions, this differential indicates the relatively poor ability of the Party to enforce the social conformity that the Kim Il Sungist era had aimed to achieve.[90]

As the market economy shaped the rest of society so it also transformed values and norms within the military.[91] The daily lives of North Korean soldiers and their families provided a constant refutation of the Kim family propaganda that accompanied army service. Young soldiers, as many youths in communist countries had learned before them, now learned how to listen to state propaganda without comment and collude with others as unobtrusively as possible to find ways round the system. Young people no longer learned how to be model socialist citizens by way of military service but instead how to behave in everyday life in ways diametrically opposed to state directives.

Markets provided freedom of choice but also helped to institutionalise inequality as only those with independent purchasing power could afford to buy food and goods. Female domination of the retail sector did not translate into new-found economic power for women because wholesale trade was controlled by the 'big hands', linked to powerful groups in the North Korean state and Chinese trading networks.[92] Women's new-found ability to participate in market transactions meant that some ended up selling their bodies as prostitutes. Others ended up in neighbouring China as bargirls, prostitutes or by agreeing or being coerced into becoming 'wives' for Chinese men unable to find a Chinese bride.[93]

Many state employees continued to work for next to nothing in social welfare jobs, such as health and education, but the main value underpinning the new marketised North Korea was a version of Social Darwinism that understood that in the end it would be self-help and family support

Social and Cultural Rights, 10–28 November 2003), available at www.bayefsky.com/issuesresp/rokorea_hr_cescr_none_2003_1.pdf, accessed 27 January 2012.

[86] Hong, *Analysis of 1993 Population Census Data*, p. 39.
[87] Kim, *DPR Korea 2008 Population Census*.   [88] Ibid.   [89] Ibid., p. 77.   [90] Ibid.
[91] Suh, *Economic Hardship*, pp. 29–30.   [92] Joo, 'Visualizing the Invisible Hands'.
[93] Smith, 'North Koreans in China', pp. 165–90; Lim, *The Food Crisis*, pp. 23–5.

that would enable individuals to survive and prosper. It became legitimate, in other words, for individuals to accumulate private wealth. The less savoury aspects of the pursuit of economic self-interest included the rise of economic crime. In the urban areas, including in Pyongyang, the visible signs were the proliferation of netting, plastic sheeting or other makeshift barriers erected to fence off and protect the lower balconies of apartment buildings from intruders. In rural areas the fields were guarded by makeshift sentry boxes where farmers would watch against crop theft. Inadequate social welfare nets, continuing food shortages and reliance by the government on markets to create jobs and income resulted in increasingly visible inequality between those who had money and those who did not

By 2014, two generations of North Koreans had experienced poverty and the constant anxiety of wondering where the year's food would come from, so for simple survival purposes every North Korean had to practise a lifestyle that assumed the government would not have the capacity to provide. On the other hand, each individual had to simulate belief in the greatness of the Kim family because to indicate otherwise would be to risk prison and exile as a political dissident. The results of such obvious dissonance between rhetoric and reality were a crisis of legitimacy for the regime and the rise in political and personal cynicism as a framework for day-to-day survival.

The resilience of marketisation

The government never fully acknowledged that the state could not and did not provide basic welfare functions for most of its population, including enough food to eat. Consequently it never fully acknowledged that engaging in private trading was not a choice but a necessity for all the population.

Economic transformation was accompanied by a social transformation that loosened the ability of the Party to inculcate ideological fervour and revolutionary discipline in the population at large. Ideas and information from abroad and disillusionment with the government encouraged the rise of individualism, although North Koreans also conceived of themselves as bound by important relationships that included 'natural' duties and obligations to family and, in some instances, to local communities.[94] Nevertheless the turn to market values represented a significant shift in societal norms.

[94] For discussion on the rise of 'Mammonism' in the DPRK, see Kim, *Economic Reform in North Korea*, pp. 26–8.

The self-help society created in North Korea was much more of a genuine exercise in local self-reliance than the state-controlled, top-down model of Kim Il Sungist *Juche* ideology. North Koreans moved from being without hardly any economic agency to being more proactively involved in the market than most people living in market democracies, whose market activity tends to remain on the purchasing side of the market equation. For almost all the population the informal economy was not only the most reliable source of food but also the most rational way of making money and the population never again trusted the state to provide a reliable source of food supply after their experience of famine in the 1990s. Marketisation proved extraordinarily resilient in the face of military rule from above that periodically sought to suppress and contain the marketisation of the economy and the society.

10   Military rule from above

The goal of military-first politics was regime survival. The idea was to embed regime security against dissent at home and threats from abroad in a new system of politics in which the interests and survival of the Kim family were institutionally folded into the interests and survival of the military. Military-first politics was a response to instability generated by the famine and economic collapse of the mid-1990s, although, in an effort to secure legitimacy for military-first politics, some North Korean publications read back the foundations of military-first politics into history, at least as far as 1960.[1] Other North Korean sources are more accurate with one Pyongyang publication attributing the first articulation of 'Songun' or 'military-first politics' to a 1995 New Year's Day speech made by Kim Jong Il to a military unit.[2]

Military-first politics provided the means to achieve and operationalise regime security priorities.[3] For the first time in the brief history of the North Korean state, the military assumed executive authority over the political sphere.[4] Communist institutional models that conflated state

[1] *Korea Today*, 'Songun Idea with Deep Roots', No. 4, 2011, pp. 24–5.
[2] Chol U Kim, *Songun Politics of Kim Jong Il* (Pyongyang: Foreign Languages Publishing House, 2008).
[3] Ibid.
[4] There is a debate in the literature as to the extent of military dominance of domestic politics in the post-famine era but little disagreement that there has been a shift in power in domestic politics towards the military. Young-Tai Jeung argues, for example, that the structure can still be characterised as 'Party-commands-the-military'. See Young-Tai Jeung, *North Korea's Civil-Military-Party Relations and Regime Stability* (Seoul: Korea Institute for National Unification, 2007), p. 20. My view is that the Party has become marketised such that it is a different entity than it was in the Kim Il Sung period. It still operates as a transmission belt for state priorities such as carrying out vaccination campaigns but the economic interests of Party members and officials mitigate effectiveness as a political/security institution whose function is to implement state restrictions on the market and the society. In the context of the scope of this book, the point need not be argued here, but it should be recorded that there is an on-going debate about the extent of military power in domestic politics in the military-first era and the extent to which the balance of power between various institutions of the state changed over time. See Park and Lee, *Continuities and Changes*; Jeung, *Internal and External*

and Party were maintained but the government stressed that military-first politics was a new form of political organisation. Constitutional changes in 1998 and in 2009 embedded military-first principles in law. There was no question of a switch to a democratic system based on multiparty elections. Military-first governments did not engage in structural reform of the judicial or penal system although some modernisation of the criminal law took place.

Military-first economic planning aimed to reconstruct the old command economy founded on the resuscitation of heavy industry for the same reasons that underpinned Kim Il Sungist policy. The aim was an economy that could support a military capacity that could deter or, in the worst-case scenario, defend against military intervention from abroad. Military-first era governments remained ideologically opposed to implementing a radical 'marketisation from above' but in practice relied on the *de facto* marketisation that had emerged 'from below' to deliver key priorities, including food security. Foreign investment policy remained guided by national security policies that shunted foreign investment and foreigners into 'enclaves' that could be literally fenced off from the rest of the country.[5] The institutionalisation of military-first politics embedded a national security mentality such that economic policy was subordinated to a militarised understanding of national security.

Military-first politics

Military-first politics were designed to achieve symbiosis of the interests of the Kim family with those of the military; to promote and secure the interests of the military as an institution; and to legitimise regime goals through the promotion of a nationalist ideology as well as the continued glorification of the Kim family. Kim Jong Il aimed to constitute military-first politics such that regime survival entailed the survival of the Kim family as the dominant political group. Kim Jong Un succeeded his

Perceptions; Choi and Shaw, 'The Rise of Kim Jong Eun'; Dongmin Lee, 'The Role of the North Korean Military in the Power-Transition Period', Background Paper Series (Seoul: Ilmin International Relations Institute, July 2011); Lee *et al.*, *Changes in North Korea*; Ken E. Gause, *North Korean Civil-Military Trends: Military-First Politics to a Point* (Carlisle, PA: Strategic Studies Institute, US Army War College, 2006), unpaginated but pp. 59–110 on pdf; available at www.nkeconwatch.com/nk-uploads/dprkpolicyelites.pdf, accessed 2 November 2014; Joseph S. Bermudez, 'Information and the DPPK's Military and Power-holding Elite', in Kongdan Oh Hassig (ed.), *DPRK Policy Elites* (Alexandria, VA: Institute for Defense Analyses, 2004), unpaginated but pp. 15–58 on pdf; available at www.nkeconwatch.com/nk-uploads/dprkpolicyelites.pdf, accessed 2 November 2014.

[5] Helgeson and Høyrup, *North Korea 2007*, pp. 41–3.

father in 2011 as the designated inheritor of strategy that prioritised the military. He remained committed to regime survival techniques that relied on the militarisation of society and foreign policy.

When Kim Il Sung died in 1994, Kim Jong Il became state Leader by virtue of his status as Chairman of the National Defence Commission and leadership of the armed forces. Kim Jong Il was not formally appointed as President so the DPRK state remained without an official head of state. The younger Kim was not seen in public until 1997. Photographs of Kim inspecting military installations were periodically published in the local media but there was no certainty that these were contemporary pictures. Kim Jong Il's absence from public view coincided with the height of the famine and until 1997 there was some doubt as to whether Kim Jong Il was actually running the country. When Kim Jong Il finally emerged into the public arena it was to announce that from henceforth the country would be run according to 'military-first' politics.[6] The official explanation for Kim's absence was that he had been observing a traditional three-year mourning period for his father, but whether from *force majeure* on the part of the military, leadership agility or a combination of the two, after 1997, Kim Jong Il's interests, status and future became symbiotic with those of the military.

In 1997 Kim Jong Il consolidated his leadership of the Party after taking the position of General Secretary of the Workers' Party of Korea.[7] Kim Jong Il maintained control of the powerful Organisation and Guidance Department of the Party that he had transformed during the Kim Il Sung era into a means of exercising personal power and which was responsible for nominating cadres for Party, government and military appointments as well as surveillance and discipline.[8] Kim Jong Il was not merely an instrument of the military but the strategic alliance between the Kim family and the military as an institution meant that Kim did not have free rein to ignore their views and interests.[9] Kim Jong Il was

[6] Kim, *Songun Politics*, pp. 5 and 7. McEachern dates the announcement of the military-first policy to a *Rodong Sinmum* (the Party's daily newspaper) article of 22 August 1998. See McEachern, *Inside the Red Box*, p. 62, but dates the introduction 'The Military First Concept' to 1997, p 71.
[7] Délégation générale de la RPD de Corée en France, *Bulletin d'information, Special Issue No. 37/1097* (Paris: Délégation générale de la RPD de Corée en France, 28 January 1991), pp. 1–3.
[8] *New Focus International*, 'Insider Perspective: The Removal of Jang Song Taek (Update)', 9 December 2013, available at http://newfocusintl.com/insider-perspective-the-removal-of-jang-song-taek-update, accessed 14 January 2014; *New Focus International*, 'This is it: North Korea's Hidden Power System', 31 December 2013, available at http://newfocusintl.com/north-koreas-hidden-power-system/#comments, accessed 15 January 2014.
[9] Choi, 'The North Korean Domestic Situation', p. 11.

surrounded by military advisers who influenced his agenda and controlled access to the Leader.[10]

In 2010, the year before he died, Kim Jong Il promoted 185 persons into new military ranks, as part of the effort to consolidate the military as an effective instrument of regime security for Kim Jong Un and to reinforce the centrality of the military as the core institution in the North Korean polity.[11] Kim Jong Il endowed the status of Four Star General on his sister, Kim Kyong-Hui and on Kim Jong Un, despite neither having any significant military experience, and promoted both to membership of the National Defence Commission.[12] When Kim Jong Il died, Kim Jong Un was immediately appointed as Supreme Commander of the Korean People's Army and ruled as First Vice-Chairman of the National Defence Commission. Civilian officials in the Kim Jong Un government, including those with economic portfolios as well as state security officials, were given military rank and existing military personnel were promoted to the rank of general.[13]

Organisational change and continuity

North Korean texts made clear that military-first politics should be understood as a substantive redirection of the state structure 'to establish the political system that gives weight to the army'.[14] Military-first politics entailed an explicit commitment 'to give priority to the army over the working class' and to ensure that the 'country's manpower and material resources are mobilised in boosting military capabilities on a priority basis'.[15] Economic reconstruction was to be pursued in military-first politics but only in the context of giving 'primary importance to the military affairs' to which 'all the issues arising in the revolution and construction are subordinated'. The message for domestic and foreign consumption was that, in a continuing era of limited resources, the military as an institution would be prioritised, protected and nurtured.[16]

---

[10] Mansourov, 'Inside North Korea's Black Box', p. 29.

[11] Kyo-duk Lee, Soon-Hee Lim, Jeong-Ah Cho and Joung-Ho Song, *Study on the Power Elite of the Kim Jong Un Regime* (Seoul: Korea Institute for National Unification, 2013), pp. 56–8.

[12] BBC News Asia Pacific, 'North Korean Leader Kim Jong-Il's son "made a general"', 28 September 2010, available at www.bbc.co.uk/news/world-asia-pacific-11417016, accessed 3 November 2014.

[13] Lee *et al.*, *Study on the Power Elite*, pp. 58–61.

[14] Kim, *Songun Politics of Kim Jong Il*, p. 7.

[15] Chun Gun Kim, 'Principles in Songun revolution', *The Pyongyang Times*, 1 October 2011, p. 2.

[16] Ibid.; Hong Su Ri, 'Songun Politics, Unique Mode of Politics', *The Pyongyang Times*, 19 November 2011, p. 3.

Constitutional changes of 1998 and in 2009 fundamentally altered state structures to reflect the dominance of the military in domestic politics.[17] These were of a different order from the 1992 constitutional amendments. The 1998 Constitution confirmed the status of the National Defence Commission as supreme executive authority within the state.[18] The 1998 Constitution subordinated institutions of governance, including the formerly powerful Cabinet of Ministers, previously known as the State Administration Council, to the National Defence Commission.[19] The 2009 Constitutional amendment solidified the priority of military interests in state policy in its reminder that the Chairman of the National Defence Commission is the 'supreme leader' of the state and has the duty and authority to, among other things, 'guide overall affairs of the state'.[20] The Chairman of the NDC should be understood as the head of state as 'the mission of the chairman of the National Defence Commission is the highest official duty of the state … [it] constitutes a sacred official duty symbolic and representative of the glory of the motherland and the nation's dignity'.[21]

Military-first politics did not represent a fundamental change in political and legal philosophy or entail change to the administrative structure of government. Politics remained authoritarian, and fundamentally antithetical to liberal notions. The rights of individuals to challenge the state through recourse to the rule of law, as in liberal democratic systems,

---

[17] For discussion see Dae-Kyu Yoon, 'The Constitution of North Korea: Its Changes and Implications', *Fordham International Law Journal*, Vol. 27, No. 4, April 2004, pp. 1289–305; Marion P. Spina, Jr., 'Brushes with the Law: North Korea and the Rule of Law', in *Academic Series Papers on Korea* (Washington, DC: Korea Economic Institute, 2008), pp. 75–97, available at www.keia.org/Publications/OnKorea/2008/08Spina.pdf, accessed 9 February 2014. For texts of the Constitutions in English see Foreign Languages Publishing House, *Socialist Constitution of The Democratic People's Republic of Korea* (Pyongyang: Foreign Languages Publishing House, 1993); Supreme People's Assembly, *DPRK's Socialist Constitution* (full text), amended and supplemented Socialist Constitution of the DPRK, adopted on 5 September 1998 (Pyongyang: DPRK Government, 1998), available at www.novexcn.com/dprk_constitution_98.html, accessed 23 January 2014. An unauthorised translation of the 2009 DPRK Constitution 'by a team of American analysts specializing in North Korean politics' can be found on a blog entitled 'NorthEast Asia Matters' on http://asiamatters.blogspot.com/2009/10/north-korean-constitution-april-2009.html, accessed 19 June 2011.

[18] Ibid. For discussion see Gause, *North Korean Civil-military Trends*.

[19] Supreme People's Assembly, *DPRK's Socialist Constitution*. For discussion see Gause, *North Korean Civil-military Trend*.

[20] An unauthorised translation of the 2009 DPRK Constitution 'by a team of American analysts specializing in North Korean politics' can be found on a blog entitled 'NorthEast Asia Matters' at http://asiamatters.blogspot.com/2009/10/north-korean-constitution-april-2009.html, accessed 19 June 2011.

[21] See Sung Ung Kim (ed.), *Panorama of Korea* (Pyongyang: Foreign Languages Publishing House, 1999), p. 52.

remained non-existent.[22] North Korea charged that global human rights campaigns were designed for the purpose of upturning its national sovereignty, arguing in a report to the United Nations Human Rights Council, the DPRK stated that

The [DPRK] Government respects the principles of the Charter of the United Nations in respect of human rights and international human rights instruments, and maintains the principle of recognizing the universality of human rights, while taking due account of the political and economic systems of different countries and nations, and the level of their development, peculiarities, characteristics and diversity of their historical and cultural traditions. It welcomes and encourages, in dealing with international human rights issues, dialogues and cooperation based on respect for sovereignty and equality, rejects the application of double standard, and calls for strict observance of the principle of impartiality, objectivity and non-selectivity. It is of the view that as human rights are guaranteed by sovereign States, any attempt to interfere in others' internal affairs, overthrow the governments and change the systems on the pretext of human rights issues constitutes violations of human rights. In this sense, the DPRK holds that human rights immediately mean national sovereignty.[23]

Legal reforms brought some modernisation, although not to the extent of allowing political dissent and/or criticism of the leadership.[24] In 2004 the government introduced the principle of *nullum crimen sine lege*, that is, the principle that the offence for which an individual is charged must be specified.[25] Previously the DPRK, as other socialist countries, had relied on vague wording to describe groups of crimes; vagueness which contributed to the arbitrary application of the law. From 2004, the DPRK iterated and specified a large number of crimes, including large numbers of economic offences. The reforms allowed for the substitution of life-imprisonment as an alternative to the death penalty for hitherto capital crimes. From 2004, 'labour-training' of up to two years in a variety of workplaces, including mines, factories and farms, became the most common penalty for legal transgressions.[26] 'Labour-training' did not

---

[22] A careful analysis of human rights concerns is in Richard Kagan, Matthew Oh and David Weissbrodt, *Human Rights in the Democratic People's Republic of Korea* (Minneapolis/Washington, DC: Minnesota Lawyers International Human Rights Committee/Asia Watch, 1988).

[23] Human Rights Council, 'National Report Submitted in Accordance with Paragraph 15 (A) of the Annex to Human Rights Council Resolution 5/1: Democratic People's Republic of Korea', Geneva, 30 November–11 December 2009.

[24] Patricia Goedde, 'Law of "Our Own Style": The Evolution and Challenges of the North Korean Legal System', *Fordham International Law Journal*, Vol. 27, 2003–4, pp. 1265–88; Spina, Jr., 'Brushes with the Law'.

[25] In Sup Han, 'The 2004 Revision of Criminal Law in North Korea: A Take-off?', *Santa Clara Journal of International Law*, Vol. 5, No. 1, 2006, pp. 122–33.

[26] Ibid., pp. 125–6.

entail incarceration and therefore represented marginal liberalisation of the judicial system.

The provinces continued to provide the higher level body of local government and counties and their urban equivalent, the districts, provided the lower level of government authority. At the start of the military-first era there were twelve provinces but local government reorganisation brought this down to ten in 2004 as Nampo and Kaesong, respectively, were incorporated into North Hwanghae and South Pyongan.[27] Local government continued to be delegated to 208 rural counties and urban districts (as at 2013), which were divided into smaller geographical areas, known as the *ri* in rural areas and the *dong* in urban areas, although these smaller geographical units were administrative divisions and were not repositories of local government authority.[28] The government gave 'special status' to the areas in which foreigners were permitted to work, including the free trade area of Rajin-Sonbong located in the north-east of North Hamgyong province, and the South Korean-funded Kaesong Industrial Zone in North Hwanghae provinces. These were administrative changes and did not represent radical organisational change.

The intent of military-first organisation was to ensure that government and society was prepared for war. Military-first politics was justified because 'military affairs [were] the most important of all state affairs ... Preparing an unconquerable army to forestall the aggressive attempt of the forces of imperialism and domination and continuing to advance socialism by relying in the powerful army is his [Kim Jong Il's] far-sighted political strategy.'[29] The core organisational message was that the entire society should learn to operate as a well-drilled military force while the armed forces were supposed to contribute to economic development as well as to carry out their military duties. Military-first organisation of society did not mean that North Korea became a militarised society in the sense that the streets became full of gun-toting soldiers. Soldiers and the police did not normally carry arms in North Korea.

Songun politics meant that 'all members of the society should model [*sic*] after the traits of soldiers'.[30] Highly valued traits were obedience, discipline and subordination to the leadership. In the new era of the 'military-led' society 'working people ... should put the interests of

[27] For more detail on local government structures see UNICEF, *Situation Analysis of Women and Children*.
[28] UNICEF, *DPRK at a Glance 2013* (Pyongyang: UNICEF, 2013), available at www.unicef.org/dprk/DPRK_at_a_glance_April_2013.pdf, accessed 7 February 2014.
[29] Kim, *Songun Politics of Kim Jong Il*, p. 6.
[30] *Korea Today*, Editorial, 'Make this a Year of Brilliant Victory,' No. 3, 2004.

society and the collective above their own.'[31] As in the military, orders were to be obeyed without question and control was, ultimately, by the threat of force. These were not new methods of operation as Kim Il Sungist mass mobilisation techniques had relied heavily on a military level of organisation. Military-first era organisation was, however, less well accepted as a normative good as it offered few rewards to compensate for the physically arduous compulsory labour that occupied time which could have been better spent in income generation activities.

Duties of the armed forces include being at 'the forefront of the work to build factories and enterprises which will be exemplary in modernising the country's economy'.[32] Uniformed military constructed buildings, dams and monuments.[33] They were involved in the lucrative *Arirang* mass games, held every year to generate hard currency for the state.[34] Economic activities were not, however, prioritised over military drills and preparation for potential conflict as 'the DPRK's revolutionary armed forces are in full preparedness for launching a do-or-die battle against any act of military provocation'.[35] Kim Jong Il made repeated visits to military units to emphasise the military readiness of the DPRK armed forces. In November 2011, just weeks before his death, Kim Jong Il was reported as visiting an air force base where 'he highly praised again the men and officers ... for conducting training without slackening the militant spirit while being on the alert for the enemy's aggressive moves'.[36] After Kim Jong Il's death, Kim Jong Un was similarly reported in the DPRK media as a regular visitor to military bases, in an effort to shore up his military credentials and to demonstrate that the Korea People's Army continued to provide the focus of national priorities.[37]

The armed forces were tasked with suppressing political dissent and dissatisfaction with state failure to prevent famine, continued economic

---

[31] Ibid.

[32] Editorial Board, 'Creators of Happiness', *Democratic People's Republic of Korea*, No. 660, April 2011, p. 15.

[33] For a list of infrastructure built by the Korean People's Army between 1995 and 2005 see Park and Lee, *Continuities and Changes*, p. 21.

[34] For details on costs for travel and a visit to the mass gymnastic displays see www.korea-dpr.com/travel.htm, accessed 26 June 2011.

[35] Supreme Command Korean People's Army, 'Press statement', *The Pyongyang Times*, 26 November 2011, p. 1.

[36] Ibid.

[37] For example, Korean Central News Agency (KCNA), 'Kim Jong Un inspects Command of KPA Unit 534', 12 January 2014, available at www.kcna.co.jp/index-e.htm, accessed 15 February 2014; KCNA, 'Kim Jong Un Guides Night Exercise of KPA Paratroopers', 20 January 2014, available at www.kcna.co.jp/index-e.htm, accessed 15 February 2014; KCNA, 'Kim Jong Un Guides Tactical Exercise of KPA Unit 323', 23 January 2014, available at www.kcna.co.jp/index-e.htm, accessed 15 February 2014.

deterioration and the poverty of daily life.[38] Official pronouncements continued to trumpet the superiority of the political and social system, yet every government proclamation contrasted with the lived, daily reality of poverty and hunger. Dissatisfaction with the government was prevalent. In 1999, the army crushed anti-government demonstrations in Onsong, in the northern province of North Hamgyong, with an unknown number of deaths and casualties.[39] Kim Jong Il continued to face opposition from within and reportedly eradicated army generals accused of plotting a coup in 1998.[40] Elite consensus was that the regime could be best secured by way of reliance on the military but this did not mean that all of North Korea's upper echelons supported the Kim family in every aspect of policy. Nevertheless, penalties against political dissent remained brutal. Kim Jong Un's sanctioning of the execution of his uncle, Jang Song-thaek, in 2013, demonstrated the absence of fundamental political change in the DPRK.

The nationalist tropes

The central ideological messages of the military-first era were founded in nationalist tropes, reinforcing an ideological orientation that had already been prominent during the Kim Il Sung era. The propaganda emphasis shifted further away from the communist heritage towards an insistence on the unique nature of *Juche* tradition, or spirit of self-reliance. An article published under the name of Kim Jong Il in the Party's theoretical journal, *Kulloja*, in 1996, sternly warned that North Korean scientists who argued that *Juche* was embedded in 'Marxist dialectical materialism' were guilty of 'a deviation'.[41] The 2009 constitutional amendment that dropped reference to communism therefore reflected the long-established position that argued for the inadequacies of Marxist philosophy and the originality of the *Juche* idea.

[38] Mansourov, 'Inside North Korea's Black Box', VA, pp. 28–9.

[39] Reports of the Onsong riot in 'Chinese Influence on the Rise in Pyongyang', *Sratfor.con Global Intelligence Update*, 5 November 1999, available at www2.gol.com/users/coynerhm/chinese_influence_on_pyongyang.htm; *NAPSNet Daily Report*, 2 November 1999, available at www.nautilus.org/napsnet/dr/9911/NOV02.html#item7; Bradley Martin, 'The Koreas: Pyongyang Watch: The Riot Act?', 3 November 1999, available at www.atimes.com/koreas/AK03Dg01.html, accessed 15 December 2014.

[40] Mansourov reports serious criticism of Kim Jong Il by senior officials in 1998. See Mansourov, 'Inside North Korea's Black Box', pp. 28–9. For disaffection after the famine see Jeung, *Internal and External Perceptions*, pp. 2–4.

[41] Kim Jong Il, 'The Juche Philosophy is an Original Revolutionary Philosophy', *Kulloja*, 26 July 1996 (in English) (Paris: Délégation générale de la RPD de Corée en France, 1996), p. 10.

Military-first politics was portrayed as the only way to guard against the machinations of foreign countries attempting to intervene in North Korea, especially the United States and Japan.[42] The ideological justification was that the armed forces provided the only guarantor of Korean independence, which was threatened by imperialist enemies.[43] These messages were contextualised in nationalist polemics that proclaimed that the only independent Korea was the DPRK and that the DPRK only existed because of the beneficent leadership of the Kim dynasty.[44] The deceased Kim Il Sung was designated 'Eternal President of the Republic' in the revised Constitution of 1998, so as to symbolise the continuity of Kim family rule.[45]

North Korean publications portrayed the regime as giving embattled leadership to the entire Korean peninsula and to Koreans everywhere, with the North Korean government the embodiment of a pan-national Korean independence. National holidays recalling specifically North Korean anniversaries, including Kim Il Sung's birthday on 15 April, were celebrated but traditional festivals such as 'Chusok', where ancestors are remembered on the fifteenth day of the eighth lunar month, that are also celebrated in South Korea, were also acknowledged and given prominence by the state.[46]

Military-first economics

The nominal goal of economic planning was to encourage balanced development combining industrialisation, agriculture and the development of trade. Defence expenditure was protected and this is not surprising given the absolute priority of national security to all aspects of state strategy. Military-first priorities also skewed economic policies in other ways. Marketisation was viewed as a threat to regime security and foreign economic investment a security threat.

The growth strategy of military-first governments entailed encouraging foreign investment because it could not redevelop moribund and decaying economic infrastructure, including roads, railways, telecommunications, power grid and buildings, purchase advanced technology and resuscitate the heavy industrial sector, from domestic resources.[47] Yet government practice contradicted the aim of securing foreign investment

---

[42] Kim, *Songun Politics of Kim Jong Il*, pp. 77–92.   [43] Ibid., p. 7.   [44] Ibid., pp. 14–18.
[45] Supreme People's Assembly, *DPRK's Socialist Constitution*.
[46] For discussion of *Chusok* see *Korea Today*, '*Chongmyong* and Related Customs', Vol. 4, 2011, p. 41.
[47] Joo, 'Visualizing the Invisible Hands', p. 123.

as national security priorities always trumped economic priorities where a
conflict between the two arose. While the government offered generous
terms to foreign investors for the repatriation of profit, low taxation and a
controlled and cheap workforce, it tried very hard to maintain political
control over any possible liberalising influences from foreigners and
foreign ways of doing business. Contracts were sometimes unilaterally
and abruptly changed, terminated or not honoured for reasons that were
often not made explicit but which appeared led by security policy.[48]

The government succeeded in ending the precipitous freefall of the
economy of the 1990s but failed to achieve substantial economic growth.
Its aim was to build a 'strong and prosperous country' by 2012, the
hundredth anniversary of the birth of Kim Il Sung.[49] United Nations data,
however, showed that per capita income fell from $735 in 1990 to $583
per annum in 2012, with the DPRK only achieving a high of $638 per
capita income in 2011.[50] The Bank of Korea calculated that average per
capita income was $1,150 in 2009, compared to average per capita income
of just under $20,500 in South Korea in the same year.[51] The numbers
differed but the direction of travel of all the figures indicated a low- to
middle-income economy whose population was struggling to maintain a
decent standard of living.

United Nations data showed that aggregate gross domestic product
(GDP) growth took place between 1999 and 2005, but that the economy
went into recession in 2006, 2007 and 2010.[52] In 2011 and 2012 negligible growth was recorded, at 0.8 per cent and 0.3 per cent
respectively.[53] The economy stabilised but continued to operate at a very

---

[48] There is a favourable report on the success of South Korean business in non-enclave
North Korean business initiatives in Pyongyang, Nampo and Sinuiju, in *Korea Now*, '80
Percent Post Profits in Inter-Korea Trade', Seoul, 24 August 2002. This should be
contrasted with the more sober assessment of Young-Yoon Kim in 2005 who reports
that 65 per cent of South Korean businesses operating in the DPRK 'considered that
their business ... was not going well'. Young-Yoon Kim, *Evaluation of South-North
Economic Cooperation and Task for Success* (Seoul: Korea Institute for National
Unification, 2005), p. 31.
[49] Moon-Young Huh (ed.), *Basic Reading on Korean Unification* (Seoul: Korea Institute for
National Unification), p. 186.
[50] United Nations Statistics Division, 'Per Capita GDP at Current Prices in US Dollars (all
Countries)', National Accounts Main Aggregates Database, available at http://unstats.
un.org/unsd/snaama/dnlList.asp, accessed 15 February 2014.
[51] Bank of Korea, *Gross Domestic Product of North Korea in 2009* (Seoul: Bank of Korea,
2010), available at www.nkeconwatch.com/nk-uploads/bok-dprk-gdp-2009.pdf,
accessed 30 April 2011, p. 3.
[52] United Nations Statistics Division, 'Growth Rate of GDP/Breakdown at Constant
2005 Prices in Percent (all countries)', National Accounts Main Aggregates Database,
available at http://unstats.un.org/unsd/snaama/dnlList.asp, accessed 15 February 2014.
[53] Ibid.

low level of economic activity and output.[54] In 2009 all major sectors of the economy, including agriculture, forestry and fisheries, and mining and manufacturing, including light and heavy industry, declined in output.[55] Only construction and services showed growth, at a low level, of 0.8 per cent and 0.1 per cent respectively.

The consequences of the military-first policy designed to 'enable[s] liberal investment in increasing defence power and improve[s] the weapons and equipment of the armed forces to the maximum', was that resources that could have been used for national reconstruction were swallowed up by defence priorities that also took around a million potentially economically productive young men and women out of the workforce every year.[56] Chronic labour shortages prevailing in every sector of the economy were exacerbated.[57]

The armed forces were the best-resourced and best-organised political and social institution in the country.[58] Government investment in the successful potato production project in Taehongdang County, Ryanggang province was designed, for example, as both a means to increase national grain production and a place of work for demobilised soldiers.[59] Taehongdang County was one of a tiny number of farms in the DPRK where sophisticated mechanisation was visible.[60] Yet the high percentages of government spending that went to defence was not sufficient to feed, clothe and shelter the large numbers of young soldiers, never mind fund the hardware and software necessary to support a viable modern army.

Official figures show that the percentage of the national budget allocated to the military rose from a low of 11.4 per cent in 1994 to 14.6 per cent in 1998.[61] Defence spending did not return to the historic

---

[54] Helgesen and Høyrup, *North Korea 2007*; Bank of Korea, *Gross Domestic Product*.

[55] Ibid., p. 2.   [56] Kim, *Songun Politics of Kim Jong Il*, p. 10.

[57] Helgeson and Høyrup, *North Korea 2007*, pp. 34–5; Suh, *Economic Hardship*, p. 13.

[58] Gause, *North Korean Civil-Military Trends*.

[59] Reference to military involvement in construction and agricultural development, including the large potato project in Taehongdan County, is in Kim, *Songun Politics of Kim Jong Il*, pp. 27–8. Taehongdan County was noted for its successful agricultural investment in potato production before the famine and became the target of international humanitarian assistance by various donors in early 2000s. See Ryon Hui Yang, 'Taehongdan County Integrated Farm on Paektu Plateau', *The Pyongyang Times*, 13 August 1994, p. 4. This author visited the potato project in Taehongdan County in October 2000 when she was working for the UN WFP.

[60] Author's observations from travel in and through every province in the DPRK, ecxept Chagang, 1999–2001.

[61] Chung-in Moon and Sangkeun Lee, 'Military Spending and the Arms Race on the Korean Peninsula', *Asian Perspective*, Vol. 33, No. 4, 2009, pp. 80–1.

highs of around 30 per cent of the late 1960s, but neither did it fall to the levels of the early 1990s.[62] Defence spending remained at between 14 per cent and 16 per cent of government expenditure from the 2000s onwards.[63] Non-DPRK sources suggested that the percentage of government resources spent on defence was nearer 50 per cent and, if military involvement in ancillary industries were to be included, these higher estimates would not be unreasonable.[64]

International Institute of Strategic Studies (IISS) data suggest that, in 2010, North Korea's army comprised 1,190,000 active forces along with 600,000 reservists.[65] If the entirety of defence expenditure was allocated to only the active military, $3,680 a year was spent on each soldier, but if real exchange rates are used the figures are deflated considerably to defence spending at less than $300 per soldier. In 2011 the *won* was trading at between 2,500 and 5,000 to the dollar compared with the official exchange rate at around 150 *won* to the dollar.[66] Given that the North Korean military leadership probably did not allocate all its funds to the upkeep of its military personnel, the amount of government allocated to cover the basic living requirements of each soldier must have been pitifully small.

Economic legislation as a means of control

Economic legislation reflected the competing aims of encouraging growth and at the same time controlling and channelling the private sector in the interests of military-first security priorities. Military-first governments understood that market operations were by their very nature private and spontaneous and thus tended to undermine authoritarian methods of command and control. The *de facto* marketisation within which the whole country operated was therefore only tolerated as a temporary necessity even as the pursuit of profit was lauded as a new aim for enterprises. The government rejected suggestions that it might benefit from a fundamental shift in economic philosophy. Legislation was designed to manage marketisation and did not represent a political decision to engage in profound economic restructuring.[67]

---

[62] Ibid.   [63] Ibid.   [64] Ibid.

[65] International Institute of Strategic Studies (IISS), *The Military Balance 2011* (London: Routledge, 2011), p. 249.

[66] Author's observations and interviews, Pyongyang, May 2011.

[67] A contemporaneous analysis of the 2002 reforms gives useful data and also notes that the intention was to maintain government control over pricing. See Ihk-pyo Hong, 'A Shift toward Capitalism? Recent Economic Reforms in North Korea', *East Asian Review*, Vol. 14, No. 4, Winter 2002, pp. 93–106. For a view that is more positive about the

In 1998, economic reforms in other socialist countries, such as Vietnam, were denounced as 'Americanization'.[68] In 1999, an editorial in the English-language publication, the *Pyongyang Times*, reproduced a long article originally published in the Party's theoretical journal that called on its readers to 'reject imperialists' ideological and cultural poisoning'. The statement appeared at the same time as the relatively large numbers of humanitarian organisations resident in North Korea were discussing with the government ways and mechanisms of economic development, although suggestions of policy change to encourage incentives by way of supporting market activity were understood by the government as threatening the basis of its existence. The 1999 article, read widely by humanitarian officials in Pyongyang, warned that '[The] bourgeois publications that find their way into socialist countries mainly preach on "liberalism" and "democracy". If one dances to the tune of their version of "liberalism" and "democracy", we will become a degenerate riffraff without an iota of faith in the Party and socialism.'[69]

Legal reforms lagged behind *de facto* economic transformation on the ground. In 1998 Constitutional changes allowed legal ownership rights to social organisations in recognition of the post-famine practices of enterprises and local Party organisations, which had started to buy and sell goods outside state mechanisms. Individuals were also given rights to travel.[70] Legal changes followed the market reality. Individuals had been wandering the countryside since the mid-1990s without the requisite paperwork; seeking food, income and trading opportunities. The 1998 constitutional changes authorised the population to lead their lives, within certain constraints, as market-driven actors.

The government implemented a raft of economic legislation in July 2002 in an attempt to control and manage market operations. The reforms included a partial freeing of price and wage controls, the reduction of subsidies on a number of public services, including housing and utilities, and a commitment that enterprises should operate according to profit and loss criteria.[71] Wages were hiked up dramatically so that waged workers could afford to buy the much more expensive food. The reforms

---

2002 reforms as a decisive change in government policy see Helgeson and Høyrup, *North Korea 2007*.

[68] CNS, DPRK Report No. 15, November–December 1998, available at http://cns.miis.edu/pubs/dprkrprt/98novdec.htm.

[69] Rodong Sinmun and Kulloja, 'Reject Imperialists' Ideological and Cultural Poisoning', *Pyongyang Times*, 12 June 1999.

[70] Yoon, 'The Constitution of North Korea',.

[71] Kim, *Economic Reform in North Korea*, pp. 17–24; Choi, *Structure of Industry*, pp. 31–2.

institutionalised and legitimised the pursuit of profit, rational accounting and increased independence for enterprises. The 2002 reforms sanctioned the idea that autonomous, profit-directed enterprise was conducive to national economic regeneration and thus gave legitimacy to grey-area economic developments, including the growing numbers of semi-public/semi-private trading companies.[72] In 2003, the government also recognised the *de facto* expansion of markets that had taken place over the previous decade by redesignating 'farmers' markets' as 'general markets'.[73]

In 2004, penalties for crossing the North Korea/China border without papers to obtain food and income were reduced, with these activities more or less now understood as misdemeanours rather than crimes.[74] Harsher sanctions were reserved for those judged to be crossing the border to engage in anti-state activities or espionage, which could still result in life-imprisonment or the death penalty.[75] The notorious penalties for listening to foreign broadcasts and media were reduced so that isolated incidents were exempt from penalties, although the state still regarded the 'systematic' listening to such material as criminal activity. These legal changes reflected an incremental realisation that not all North Koreans were travelling to China to foment anti-government dissent. Most trading activities did not threaten the regime and in some ways strengthened it by providing an economic safety-valve for thousands of poor North Koreans. North Koreans devoured South Korean movies but were less interested in listening to overt political propaganda and much more in enviously observing trends in South Korean fashion and consumer culture.

The government relied on market transactions as it received taxes from the licensing of large marketplaces and trading companies.[76] Military-first governments were also freed from the necessity to expend state resources on social expenditures, such as food and medicine, as long as individuals were able to buy and sell these goods through non-state channels. Nevertheless, the government tried on a number of occasions to manage and control the scope and scale of non-state directed economic transactions.

In 2009, the government revalued the currency without warning to try to eradicate private markets. These private trading networks revived within a few weeks as the state was not able to resuscitate state trading and distribution networks so as to provide food and goods that had

---

[72] Park, *North Korea, Inc.*   [73] Kim, *Economic Reform in North Korea*, p. 19.
[74] Han, 'Criminal Law in North Korea', pp. 122–33.
[75] Ibid., p. 129–31.   [76] Park, *North Korea, Inc.*

more or less entirely been provided through market channels.[77] The policy failed to control marketisation but the currency revaluation decimated the value of each individual's savings and antagonised the entire population, even those who may never before have criticised the leadership.[78]

The cooperative farms that produced most of the country's grain remained tightly integrated into state-controlled agricultural supply chains, and incentives for increases in cooperative farm production remained minimal.[79] In 2012 the United Nations reported that 'no radical reform relating to agriculture is expected'.[80] Agriculturally productive farms were compelled to surrender all cereals, soybean and potato production over and above the rather meagre government grain allowances allocated to farmers after the harvest.[81] There was thus no incentive to increase production and every incentive to try to siphon off grain surpluses into the parallel markets where grain could be sold for high prices. In response, the government periodically attempted to keep grain out of the markets and to reinstitute grain sales only through the public distribution centres and state shops. These attempts to take back control were never completely successful as there were too many countervailing forces that encouraged farmers and officials to engage in profit-seeking opportunities, even though this behaviour still risked penal retribution.[82]

Agricultural privatisation was not contemplated because the government aimed to maintain state control over an industry that was primarily understood in terms of how it could support defence and, potentially, war-fighting. The government therefore only permitted marginal changes to agricultural organisation. It tinkered with the agricultural system by promoting fish farming, sweet potato production, double cropping and the development and propagation of new seed varieties. The government allowed sub-work teams to be rewarded for productivity increases and an expansion of the size of private plots where farmers were allowed to cultivate for the market as well as for their own consumption. The government did not go so far as to admit, however, that wholesale privatisation might bring productivity increases, even without massive new investment, even though the implementation of marginal changes

---

[77] Soo-ho Lim, 'North Korea's Currency Reform a Failure?', *SERI Quarterly*, April 2010, pp. 115–19.

[78] FAO/WFP, *Crop and Food Supply Assessment Mission*, 16 November 2010, p. 6

[79] United Nations, *DPR Korea Common Country Assessment 2002* (Pyongyang: UNOCHA, February 2003), p. 14.

[80] FAO/WFP, *Crop and Food Supply Assessment Mission*, 12 November 2012, p. 9.

[81] Ibid., pp. 9–10.   [82] Joo, 'Visualizing the Invisible Hands, p. 117.

showed that yields on private plots were higher than yields from the same crops on the cooperative farms.[83]

The security preoccupations of the government prevented the development of the fishing industry as much of the coast was mined, fenced and guarded, ostensibly to deter foreign spies sneaking into the country. Large-scale coastal fishing remained the remit of quasi-government entities such as fishing cooperatives and medium-sized enterprises. Boats and fuel were expensive, electricity supplies unreliable and refrigerated trucks and refrigeration capacity very scarce, so fish traded at major ports could not travel far within North Korea.[84] Some of these fishing enterprises developed as export business but the chronic infrastructural degeneration militated against the development of fishing as a major source of employment and fish as a major part of the diet in North Korea.

The food priority

Military-first governments maintained the objective of food self-sufficiency through domestic agricultural production despite the intrinsic difficulties of achieving this goal.[85] In 2006, the United Nations commented that the 'country has opted, in spite of climatic factors (long winters, vulnerable location in regard to such natural occurrences as typhoons, tidal surges, hail and droughts) and a scarcity of arable lands, to produce food crops and orient policies towards agricultural self-sufficiency when other nations might possibly have opted for increased food importation'.[86]

---

[83] FAO/WFP, *Crop and Food Supply Assessment Mission*, 16 November 2010, p. 12. For evidence that maize grown in private plots was much more efficiently cultivated than maize in the cooperative farms, see FAO/WFP, *Democratic People's Republic of Korea Joint WFP/FAO Rapid Food Security Assessment Mission* (Rome: FAO/WFP, 9–30 June 2008).

[84] Helgesen and Høyrup, *North Korea 2007*, pp. 67–73.

[85] For discussion on agricultural supply and demand in the early years of the Kim Jong Il administration, see Woon-Keun Kim, 'Recent Changes in North Korean Agriculture Policies and Projected Impacts on the Food Shortage', *East Asian Review*, Vol. 3, No. 3, Autumn 1999, pp. 93–110; Phillip Wonhyuk Lim, 'North Korea's Food Crisis', *Korea and World Affairs*, Winter 1997, pp. 568–85. On the precariousness of food self-sufficiency policies in North Korea, see Tae-Jin Kwon and Wook-Keun Kim, 'Assessment of Food Supply in North Korea', *Journal of Rural Development*, 22, Winter 1999, pp. 47–66; FAO/WFP, *Crop and Food Supply Assessment Mission*, 16 November 2010; United Nations, *DPR Korea Common Country Assessment 2002*, Pyongyang, mimeo, February 2003.

[86] United Nations, *Strategic Framework for Cooperation Between the United Nations and the Government of the Democratic People's Republic of Korea 2007–2009* (Pyongyang: United Nations, September 2006), p. 12.

Military-first policies did not succeed in achieving food self sufficiency but production increased so that by 2012 the 'food gap' was the narrowest it had been since the famine years. In 2012 the United Nations estimated that the country would need 200,000 tonnes of food support that year, much less than the half a million tonnes that had regularly constituted the cereal deficit since the late 1990s.[87] In 2013, the food gap narrowed further so that the United Nations argued that only 40,000 tonnes would be required to compensate for insufficient domestic agricultural production.[88] These aggregate figures, however, were based on minimum requirements to meet survival needs, and increases in cereal production were not sufficient to engender significant tradable surpluses. The emphasis on cereal production also meant that although North Korea no longer suffered from a food or public health emergency by 2014, the lower priority given to the production of livestock and quality food and vegetables meant that the diet of the average North Korean was deficient in the protein, vitamins and minerals necessary for healthy growth.[89]

Food allocation and distribution policy changed under military-first governments which, in practice, gave up their role as the primary providers of food for all the population, all of the time. Intermittent attempts to revive the public distribution system as an exclusive means of food allocation and distribution all failed. The government could only manage a general distribution of food to the entire population on national holidays and then only for a few days.[90] When food was available for the general public, it was no longer allocated via differential rations based on occupation, age and gender. The system changed to one based on a flat-rate minimum ration of around 300 grams per day. Government policy was to provide a food ration for vulnerable groups including children under the age of seven, pregnant and nursing women and the elderly. In the military-first era, food to these social groups was not distributed on a regular basis and depended on availability.

By 2008, military-first food policy focused on the provision of a food ration to some two million key workers; the ration did not include a food allocation for their families. In 2011, key workers included 439,586 males and 284,592 females who worked in the military, public administration and as 'compulsory social security workers'; and 718,195 people who worked in mining and quarrying; as well as 367,650 construction

---

[87] FAO/WFP, *Crop and Food Supply Assessment Mission*, 12 November 2012, p. 4.
[88] FAO/WFP, *Crop and Food Supply Assessment Mission*, 28 November 2013, p. 4.
[89] Ibid.   [90] *The Changes of Everyday Life*, pp. 25–6.

workers.[91] Key workers were guaranteed a ration of 700 grams of grain per day.[92] The public distribution system was thus transformed from a primary source of food for the entire non-farming population, based on finely tuned allocations, to that of providing flat-rate rations to key workers.

Food rations were not free but until the economic reforms of 2002 they were sold at well below market price. After 2002, rationed food had to be paid for at prices linked to the Chinese rice price.[93] The huge subsidies that the government had hitherto provided were abolished.[94] As Chinese rice was sold at near world prices, this innovation introduced real market pricing into the heart of government food policy and the value of the food ration to the individual became less its low price but more the guarantee of supply.

The goal: foreign investment without foreign influence

The government attempted to reconcile national security and economic development priorities by trying to secure foreign investment while minimising foreign influence and foreign ideas. The central plank of foreign economic investment policy became the provision of geographically demarcated, fenced-off economic enclaves in which foreigners and the local population with whom they came into contact could be monitored and supervised. A major objective was to prevent North Koreans obtaining access to information that would contradict the government depiction of foreign countries, especially South Korea, which it had presented as having an inferior level of social, cultural and economic achievement to that of North Korea. An unmediated exposure to large numbers of foreigners, even those who did not speak Korean, would have exposed this picture of the outside world as false. Given the government's continued anxiety to present itself to its own population as the only legitimate representative of the Korean nation, and given that South Koreans by definition could speak Korean and had therefore relatively easy means of conversation with North Koreans, the enclave policy was strictly applied to South Korean investment.

---

[91] WFP/FAO/UNICEF, *Special Report: Rapid Food Security Assessment Mission to the Democratic People's Republic of Korea, 24 March 2011* (Rome: WFP, 2011), p. 18, available at http://ko.wfp.org/sites/default/files/english_rfsa.pdf, accessed 22 June 2014.

[92] Ibid.

[93] For knowledgeable discussion on the North Korean economic changes of the 2000s, see Park (ed.), *The Dynamics of Change.*

[94] Jung-Chul Lee, 'The Pseudo-Market Coordination Regime', in Phillip H. Park (ed.), *The Dynamics of Change in North Korea: An Institutionalist Perspective* (Boulder, CO: Lynne Rienner Publishers, 2009), pp. 199–201.

North Korea's first experiment in closed-off enclave zones had taken place in the Kim Il Sung era when the government had agreed a joint free trade zone in the far-off north-east of the country, in Rajin-Sonbong, where the DPRK bordered the then Soviet Union and China.[95] The lack of infrastructure, including decent roads and reliable rail transport into North Korea and out through China and Russia, poor telecommunications, irregular and inadequate electricity and general underdevelopment contributed to a failure to attract much more than minimal investment, less than a hundred million dollars between 1990 and 2000.[96] The North Korean government also deliberately discouraged interelinkage backwards into the DPRK society and economy. The inhospitable mountains separating Rajin-Sonbong from the rest of the country were seen by the North Korean government as a positive rather than a negative factor in the promotion of Rajin-Sonbong as an enclave for capitalist enterprise, as foreigners were thus prevented from contact with the North Korean population. The foreigners who visited Rajin-Sonbong, of which there were 90,000 in 1999, were kept under close scrutiny, with South Koreans particularly subject to suspicion.[97]

The next enclave development was in Kumho, located in the east of the country, near the coastal city of Wonsan, where the two nuclear power reactors funded by the Korea Peninsula Energy Development Organisation (KEDO), as agreed in the 1994 Geneva Agreement, were to be built.[98] The North Korean government physically cleared the site of the local population. Only North Korean technicians and service workers were permitted to remain. KEDO agreed to North Korean strictures that prevented foreign workers from leaving the Kumho construction site, which was absent any but the most basic facilities, during the entire year-long contract that foreign workers spent in the DPRK. KEDO-employed Uzbeki workers were paid less than $200 a month so did not have the option of leaving the site by paying for trips home during the duration of

[95] Délégation générale de la RPD de Corée en France, 'Rajin-Sonbong Zone Appealing to Investor', in *Bulletin d'information*, 25/1096 (Paris: Délégation générale de la RPD de Corée en France, 7 October 1996), p. 3; Délégation générale de la RPD de Corée en France, 'Bright Future of "Golden Triangle"', in *Bulletin d'information*, 28/0197 (Paris: Délégation générale de la RPD de Corée en France, 26 January 1997), pp. 2–3.

[96] Tumen Secretariat, *Tumen Update No. 3* (Beijing: Tumen Secretariat, October 2000).

[97] South Korean academic staff at Yanbian University of Science and Technology, in the Yanbian area of China, informed me in 2002 that two of their number had been arrested and imprisoned in Rajin-Sonbong after their deliveries of food and goods to children's nurseries had brought them under suspicion of spying.

[98] Alexandre Y. Mansourov, 'North Korea Stressed: Life on the Hamster Wheel', *International Journal of Korean Unification Studies*, Vol. 14, No. 2, 2005, p. 97.

their contracts.[99] President George Bush called a halt to KEDO activities in 2005 but the enclave modalities of fenced-off sites, with foreigners physically separated from North Korean nationals, remained a feature of North Korean government approaches to capital transfers from abroad.

In September 2002 the government proposed another enclave development in the form of a free trade zone in Sinuiju City, on the northwestern border with the Liaoning province, a prosperous and rapidly developing part of China.[100] Intrinsic to the plan was the non-voluntary relocation of the entire population of Sinuiju, some 340,000 people, from their homes to what would have been a newly created residential area. The government also planned to build a wall to prevent anything other than minimal contact of the displaced population with foreigners. The Sinuiju free trade zone would have been excluded from DPRK domestic economic regulation and the intention was that it should be headed up by a Dutch-Chinese citizen, Yang Bin.

The absence of a settled rule of law in the DPRK meant that even without malice aforethought, Sinuiju could have become a magnet for East Asian transnational organised crime including the proximate Chinese snakeheads (people smugglers), Russian criminals based in Vladivostok and Japanese *yakuzas* (gangsters) – not to mention home-grown North (and South) Korean criminal elements. China's response to the announcement of the free trade zone in Sinuiju was swift and publicly humiliating for the DPRK government. The Chinese authorities arrested Yang Bin on charges of bribery, forging documents, illegal use of land and fraudulent contracts, with the Liaoning People's court sentencing him to eighteen years' imprisonment in July 2003.[101] The message to Pyongyang was that China would not tolerate potentially harmful developments on its border as a result of unilateral DPRK actions.

The setbacks did not prevent adoption of the enclave model as the template for inter-Korean economic cooperation.[102] In the late 1990s,

---

[99] Uzbeki sources report that Uzbeki workers were paid just $110 a month. See http://uzland.freenet.uz/2001/march/19.htm. North Korean workers had been paid $110 a month and when they demanded more money, KEDO refused to pay and imported Uzbeki workers who were also paid low wages. The figure of $200 is from my interviews with KEDO officials.

[100] Hazel Smith, 'Asymmetric Nuisance Value: The Border in China–Democratic People's Republic of Korea Relations', in Timothy Hildebrandt (ed.), *Uneasy Allies: Fifty Years of China–North Korea Relations* (Washington, DC: Woodrow Wilson Center Asia Program Special Report, September 2003), pp. 18–25.

[101] *China Daily*, 'Tycoon Given 18 Years Behind Bars', 15 July 2003, reproduced online at 'China Through a Lens', www.china.org.cn/english/2003/Jul/69917.htm, accessed 15 December 2014.

[102] The discussion on the enclave policy is derived from research I published originally in Hazel Smith, 'How South Korea Means Support North Korean Ends: Crossed

Hyundai sponsored the Mount Kumgang tourism project, where South Korean tourists were bussed from South Korea to enjoy the scenery from one of Korea's most famous mountains. The South Korean government also sponsored a joint industrial zone in Kaesong, in which South Korean small and medium-sized enterprises were encouraged to set up shop. The Mount Kumgang project was intended to generate millions of dollars of hard currency, while the Kaesong project was viewed as providing a vehicle through which North Korea could access large-scale capital and high-end technology.

The government implemented the Kumgang and Kaesong enclaves in the same way as they had administered enclave development in Rajin-Sonbong and Kumho. The local population was excluded from both sites except if they were needed as workers. Foreigners, whether as tourists to Mount Kumgang or employees in Kaesong and Mount Kumgang, faced strict controls in terms of their interaction with local counterparts and North Korean workers.[103] Politically driven macro modalities were mirrored by politically driven 'micro-modalities' that sought to maintain a one-sided control over business dealings.[104] These included the North Korean government's insistence on cash transfers, refusal to permit productivity-linked wages, one-sided arbitrary decision-making and opacity in accounting procedures. South Korean businesses were not permitted to hire and fire the labour they employed.

The Mount Kumgang venture was suspended when a South Korean woman tourist, Park Wang-ja, was shot dead in July 2008 by a North Korean soldier for allegedly venturing into a military zone, and had not been reopened by 2014. The shocked and angered South Korean government demanded an inquiry, which the North Koreans refused.[105]

Purposes in Inter-Korean Cooperation', *International Journal of Korean Unification Studies*, Vol. 14, No. 2, 2005, pp. 21–51.

[103] Lim and Lim argued in 2005 that South Korean businesses had greater autonomy in labour management in Kaesong than in the past. This may have been true in relative terms but as Lim and Lim acknowledged, all decisions regarding labour policies had to be negotiated with the 'representatives of Kaesong SEZ workers', which in the context of North Korea meant the North Korean government. See Kang-Taeg Lim and Sung-Hoon Lim, *Strategies for Development of a North Korean Special Economic Zone through Attracting Foreign Investment* (Seoul: Korea Institute for National Unification, 2005), pp. 47–8. Lim and Lim's generally rather optimistic analysis of the potential for SEZs in North Korea also noted, prior to the shooting of a South Korean tourist in 2008, that one of the problems in the Mount Kumgang tourism zone was the restriction on South Korean tourist freedom of movement when they stated that 'more free activity to individual tourists' needed to be permitted, ibid., p. 38.

[104] Dick K. Nanto and Mark E. Manyin, *The Kaesong North-South Korean Industrial Complex* (Washington, DC: Congressional Research Service, 17 March 2011).

[105] Jonathan Watts, 'South Korean Tourist Shot Dead in North Korea', *The Guardian*, 11 July 2008, available at www.guardian.co.uk/world/2008/jul/11/korea, accessed 22 June 2014.

The Kaesong Industrial Development zone was temporarily closed in April 2013 due to inter-Korean security tensions but reopened in September of that year. South Korea was reluctant to shut down one of its few channels of direct contact with the North and the North Korean government obtained around $200 million a year from the Kaesong Industrial Development zone.[106] This was a small sum for a rich, industrial country but a significant sum for an impoverished economy such as North Korea.

The enclave policy failed to achieve key objectives because although many of North Korea's population were prevented from meeting foreigners and imbibing Western ideas, many were not. China became an unmediated source of capitalist goods, ideas and sources of information as Chinese traders were given more latitude to travel and work in the country than other nationals.[107] Chinese traders from Korean-speaking areas in China had the comparative advantage of knowing the Korean language as well as Chinese. They functioned reasonably efficiently as they had experience of working around politicised decision-making in economic affairs in China. They found their way around the new North Korean system by relying on cash transactions and petty or major corruption and were able to cope with the degree of opacity required by North Korean interlocutors.

Tactical success and strategic failure

Military-first policies were partially successful in that the country did not experience military intervention, although government insecurities as to its vulnerability were never allayed. Military-first politics protected the regime internally although they did not prevent serious intra-elite conflict even as the system maintained political continuity. Government interventions that ignored, downplayed or tried to reverse the marketised reality upon which people depended for survival reinforced the sense of alienation of the population from the government. Popular uprisings were prevented, partly by the threat of punitive sanctions but also because the priority of the vast majority of the population remained the securing of food and income to stave off the persistent threat of hunger-related disease and illness.[108]

---

[106] Nanto and Manyin, *The Kaesong North-South Korean Industrial Complex.*
[107] Information in this paragraph from author's interviews with Chinese traders based in Dandong, China, and Pyongyang, DPRK, 2000–1.
[108] There is an important debate in the literature about the causation of revolutions but probably little disagreement that when individuals, families and communities are facing starvation or severe malnutrition this may create the conditions for sporadic uprisings,

The economic strategy failed to generate the billions of dollars needed for reconstruction of the economic infrastructure. The Chinese-dominated trading networks upon which the whole country had come to rely operated at a relatively low level of economic activity and by their nature could not bring the quantity of foreign capital and advanced technology that the DPRK needed to support national redevelopment. South Korean investors had channelled some two million dollars into geographical enclaves by 2005 and these were significant sums of money for North Korea but it was just not enough.[109] The perceived lack of political stability and governmental and institutional opacity, and the multilateral economic sanctions imposed from 2006 onwards, deterred large-scale foreign investment. The contradiction at the heart of military-first politics was that economic development was required for regime security but that military-first politics by their nature provided disincentives and obstacles to the foreign investment that was necessary for development to take place.

North Korea's decision to promote military-first priorities in politics and the economy had the paradoxical result of setting up a competition that it could not win. South Korea's conventional defence capacity remained hugely superior to that of North Korea defence, spending five times as much as North Korea in 2009.[110] In the same year North Korea's gross national income (GNI) was $22.4 billion compared with a GNI of $837.2 billion for South Korea, making the South Korean GNI 33.7 times more than that of the DPRK.[111] The burden of defence spending was therefore much less for South Korea, where it remained at just under 3 per cent of gross

but is not the optimal condition for successful political mobilisation against a state that is able to command the allegiance of organised military forces. For summary on revolutions see Fred Halliday, *Revolution and World Politics: The Rise and Fall of the Sixth Great Power* (London: Macmillan, 1999). For empirical examples of famine-stricken communities, uprisings and the use of military state power to repress such uprisings see Mike Davis, *Late Victorian Holocausts: El Niño Famines and the Making of the Third World* (London: Verso, 2001).

[109] For discussion of the two million dollars of South Korean investment see Young-Yoon Kim, *Evaluation of South-North Economic Cooperation and Task for Success* (Seoul: Korea Institute for National Unification, 2005), p. 25.

[110] Chung-in Moon and Sangkeun Lee, 'Military Spending and the Arms Race on the Korean Peninsula', *Asian Perspective*, Vol. 33, No. 4, 2009.

[111] Ministry of Defense, *2010 White Paper* (Seoul: Ministry of Defense, 2010), p. 341, available at www.nti.org/media/pdfs/2010WhitePaperAll_eng.pdf?_=1340662780, accessed 8 November 2014.

domestic income, than for the North.[112] More tellingly for North Korean national security anxieties, the South Korean defence budget of $22.4 billion in 2009 amounted to almost exactly the total GNI for North Korea in the same year.[113]

---

[112] *The Military Balance 2011* IISS, p. 251.

[113] For the GNI figure, see Ministry of Defense, *2010 White Paper*, p. 341. The figure used for defence spending in the calculation is $22.4 billion and is cited in IISS, *The Military Balance 2011*, p. 251. The Ministry of Defence and IISS give different but, in both cases, higher figures for the 'defence budget', compared to 'defence expenditure', at, respectively, $24.5 billion (White Paper) and $22.5 billion (IISS). See Ministry of Defense, *2010 White Paper*, p. 339; IIS, *The Military Balance 2011*, p. 251.

11   The marketisation of well-being

Military-first governments did not abandon social policy but refocused on priority areas, including food security, public health and education. Living standards improved compared to the famine years but not enough to allow most of the population freedom from economic insecurity. The core of government social policy was designed to improve food security and the core social group to which food security policies were addressed was children. Nutritional standards improved so that the threat of starvation as measured by what nutritionists call 'wasting', which is a measure of the ratio of weight to height, fell below that of East Asia and the Pacific Asia as a whole.[1] Improvements in nutrition were partly due to government interventions and partly because access to market opportunities for some of the population provided a safety-net that had not existed in the famine years.

Life expectancy diminished for men as well as women but the physical burden of market participation was disproportionately carried by women, especially mothers of young children who worked in markets and bore the brunt of heavy physical work in the home. One consequence was the persistently high maternal mortality rate and infant mortality rate (the death rate of children under one year old) that correlated with the poor health of mothers. Nevertheless, the under-five mortality rate, a standard international indicator of child well-being, steadily improved and this was partially because of the successful campaigns against tuberculosis, malaria and the effective national immunisation campaigns.

The government expanded education provision but educational facilities were under-resourced and nurseries, schools and colleges

---

[1] UNICEF, *The State of the World's Children 2013: Children with Disabilities* (Geneva: UNICEF, 2013), pp. 105–7, available at www.unicef.org/sowc2013/files/SWCR2013_ENG_Lo_res_24_Apr_2013.pdf, accessed 20 April 2014. The data refers to the most recent year available in the years 2007–11 except for India where a footnote implies the data is for 2005/6.

became reliant on locally acquired inputs. Enrolment remained high but attendance suffered as the educational institutions were without sufficient material resources and enough staff, many of whom had disappeared into the market. Children benefited from the decreased ability of the state to exert suffocating levels of social control in the education system but parents had extra burdens as they had to help provide resources for schools in lieu of state-supplied inputs. The elderly lost out as they did not receive priority for state resources, but the very worst-off groups in military-era society were those without family support, who had to depend entirely on the state. State-run residential care institutions for children and the elderly expanded to provide basic care for the most destitute but, as in many poor countries, these institutions were massively under-resourced and did not deliver a decent quality of life for their inhabitants.

Malnutrition

The World Health Organisation announced in 2012 that the levels of malnutrition in North Korea although 'worrisome' were 'acceptable' and no longer justified emergency humanitarian operations because acute and chronic malnutrition had fallen dramatically since the famine years.[2] Improved nutrition was due to a combination of factors that included the recovery of the agricultural sector, the increase in market access to food, the continued social expectations that children should remain in education and not enter the labour market and successful public health campaigns.

As in most countries, the DPRK government and international organisations used child and maternal nutrition as proxy indicators for national nutritional status as these groups were held to be the most vulnerable to food insecurity. Acute malnutrition as measured by wasting fell steadily; from 8.3 per cent in 2002 to 7.5 per cent in 2004 and to 5.2 per cent in 2012.[3] Stunting rates – an indicator of chronic malnutrition – also fell, to 39 per cent in 2002, 36 per cent in 2004, and 32 per cent in 2012.[4]

[2] Central Bureau of Statistics, *Democratic People's Republic of Korea Preliminary Report of the National Nutrition Survey, October 2012* (Pyongyang: Central Bureau of Statistics, 2012), p. 26.

[3] Central Bureau of Statistics, *Report on the DPRK Nutrition Assessment 2002* (Pyongyang: Central Bureau of Statistics, 20 November 2002); Central Bureau of Statistics, *DPRK 2004 Nutrition Assessment* (Pyongyang; Central Bureau of Statistics, Institute of Child Nutrition, February 2005); Central Bureau of Statistics, *National Nutrition Survey, October 2012*, pp. 26 and 29.

[4] Central Bureau of Statistics, *Nutrition Assessment 2002*; Central Bureau of Statistics, *DPRK 2004 Nutrition Assessment* (Pyongyang; Central Bureau of Statistics, Institute of

In 2012, children in North Korea were less likely to suffer from acute malnutrition than children who lived in the wealthy and democratic states of India and Indonesia, whose wasting rates in 2012 stood at, respectively, 20 per cent and 13 per cent.[5] Chronic malnutrition rates fell below the South Asia average of 39 per cent but remained much worse than the average for East Asia and the Pacific of 7 per cent. These levels of stunting were symptomatic of pervasive poverty and reflected a shortage of decent-quality food for North Korea's children.[6]

Gender differentials in nutrition were recorded but the data was sometimes contradictory and did not support conclusive explanations. By contrast 2004 nutrition survey found that rates of acute malnutrition were similar in girls and boys while the prevalence of stunting, an indication of long-term poor nutrition, was found to be higher for boys than girls.[7] A 2009 UNICEF survey found that there were no statistically significant differences in malnutrition between boys and girls while a 2012 survey found that boys, similarly to the 2004 survey, were slightly more likely to be malnourished than girls.[8]

Very little data was available on male malnutrition although one refugee and migrant survey showed worse malnutrition in adult males than adult females in 2001. The paucity of data means that meaningful conclusions could not be drawn about the scale and reasons for male malnutrition.[9] The scale and causation of female malnutrition was, however, well understood and well documented.[10] One known and disturbing

Child Nutrition, February 2005); Central Bureau of Statistics, *National Nutrition Survey, October 2012*, pp. 26 and 29.
[5] UNICEF, *The State of the World's Children*, pp. 105–7. The data refers to the most recent year available in the years 2007–11 except for India where a footnote implies the data is for 2005/6.
[6] Central Bureau of Statistics, *Nutrition Assessment 2002*; Central Bureau of Statistics, *2004 Nutrition Assessment*, p. 43; Central Bureau of Statistics, *National Nutrition Survey, October 2012*; UNICEF, *The State of the World's Children*, p. 107.
[7] Central Bureau of Statistics, *DPRK 2004 Nutrition Assessment*.
[8] Central Bureau of Statistics/UNICEF, *The Democratic People's Republic of Korea Multiple Indicator Cluster Survey Final Report 2009* (Pyongyang: CBS, 2010), p. 31; Central Bureau of Statistics, *National Nutrition Survey, October 2012*.
[9] W. Courtland Robinson, Myung Ken Lee, Kenneth Hill, Edbert Hsu and Gilbert Burnham, 'Demographic Methods to Assess Food Insecurity: A North Korean Case Study', *Prehospital and Disaster Medicine*, Vol. 15, No. 4, 2001, pp. 286–93.
[10] Central Bureau of Statistics, *National Nutrition Survey, October 2012*; United Nations, *DPR Korea Common Country Assessment 2002* (Pyongyang: UNOCHA, February 2003); UNICEF, *Country Programme of Cooperation between the Government of the Democratic People's Republic of Korea and the United Nations Children's Fund 2004–2006 Strategy Document* (Pyongyang: UNICEF, February 2003); Hazel Smith, *WFP DPRK Programmes and Activities: A Gender Perspective* (Pyongyang: WFP, 1999); Soon-Hee Lim, *The Food Crisis and Life of Women in North Korea* (Seoul: Korea Institute for National Unification, 2005).

phenomenon was the uniformity of the prevalence of malnutrition in women; in 2009 a UNICEF survey showed no significant differences between urban and rural areas or between levels of educational background.[11]

When food rations were short, mothers, as is common in many countries, sacrificed their own food so that family members could eat.[12] In 2012, 5 per cent of women between the ages of 15 and 49 were severely (acutely) malnourished and this figure had barely changed since 2009.[13] Maternal malnutrition remained persistently high with insufficient and inadequate diets leading to women becoming dangerously anaemic during pregnancy. Poor diets and poor quality obstetric care contributed to the worsening of maternal mortality rates.[14] In 1993, 54 maternal deaths per 100,000 live births were reported, compared to 105 in 1996 and a reduced though still high figure of 77 in 2008.[15] These figures showed an increase of 42 per cent in maternal deaths between 1993 and 2008, in just 15 years.[16]

The marketisation and fragmentation of nutritional outcomes

The joint national and international surveys that took place from 1998 onwards showed that some provincial populations were more likely to face malnutrition than others, even as malnutrition rates diminished both nationally and in every province.[17] With the exception of Pyongyang, where malnutrition rates were consistently lower than the rest of the country, there was, however, no linear association between province and malnutrition rate, which varied between provinces and over time. Major differences in malnutrition outcomes were most prominent

[11] Central Bureau of Statistics/UNICEF, *The Democratic People's Republic of Korea Multiple Indicator Cluster Survey Final Report 2009* (Pyongyang: CBS, 2010), p. 69.
[12] Soon-Hee Lim, *The Food Crisis and Life of Women in North Korea* (Seoul: Korea Institute for National Unification, 2005), pp. 26–7.
[13] Central Bureau of Statistics, *National Nutrition Survey, October 2012*, p. 23.
[14] UNICEF's programmes focused on 'safe motherhood' in its work in the DPRK that began in 1987 and is on-going. Frequent reports identified the causation of maternal malnutrition and maternal mortality rates. See for example UNICEF, *A Humanitarian Appeal for Children and Women* (Pyongyang: UNICEF, 2002), p. 12.
[15] 1993 and 2008 figures from Central Bureau of Statistics, '2008 Census of Population of DPRK: Key Findings', available at www.unfpa.org/webdav/site/global/shared/documents/news/2010/dprk08_censuskeyfinds.pdf, accessed 22 June 2014; 1996 figures from UNICEF, *An Analysis of the Situation of Children and Women in the Democratic People's Republic of Korea 2000* (Pyongyang: UNICEF, December 1999).
[16] Central Bureau of Statistics, '2008 Census'.
[17] For work that analyses provincial nutritional outcomes subsequent to the famine years, see Hazel Smith, 'North Korea: Market Opportunity, Poverty and the Provinces', *New Political Economy*, Vol. 14, No. 3, June 2009, pp. 231–56.

between rural and urban locations; in 2008 chronic malnutrition in rural areas was a high 45 per cent compared with 23.4 per cent in urban areas.[18] These high levels of stunting were compatible with receiving enough food to avoid actual starvation but not enough nutrients to live a healthy life.[19]

Pyongyang's children were not exempt from poverty and children living in the north-eastern border provinces were sometimes better-off than if they lived in an agriculturally productive farming area in the south. Pyongyang's children were less likely to be hungry than children in other provinces, although the capital continued to be home to significant numbers of malnourished and poor people.[20] In 2002, 4 per cent of Pyongyang's children, that is 14,600 children, suffered from severe malnutrition.[21] In 2009 some 2.3 per cent of children under 5, that is over 5,000 children, still suffered from severe malnutrition.[22] In 2012, just over 2 per cent of Pyongyang's population of children aged under 5 years old were severely malnourished, that is, about 5,000 children.[23] The malnutrition figures for Pyongyang were lower than those of other provinces, but they were not low in terms of the absolute numbers of malnourished children or compared with more prosperous countries, including China, where the severe malnutrition rate was 1 per cent in 2002.[24]

In the military-first era, the breadbasket provinces of South Hwanghae and North Hwanghae were the only provinces consistently to produce more than enough grain to feed their population, and yet the population suffered disproportionately high malnutrition rates.[25] In 2002 the child population of South Hwanghae, the most agriculturally productive province in the country, experienced levels of severe malnutrition worse than

[18] Central Bureau of Statistics/UNICEF, *Multiple Indicator Cluster Survey*, p. 31.
[19] On urban food insecurity, see Central Bureau of Statistics, *National Nutrition Survey, October 2012.*
[20] UNICEF, DPRK *Social Statistics:* (Pyongyang: UNICEF, 1999); UNICEF, *Children and Women*; EU, UNICEF and WFP in partnership with the Government of DPRK, *Nutrition Survey of the Democratic People's Republic of Korea* (Rome/Pyongyang: WFP, 1998); Central Bureau of Statistics, *Nutrition Assessment 2002*; Central Bureau of Statistics, *DPRK 2004 Nutrition Assessment.*
[21] World Food Programme (WFP), *Statistics of DPRK Population 2002* (Pyongyang: WFP, 2003).
[22] Central Bureau of Statistics/UNICEF, *Multiple Indicator Cluster Survey*, p. 31; Pyongyang child population figures from Chang Su Kim, *DPR Korea 2008 Population Census National Report* (Pyongyang: Central Bureau of Statistics Pyongyang, 2009).
[23] Central Bureau of Statistics, *National Nutrition Survey, October 2012*, p. 17; numbers of children derived from 2008 population figures in Kim, *2008 Population Census*, p. 31.
[24] Central Bureau of Statistics, *Nutrition Assessment 2002.*
[25] Smith, 'North Korea: Market Opportunity', pp. 231–56.

any in the country except for the industrial north-eastern province of
South Hamgyong.[26] In 2004, three north-eastern provinces of Ryanggang, North Hamgyong and South Hamgyong demonstrated worse rates
of severe malnutrition than other provinces, but North Hwanghae, the
second most agriculturally productive province in the country, was not
far behind.[27]

In 2012, the children of North Hwanghae, which that year produced
306 kilograms per person of grain – well above the requirement of
127 kilograms per capita needed for survival purposes – had the same
levels of chronic malnutrition as children living in North Hamgyong,
which only produced 117 kilograms per capita of grain in that year.[28] In
2012, Ryanggang province had the highest levels of acute and chronic
malnutrition in the country, followed by Chagang and South Hamgyong.[29] The fourth worst-off province was, however, North Pyongyan,
a south-western province containing agricultural areas and which
bordered Pyongyang. The population was worse off than the population
of North Hamgyong, which shared a border with China and which had
suffered terribly during the famine years.[30]

The reason for relatively high levels of child malnutrition in the agriculturally productive provinces was that national security priorities left
the south-east's population with few opportunities to leverage better
agricultural conditions into economic prosperity. The two breadbasket
provinces are easily accessible from Pyongyang, road links over the more
or less flat plains are relatively good and it was a straightforward exercise
for the government to appropriate agricultural production for the military
and other key workers. Where the state could, it took all but the minimum needed by farming households to survive and for basic seed
requirements.

Government policy to South Hwanghae was highly militarised and
governed by national security priorities that militated against the development of market access for the population of the province. South
Hwanghae's agricultural capacity was of strategic importance to the
government as was its geographic location as a border province to South
Korea. South Hwanghae did not have the same sorts of topographical
barriers to potential invading forces as Kangwon province, its eastern
neighbour, which is one reason for the oxymoronic demilitarised zone

[26] Ibid.   [27] Ibid.
[28] Central Bureau of Statistics, *National Nutrition Survey, October 2012*, p. 26; FAO/WFP,
*Crop and Food Supply Assessment Mission to the Democratic People's Republic of Korea,
Special Report* (Rome: FAO/WFP, 12 November 2012).
[29] Central Bureau of Statistics, *National Nutrition Survey, October 2012*, p. 26.
[30] Ibid.

(the DMZ), that was heavily mined and guarded on both sides by concentrations of troops and weapons. No clandestine border trade was possible. Haeju, South Hwanghae's major port, was heavily militarised, because of its proximity to the South Korean border and its strategic importance, which meant that that there were few possibilities for the development of private commercial initiatives as had occurred in other port cities. Nampo, for instance, one of the country's major ports and just a few kilometres north of Haeju, had seen the development of restaurants, shops and petty commerce to serve seamen, port employees and some of the local residents.

The northern provinces suffered high rates of malnutrition in the military-first era but not quite as high as might have been expected given the large grain deficits in the region and the end of grain redistribution from the breadbasket provinces. This was because many of the inhabitants of North Hamgyong had relatively easy access to market opportunities, especially if they lived near the China border. The Chinese and North Korean government allowed special privileges to North Koreans and Chinese citizens who lived near the border to travel between the two countries for limited distances without passports but with locally issued papers. Poor transport and communication links between Pyongyang and the north-east also made it difficult for the central state to exercise systematic controls over the northern border provinces.

The nutritional differentials between the provinces were significant but there was also considerable intra-provincial variability in well-being outcomes. Not everyone who lived in the breadbasket provinces had access to a private plot on which they could grow food for personal consumption or to sell on the market, and not everyone living in the capital had access to foreigners from whom they might obtain foreign currency. Some of those living in parts of the poorest provinces had locational advantages that were unavailable even for many Pyongyang residents. The inhabitants of Hyesan, for example, which is the provincial capital of Ryanggang and has a bridge running from the town centre into China, benefited from cross-border opportunities, even as those living in the remote and difficult to access southern part of the province were some of the worst off in nutritional terms in the whole country.

At the micro-locational level, if an individual could keep chickens on the balcony and had a colleague who could make use of an official car for private business and perhaps lived in a small urban town in the north where central state constraints on private trade were no longer enforced all the time, and that person happened to be a woman and so could more easily take time away from the workplace, she might be able to improve her economic status by selling and swapping eggs. If that person lived in

Pyongyang, perhaps with an overzealous neighbour with good connections to the security apparatus, they might see those chickens confiscated and suffer penalties for speculation. In both cases entrepreneurship was risky but necessary and the advantages and disadvantages of geographical location a question of politics as well as physical domicile.

In sickness and in health

Patients still received free health care. Nevertheless, the quality of hospitals and clinics was not good as buildings were not well constructed and had inadequate heating, water and basic supplies, including medicines. The United Nations World Food Programme reported in 2011 that that only 30 per cent of essential drugs were being supplied.[31] Life expectancy rates fell from 72.7 years in 1993 to 69.3 years in 2008; figures that would have been much worse without the improvements in nutrition that took place, the successful public health campaigns that vaccinated children and the campaigns to reduce the incidence of diseases associated with poverty, including the potentially fatal illnesses of malaria and tuberculosis.[32] Under-five child mortality rates improved partly because of the systematic nationwide vaccination campaigns were the major outcome of public health priorities.

Men's life expectancy remained less than that of women; in 2008 women's life expectancy was seven years more than men's.[33] Women experienced a more rapid reduction in life expectancy, however, by 3.3 years compared to 2.8 years for males, between 1993 and 2008.[34] A major cause of poor health in women was marketisation that meant that women worked hard to earn income and had also to carry out physically onerous domestic functions to support the family. Women suffered ill-health and premature death partly because of their maternal role and responsibilities.

Using adjusted figures, UNICEF reported in 2013 that North Korea's maternal mortality rate was 81 maternal deaths per 100,000 live births,

[31] WFP, *Overview of Needs and Assistance in DPRK 2012* (Rome: World Food Programme, 2012), p. 16.
[32] The 2008 census did not offer figures on life expectancy rates. These were calculated by commentators and reported in various media. The UNFPA, however, which had sponsored and guided the 2008 census, reported the life expectancy rates quoted here on its official webpage, albeit with the conventional disclaimer that 'UNFPA is not responsible for the accuracy or content of independent media reports displayed for reference purposes only'. See UNFPA in the News, 'Democratic People's Republic of Korea: Census Finds Drop in Life Expectancy', 21 February 2010, available at http://inthenews.unfpa.org/?p=1005, accessed 15 December 2014.
[33] Central Bureau of Statistics, '2008 Census'.   [34] Ibid.

while the equivalent rates were 16 for South Korea, 21 for the United States and 12 for the United Kingdom.[35] North Korea's maternal mortality rate was close to the average of 82 for East Asia and the Pacific and representative of maternal mortality rates in other middle-income developing countries.[36] By contrast UNICEF data reports a maternal mortality figure of 200 and 220, respectively, for the wealthier Asian countries of India and Indonesia.[37] North Korea's maternal mortality rates required substantial improvement, but they were not near the shocking figures UNICEF reported for Somalia, at 1,000 maternal deaths per 100,000 live births, or Chad, that in 2013 had the worst maternal mortality figures in the world at 1,100 maternal deaths per 100,000 live births.[38]

The total fertility rate declined between 1993 and 2008. The reason for decline was not, as in developed countries, the product of increased economic advantages and the use of reliable contraception.[39] In North Korea, where contraceptive methods were primitive, North Korean women were aborting once pregnant, in 2009 at a high rate of 121 abortions per 1,000 live births. Women were doing their best to avoid pregnancy and not ovulating due to under-nutrition.[40]

The paucity of data on men's health and male malnutrition means that the reasons for the decrease in life expectancy for men are not as well understood as those for women, although the contributory factors to male ill-health are well known. They include the widespread practice of heavy smoking, which is almost entirely confined to men because of strongly gendered social norms that made it unthinkable for women to smoke in public and in private.[41] In 2002 the World Health Organisation

---

[35] UNICEF, *The State of the World's Children*, pp. 128–31.
[36] Ibid.   [37] Ibid., p. 129.   [38] Ibid., pp. 128–31.
[39] The summary of findings published by the DPRK in conjunction with UNFPA states that the use of contraception is one reason for the decline in fertility rate. My view is that there is no evidence for the widespread use of contraception, as indicated by UNFPA itself in UN reporting. See Central Bureau of Statistics, '2008 Census of Population', abortion figures in UNOCHA, 'Joint UNCT submission for the UN Compilation Report Universal Periodic Review – Democratic People's Republic of Korea (DPRK) 6th session (30 November–11 December 2009)', available at http://lib.ohchr.org/HRBodies/UPR/Documents/Session6/KP/UNCT_PRK_UPR_S06_2009.pdf, accessed 22 June 2014.
[40] Ibid., p.4.
[41] Author's observations, DPRK, 1990–2011; World Health Organisation (WHO), *Democratic People's Republic of Korea: National Health System Profile* (Pyongyang: WHO, undated but probably 2006). The textbook provides a handbook on good health for a broad North Korean audience and warns of the dangers of smoking throughout the book but only pictures men smoking. The book was produced in Korean but a small number was translated into English. See Thae Sop Choe, *Topics on Health*, English edition (Pyongyang: Korea Publications Exchange Association, 1999).

reported that smoking was the main cause in the rise in non-communicable disease in North Korea and that hypertension and heart disease were the major causes of death.[42]

The health of young men was adversely affected by their years living in spartan conditions during the period of their military service.[43] The 662,349 men and 40,023 women reported in the 2008 census as based in institutional living quarters, including military camps, received only basic rations.[44] These young people were deliberately mobilised away from their natal home; one consequence was that official rations could not be compensated by food assistance from the family.

Child health

The conditions of life for children were tough for the same reasons that they were tough for most of the rest of the population; inadequate food, low income and poorly resourced state services. High rates of maternal malnutrition jeopardised the health of women and infants who depended almost entirely on their mothers.

In 2011, the infant mortality rate, measured as the probability of dying between birth and one year, was similar to a diverse range of low to middle-income countries, including Guatemala, Iran, Iraq, Kazakhstan and the Philippines.[45] These countries, however, demonstrated a downward trend, while in North Korea the trend was upwards.[46] The infant mortality rate worsened from an estimated 9.2 per 1,000 live births in 1990, to 23 per 1,000 in 1998, to 26 in 1,000 live births in 2008.[47]

The main reason for the rise in infant mortality was the persistence of poverty and malnourished mothers, who had difficulty breast-feeding and accessing breast-milk substitutes.[48]

Infant formula was expensive and not widely available as well as risky for child health because of the absence of safe water supplies.[49] Mothers

---

[42] World Health Organisation, *Democratic People's Republic of Korea: National Health System Profile* (Pyongyang: WHO, undated but probably 2006), p. 4.

[43] Young-Tai Jeung, *Internal and External Perceptions of the North Korean Army* (Seoul: Korea Institute for National Unification, 2005), p. 35.

[44] Figures derived from Kim, *2008 Population Census*, pp. 14–22.

[45] UNICEF, *The State of the World's children*, pp. 100–3.

[46] WFP, *Overview of Needs*, p. 15.

[47] 1990 and 1998 figures in Dilawar Ali Khan, *Improving the Quality of Basic Social Services for the Most Vulnerable Children and Women: Executive Summary* (Pyongyang: UNICEF, April 2001), p. 5. Figures for 2008 in WFP, *Overview of Needs*, p. 15.

[48] UNICEF, *Nutrition Situation in DPR Korea* (Pyongyang: UNICEF, November 2000).

[49] UNICEF, *An Analysis of the Situation of Women and Children in the Democratic People's Republic of Korea, Draft* (Pyongyang: UNICEF, May 1998), p. 20; UNICEF, *Situation Analysis of Women and Children*.

could also not always secure appropriate semi-solid food at the weaning stage of child development. Cooked rice was the culturally preferred commodity for this purpose but rice and fuel for cooking were not always accessible to North Koreans. In 2009, a UNICEF survey showed that less than half of all infants aged six to twenty-three months received an appropriate mix of food.[50] Insufficient food, the absence of safe clean water, shortages of fuel to heat water and a health service that was staffed with medical personnel but which was without medicines meant that babies and infants were dangerously vulnerable to diarrhoeal and respiratory illnesses, the two leading causes of death of children worldwide.[51]

The under-five mortality rate, that is, the probability of dying between birth and 5 years of age, improved from a reported 45 per 1,000 live births in 1990 to 33 per 1,000 in 2011.[52] North Korea's under-five mortality rate did not, however, improve to the levels of its north-east Asian neighbours, including Mongolia and China, which had an under-five mortality rate of, respectively, 31 and 15, in the same year.[53] North Korean children fared very badly compared to South Korean children. In 2011 in South Korea, the under-five mortality rate of just 5 was the same as that of the United Kingdom and better than the United States, at 8 deaths per 1,000 live births.[54] South Korea's under-five mortality rate was improved on by only twenty-seven other countries globally.[55] Compared to countries at similar levels of economic development, however, North Korea's under-five mortality rate was typical and in some instances showed better survival rates for under-fives. In South Asia, for example, the under-five mortality rate stood at 62 deaths per 1,000 live births in 2011.[56]

Public health campaigns

In the 1990s, tuberculosis and malaria had become major public health risks and these two diseases provided the focus of health policy during the 2000s.

Tuberculosis deaths were reduced from a reported 19,000 in 1990 to 5,700 in 2010, with the prevalence and incidence of the disease also decreasing between 1990 and 2010.[57] The control of tuberculosis can

[50] Central Bureau of Statistics/UNICEF, *Multiple Indicator Cluster Survey*, pp. 37–40.
[51] Ibid., pp. 46–52.   [52] UNICEF, *The State of the World's Children*, p. 100.
[53] Ibid., p. 99.   [54] Ibid.   [55] Ibid.   [56] Ibid., p. 95.
[57] WHO, *Global Tuberculosis Control: WHO Report 2011* (Geneva: World Health Organisation, 2011), p. 215.

only be successful in any country by way of sustained and systematic organisational efforts that prevent contagion and monitor the disease. North Korea's success in controlling the spread of tuberculosis in the 2000s indicated two things; that the government had recovered nation-wide organisational capacity and that the government prioritised public health programmes.

The emphasis on public health was evidenced in the campaign to reduce malaria and the outcome, which was that North Korea was one of only a small number of countries that cut the incidence of malaria by over 50 per cent between 2000 and 2009.[58] In 2010, the World Health Organisation classed North Korea as in the 'pre-elimination' stage of malaria eradication after a major fall in suspected cases, from 296,540 in 2001 to 14,845 in 2009.[59] The World Health Organisation attributed success to effective societal organisation, whereby each active malaria case was followed-up and monitored.[60] The achievement of reducing the incidence of malaria from almost epidemic levels to almost eliminating the disease in less than ten years was quite remarkable even if North Korea had some way to go to achieve the successes of its southern compatriots. In South Korea malaria was virtually eradicated by 2010, with only 1,343 cases reported as confirmed in 2009.[61]

The government maintained a focus on systematic, nationwide immunisation campaigns designed to wipe out vaccination-preventable diseases. In 2010, North Korea's vaccination coverage was as high as that of the rich countries of the world.[62] Vaccination rates for polio and measles rose to 99 per cent and to 98 per cent for the Bacille de Calmette et Guérin (BCG) vaccination against tuberculosis.[63] These were higher vaccination rates than South Korea, where UNICEF and the World Health Organisation recorded a vaccination rate of 98 per cent for measles, 95 per cent for polio and 96 per cent for the BCG vaccination in the same year.[64] Vaccination rates were only slightly lower than South Korea for Hepatitis B, at 93 per cent as against 94 per cent.[65] Similarly North Korea showed only marginally less coverage than South Korea for the full course of Diphtheria, Pertussis and Tetanus (DPT) vaccination, at 93 per cent as against 94 per cent.[66]

Vaccination campaigns bypassed the day-to-day deficiencies of the health services as they were organised around mass mobilisation of

---

[58] WHO, *World Malaria Report 2010* (Geneva: World Health Organisation, 2010), p. 41.
[59] Ibid., p. 192.   [60] Ibid., p. 50.   [61] Ibid., p. 193.
[62] UNICEF/WHO, *Immunization Summary: A Statistical Reference Containing Data Through 2010* (New York: UNICEF/World Health Organisation, 2012), pp. 90–1, available at www.childinfo.org/files/immunization_summary_en.pdf, accessed 22 June 2014.
[63] Ibid.   [64] Ibid.   [65] Ibid.   [66] Ibid.

communities throughout the whole country on specified days every year. A typical campaign in 2001 mobilised the entire population on three 'health days' in May, October and November.[67] The first delivered Vitamin A supplements and de-worming pills; the second polio vaccinations; and the third all three combined.[68] In all, a remarkably high 2.5 million, that is 95 per cent, of children below five were reached.[69] These campaigns benefited from funding from the World Health Organisation, UNICEF and the Bill Gates Foundation, as well as the state's capacity to organise the population for short-term specific objectives.

The fragmentation of education provision

Education was a national policy priority because an educated youth was understood as the key to a prosperous future for the entire society. Nevertheless, many of the nation's schools struggled to secure basic resources, as the DPRK government reported to international organisations.[70] The education system became fragmented as elite schools became highly competitive while most schools became 'self-help' organisations that were reliant on local communities and families for funding and support.

In 2012 the DPRK expanded free, compulsory state schooling from an already impressive eleven years to twelve years duration, so that all children would attend school from age 5 to 17.[71] Nursery education was open to children from a few months old until they started kindergarten at age five; although not mandatory almost all children continued to be registered for nursery care, with 1,574,000 children enrolled in 27,017 'nursery schools' in 1998.[72] The government supported specialist schools in subjects that included language training and computer studies. Unlike many poor countries, North Korea continued to enrol all girls in school as well as all boys. Child labour remained virtually non-existent, except at transplanting seasons when entire communities were mobilised.

---

[67] UNICEF, *DPRK Donor Update* (Pyongyang: UNICEF, 4 February 2002), p. 2.
[68] Ibid.   [69] Ibid.
[70] DPRK Ministry of Education, *The Development of Education: National Report of the Democratic People's Republic of Korea* (Pyongyang: Ministry of Education, 2004), available at www.ibe.unesco.org/International/ICE47/English/Natreps/reports/dprkorea.pdf, accessed 7 February 2014.
[71] Kyu-won Kim, 'North Korea Announces Education Reforms, Silent on Economy', *The Hankyoreh*, 26 September 2012, available at http://english.hani.co.kr/arti/english_edition/e_northkorea/553442.html, accessed 27 February 2012.
[72] National EFA 2000 Assessment Group, *Democratic People's Republic of Korea, National EFA Assessment Report: The Implementation of the 'World Declaration on Education for All'* (Pyongyang: National EFA 2000 Assessment Group, 1999), p. 78.

Marketisation and economic transformation impacted on the education system directly in that the numbers of nurseries were reduced as the workplaces in which they were located ceased operating. Although enrolment remained high, attendance at nurseries decreased, with North Korean government data showing only 993,000 children of the 1,574,000 registered as attending nurseries in 1998.[73] In-country international organisations repeatedly reported low attendance at schools and nurseries. In 1999, the World Food Programme reported that during the periods before the harvest, when food was short, 'educational institutions in urban areas experience a reduction in attendance, as a certain percentage of urban families go for extended visits to relatives in rural areas, where access to food is more likely'.[74] In 2000 UNICEF reported declining attendance rates, dropping to between 60 and 80 per cent from informal reports, due to 'poor heating, lack of food, teaching and learning materials and low teacher motivation'.[75] In 2002, UNICEF reported that a 'lack of basic school supplies is leading to increasingly intermittent attendance and compromising quality of learning'.[76]

The quality of teaching and basic care of children deteriorated as women, who had provided 100 per cent of staff in nurseries and kindergartens and the majority in primary schools, swapped their official employment for more remunerative market trading.[77] UNICEF reported that 'when carers must cope with increased illness, lack of available clean water, inadequate sanitation, lack of food and lack of medical supplies, even basic care functions [are]... threatened. Demotivated care givers, working in stressful environments in which food, medicines, heating, regular and safe water suppliers are in scarce supply, are often not able to provide the standard of care required.'[78]

Irregular teaching and poor resources resulted in less regimentation than in the Kim Il Sung era. The curriculum changed little in formal terms but the lack of resources and insufficient staff also reduced the ability of the care and educational institutions to inculcate government ideology in children.[79] Teachers had little incentive to carry out much

[73] UNICEF, *Women and Children*, p. 49.
[74] WFP, 'Protracted Relief and Recovery Operation – DPR Korea 6157.00', in WFP, *Projects for Executive Board Approval, Agenda Item 7, 19–22 October 1999* (Rome: WFP, 1999), p. 5.
[75] UNICEF, *Annual Report 2000 Democratic People's Republic of Korea* (Pyongyang: UNICEF, 2000), p. 6.
[76] UNICEF, *A Humanitarian Appeal*, p. 3.
[77] UNICEF, *Women and Children*, p. 40; Smith, *WFP DPRK Programmes and Activities*.
[78] UNICEF, *Women and Children*, p. 84.
[79] The DPRK government, in reporting on its progress on implementing its commitments under the International Convention on the Rights of the Child, which it ratified in 1991,

more than pro forma ideological socialisation as they had their own economic worries and priorities, given their low pay and lack of priority for food rations. Marketisation, therefore, reduced the capacity of the education system to enforce all-encompassing ideological education all of the time. The diminished availability of female staff also meant that Party-led extracurricular activities were less frequent and the formerly active Children's Brigades became less effective as vehicles for Kim Il Sungist socialisation.

Young people were encouraged to carry on with their education after the mandatory period of schooling. High school and college youth were meant to provide the intellectual input to devise ever more innovative solutions to chronic economic stagnation so as to contribute to achieving the goal of building a 'strong and prosperous nation'.

Young women and young men emerged from the schools as equally numerate and literate. A commendable one in twelve women had completed university education by 2008 but compared to men, whose graduation rate was one in seven, female graduation rates were low.[80] The comparative lack of success placed women at a disadvantage in employment. The domination of men in professional and managerial occupations was therefore partly a result of the availability of better-qualified men.[81] Men were also more likely to be channelled into subjects at university that led to high status and relatively highly paid work.[82] Men, for example, predominated in engineering faculties while women gravitated towards teacher training and education.[83]

The failure of state and market

In marketised North Korea, the worst off were the elderly, and adults and children who could not call on family support and therefore lived in state-run residential institutions. At the level of policy pronouncements,

---

noted that the economic crisis of the 1990s had, among other things, compromised the quality of education because of 'irregularities in provision of textbooks and other educational and learning materials'. See Democratic People's Republic of Korea, *National Report*, written for the 5th Ministerial Consultation for the East Asia and Pacific Region, mimeo, May 2000. Damage to schools and educational institutions was outlined in National EFA 2000 Assessment Group, *National Assessment Report*, pp. 33–4.

[80] Central Bureau of Statistics, '2008 Census'.
[81] Chang Su Kim, *2008 Population Census*.
[82] Moosuk Min and Jehee Ahn, *A Study of Education for Women in North Korea* (Seoul: Korea Women's Development Institute, 2001), available at www.kwdi.re.kr/data/02forum-4.pdf, accessed 22 June 2014.
[83] Central Bureau of Statistics, '2008 Census of Population'.

the state supported the elderly, including the indigent. In practice the elderly were not a priority for military-first social policy.

In the world of marketised social relations and military rule, those living in residential institutions were handicapped three times over. Firstly, they were without the family support that enabled the rest of the population to survive and function. Secondly, those living in residential institutions had few market options because they could not fend for themselves within the market. Thirdly, these institutions were not resourced by the central state and were largely left to the provincial administrations to manage and supervise. Provincial administrations did not receive resources from central government and had no formal local taxation powers so could not guarantee stability of provision of food and goods to these institutions.

The elderly

The percentage of the population aged over 65 grew from 5.4 per cent in 1993 to 8.7 per cent in 2008, with much higher numbers of women than men.[84] In 2008, the over-75 age group comprised the Korean War generation in which millions of men had died, so it was not surprising that the gender ratios were skewed towards female predominance. In 2008, the 64 people reported as aged between 100 and 110 were all women.[85] Of the population aged between 75 and 100, there were 416,713 women compared to 103,940 men, a ratio of 4 to 1.[86] In 2008 the census showed that some 1.17 million women over 60 were widowed, out of a total female population aged over 60 of just less than two million.[87] By contrast a much smaller number of men of any age (not just elderly men), just 106,809, were identified as widowers in 2008.[88] The predominately female elderly population was a predominantly single population.

The government passed legislation in 2007 entitled the 'Law of the Democratic People's Republic of Korea on the Care of the Elderly'.[89] The government's official view was that 'the elderly are regarded as the

[84] Sun Won Hong, *Analysis of 1993 Population Census Data DPR Korea* (Pyongyang: Population Center, DPRK, 1996); Kim, *2008 Population Census*, p. 16; Central Bureau of Statistics, '2008 Census of Population', p. 2, available at www.unfpa.org/webdav/site/global/shared/documents/news/2010/.
[85] Kim, *2008 Population Census*, pp. 16–17.   [86] Ibid., p. 16.
[87] Central Bureau of Statistics, '2008 Census of Population', p. 2.
[88] Kim, *2008 Population Census*, p. 33.
[89] UNESCAP, 'Report by the Delegation of the Democratic People's Republic of Korea', in Economic and Social Commission for Asia and the Pacific, 9–11 October 2007, p. 3.

forerunners who devoted their lives to the rising generation and to respect them is an obligation as well as lofty moral duty of the rising generation, and the state is paying its primary attention to the promotion of the traditional virtue of revering the elderly. The elderly are regarded as the former generation, revolutionary forerunners, seniors of the society, and heads of their families who devoted their talents and enthusiasm to the stable development of the state and the society as well as to the creation of the economic and cultural wealth.'[90]

The pension, which a woman received at 55 and a man at 60, became literally worthless in the military-first period and the reduced food rations to which the elderly were formally entitled were only sporadically available from the 1990s onwards.[91] Those living in the country with access to land had opportunities to grow food but the urban elderly and a sizeable number of poor rural dwellers depended on handouts from family.

The last resort for those elderly who had no immediate family support or who could not receive help from neighbours or friends was to move to one of the state's twenty-four residential homes for the elderly.[92] Those were completely inadequate.[93] Like the children's institutions, residential institutions for the elderly received few inputs from the state and relied on international humanitarian organisations, like the French non-governmental organisation, Triangle, which rehabilitated six of these homes to provide basic heating, sanitation facilities and medical facilities.[94]

Children in residential institutions

North Korea had closed down orphanages that had been established in the wake of the Korean War and implemented an adoption policy that placed orphaned children in families. The state reopened the children's institutions after the economic collapse of the 1990s meant that families could no longer afford to look of the adopted children. The children's

---

[90] Ibid., p. 4.
[91] WFP, *Emergency Operation (EMOP 200266): Emergency Food Assistance to Vulnerable Groups in the Democratic People's Republic of Korea* (Rome: WFP, undated but 2011), p. 6, available at http://reliefweb.int/sites/reliefweb.int/files/resources/Full_Report_454.pdf, accessed 8 November 2014.
[92] Triangle webpage, www.trianglegh.org/English_TGH/html/Programmes/Missions Humanitaire/NorthKorea/NorthKoreaREA_gb.html, accessed 30 November 2011.
[93] Triangle Génération Humanitaire, *Annual Activity Report Year 2009*, p. 27, available at www.trianglegh.org/ActionHumanitaire/PDF/PDF-Rapport-Activite/Rapport-TGH-2009-FR.pdf, accessed 22 June 2014.
[94] Ibid.

residential institutions became home to destitute children, some of whom had been wandering the streets in the wake of the collapse of families and community support during the famine. These 'street-children' were placed in the provincial children's institutions that were termed generically as 'orphanages'. The term was somewhat misleading as children were housed in these institutions because their parents could not cope, normally because of poverty or ill-health or a combination of the two, as well as when both parents had died. In 1998, UNICEF estimated that about 50 per cent of children in these residential institutions were orphans.[95]

The initial idea was that these would be temporary facilities to cope with a temporary problem but as economic crisis and poverty became the norm, these institutions became permanent. Almost every province provided some facility for the care of children without parental support and these homes were organised to match school age cohorts.[96] Nursery-age children from birth to five years old were housed in thirteen 'baby homes' throughout the country.[97] The nine residential homes that housed kindergarten-age children, from age six to seven years, were, somewhat confusingly, sometimes known in the humanitarian community as 'orphanages'.[98] The eleven 'boarding schools' were home and school to children of primary and secondary level age, from 8 to 17 years old.[99] In 1998 around 10,200 children were reported to be living in residential institutions and these same numbers were reported to the World Food Programme (WFP) in 2011, albeit with more children reported by the government as living in the boarding schools for older children and fewer in the baby homes.[100]

Provincial and county authorities were supposed to provide food and goods to these institutions but provision was never other than utterly basic. Residential homes were housed in decrepit buildings without adequate heating, sanitation or kitchen facilities and with poorly trained staff. Residential homes remained under-resourced and relied on the charity of foreigners to sustain basic living standards.[101] Carers were low paid and endeavouring to compensate for low state wages with activity in the informal economy. Basic care and nutrition was provided to the children but the often ill-trained female staff did not cope well with the malnourished and sick children they looked after, especially the infants who needed constant nursing care.

---

[95] UNICEF, *Draft Master Plan of Operations* (Pyongyang: UNICEF, 1999), p. 38.
[96] UNICEF, *Situation Analysis of Women and Children.*
[97] Ibid., p. 74.   [98] Ibid., p. 75.   [99] Ibid., p. 76.
[100] WFP, *Emergency Operation (EMOP 200266)*, p. 10.
[101] Hazel Smith, *Hungry for Peace.*

The children's institutions housed children, by definition without family support, who were often as a consequence in poor health, almost always accompanied by visible signs of chronic malnutrition and often with acute malnutrition. In the family context food would normally be shared so that the child would receive some food even if it was insufficient. Extended families, neighbours and the wider community might also provide food for poor families. In the residential institutions, children were entirely dependent on inputs from the local authorities, which had numerous other urgent priorities and which had to rely on recruiting resources from local communities in the absence of reliable state supplies. There were few spare resources in most localities, so food remained scarce for these children.

The marketisation of well-being

Military rule did not bring sustainable improvements in well-being but neither did the society collapse into the absolute poverty that had characterised the famine years. Military-first governments did not abandon social policy to the market but neither were they successful in restoring the relatively egalitarian social provision that had characterised the Kim Il Sungist era. Social policy interventions were insufficient to prevent the great transformation in social structure that was the unanticipated consequence of marketisation.

12   The marketisation of the social structure

The Kim dynasty remained at the apex of the restructured social hierarchy but the social structure over which the Kim family presided became more fragmented and less stable. The formal occupational structure remained similar to that which existed in the Kim Il Sungist era but there was no longer a reliable correlation between occupational and social status.[1] Party members found that political status still counted for something in North Korea but, in the context of market realities, perennial food shortages, low incomes and high prices, economic entrepreneurial skills mattered more.

Women as a social group remained in low-status, physically arduous and dirty jobs; over half a million women worked as labourers in 2008. A minority secured good jobs and high-status positions but low pay pushed many women into the marketplace to supplement their income. Formerly high-status groups found that they were no longer privileged economically and socially. Professionals, the industrial working class, farmers on agriculturally productive farms and the ranks of the armed forces saw their fortunes plummet. A new class of *nouveau riche* emerged whose ostentatious lifestyle was based around the capacity to privately accumulate wealth.

The government viewed young people as the social group most likely to become politically disaffected and refocused mass mobilisation policies to an almost exclusive concentration on young people. Military-led command-and-obey organisation supplanted previous Party-led

---

[1] For discussion of the new market priorities and the transformation of social class structure, see Choong-Yong Ahn (ed.), *North Korea Development Report 2003/2004* (Seoul: Korea Institute for International Economic Policy, 2003/4), pp. 307–8. See also Jeong-Ah Cho, *The Changes of Everyday Life in North Korea in the Aftermath of their Economic Difficulties* (Seoul: Korea Institute for National Unification, 2007); Jae-Jean Suh, *Economic Hardship and Regime Sustainability in North Korea* (Seoul: Korea Institute for National Unification, 2008); Andrei Lankov, 'North Korea in Transition: Changes in Internal Politics and the Logic of Survival', *International Journal of Korean Unification Studies*, Vol. 18, No 1, 2009.

techniques that had offered rewards as well as penalties for participation in mass mobilisation into the military, civil defence and economic construction. Forced mobilisation served to keep young people occupied and managed but could not hide the obvious failings of the government. Inefficacy of the propaganda machine and greater understanding of the outside world only confirmed the bankruptcy of government policies.

The fragmentation of the old elites

During the military-first era, a narrowly based, non-accountable and interdependent civilian and military elite continued to preside over the state and society. Power and politics continued to coalesce around a network of oligarchies, the most important of which was the Kim Il Sung dynasty.[2] Social status at the top was dependent on political loyalty but good political connections no longer automatically led to positive well-being outcomes for all elite members.

The core of the North Korean elite were those families headed by comrades of Kim Il Sung, who had fought with him in the anti-Japanese struggle and/or had trusted political relationships with Kim Il Sung of a long duration.[3] The children of the old political elites received the same benefits as their parents of access to elite Pyongyang schools, preferential access to the best universities and, sometimes, the option of travel abroad; but not all were well-off. A senior member of a ministry could expect to take home $300 a month in 2011.[4] This amount of money was much more than most North Koreans earned, which was about a dollar a day, but much less than required to be comfortable, especially as prices were not much different from those prevailing in China. Even the old elites needed to find ways to leverage their position for private gain.[5]

[2] An account of the interlinkages between key figures can be found in Kyo-duk Lee, Soon-Hee Lee, Jeong-Ah Cho and Joung-Ho Song, *Study on the Power Elite of the Kim Jong Un Regime* (Seoul: Korea Institute for National Unification, 2013). Another informed analysis is Alexandre Y. Mansourov, 'Inside North Korea's Black Box: Reversing the Optics', in Kongdan Oh Hassig (ed.), *North Korean Policy Elites* (Alexandria, VA: Institute for Defense Analyses, 2004) unpaginated but pp. 159–226 on pdf, available at www.nkeconwatch.com/nk-uploads/dprkpolicyelites.pdf, accessed 2 November 2014.
[3] Joseph S. Bermudez, 'Information and the DPRK's Military and Power-holding Elite', in Kongdan Oh Hassig (ed.), *DPRK Policy Elites* (Alexandria, VA: Institute for Defense Analyses, 2004), unpaginated but p. 1–2 on pdf; available at www.nkeconwatch.com/nk-uploads/dprkpolicyelites.pdf, accessed 2 November 2014.
[4] Author interviews, Pyongyang, May 2011.
[5] Jae-Jean Suh, *Economic Hardship and Regime Sustainability in North Korea* (Seoul: Korea Institute for National Unification, 2008), pp. 15–17.

Ideology and institutional conflicts of interest between the Party and the military did not, however, provide the basis for intra-elite conflict. For one thing elite members routinely held positions in both civilian and military hierarchies so that they had loyalties to both institutions.[6] Elite families also remained bound together by a common awareness that they stood to face ruin and reprisals from home and abroad if the regime were to collapse. Instead it was personal and family interest that provided the rationale for tension as expanded elite numbers, from new generations and marriage into the core elite families, engendered cross-cutting family loyalties.

The second and third generation of politically important families had grown up with no personal experience of colonialism, war or individual hardship and had access to power and privilege because of family status rather than merit or demonstrable political skills.[7] International sanctions and global security services interest in the North Korean elite meant that family money could not easily be used outside the DPRK, so this generation, many of whom had been educated abroad and used to living a privileged life, had few options other than to look for a future in the DPRK. The third generation of elite families had a lot to lose from regime transformation and therefore were collectively committed to the overriding goal of regime security. On the other hand, these new generations had fragmented and conflictual personal interests. Unconstrained by ideology or institutional loyalties, individual allegiances became opportunistic and unstable.

The new unpredictability of dynasty politics

The Kim dynasty was far from monolithic, given the multiple marital relationships of Kim Il Sung and Kim Jong Il, which produced children from different women for both father and son.[8] Not all members of the Kim family participated in North Korean politics, most notably Kim Jong Il's older son, Kim Jong Nam, who lived outside the DPRK, from where he gave media interviews in which he distanced himself from family politics.[9] Overlapping family relationships, amplified by in-law

[6] The military elite held office in civilian institutions, including security agencies and the Party, as well as in the armed forces. See Bermudez, 'Information'.
[7] Kyo-duk Lee et al., Study on the Power Elite.
[8] A pithy summary of the Kims' marital relationships is in Andre Lankov, The Real North Korea: Life and Politics in the Failed Stalinist Utopia (Oxford University Press, 2013), pp. 54–6.
[9] The Chosunilbo, 'Kim Jong-nam Says N. Korean Regime Won't Last Long', 17 January 2012, available at http://english.chosun.com/site/data/html_dir/2012/01/17/201201170 1790.html, accessed 25 January 2014.

networks, generated potentially divisive and competing loyalties among different power centres within the extended Kim family dynasty. Kim Jong Il delayed choosing a successor until after he suffered a stroke in 2008, when his ill-health precipitated a decision to designate Kim Jong Un as next leader. Unlike Kim Jong Il, who had spent twenty years understudying his father, Kim Jong Un came into office when Kim Jong Il died with little experience and without having built up a powerful constituency of support.[10]

When Kim Jong Il was alive, the most politically significant in-law relationships in the Kim dynasty were those centred on Kim Jong Il's sister's husband, Jang Song-thaek, whom Kim Jong Il promoted along with Jang's two brothers, although he also removed Jang from power on two occasions.[11] Jang accumulated power as Kim Jong Il's authorised representative in foreign trade and business links and suppressed political rivals in the name of the Kim dynasty.[12] In 2008, Kim Jong Il promoted Jang to Vice-Chairman of the National Defence Commission, a move that effectively made Jang second in command of the state.[13]

After Kim Jong Il's death in 2011, Jang Song-thaek was progressively isolated by other elite families and in December 2013 he was arrested and accused of profiteering and corruption. Pictures of Jang's arrest were broadcast around the world, as was the news of his subsequent execution. A beneficiary of Jang Song-thaek's eradication from DPRK politics was Choi Ryong-hae, a former protégé of Jang Song-thaek and son of Choi Hyon, a trusted confidant of Kim Il Sung from their guerrilla days in the anti-colonial struggle in Manchuria.[14] Choi had been promoted to the status of general by Kim Jong Il in 2010 but had no background in military operations, and the suggestion was that his compliance with Jang's execution improved his standing with the military.[15]

Kim Jong Un was credited by the North Korean media with authorising Jang's execution, although well-placed observers described Kim Jong Un as a powerless 'avatar' for the North Korean state and Jang's execution

[10] Lankov, *The Real North Korea*, pp. 132–5.
[11] Mansourov, 'Inside North Korea's Black Box', p. 17.
[12] *New Focus International*, 'Insider Perspective: The Removal of Jang Song Taek (Update)' 9 December 2013, available at http://newfocusintl.com/insider-perspective-the-removal-of-jang-song-taek-update, accessed 14 January 2014.
[13] Jinwook Choi and Meredith Shaw, 'The Rise of Kim Jong Eun and the Return of the Party', *International Journal of Korean Unification Studies*, Vol. 19, No. 2, 2010, pp. 175–202.
[14] Lee *et al.*, *Study on the Power Elite*, p. 34. On Choi Hyon and the friendship with Kim Il Sung, see Robert A. Scalapino and Chong-Sik Lee, *Communism in Korea: The Movement* (Berkeley: University of California Press, 1972), p. 392.
[15] *New Focus International* 'Insider Perspective'.

as a 'coup'.[16] Internal political dynamics in North Korea remained too opaque to assess the autonomous capacity of Kim Jong Un but what was evident was that close family connections to the Kim dynasty no longer provided an automatic guarantee of personal protection.

The marketisation of the occupational structure

The 2008 census abandoned the old Kim Il Sungist social classification scheme of worker, farmer and official and adopted modern, internationally standard industrial classifications to analyse employment.[17] The census, which was conducted with the help of the United Nations Population Fund (UNFPA) under-recorded social transformation even as it provided a useful picture of the DPRKs changing industrial structure. This is because the figures included the fully employed, underemployed and the unemployed and only indicated formal employment categories. Government policy was that all able-bodied adults of working age should be allocated a specific workplace but there were also incentives for individuals to maintain workplace registration. Workplace affiliation was the only conduit to state benefits, including maternity benefits, sick benefits, healthcare, adult education, cultural opportunities and access for the workers' children to nurseries, kindergartens and schools. The workplace was the channel for the allocation of state provision of food and goods if and when they became available, for instance on national holidays.

The 2008 census reported that the majority of the working age population, nearly four and a half million, was located in the agriculture, fisheries and food sector, with the next highest industrial sector being manufacturing, including light industry, employing just less than three million people.[18] It also reported that public sector employment remained as extensive as in the Kim Il Sung era. In addition to the 700,000 or so military, about three-quarters of a million people were employed in public administration, defence and compulsory social security; half a million in education; a third of a million in human health and social work activities; 100,000 in information and communication; and another half million in administrative and support service activities.[19]

---

[16] *New Focus International*, 'We have Just Witnessed a Coup in North Korea', 27 December 2013, available at http://newfocusintl.com/just-witnessed-coup-north-korea, accessed 14 January 2012.

[17] Chang Su Kim, *DPR Korea 2008 Population Census National Report* (Pyongyang: Central Bureau of Statistics Pyongyang, 2009), p. 8.

[18] Ibid., p. 195.

[19] Ibid.

The 2008 census showed broadly similar gender patterns in official employment as those reported in the 1993 census. The workforce comprised 6,359,938 men and 5,824,782 women with more than two-thirds employed in the agriculture and manufacturing sectors.[20] The census recorded slightly more women than men working in 'agriculture, forestry and fishing', where 2,304,598 women, compared with 2,082,297 men, were employed; a change from 1993 when slightly more men than women were recorded in this sector.[21] Slightly more men than women, at 1,507,014 and 1,375,968 respectively, were registered as employed in the manufacturing industry – a difference from 1993 when slightly more women than men were employed.[22]

The 2008 census showed that women comprised by far the majority of the workforce in the occupation categories of wholesale and retail trade, including 'repair of motor vehicles; accommodation and food service activities; and human health and social work activities.'[23] With the exception of the sub-category 'repair of motor vehicles', which would have been almost exclusively a male occupation in North Korea, female-dominated categories reflected caring, serving and support roles.

Perhaps surprisingly, the 2008 census shows women worked in substantial numbers in male-dominated occupations including mining and quarrying; construction; transportation and storage; electricity, gas, steam and air conditioning supply; and water supply, sewerage, waste management and 'remediation' activities.[24] Within the manufacturing sector more women worked in mining and minerals as plant operators than men – some 87,651 women as against 76,649 men.[25] In coal and ignite mining, women workers amounted to 123,678 compared with 197,647 men.[26]

Many of those formally registered in official workplaces did not receive a living wage from the government and were of necessity supplementing their income in the informal economy. A 'double economy' existed in which the numbers of those employed in the formal economy were grossly exaggerated and census returns could not fully account for those employed in the informal economy. The 1993 census had shown 508,630 persons employed in 'commerce' but in 2008 the analogous category of 'wholesale and retail trade; repair of motor vehicle' reported

---

[20] Ibid.   [21] Ibid.   [22] Ibid.   [23] Ibid.
[24] Ibid. It is not clear from the text what is meant by 'remediation' but it probably refers to the cleaning of industrial sites.
[25] Ibid, p. 201.   [26] Ibid, p. 193.

just 557,355 persons, only a small increase and therefore providing a misleading underestimate of those earning their living from market activity.[27]

The 2008 census recorded 300,172 women and 6,472 men employed as market salespersons but these numbers did not include participants in the informal economy, including the army of petty traders, street corner pedlars and employed, unemployed and retired persons who traded on the side.[28] One indication of the numbers involved is in the figure of one million non-retired adults, most of whom were women, who reported that their main economic activity was household work.[29] In the absence of a functioning welfare state to provide income and food and with the majority of the population living in poverty, it would be a reasonably safe assumption that these women were active participants in the informal economy.

Census returns show that women's participation in waged work decreased exponentially between 1993 and 2008.[30] The fall from 89 per cent in 1993 to just over 62 per cent in the 2008 census was probably, however, an underestimate.[31] Official figures included those who were only nominally still attached to a workplace or who only occasionally participated in waged work. The real drop in female participation in the waged workforce was likely much higher as women did not stop working outside the home but instead moved to work in the markets.

Women were employed in large numbers in some of the toughest and dirtiest manual work in the country. UNICEF officials reported in 2002 that the country had become more reliant on women's unskilled labour, and 'the loss of industrial capacity... and the workforce, which includes many women, is frequently engaged in labour-intensive/low output activity'.[32]

In 2008, 546,942 women labourers as compared to 774,117 men were employed in road and irrigation construction, manually shovelling and shifting heavy loads in dirty, unhygienic and physically demanding conditions.[33] This pattern of labour activity was consistent with the Kim Il

[27] Ibid, p. 195; Sun Won Hong, *Analysis of 1993 Population Census Data DPR Korea* (Pyongyang: Population Center, DPRK, 1996), p. 69.
[28] Kim, *DPR Korea 2008 Population Census*, p. 200.
[29] Central Bureau of Statistics, '2008 Census of Population of DPRK: Key Findings', available at www.unfpa.org/webdav/site/global/shared/documents/news/2010/dprk08_censuskeyfinds.pdf, accessed 22 June 2014.
[30] Ibid.   [31] Ibid.
[32] UNICEF, *A Humanitarian Appeal for Children and Women* (Pyongyang: UNICEF, 2002), p. 1.
[33] Kim, *DPR Korea 2008 Population Census*, p. 201; Author's observations, 1990–2011, DPRK.

Sung era and the reasons for it were also the same.[34] The predominance of women in labouring work reflected their substitution for the young men conscripted into the army who might otherwise have been engaged in this type of work. Women's work in nursing and the care professions involved lifting and carrying while, in the absence of mechanisation, women's work in agriculture was back-breaking and highly physically demanding.

Women were predominantly, but not uniformly, employed in low-status jobs. In 2005, in the sectors in which the workforce was predominantly women, that is, public health, commerce and childcare, 70 per cent of managers were women.[35] In education, communication and culture, just 34 per cent of managers were women, while in industry, agriculture and construction just 15 per cent of managers were women.[36] The DPRK government reported in 2005 to the international monitoring body of the Convention on the Elimination of Discrimination Against Women (CEDAW) that just 10 per cent of government officials were women and that the 'proportion of female officials is high at medium or lower positions [but] ... is comparatively low at the level of department directorship of government'.[37] Women, however, were as well represented in governmental positions as in some of the developed countries. In 2004, 32.9 per cent of those holding government offices were women, compared to 29.5 per cent in 1995.[38] Women comprised 20.1 per cent of deputies to the eleventh Supreme People's Assembly and 21.9 per cent of deputies to the local people's Assemblies.[39]

Losers and winners

Marketisation fragmented formerly well-understood and transparent occupational hierarchies, as previously coveted occupations no longer automatically provided decent pay and benefits and those who prospered in the military-first era did so because of their success in private trade. Those who could not easily access income from private production and trade included professionals, the industrial working class, farmers on

---

[34] The terminology of the 1993 census was not directly analogous to the 2008 census but the 1993 census reported that 66 per cent of 'semi-specialists' were women and 42 per cent of 'specialists' were women, indicating the relative concentration of women in unskilled jobs. See Hong, *Analysis of 1993 Population Census Data*, p. 116.

[35] Committee on the Elimination of Discrimination against Women, *Written Replies by the Democratic People's Republic of Korea Concerning the Responses to the List of Issues and Questions. PSWG/ 2005/II/CRP.2/Add.3* (New York: UN Women, 15 April 2005), p. 6, available at www.un.org/womenwatch/daw/cedaw/cedaw33/responses/kor/kor-E.pdf, accessed 22 April 2014.

[36] Ibid.   [37] Ibid.   [38] Ibid., p. 9.   [39] Ibid.

agriculturally productive farms and the majority of those serving in the armed forces. These social groups faced destitution in the military-first era.

In 2008, the United Nations Food and Agriculture Organisation reported that 'even officials appeared to be affected by the current food shortages and in some cases appeared to face greater food security challenges than those [family] whose members have full-time informal jobs'.[40] On the other hand, those officials and private individuals with entrepreneurial skills and the ability to leverage political connections could do very well, even if they did not hold senior Party positions. These entrepreneurs formed the nucleus of the *nouveau riche*, who successfully exploited the market for private gain.

Doctors, engineers, judges, teachers and other qualified professionals and their families had formerly had access to guaranteed food rations, basic goods and income, but in the military-first era these were nominal and state-supplied food minimal.[41] Urban professionals were worse off than their rural counterparts in that they had less access to home-grown food.[42] Unless they had relatives in the country and the ability to communicate with those relatives or were one of the lucky few whose work gave them opportunities to make some money from trade, these individuals could be in a very difficult position. Doctors, teachers and professionals accepted 'gifts'; social, welfare and education services, although nominally still free at the point of use, depended on consumers of the services to feed and fund staff through these ex-gratia payments.[43] Many professionals did not possess even a partial safety net. Those who had little contact with the public such as, for example, engineers and accountants, and who could not supplement their income through petty trade, faced a high risk of poverty and malnutrition.

The government expropriated agricultural production from the agricultural cooperatives located in the breadbasket provinces of South Hwanghae and North Hwanghae to feed the military and city-based officials.[44] The government paid below the market price for official grain

---

[40] FAO/WFP, *Crop and Food Supply Assessment Mission to the Democratic People's Republic of Korea, Special Report* (Rome: FAO/WFP, 8 December 2008), p. 28.

[41] Cho, *The Changes of Everyday Life*, pp. 45–6.

[42] FAO/WFP, *Crop and Food Supply Assessment Mission*, 8 December 2008, pp. 28–9.

[43] On changes in the education sector and the practice of parents providing teachers with food, see Kyo-Duk Lee, Soon-Hee Lim, Jeong-Ah Cho, Gee-Dong Lee and Young-Hoon Lee, *Changes in North Korea as Revealed in the Testimonies of Saetomins* (Seoul: Korea Institute for National Unification, 2008), pp. 57–71.

[44] For state controls in respect of grain sales, see FAO/WFP, *Crop and Food Supply Assessment Mission to the Democratic People's Republic of Korea, Special Report* (Rome: FAO/WFP, 16 November 2010).

expropriations and nothing at all for the 'patriotic contributions' that were nominally voluntary and in practice compulsory. Farmers were supposed to be left with a cereal ration sufficient to keep themselves and their families and to provide seeds for the following year, and were supposed to be supplied with low-cost fixed-price inputs.[45] In practice, necessary farming inputs were not made available in adequate quantities through government channels and farmers had to resort to the market and pay market prices. Farmers, like the rest of the population, also had to pay market prices for their daily living expenses. Low fixed incomes combined with high market prices resulted in these formerly well-off farmers facing destitution in marketised North Korea.

The industrial working class lost secure incomes, guaranteed food rations, relatively high social status and guaranteed employment. In 2008, the marginal recovery of the economy brought a reported utilisation of industrial capacity to only between 20 and 30 per cent.[46] Unlike the officials, whose social status diminished but who still remained of some importance within formal and informal social structures, the industrial working class collapsed as a political and economic force. Manufacturing enterprises could not make the profits out of which they were supposed to pay workers after the economic reforms of 2002.[47] The industrial working class lost political influence as the organisational structure in which it had operated – the workplace as an important focus of political organisation – all but disappeared. The role of heavy industrial workers as the ideological vanguard of the working class lost relevance as market realities replaced ideology.

The industrial working class that lived in the big north-eastern cities faced mass unemployment and underemployment. Environmental conditions were poor in the densely populated cities as the crumbling apartment blocks in which people lived suffered from little or no maintenance, and poor water, sanitation and electricity supplies. In Hamhung, site of North Korea's run-down chemical industry, unknown chemicals seeped into the ground and water supplies, affecting health and causing long-term environmental degeneration.

Despite the eponymous doctrine, military personnel were not well-off and did not benefit personally from military-first politics. Young people in military service lived in difficult conditions that would not be much

[45] FAO/WFP, *Crop and Food Supply Assessment Mission to the Democratic People's Republic of Korea, Special Report* (Rome: FAO/WFP, 28 November 2013), p. 35.
[46] Geir Helgeson and Nis Høyrup, *North Korea 2007: Assisting Development and Change* (Copenhagen: Nordic Institute of Asian Affairs, 2007), p. 30.
[47] Soo-Young Choi, *A Study on the Structure of Industry in North Korea* (Seoul: Korea Institute for National Unification, 2006), p. 34.

different than those they had left at home but nevertheless they and their families resented these unproductive years in which they could neither earn money nor advance in their lives. The families of military personnel did not receive preferential food allocations and the absence of a potential income earner from home provided an impediment to the main task exercising every family, of making money.[48]

Demobilised troops lost the opportunities open to former military in the Kim Il Sungist era.[49] Rather than ending up on productive farms or as in the Kim Il Sung era with good jobs in the heavy industrial sector, ex-military often ended up in miserable conditions of employment. In lieu of the technology that remained in perennial short supply, the state especially required labour in dirty, dangerous industries like mining, power generation and construction and these sectors provided a common destination for demobilised soldiers in the military-first era. These jobs were low-paid, subject to endless demands for 'voluntary', meaning unpaid, extra labour and workers could not rely on a stable food supply even though the state formally guaranteed food rations to 'key workers'.

The rise of the nouveau riche

Marketisation brought the opportunity for significant wealth creation for a small minority even though most North Koreans engaged in the market only as petty traders.[50] The importance of this new social group was that it generated income and wealth through non-state-directed and 'grey-area' activities and that the government encouraged these new entrepreneurial elements, despite the fact – indeed because of the fact – that they were capitalists in practice and morality.[51] The government thus normatively sanctioned the new ethos that, without too much of an exaggeration, could be understood as 'greed is good'.

Some of those who became rich from North Korean marketisation were not Korean but Chinese – known as the 'Big Hands' for their ability to marshal sufficient resources to finance and direct trading networks.[52]

---

[48] Lee *et al.*, *Changes in North Korea*, pp. 54–5.
[49] Ibid.
[50] Colin Dürkop and Min-Il Yeo, 'North Korea after Kim Jong Il: Political and Social Perspectives ahead of the Expected Change of Power', *KAS International Reports*, August 2011, available at www.kas.de/wf/doc/kas_23605-544-2-30.pdf? 110811143245, accessed 29 August 2011; Hyung-min Joo, 'Visualizing the Invisible Hands: The Shadow Economy in North Korea', *Economy and Society*, Vol. 39, No. 1, February 2010, pp. 110–45; Lankov, 'North Korea in Transition', pp. 10–11.
[51] Suh, *Economic Hardship*, pp. 30–2.
[52] Joo, 'Visualizing the Invisible Hands'.

Some individual entrepreneurs were the Koreans 'from Japan' who remained in close contact with the pro-North Korean organisations in Japan and had access to capital.[53] Urban wholesalers tended to be North Koreans who had either made enough money to set themselves up in business or were supported by relatives living abroad, including in South Korea.[54] Party officials who proved successful in leading or working for the arm's-length businesses created by the state, Party and military in the wake of the government's economic legislation of 2002 joined the ranks of the new rich.[55]

The *nouveau riche* flaunted their wealth; buying caseloads of cigarettes and alcohol from the hard currency shops operating in Pyongyang and other major cities, and consumer goods such as refrigerators, bicycles and second-hand cars from abroad. The *nouveau riche* assumed a politically precarious, socially envied and highly visible status in the society. Officially and legally, the government banned 'speculation' and occasionally made an example of those that it considered had gone too far in enriching themselves, by instigating penal sanctions. On the whole, however, this social group was envied for their visible economic success. The new rich engaged in conspicuous consumption in restaurants, hotels and shops, and had access to the latest technology, including mobile phones, cameras and computers. They did not, however, form a political class in themselves as the authoritarian nature of the state pre-empted any political opposition and the primary aim of these individuals was not political access and advancement, but economic and monetary gain.

This new social group existed in an interdependent relationship with the political classes at local and national level. The new entrepreneurs needed political protection in order to stave off state political interference and the old political elites needed to find ways of making money. Market participation was dependent on achieving political 'cover' by ensuring that Party and security officials colluded with market activities.[56] After the economic reforms of 2002, government policy pursued 'profitability' as well as 'self-reliance' and these slogans were used by entrepreneurs to justify their activities as in line with government objectives.

[53] Sonia Ryang, *North Koreans in Japan: Language, Ideology and Identity* (Boulder, CO: Westview, 1997); Emma Chanlett-Avery, *North Korean Supporters in Japan: Issues for US Policy* (Washington, DC: Congressional Research Service, 7 November 2003), available at www.ncnk.org/resources/publications/CRS_Chosen_Soren_2003_RL32137.pdf, accessed 1 April 2014.
[54] Joo, 'Visualizing the Invisible Hands', pp. 127–8.
[55] Suh, *Economic Hardship*, pp. 20–3.
[56] Cho, *The Changes of Everyday Life*, pp. 41–6.

The regimentation of young people

The government viewed youth – late adolescents and young adults – as a key physical and political resource for regime maintenance but also as a potential threat to regime stability.[57] Young people experienced as much, if not more, regimentation as in the Kim Il Sung era, but lost the perks from which young people had previously benefited. In the military-first era the element of compulsion was practically all that remained of youth policy. Youth mobilisation comprised participation in cheerless, physically onerous activities that were understood by both government and the youth as a means of social and political control. The government was constantly on guard against the potential of dissidence and rebellion from young people, who were aware of both the economic and political deficiencies of the society in which they lived.[58]

In the face of continuing shortages of technology and capital, young people were organised in quasi-military structures to provide a second arm of national defence, alongside the regular military.[59] In January 1996, the government reorganised the League of Socialist Working Youth of Korea as the Kim Il Sung Socialist Youth League to function as a vehicle for regimented contributions to construction, agricultural production, civil defence and military mobilisation.[60] The central committee of the revamped Youth League was named the 'youth vanguard' and its governance reinforced by the creation of posts of secretary and deputy-secretary at province, city, county and 'primary organisation' level.[61] Strengthening of the youth organisation was supposed to produce 'a fresh militant contingent that constitutes the driving force of the revolution' and as a key resource in the defence and maintenance of the state.[62]

The youth organisation was meant to protect 'youth and children from the infiltration of all sorts of unsound, corrupt and reactionary ideas and

---

[57] Young people are an under-researched topic in the study of North Korea. For discussions that touch on some of the changes in young people's lives, seeJae-Jean Suh, *North Korea's Market Economy Society from Below* (Seoul: Korea Institute for National Unification, 2005); Suh, *Economic Hardship*; Lee et al., *Changes in North Korea*; Soon-Hee Lim, *Value Changes of the North Korean New Generation and Prospects* (Seoul: Korea Institute for National Unification, 2007).

[58] Lim, *Value Changes*, pp. 7–9.

[59] Author's interviews and observations, Pyongyang May 2011.

[60] Délégation générale de la RPD de Corée en France, *Bulletin d'information, No. 14/0196* (Paris: Délégation générale de la RPD de Corée en France, 22 January 1996), p. 3.

[61] Ibid.

[62] Kim Jong Il, *Let us Exalt the Brilliance of Comrade Kim Il Sung's Idea on the Youth Movement and the Achievements Made under his Leadership* (Pyongyang: Foreign Languages Publishing House, 1996), p. 2.

culture'.[63] Mass mobilisation was used to maintain surveillance over young people who were herded into the 'military first general youth mobilisation' rallies and 'Oath pledging parades of youth vanguards' that took place throughout the country after the death of Kim Jong Il in December 2011.[64] The aim was that the military-first youth organisation would inculcate the ideological training that in the previous era had been transmitted through hegemonic practices in every arena of society. Military-first youth policy was to mobilise young people in the quasi-military youth league and to insist that young people must subordinate their individual lives to military-first discipline as directed by the leadership.

The policy failed to achieve the objective of creating a willing and able group of physically and ideologically prepared young people prepared to defend the Kim family at all costs. Young people met outside the constraints of work and political activity, in train stations and parks and at the movies and sporting events, and were less subject to intrusive surveillance outside political activities than in the Kim Il Sungist era. Security personnel were less motivated to monitor and check casual conversations and lifestyles that might hint at lack of revolutionary fervour as they themselves were trying to find ways round state strictures in order to feed their own families.

Young people expressed themselves in a more individualistic manner, particularly through clothing and hairstyles. In Pyongyang in 2011, for example, fashionable young male students visibly cultivated the louche look of South Korean pop stars – with floppy hair styled to fall casually over the face and wearing their state-issued formal suit jackets with sleeves pushed up to just below the elbow.[65] Young women's dress was less uniform than in the previous era, although dress remained conservative. Skirts remained knee length and cleavage and bare legs were never on show, although this was as much a product of historically founded conservative cultural conventions as of military-first state directives.

Young people grew up with a different relationship to the state than their parents and grandparents. In the Kim Il Sung era, it had been necessary to obey and participate in order to have a chance of a decent and prosperous life. In the post-Kim Il Sung era, to have any chance of

[63] Kim Jong Il, 'Let us Exalt the Brilliance of Comrade Kim Il Sung's Idea on the Youth Movement and the Achievements Made under his Leadership', in Délégation générale de la RPD de Corée en France, *Bulletin d'information, Special Issue No. 23/0896* (Paris: Délégation générale de la RPD de Corée en France, 31 August 1996), p. 4.

[64] Jin-Ha Kim, 'On the Threshold of Power, 2011/12 Pyongyang's Politics of Transition', *International Journal of Korean Unification Studies*, Vol. 20, No. 2, 2011, p. 10.

[65] Author's observations, Kim Il Sung University, Pyongyang, May 2011.

securing a decent future, it was often a much more rational act to avoid and ignore state directives.

The end of the monolith

The regime survived but not in the form of the all-encompassing state/Party/society model of the past. In its place rose a state that was as politically repressive as its Kim Il Sungist predecessor but less capable of controlling every aspect of private and civic life than had been the case prior to the famine. Social structures were re-ordered around a matrix of old politics and new market opportunities, and the *nouveau riche* provided new role models for young people despite the efforts of military-first policy to insulate the youth from the social dynamics of marketisation.

13   Going nuclear

Military-first era governments used diplomacy and military deterrence to pursue regime security goals but, in the absence of a strong civilian or political counterweight to military-first logic, foreign policy evolved into that of 'nuclear deterrence first – diplomacy second'.[1]

The central goal of early military-first era foreign policy was to achieve normalisation of diplomatic relations with the United States. Military-first foreign policy pursued bilateral engagement with the United States and also engaged in diplomatic outreach worldwide to states of all ideological hues. The objective was to reduce North Korea's diplomatic isolation abroad, to enhance regime security and to obtain support for economic redevelopment. Kim Jong Il's government presided over a historic rapprochement with South Korea and rebuilt relationships with Russia and China.

Military-first government recalibrated their security policy after the 2000 election of George Bush, as DPRK decision-makers viewed activist United States foreign policy as heralding a military attack on North Korea. Military-first governments were not confident that their conventional armed forces could withstand military intervention and reasoned that they could use scientific expertise, technology and the fissile materials they possessed to develop a nuclear weapons capacity. The aim was to provide effective deterrence against foreign invasions. North Korea's decision to vigorously pursue the development of nuclear weapons precipitated what became known as the 'second nuclear crisis'.[2]

---

[1] This chapter draws on my previous publications on North Korean foreign policy. See, for example, Hazel Smith, 'North Korean Foreign Policy in the 1990s: The Realist Approach', in Hazel Smith, Chris Rhodes, Diana Pritchard and Kevin Magill (eds.), *North Korea in the New World Order* (London: Macmillan, 1996), pp. 93–113; Hazel Smith, 'North Korea's Security Perspectives', in Andrew T. H. Tan (ed.), *East and South-East Asia: International Relations and Security Perspectives* (London: Routledge, 2013), pp. 121–32.

[2] There is a large literature, mainly American, on the second nuclear crisis. The most useful and well-informed account is, however, written by a non-American. See Yoichi Funabashi, *The Peninsula Question: A Chronicle of the Second Korean Nuclear Crisis*

The military logic that underpinned DPRK domestic and foreign policy viewed political problems through a militarised lens in which the first choice of solution was via military means. Military-first era national security policy evolved to explicitly constitute regime security around the possession of an independently controlled nuclear weapons capacity. In 2013 Kim Jong Un announced that diplomacy and deterrence remained the foreign policy instruments of the military-first era but, in practice, the balance between the two was skewed so that nuclear deterrence remained the core of security policy.[3]

Inching towards normal: DPRK diplomacy and the United States

The DPRK government had very high hopes that the 1994 Geneva Agreement presaged a 'normalisation' of relations with the United States. North Korean strategists believed that it was only with 'normal' diplomatic relations that the threat of military intervention would recede. The North Korean government did not believe that Japan or South Korea would undertake military action against the North without the prior agreement of the United States and the evidence of malign intent and imminent threat from the United States seemed clear to North Korean policy-makers, as did their vulnerability to attack. Normalisation was also important for economic reasons. North Korea understood that other countries and international institutions would only be persuaded to invest in North Korea if the United States did not oppose such investment.

North Korea hoped that within the ten-year period that it would take for KEDO to provide the light water reactors specified in the Geneva Agreement that '[North] Korea and the United States would develop their relations in different fields based on the bridge of the LWR [Light water reactors]'.[4] All contacts with United States organisations of any

---

(Washington, DC: Brookings Institution Press, 2007). See also Chae-Jin Lee, *A Troubled Peace: US Policy and the Two Koreas* (Baltimore, MD: The Johns Hopkins Press, 2006); Bruce Cumings, 'Creating Korean Insecurity: The US Role', in Hazel Smith (ed.), *Reconstituting Korean Security: A Policy Primer* (Tokyo: United Nations Press, 2007), pp. 21–42; for a view from a United States official and analyst who negotiated with North Korea during the second nuclear crisis, see Victor Cha, *The Impossible State: North Korea Past and Future* (London: The Bodley Head, 2012).

[3] Kim Jong Un persisted with calls for unification through cooperation with the South. See Kim Jong Un, *Kim Jong Un Makes New Year Address* (Pyongyang: Korean Central News Agency, 1 January 2013), available at www.kcna.kp/goHome.do?lang=eng, accessed 3 January 2013.

[4] Chol Nam Jon, *A Duel of Reason Between Korea and US: Nuke, Missile and Artificial Satellite* (Pyongyang: Foreign Languages Publishing House, 2000), p. 185.

sort – whether governmental or non-governmental – were viewed as potentially contributing to the aim of improved relations between the DPRK and the United States. Contacts that were not especially high-level from the United States side were understood disproportionately by North Korea as evidence of success in moving towards the goal of normalisation. These included military-to-military relations and contact with United States non-governmental organisations as well as the occasional contact with American journalists, among others.[5] A Pyongyang publication noted approvingly that between 1994 and 1997 'more than one hundred US Congressmen, military officials, financial and economic figures as well as civilians visited the Republic [North Korea]'.[6]

The Korean People's Army (KPA) collaborated with the United States army throughout the 1990s and early 2000s. Several dozen US military personnel spent repeated periods of time in North Korea searching for the remains of missing service personnel.[7] For the North Korean government, this was partly an income generation project; between 1995 and 2003 the United States Department of Defense paid $15 million for the privilege of sending investigators into the country.[8] These joint activities were viewed by the North Korean government as one means of normalising DPRK–US relations but instead the constraints placed on resident United States military personnel and the wariness in which they were held consolidated the deep divide between the two countries.[9]

The DPRK never expected that the easing of United States sanctions that followed the Geneva Agreement would lead to much in the way of expanded trade with the United States. The North Korean government valued the lifting of economic sanctions much more for their indirect economic impact. With normal relations with the United States, North Korea would be able to access major investment from the international financial institutions like the World Bank. The North Korean government consistently argued that United States sanctions were a crucial factor in

---

[5] For discussion of the relationship with US NGOs, see Hazel Smith, *Overcoming Humanitarian Dilemmas in the DPRK*, Special Report No. 90 (Washington, DC: United States Institute of Peace, July 2002).

[6] Nada Takashi, *Korea in Kim Jong Il's Era* (Pyongyang: Foreign Languages Publishing House, 2000), p. 98.

[7] Ibid., pp. 97–8.

[8] Mark E. Manyin, *US Assistance to North Korea: Fact Sheet* (Washington, DC: Congressional Research Service, 2005) updated 11 October 2006, available at http://assets.opencrs.com/rpts/RS21834_20061011.pdf, accessed 7 June 2012.

[9] Takashi, *Korea in Kim Jong Il's Era*, p. 97; US military personnel in the DPRK lived in difficult conditions as they worked in physically remote areas and they were also treated with suspicion by their North Korean interlocutors. Author's interviews, Pyongyang, 2001.

explaining North Korea's economic woes, but United States sanctions were mostly bilateral; they did not inhibit trade with other wealthy countries, including the western Europeans and the capitalist countries of South and South-east Asia.

North Korea received generous humanitarian aid from adversaries, including the United States, Japan and South Korea, which collectively donated over one million tonnes of food in just one year – 2000 to 2001 – enough to feed eight million North Koreans, or a third of the population, for one year.[10] The United States alone donated just over a billion dollars' worth of humanitarian aid from the United States between 1995 and 2002.[11] Most of this was in the form of high volumes of food aid; ranging from 177,000 metric tonnes of food aid in 1997 to a high of 695,194 metric tonnes in 1999.[12]

The North Korean government valued the humanitarian aid programme for its substantive content but also because it hoped that the process of interaction with United States government officials would contribute to normalisation of bilateral diplomatic relations. The donor status of the United States meant that State Department and other governmental officials, American NGO workers and some interested American politicians, such as Congressman Tony Hall, sustained direct and indirect contact with North Korean officials from the mid-1990s onwards. For the North Korean government, a high point of persistent efforts at 'normalisation' was when President Clinton's Secretary of State, Madeleine Albright, visited Pyongyang in October 2000 to meet with Kim Jong Il. Photos of the meeting were posted all over North Korea in public places.

Strategic recalculations

Senior North Korean diplomats, many of whom had negotiated with successive United States administrations for over a decade, understood that the election of President George W. Bush in 2000 brought to office a Republican administration in which important domestic constituencies – particularly the so-called 'neo-conservatives' or 'neo-cons' – were

---

[10] Hazel Smith, *Hungry for Peace: International Security, Humanitarian Assistance and Social Change in North Korea* (Washington, DC: United States Institute of Peace Press, 2005); Smith, *Overcoming Humanitarian Dilemmas*, p. 16.

[11] Mark E. Manyin and Ryun Jun, 'US Assistance to North Korea: Fact Sheet', CRS Report for Congress (Washington, DC: Congressional Research Service, 17 March 2003), p. 24.

[12] Mark Manyin and Mary Beth Nikitin, *Foreign Assistance to North Korea* (Washington, DC: Congressional Research Service, 2012), p. 3, available at www.fas.org/sgp/crs/row/R40095.pdf, accessed 24 September 2012.

viscerally anti-communist and anti-DPRK, and saw diplomatic dealings with the DPRK as akin to supping with the devil. Nevertheless, the military-first policy of the early 2000s was to persist with bilateral talks with the United States even as relations between the two deteriorated and even though they were characterised by mistrust and suspicion. North Korean officials allegedly confirmed to Bush administration officials at a meeting in Pyongyang that it was developing a clandestine nuclear programme – an admission later denied by North Korean officials.[13]

From North Korea's perspective, diplomacy was achieving very little in the early 2000s. North Korean officials complained that the United States was not implementing its side of the bargain to institute 'normal' diplomatic relations between the two countries. At the same time, not all of North Korean policy-makers were convinced that diplomacy could ever achieve desirable outcomes. United States policy-makers regularly invoked the development of weapons of mass destruction as the rationale for war with Iraq. For North Korean officials, the United States seemed to be making an indirect case for war with the DPRK.

The North Koreans were conscious that the 9/11 attack on New York in 2001 and the subsequent invasion of Afghanistan made the United States more likely to engage militarily abroad. One of North Korea's senior foreign policy negotiators, Jong In-Chan, was in Manhattan on 9/11 and witnessed first-hand the atrocity and the reaction to it by the public and the government. The tough external environment in which the United States considered itself enmeshed in a 'global war on terror', in which states were either friend or foe, did not facilitate compromise. North Korea's hopes for of an imminent 'normalised' diplomatic relationship with the United States finally evaporated after President Bush denounced North Korea as part of the 'axis of evil' in 2002, along with Iran and Iraq, and withdrew support from the 1994 Geneva or KEDO agreement, which was suspended in 2003.

North Korea's officials made little diplomatic progress in their efforts to persuade the Republican Bush administration that North Korea was a reliable negotiating partner, but the tipping point was the United States intervention in Iraq. The heavy bombing of Baghdad in March 2003 and the ensuing involvement of US and allied troops on the ground dispelled any notion, fostered after the withdrawal of United States troops from Somalia in disarray in 1995, that the US could not sustain battlefield losses because domestic public opinion would not allow such losses.

---

[13] For the DPRK account see *People's Korea*, 'J. Kelly Failed to Produce "Evidence" in Pyongyang; Framed Up Admission Story', 19 January 2003, available at www.korea-np. co.jp/pk/188th_issue/2003013001.htm, accessed 9 June 2012. For the US perspective, see *Korea Now*, 'Peaceful Solutions First', 30 November 2002, p. 7.

The disintegration of the Iraqi army in the face of United States military action also caused military-first strategists to reconsider the efficacy of North Korea's armed forces. The Iraqi army was formed from conscripts, not unlike the North Korean army which, although not formally conscripted, in practice, was full of unwilling young 'volunteers'. The defeat of the Iraqi army, following the disintegration of Iraqi armed forces in 1991, again called into question a deterrence policy based on large numbers of poorly equipped, ill-fed young people who, if war broke out, might not be ideologically motivated to defend the regime. It also made the option of military deterrence via the development of a viable nuclear capacity more attractive.

The lesson that North Korea drew was that nuclear armed states were never attacked by foreign invaders. Nuclear deterrence is not a very sophisticated military policy but it is widely understood within Western political theory and military practice, most noticeably by Thomas Schelling, as providing effective defence. At its core, deterrence theory argues that nuclear weaponry has only ever been used in war once, when the United States dropped atom bombs on Hiroshima and Nagasaki in Japan in 1945, and that nuclear weapons work mainly to intimidate or deter adversaries from military attack.

In the early to mid-2000s, military-first policy ambivalence in respect to the open pursuit of nuclear deterrence remained as the government continued to deny an intention to develop nuclear weapons. Announcements that the country was building its own 'deterrent' capacity were combined with other statements to the effect that North Korea did not intend to develop nuclear weapons. North Korea announced withdrawal from the Nuclear Non-Proliferation Treaty (NPT) in 2003 even as it continued to participate in multilateral diplomatic negotiations along with the United States, Russia, Japan, China and South Korea. These six-party talks did not defuse the conflict and often merely provided a vehicle for the DPRK and the United States to expose to the world how far apart they were from each other. In 2006 North Korea divested itself of all nuclear ambiguity: it staged a test of a nuclear weapon.[14]

The nuclear test precipitated sustained North Korean re-engagement with the United States but talks ended acrimoniously in 2007 as North Korea refused to entertain the tough verification measures demanded by the United States. North Korea's view was that it showed good faith by handing over 18,000 pages of information relating to its nuclear programme. It also argued that the United States insisted on such a

[14] Gary Samore and Adam Ward, 'Living with Ambiguity: North Korea's Strategic Weapons Programmes', in Hazel Smith (ed.), *Reconstituting Korean Security: A Policy Primer* (Tokyo: United Nations Press, 2007), pp. 43–64; Cha, *The Impossible State*.

broad brush interpretation of the notion of verification that, effectively, the United States would only be satisfied if United States officials physically took over North Korean ministries and military establishments. For North Korea this was regime change through the back door.

The multilateral six-party talks were suspended in 2007. North Korea did not respond in a conciliatory manner to President Obama's policy of 'strategic patience' that entailed a suspension of initiatives towards North Korea. Military-first governments continued to interpret United States political and military activism abroad as intent to invade the DPRK. Western support for transitions to democracy in Georgia and the Balkans, involvement in Afghanistan and Iraq, support for the Arab Spring in 2010 and 2011 and Western intervention in Libya, consolidated a siege mentality in Pyongyang.[15] The consensus in Pyongyang was that if Muammar Quaddafi had not given up Libya's nuclear weapons, the Libyan regime would not have fallen.[16] Military-first governments hardened their view that the regime would only be secure from invasion if North Korea possessed a credible nuclear deterrence capacity. The DPRK tested nuclear weapons in 2009 and again in 2013.[17]

North Korea accompanied its nuclear programme with ballistic missile development.[18] North Korea had a known short-range missile capacity of up to a 500 kilometre range, although not all analysts were convinced that even these successful short-range missile tests meant that North Korea had much of an indigenous missile production capacity. One suggestion was that North Korea's short-range missiles were slightly altered scuds purchased from the former communist bloc decades previously.[19] North

[15] Andrei Lankov, 'North Korea: The Logic of Survival', in Christoph Bluth and Hazel Smith (eds.), 'North Korea at the Crossroad', *Journal of International and Strategic Studies*, No. 5, 2012, p. 11 available at http://ceris.be/fileadmin/library/Publications/Journal-NS-E.pdf, accessed 2 November 2014.

[16] Ibid.

[17] Emma Chanlett-Avery and Ian E. Rinehart, *North Korea: US Relations, Nuclear Diplomacy, and Internal Situation* (Washington, DC: Congressional Research Service, January 2014), available at www.fas.org/sgp/crs/nuke/R41259.pdf, accessed 27 April 2014.

[18] David C. Wright and Timur Kadyshev, 'An Analayis of the North Korean Nodong Missile', *Science and Global Security*, Vol. 4, No. 2, 1994, pp. 129–60.

[19] Christoph Bluth, 'The North Korean Missile Program: Origins, Capabilities and Future Trajectories', mimeo (Leeds University, 2011); Sang-Hun Choe, 'New North Korean Missile is Called into Question', *New York Times*, 27 April 2012, available at www.nytimes.com/2012/04/27/world/asia/new-north-korean-missile-is-called-into-question.html?_r=1&ref=northkorea, accessed 30 October 2012; Markus Schiller and Robert H. Schmucker, 'A Dog and Pony Show: North Korea's New ICBM', 18 April 2012, available at http://lewis.armscontrolwonk.com/files/2012/04/KN-08_Analysis_Schiller_Schmucker.pdf, accessed 30 October 2012.

Korea had only limited success with testing medium-range missiles that had a range of up to 1,600 kilometres.[20] The 1998, 2006, 2009 and April 2012 satellite launches, which relied on the same technology that could fire a long-range missile, were not successful in demonstrating a fully fledged long-range missile capacity.[21]

North Korea was not prepared to abandon what it considered its sovereign right to develop satellite technology for peaceful purposes, especially as its neighbours, including South Korea and Japan, regularly launched such satellites. The United States understood such actions as provocative and dangerous as the exact same technology used to launch satellites into space could be used to launch nuclear missiles.

North Korea's successful satellite launch of December 2012 was an engineering breakthrough for North Korea, but also a confirmation that it was prepared to act outside United Nations strictures in its pursuit of regime security.[22] North Korea's missile, satellite and nuclear programmes were unambiguously illegal under international law since the 2009 United Nations Security Council resolution subsequent to North Korea's second nuclear test prohibited North Korea from developing any form of ballistic technology.[23] If there had been any further ambiguity about North Korea's willingness to challenge the international body this was also dispelled in 2012 when the government declared that North Korea was a nuclear state.

In late 2011, after the death of Kim Jong Il, North Korea and the United States accelerated bilateral negotiations that had continued sporadically, often in off-the-record meetings, since the breakdown of six-party talks in 2007. In February 2012 North Korean negotiators agreed to suspend nuclear tests and missile launches and allow International Atomic Energy Agency officials back into the country in return for food aid.[24] On-off diplomacy was off again, however, after the April 2012 rocket launch, and did not resume in any significant manner. After North Korea's nuclear tests, which were condemned by the United Nations Security Council, the United States could argue that it had

---

[20] Chanlett-Avery and Rinehart, *North Korea*, p. 14.
[21] Ibid.   [22] Ibid., p. 8.
[23] Department of Public Information News and Media Division, *Resolution 1874 (2009) Strengthens Arms Embargo, Calls for Inspection of Cargo, Vessels if States have 'Reasonable Grounds' to Believe Contain Prohibited Items* (New York: United Nations Security Council SC/9679, 2009), available at www.un.org/News/Press/docs/2009/sc9679.doc.htm, accessed 3 January 2013.
[24] Chris McGreal and Tania Branigan, 'North Korea Pledges to Halt Nuclear Programme in Exchange for US Aid', *The Guardian*, 29 February 2012, available at www.guardian.co.uk/world/2012/feb/29/north-korea-moratorium-nuclear-programme, accessed 7 June 2012.

international law on its side. The terms of United Nations resolutions prohibited the use of ballistic technology by North Korea, even for peaceful purposes.

The new diplomacy

Military-first era pursuit of diplomacy with the United States was mirrored by efforts to achieve 'normalisation' of diplomatic relations with the rest of the world. The 'first nuclear crisis' of 1993–4 had provided North Korea with confidence in its abilities to engage in successful diplomacy and for about a decade, from the mid-1990s to the mid-2000s, the DPRK government initiated imaginative and nuanced diplomatic activity – opening up diplomatic relations with ideologically diverse states, working with international organisations and, in an unprecedented development, beginning a process of substantive economic and political engagement with South Korea, its erstwhile nemesis and alter ego. North Korea's diplomatic forays were not always successful, however, and its ineptitude and refusal to compromise alienated adversaries and allies.

North Korea established diplomatic relations with a broad range of new partners including with United States' allies in East Asia and in Europe.[25] These efforts were unconstrained by ideology or historical antagonism; instead they were pragmatic and opportunistic and generated out of necessity. North Korea sought multiple and indirect routes to diplomatic normalisation with the United States via normalising relations with US allies, but also looked to obtain resources to help rebuild its devastated economy. From 1991 to 2001, the DPRK established diplomatic relations with forty-two states.[26] These included thirteen of the European Union states, new states created from the former Soviet Union, and oil-rich Brunei, Qatar, Oman and Kuwait.[27] Most of the former communist states that had had large embassies in the DPRK during the Cold War, such as Poland and Bulgaria, did not entirely cut off old ties but instead drastically reduced the scale of their diplomatic representation in Pyongyang.

North Korea pro-actively sought to establish diplomatic relations with developed capitalist states. The North Korean government at first

---

[25] For a North Korean account of diplomatic forays towards western European states, see Jon, *A Duel of Reason*, pp. 236–8.
[26] Hazel Smith, *Hungry for Peace*, p. 181.
[27] Ibid.

designed an Asia First policy, hoping to persuade the richer Asian countries, such as Singapore, India and Thailand, to invest in North Korea in
lieu of the loss of former trading partners.[28] Asia provided a natural start to
North Korean diplomacy with the capitalist world as the DPRK had a
good deal of experience with working with some of the larger capitalist
states, like Indonesia and India, because of its activism in the non-aligned
movement.

Asia and the Middle East also provided the focus for alleged arms
trading with Pakistan, Iran and Syria. The details, however, always
remained murky as speculation in the public arena was entirely sourced
to claims from unnamed 'intelligence' officials, either from the United
States or South Korea, and which were by their nature difficult to
substantiate.[29] Uncertainty regarding volume of trade in respect of arms
trading is not unique to North Korea: earnings from any arms trade,
however, were manifestly insufficient to generate economic redevelopment. Economic outreach continued towards a very diverse range of
capitalist states; the most startlingly unconventional, perhaps, being the
sustained and serious talks with Israel and Taiwan, both of which were
motivated, from the DPRK perspective, by the possibility of gaining
economic benefits.[30]

North Korea's most visible new diplomacy was with western European
states. These outreach efforts were facilitated by the indirect contacts that
North Korea developed with major western European states that had
funded large-scale humanitarian activity in North Korea worth several
million dollars over the period 1995 to 2005. Western European states
were encouraged to establish diplomatic relations with North Korea by
South Korean president Kim Dae-Jung in the late 1990s and early 2000s,
in order to give diplomatic support to the engagement or 'sunshine'

[28] Smith, 'North Korean Foreign Policy', pp. 98–9.
[29] One account states that North Korean arms sales exceeded $500 million a year in the
1980s. See Marcus Noland, 'Prospects for the North Korean "Economy"', in Dae-Sook
Suh and Chae-Jin Lee (eds.), North Korea after Kim Il Sung (Boulder, CO: Lynne
Rienner, 1998), pp. 34–45.
[30] On Israel, see Yossi Melman, 'How the Mossad Killed a Deal with Kim Il-sung', Haaretz,
27 June 2006, available at www.haaretz.com/print-edition/features/how-the-mossad-killed-
a-deal-with-kim-il-sung-1.191489, accessed 8 November 2014; 'Oded Granot,
'Background on North Korea-Iran Missile Deal', MA'ARIV, 14 April 1996, translated by
US FBIS from Hebrew and reproduced online at www.fas.org/news/israel/tac95037.htm,
accessed 8 November 2014. On Taiwan see Ilpyong J. Kim, 'China in North Korean
Foreign Policy', in Samuel S. Kim, North Korean Foreign Relations in the Post-Cold War
Era (Oxford University Press, 1998), p. 108; Jian Chen, 'Limits of the "Lips and Teeth"
Alliance: An Historical Review of Chinese–North Korean Relations', in Timothy
Hildebrandt (ed.), Uneasy Allies: Fifty Years of China–North Korea Relations (Washington,
DC: Woodrow Wilson Center Asia Program Special Report, September 2003), p. 9.

policy. The reciprocal opening of full embassies in London and Pyong-yang was one of the most visible manifestations of the DPRK govern-ment's willingness to engage in classical diplomatic practice, based on international norms and rules.

Humanitarian diplomacy

Between 1995 and 2005, foreign aid was munificent at $1.7 billion, most of which was provided in the form of food aid.[31] The World Food Programme (WFP) contributed around $300 million of aid per year in the late 1990s, at a time when the DPRK's export earnings were hardly double that amount.[32] When relations with the United States deterior-ated in the 2000s, the government took the view that national security was jeopardised by allowing foreigners, even those employed by the humanitarian organisations, to travel, observe and analyse North Korean society.[33] In 2004 the government announced that it no longer needed humanitarian assistance, arguing that harvests were improving and that instead it wished to attract development funding.[34] North Korea had hoped that South Korea, which did not require detailed reporting and monitoring, would continue to provide bilateral aid, but the South Korean government changed policy towards the DPRK in 2008 after the election of President Lee Myun-bak. President Lee was much less inclined to give the DPRK free food or fertiliser than had the two previous South Korean administrations, and bilateral aid was much reduced.

The government used the international organisations to provide training placements for foreign ministry cadres who worked as interpret-ers, administrators and humanitarian programme officers. Many of these 'trainees' went on to use the skills developed in these organisations as Embassy officials in subsequent years, for example in Hong Kong and the United Kingdom.[35] Nevertheless, the government did not handle relationships with the humanitarian agencies well. Central government

[31] Moon-Young Huh (ed.), *Basic Reading on Korean Unification* (Seoul: Korea Institute for National Unification, 2012), p. 226.
[32] Smith, *Hungry for Peace*.
[33] For detailed discussion on the changing nature of DPRK interaction with humanitarian organisations, see ibid.
[34] Mark E. Manyin, *Foreign Assistance to North Korea* (Washington, DC: Congressional Research Service, 26 May 2005), pp. 24–8, available at www.an.af.mil/an/awc/awcgate/crs/r131785.pdf, accessed 5 November 2012.
[35] I have since come across North Korean officials, with whom I originally worked at the WFP in the DPRK on a day-to-day basis during 1998–2000, in the Hong Kong consulate and in the UK embassy. North Korean training of its officials in

often considered that requests for information and the expectations of compromise and equal partnership by international officials were threatening, intrusive and offensive.[36] At the local and working level, however, North Korean officials were sometimes more receptive to international organisation requirements. Some officials also used informal opportunities provided through international negotiations to press interlocutors to provide more food assistance.[37]

North Korean officials were ambivalent about international organisations. There was a general reluctance at every level of officialdom to expose the country's weaknesses, even though the agencies were being called upon to help deal with those weaknesses. Military-first logic interpreted the transparency that underpinned the work of these organisations as facilitating risky exposure of the country's vulnerabilities. North Korean officials also did not want to admit to being dependent on other countries and were ashamed to be aid recipients. North Koreans understood their country as having made rapid economic development since the devastation of the Korean War, were proud of the achievements they had made in education and health and were often offended at being placed in the same bracket as the countries to which they had themselves donated technical assistance in the 1970s and 1980s.

Diplomatic outreach towards Japan

In the 1990s the government developed significant backtrack diplomatic channels to Japan.[38] These two nations had not been as isolated from each other as had the United States and North Korea. For a start, the presence of around two-thirds of a million 'pro-North Korean' second-, third- and fourth-generation Koreans in Japan meant that a steady flow of commerce, investment and family visits from Japan to North Korea

international organisations is a much discussed phenomenon within those organisations although I know of no scholarly work on this issue.

[36] Smith, *Overcoming Humanitarian Dilemmas*; Smith, *Hungry for Peace.*

[37] I worked with North Korean officials between 1998 and 2001 in the DPRK for WFP and UNICEF as these organisations were largely (as in all countries where international organisations work) staffed by local officials. Officials would never of course refuse to carry out direct orders but would often show a large degree of flexibility in 'getting round' standard security procedures to get things done. I was also informed by South Korean NGO officials that North Korean negotiating partners would issue the Party line in meetings but would engineer opportunities to be alone with them to plead for the NGOs to find ways of sending food to North Korea.

[38] Gavan McCormack, 'Japan and North Korea – The Quest for Normalcy', in Hazel Smith (ed.), *Reconstituting Korean Security: A Policy Primer* (Tokyo: United Nations Press, 2007), pp. 162–81.

had taken place from the 1950s onwards.[39] Leftist political parties in Japan also had political contacts with the North Korean government, and government to government relations intermittently thawed, including in the early 1990s when substantial normalisation talks between the DPRK and Japan took place at senior levels.[40]

In 1995, the Japanese government donated one million tonnes of rice to North Korea. This was an enormous amount, enough to feed 20 per cent of the 23 million population of North Korea for one year. As part of the standard operating procedures for oversight of humanitarian assistance donations, the Japanese sent parliamentary monitoring delegations to North Korea. For any other country such visits would have few if any political implications but for North Korea, which was extremely antagonistic to Japan, such exchanges represented meaningful although small steps on the road to diplomatic normalisation with the rest of the world. Military-first governments did not demonstrate, however, a fundamental shift in attitude to Japan as they maintained a securitised view of the world that saw all Japanese officials as little more than enemy agents – even when the results of such an attitude were counter-productive. In 2000, for example, the United Nations World Food Programme persuaded the Japanese government to make another large rice donation to North Korea. The Japanese government cancelled the food donation after the North Korean government peremptorily refused visas for an official Japanese delegation to make one short visit to Pyongyang to discuss the food donation.[41]

North Korea's ineptitude on the diplomacy of food aid did not prevent it from pursuing the strategic goal of diplomatic normalisation with Tokyo.[42] North Korean officials initiated talks that resulted in September 2002 with the Japanese Prime Minister, conservative-leaning Junichiro Koizumi, travelling to Pyongyang to meet with Kim Jong Il, astounding the international media and causing raised diplomatic eyebrows in the United States.[43] The North Korean government hoped for a break-through that would allow it to receive cash as reparations for the Japanese colonial occupation, as South Korea had already received in 1965. Prime Minister Koizumi hoped to bring back Japanese citizens that had been abducted by the North Korean security services in the 1970s.

[39] Sonia Ryang, *North Koreans in Japan: Language, Ideology and Identity* (Boulder, CO: Westview Press, 1997); Tessa Morris-Suzuki, *Exodus to North Korea: Shadows from Japan's Cold War* (Lanham: Rowman and Littlefield Publishers, 2007).
[40] Smith, *Hungry for Peace*, p. 206.
[41] Author's interviews, WFP officials, Pyongyang, 2001.
[42] Smith, *Hungry for Peace*, pp. 205–11.
[43] Funabashi, *The Peninsula Question*, p. 8.

Kim Jong Il admitted DPRK responsibility but stated that the abductions had been undertaken by rogue officials. His response did not convincingly resolve outstanding concerns about possible additional abducted civilians or provide credible information in response to the questions that distraught relatives had about their missing loved ones.[44] A sceptical Japanese public refused to believe that the North Korean government was not continuing to hide further misdoings. Koizumi's two visits, which initially seemed a diplomatic triumph for the DPRK government, ended with acrimony that soured future attempts to normalise relations with Japan. The DPRK had succeeded in securing a visit from the powerful and popular Prime Minister Koizumi to Pyongyang and a public apology for colonial wrongs, but proved unable to convince a sceptical Japanese public that it regretted the abduction of Japanese civilians.[45]

Engagement with South Korea

The North Korean government entered into secret diplomatic exchanges with the South Koreans in 1999, following which in June 2000, Kim Jong Il met with South Korean President Kim Dae-Jung in Pyongyang.[46] North's Korea's domestic media widely reported the meeting of the two leaders; photos and writing about this historic exchange were posted in government offices and public places.[47] North Korea's positive response to Kim Dae Jung's unprecedented but carefully calibrated rapprochement effort was driven by economic imperatives. Diplomatic isolation, one product of the highly antagonistic DPRK relationship with the George Bush administration, provided the impetus to northern engagement with the South. A 2000 Pyongyang publication noted that, 'As is expected, this radical development of north–south contacts and dialogue is substantially melting the frozen wall between the two sides.

---

[44] A well-informed Japanese observer writes that North Korean officials anticipated the domestic backlash in Japan but that Japanese officials underestimated the possibilities. This does not belie the act that North Korean officials had no idea how to manage the issue, either in Pyongyang or after the meetings with Koizumi. See Funabashi, *The Peninsula Question*, pp. 63–8.

[45] Ibid., pp. 1–92; McCormack, 'Japan and North Korea'.

[46] Dong-won Lim, *Peacemaker: Twenty Years of Inter-Korean Relations and the North Korean Nuclear Issue* (Stanford, CA: Walter H. Shorenstein Asia-Pacific Research Center, 2012), p. 65.

[47] I worked in every province in the DPRK apart from Chagang between 2000 and 2001 for the WFP (at the time eleven out of twelve provinces), and pictures of Kim Jong Il meeting with Kim Dae Jung were on permanent public display in the lobbies of public buildings wherever I went. See also *Pictorial Korea*, 'Historical Pyongyang Meeting and Inter-Korean Summit Talks', *Democratic People's Republic of Korea No. 8*, August 2000.

However, [engagement]... is not believed to proceed smoothly. The mutual distrust rooted in the confrontation and hatred that has lasted for over half a century would not be removed overnight. This is because the basic attitudes of the two sides towards dialogue and reunification are different from each other to a considerable extent'.[48]

North Korea pursued engagement with the South even as it adopted military-first national security-centred policies that shifted the country towards a more confrontational response to the broader international community. Part of this was tactical. North Korea's channels of communication with the South enabled the North to avoid international isolation, even as the Bush administration sought to encourage its allies to close ranks against North Korea. Nevertheless, North Korea's adoption of engagement opened up channels in which conflict could be mediated and, sometimes, resolved. The dispute over the maritime border between the two countries – which erupted into a shooting match in the summer of 2002 that resulted in loss of life of North and South Koreans – did not, for example, escalate such as to stop the momentum of engagement between the two Koreas.[49] Both sides accused the other of incursion into the other's sovereign territory, but both sides also sought to keep the political engagement process on track.

A chasm to bridge

It is sometimes difficult for non-Koreans to understand the depth and breadth of estrangement of the two Koreas prior to President Kim Dae-Jung's paradigm changing visit to the North in summer 2000. Although only separated as states in 1948, Koreans in both North and South grew up relying only on government propaganda to inform them about their compatriots as it was practically impossible for northerners and southerners to meet or communicate with each other. Successive generations of Koreans in the South were taught that northerners were somehow less than human, and northerners were taught that South Koreans were miserable, oppressed and the South Korean government capable of the worst types of atrocities against its own population as well as North Koreans. These stereotypes were so extreme that when North Koreans were dying from malnutrition-related

---

[48] Jon, *A Duel of Reason*, p. 213.
[49] Jon Van Dyke, 'The Maritime Boundary between North and South Korea in the Yellow (West) Sea', *38 North* (US–Korea Institute, Johns Hopkins University School of Advanced International Studies, 29 July 2010), available at www.38north.org/?p=1232, accessed 8 November 2014.

illnesses in the mid-1990s they refused to accept medicines marked as from South Korea, as they were frightened that the South Korean government was trying to poison them.[50]

Koreans could not contact relatives from whom they had become separated after the demilitarised zone was established in 1953; telephones and postal services did not connect the two countries. North Korean officials sometimes came into contact with South Koreans abroad in diplomatic arenas, although both governments discouraged informal mixing. A handful of South Korean activists visited the North but these visits were ritualised by the northern government to maximise political messages of northern superiority at home and, where possible, to try to disseminate the same message in the South. The North Korean government persistently portrayed southern governments as mere puppets of the United States.

In comparison with the almost non-existent contact between the two states and societies since the Korean War ended in 1953, important advances and improvements in the North–South relationship occurred after the 2000 North–South summit. Some separated families met for the first time since the war, albeit under restricted circumstances. Northern governments permitted thousands of southerners to visit the North for business, culture, sport or humanitarian reasons. A North–South road and rail link was opened that crossed the previously impermeable demilitarised zone (DMZ) and the North encouraged Hyundai, the southern conglomerate, to organise visits by South Korean tourists from the South to the famous Kumgang (Diamond) Mountains in the south-east of the DPRK.

Northern engagement with the South spluttered to a virtual halt, however, in 2007 with the election of the new South Korean President Lee Myung-bak. Lee was sceptical of engagement policy and did not trust the North Korean government. The North accused President Lee of sabotage, betrayal and selling out to the United States, but North Korean governments had provided ample grounds for South Korean distrust. Military-first governments accepted South Korean investment in economic cooperation zones, but these were physically separated from the rest of the country to limit interaction of South Koreans with North Koreans. North Korean policy-makers continued to view all South Korean officials through a militarised perspective, as agents of an enemy power.

[50] Author's observations and interviews with UNICEF officials, Pyongyang, April 1998.

North Korea made no significant diplomatic advances to South Korea during the remaining period of the Lee administration, nor during the early years of the successor administration of President Park Geun-hye.

Realignment of old alliances

In the military-first era, North Korea improved relationships with Russia and benefited from low-key but strategic support from Russia in international fora. North Korea received economic assistance from both Russia and China although it was China that assumed the position of major economic provider and key international interlocutor for North Korea. North Korea renewed military pacts with China and Russia but these military accords no longer gave more or less automatic guarantees in case of war. For military-first governments this was yet another reason to go for what they conceived of as an 'independent nuclear deterrent'.

The former Soviet Union had been the key economic partner for North Korea during the Cold War as a provider of cheap oil, technology and concessional loans to the extent that by 2005, North Korea owed some $8 billion in debt to the Soviet Union, which was subsequently due to the post-Soviet Russian state.[51] Military-first governments negotiated a write-off of some $10 billion of the accrued debt of $11 billion in 2012, in a deal confirmed by the Russian Duma in 2014.[52] The Russians hoped that, in return, North Korea would support an oil and gas pipeline from Russia, through the DPRK, into South Korea. Military-first governments demonstrated therefore an ability to negotiate with a capitalist Russia with which they no longer shared a similar ideological outlook.

In the military-first era, North Korea became dependent on China economically.[53] North Koreans imported Chinese oil and goods and relied on Chinese investment and trade; by 2007 over two-thirds of North Korean trade was with China.[54] The DPRK did not receive preferential economic treatment from China as Chinese business

---

[51] Georgy Bulychev, 'Korean Security Dilemmas: A Russian Perspective', in Hazel Smith (ed.), *Reconstituting Korean Security: A Policy Primer* (Tokyo: United Nations Press, 2007), p. 186.

[52] Zachary Keck, 'Eyeing Pipeline, Russia Forgives North Korean Debt', *The Diplomat*, 22 April 2014, available at http://thediplomat.com/2014/04/eyeing-pipeline-russia-forgives-north-korean-debt, accessed 27 April 2014.

[53] Byung-Kwang Park, 'China–North Korea Economic Relations during the Hu Jintao Era', *International Journal of Korean Unification Studies*, Vol. 19, No. 2, 2010, pp. 125–50.

[54] Ibid., p. 138.

demanded market prices for trade goods.[55] Indeed, for many essential imports, including coal and oil products, the DPRK paid well over international market prices to Chinese exporters.[56] Chinese oil exports to the DPRK were fixed from 1995 to 1998 but at $126.70 per tonne they were similar to global market prices.[57]

North Korea's economic dependence on China did not translate into political dependence. Military-first governments did not consult China prior to the 2006, 2009 and 2013 nuclear weapons tests, and China did not support North Korea's nuclear activities, which Chinese officials saw as irresponsible and destabilising.[58]

Going nuclear

The overriding goal of foreign policy for military-first era governments was to assure regime survival through staving off foreign intervention. Governments sought to diversify foreign relations to obtain economic assistance but economic policy was always subordinated to national security imperatives. Military-first logic decided that a reliance on conventional military forces and diplomatic ingenuity was not enough to guarantee regime survival. The response was to 'go nuclear'. To the extent that military-first governments may have staved off military intervention – and the United States consistently denied it ever had any intentions of invading North Korea – they did so at a cost.[59] North Korea's attempts to join the nuclear club irritated allies, threatened adversaries and scared off potential foreign investors. Occasional tactical agility could not and did not compensate for strategic failure.

---

[55] Xiao Ren, 'Korean Security Dilemmas: Chinese Policies', in Hazel Smith (ed.), *Reconstituting Korean Security: A Policy Primer* (Tokyo: United Nations Press, 2007), p. 146.

[56] Nathaniel Aden, 'North Korean Trade with China as Reported in Chinese Customs Statistics: Energy Trends and Implications', *The Korean Journal of Defense Analysis*, Vol. 23, No. 2, June 2011, pp. 231–55.

[57] Ibid., p. 243.

[58] Cha, *The Impossible State*, pp. 329–32.

[59] This United States position is stated explicitly by Victor Cha, former National Security Council official, in ibid., p. 11.

14   Strategic paralysis

The United States, Japan, much of the rest of the world and a significant part of the population of South Korea viewed North Korea as constituting a threat to international security because of its very nature as an aggressor state, variously termed 'rogue', 'outlier' or just plain 'mad'.[1] From this perspective, the threat was magnified exponentially by North Korea's possession of weapons of mass destruction, including nuclear armaments. China and Russia did not share the rogue state perspective on North Korea, but they did not support North Korea's nuclear weapons programme.[2]

The United States government was understood by allies and adversaries as the necessary leader of global negotiations with North Korea given the historic, unresolved conflict between the two states and the dominant position of the United States in East Asia.[3] East Asia was important for United States governments but after 9/11 and the ensuing 'war against terror' security priorities initially shifted to the Middle East and United States policy concentrated its efforts on securing alliance structures, most notably with Japan, and focused on managing complicated relations with China, its economic partner and erstwhile political adversary.[4]

---

[1] Robert S. Litwak, *Rogue States and US Foreign Policy: Containment after the Cold War* (Washington, DC: Woodrow Wilson Center Press, 2000); Robert Litwak, *Outlier States: American Strategies to Change, Contain, or Engage Regimes* (Washington, DC: Woodrow Wilson Center Press/Johns Hopkins University Press, 2012).

[2] Georgy Bulychev, 'Korean Security Dilemmas: A Russian Perspective', in Hazel Smith (ed.), *Reconstituting Korean Security: A Policy Primer* (Tokyo: United Nations Press, 2007); Xiao Ren, 'Korean Security Dilemmas: Chinese Policies', in ibid.

[3] Hazel Smith (ed.), *Reconstituting Korean Security: A Policy Primer* (Tokyo: United Nations Press, 2007). A useful overview of US policy and practice towards North Korea is in Chae-Jin Lee, *A Troubled Peace: US Policy and the Two Koreas* (Baltimore, MD: The Johns Hopkins University Press, 2006).

[4] There is a big literature on United States, South Korean and other state relationships with the DPRK. Much of this is heavily descriptive and a good deal of it written by former diplomats and journalists and it varies in quality. Most useful is Yoichi Funabashi, *The Peninsula Question: A Chronicle of the Second Korean Nuclear Crisis* (Washington, DC: Brookings Institution Press, 2007). Important accounts of United States policy include

United States policy became one of containment as, other international priorities, combined with domestic political opposition to offering North Korea inducements, precluded radical initiatives to resolve the Korean conflict. After the United States and the DPRK came close to war in June 1994, military force was never again considered a viable policy instrument because of the fear of damaging retaliation against Seoul. United States administrations were left with few negotiating instruments other than economic sanctions and the strategic calibration of humanitarian assistance programmes to support diplomacy.

The two-term administration of President Obama developed a policy of 'strategic patience' and called for China to do more to encourage the DPRK to denuclearise. International organisations, states and campaigning non-governmental organisations (NGOs) supported the call for North Korea's denuclearisation and campaigned for human rights reform in North Korea. United States administrations delinked human rights concerns from nuclear negotiations, despite the periodic demands from sections of United States opinion that linkage should take place.[5]

The narrowing of the security agenda

United States security planners periodically discussed whether to seek a comprehensive security deal with North Korea that might take the form of a peace treaty to replace the Armistice that had ended the Korean War in 1953, but these ideas for a global settlement of outstanding disputes were never systematically pursued.[6] United States security goals focused on the discrete goal of preventing North Korea from acquiring nuclear weapons and, when that policy manifestly failed, the policy goal became to roll back nuclear weapons development. The focus on the nuclear progamme included ballistic missile technology development that, if

---

Leon D. Sigal, *Disarming Strangers: Nuclear Diplomacy with North Korea* (Princeton University Press, 1998); Joel S. Wit, Daniel B. Poneman and Robert L. Gallucci, *Going Critical: The First North Korean Nuclear Crisis* (Washington, DC: The Brookings Institution, 2005); Charles L. Pritchard, *Failed Diplomacy: The Tragic Story of How North Korea Got the Bomb* (Washington, DC: Brookings Institution Press, 2007). An analysis of the interests of regional and global powers is in Smith (ed.), *Reconstituting Korean Security.*

[5] John Kerry pointed out that Secretary Condoleezza Rice had forbidden the President's Special Envoy on Human Rights from participation in nuclear proliferation talks. See John Kerry, *Executive session, Nomination of Christopher R. Hill to be Ambassador to Iraq, Congressional Record – Senate Vol. 155 Pt. 8* (Washington, DC: Congressional Record, Proceedings and Debates of the 111th Congress, First Session, 2012), p. 10100.

[6] William Drennan, *A Comprehensive Resolution of the Korean War, Special Report* (Washington, DC: United States Institute of Peace, 2003), available at www.usip.org/publications/comprehensive-resolution-korean-war, accessed 18 April 2013.

successful, would give the DPRK the capacity to deliver nuclear weapons.[7] United States security policy also focused on proliferation, given the possibility that North Korea could act as a supplier of nuclear technology to other non-status quo states like Iran and Syria.[8] Other security concerns such as the potential capacity of North Korea to produce chemical and biological weapons were less prominent in the military-first era as the decimation of North Korea's heavy industry in the economic crisis of the 1990s made production less feasible.[9]

The Clinton, George W. Bush and Obama administrations shared the same objectives in negotiations with North Korea and had a good deal in common with regard to their negotiating patterns. Each administration began with non-action, non-contact and denunciation of the North Korean leadership. Non-engagement was followed by a period of activist diplomatic engagement, which was then derailed by a combination of North Korean intransigence and ineptitude and domestic opposition to any settlement with the DPRK in the United States. The reasons for diplomatic engagement and subsequent failure to achieve durable solutions were different, but the overall patterns of engagement meant that successive administrations had to recoup ground gained by their predecessors before they could deal with the crisis of the day.

Despite domestic controversy in the US, the 1994 Geneva Agreement achieved a number of United States goals, including a freeze on North Korea's nuclear activities. The United States reduced long-standing economic sanctions on North Korea but it did not dismantle all constraints on trade and economic relations with the DPRK. The easing of sanctions was not meant to give much away but to indicate the possibility of future rewards for North Korean cooperation.

Several rounds of negotiations produced a moratorium on missile testing in 1999 and bilateral relations warmed to the extent that Wendy Sherman, a senior United States diplomat and negotiator for the United States, reported that an agreement with the DPRK

---

[7] Emma Chanlett-Avery and Ian E. Rinehart, *North Korea: US Relations, Nuclear Diplomacy, and Internal Situation* (Washington, DC: Congressional Research Service, January 2014), available at www.fas.org/sgp/crs/nuke/R41259.pdf, accessed 27 April 2014.

[8] Jim Walsh, 'Three States, Three Stories: Comparing Iran, Syria and North Korea's Nuclear Programs', in Jung-Ho Bae and Jae H. Ku (eds.), *Nuclear Security 2012: Challenges of Proliferation and Implication* [sic] *for the Korean Peninsula* (Seoul: Korea Institute for National Unification, 2012), pp. 123–49.

[9] Most of these claims had been speculative; based on the potential of fertiliser and agricultural chemical production for dual use production of explosives and weapons. See Gary Samore, *North Korea's Weapons Programmes: A Net Assessment* (London: Macmillan Palgrave, 2004).

came tantalizingly close for President Bill Clinton in his final days in office. That agreement, when completed, would both halt North Korea's exports of missiles and related technology and stop further production, deployment and testing of long-range missiles.

The clock ran out on the Clinton administration before it could nail down the final details. For two years, the administration had pursued a practical, step-by-step policy that achieved a moratorium on missile testing by Pyongyang, gained access to an underground area suspected of being a nuclear reactor site and saw the first visit of a high-ranking North Korean military official, Vice Marshal Cho Myong Rok, to the United States.[10]

The George W. Bush administration, which succeeded the Clinton administration in 2001, distrusted the North Koreans and any agreements that had come about as the product of the previous administration. In Washington DC the term attributed to early Bush administration policy, by all sides of the political divide, was 'ABC' or 'anything but Clinton'. North Korea policy was no exception. Congressional sceptics, who considered that even talking to North Korea was to take an unprincipled position and constituted 'appeasement', received powerful backing from Vice-President Dick Cheney and the US Ambassador to the United Nations, John Bolton. These influential Bush administration officials became convinced from very early on that North Korea was 'cheating' on its obligations under the Geneva Agreement and argued that North Korea was developing a secret alternative nuclear programme, through the so-called 'highly enriched uranium' (HEU) route, which, they argued, was contrary to the letter and spirit of the 1994 agreement.

The harsh rhetoric from within the United States was accompanied by aggressive activity to isolate and pressurise the DPRK internationally. In 2002, the Spanish navy seized fifteen North Korean scud missiles at sea en route to Yemen. Spain was forced to return the missiles after the Yemeni government forcefully defended the legality of these arms transactions. The United States responded with the acceleration of the Proliferation Security Initiative (PSI) – developed outside existing multilateral institutions including the United Nations – and designed to carry out interdictions at sea of North Korea ships carrying weapons of mass destruction. The legality of interdicting ships in international waters remained unclear and China, North Korea's important ally and neighbour, refused to sign up, weakening the PSI's effectiveness in targeting North Korean shipping.[11]

---

[10] Wendy R. Sherman, 'Talking to the North Koreans', *New York Times*, 7 March 2001, available at www.nytimes.com/2001/03/07/opinion/07SHER.html, accessed 19 April 2013.

[11] Mark J. Valencia, 'The Proliferation Security Initiative: A Glass Half-Full', *Arms Control Today*, June 2007, available at www.armscontrol.org/act/2007_06/Valencia, accessed 8

Regional powers were fearful that the war of words on both sides might escalate into military conflict. The Bush administration had a reasonably good working relationship with China, especially after President Jiang Zemin offered unconditional support to the United States after 9/11, and China used its intermediary status to try to bring the United States and the DPRK back to the negotiating table.[12] In 2002, President Bush met the Chinese president at his home in Crawford, Texas, where the two discussed the denuclearisation of North Korea.[13] The product of Chinese diplomacy was the instigation of the six-party multilateral talks in Beijing in 2003, which brought the United States, the DPRK, China, South Korea, Russia and Japan into dialogue with each other.[14]

The goal of the Bush administration was the 'complete, irreversible and verifiable disarmament' of North Korea's nuclear programmes, sometimes known by the acronym of CIVD. From 2003 through 2006, United States officials could attend meetings in which North Korean officials were present, including the six-party talks, but they were instructed not to engage in even the most innocuous discussion with North Korean officials unless they agreed to denuclearise unconditionally, prior to negotiations. The policy divided United States policymakers between those who saw a deal with the Koreans as possible and necessary and those who did not. Charles Pritchard, former United States negotiator with the DPRK for the Bush administration, argued that by 2006, 'North Korea policy ... [was] fully captured by those in the administration who seek regime change'.[15] United States allies, Japan and South Korea, as well as China and Russia, were somewhat bemused as to how a negotiated solution could be found without negotiations and, perhaps not surprisingly, the DPRK did not accede to the demand of unilateral disarmament.

In 2005, the balance of political forces changed inside the Bush administration so that those advocating diplomacy gained ground against the neo-conservative forces who had adamantly opposed negotiations. The administration nuanced its policy of refusing to engage in

---

November 2014. The US Government Accountability Office identified numerous shortcomings in the implementation of the PSI, including the absence of budgets, procedures or a written strategy. See Government Accountability Office, *Nonproliferation: US Agencies have Taken Some Steps, but More Effort is Needed to Strengthen and Expand the Proliferation Security Initiative, GAO-09-43* (Washington, DC: Government Accountability Office, November 2008).

[12] Funabashi, *The Peninsula Question*, pp. 266–8.

[13] Ibid.   [14] Ibid., pp. 275–8.

[15] Pritchard, *Failed Diplomacy*, p. 131.

direct talks with the DPRK prior to denuclearisation and this change of policy gained momentum after North Korea's first nuclear test in 2006. President Bush and Secretary of State Condoleezza Rice author- ised senior career State Department official, Ambassador Chris Hill, to pursue active engagement with North Korea.[16] Hill forged an agree- ment to allow State Department officials to work with North Korean officials in Pyongyang to secure and transmit thousands of pages of documentation on North Korea's nuclear programme back to the United States. In a visible show of compliance in 2008, North Korea blew up the cooling tower of its nuclear reactor in Yongbyon in front of a watching international audience.

Despite these auspicious signs and, in relative terms, substantive progress, negotiations broke down yet again as North Korea was again accused of 'cheating' on its commitments by Washington critics. Domestic critics in the United States argued that North Korea had not produced enough documentation about its nuclear facilities and demanded that extensive and comprehensive verification practices be put in place prior to further negotiations.[17] North Korea's view was that verification modalities should be negotiated as part of the process of denuclearisation and that to open up all its military establishments, research institutes, governmental offices and any other possible sites associated with a broad interpretation of verification, would be to surrender its sovereignty to the United States.

Some in Washington considered North Korea's arguments as provid- ing an excuse for non-cooperation. Persons of influence in the Bush administration, frequently, vocally and unequivocally re-asserted that the nuclear problem could not ever be negotiated away with the North Korean regime and could only be solved by the eradication of the regime in North Korea. From this perspective, the demise of the North Korean regime provided the only effective verification of a nuclear deal – pre- cisely what the North Koreans suspected was the underlying objective of United States policy.

Occasional bilateral meetings between United States and North Korean officials took place after 2008 but the six-party talks were not resumed as neither the United States nor North Korea considered that the other side was negotiating honestly or prepared to compromise sufficiently such as to achieve a deal. The administration of President

---

[16] Jonathan D. Pollack, *No Exit: North Korea, Nuclear Weapons and International Security* (Abingdon/London: Routledge/International Institute for Strategic Studies, 2011), pp. 151–3.
[17] Ibid., pp. 154–5.

Obama, which took office in 2009, cultivated a policy of 'strategic patience' that entailed waiting for North Korea to give up its nuclear weapons and missiles.[18] North Korea was not a priority for the Obama administration as it was preoccupied with the severe economic downturn at home and ending the Iraq War abroad.

Nevertheless the Obama administration renewed negotiations in 2011 in a diplomatic initiative that produced the 'Leap Year Agreement' of February 2012. Details were not made public but it was understood to involve the provision of large volumes of food aid to North Korea in exchange for an end to missile tests. In 2012 the North Korean government agreed to a visit to Pyongyang by Robert King, a United States envoy, whose explicit mission was to promote human rights in North Korea. In April 2012, however, the *status quo ante* was resumed, as North Korea launched what they called a satellite and what the United States characterised as a long-range missile test. The United States accused North Korea of abrogating the February agreement and diplomatic engagement between the two adversaries once again ground to a halt. For the Obama administration, North Korea remained a low priority behind Iran and Syria, Iraq, Afghanistan and Pakistan, and during the second Obama administration, no substantial progress took place in any area of conflict with the DPRK, including the nuclear issues.

United States policy shifted towards giving South Korea the lead on North Korean policy at the same time as South Korea changed its approach to the DPRK. During most of the 2000s, South Korea had implemented a strategy in which bilateral economic and diplomatic engagement was conceived as providing the foundation for an incremental process of confidence-building.[19] In turn these 'habits of cooperation' were designed to 'spill-over' into the harder areas of military and national security. President Lee Myun-bak, who took office in 2008, rejected the engagement policies of his two predecessors, Kim Dae-Jung and Roh Moo-Hyung, arguing that the engagement, or 'sunshine' policies, of the 2000s had not achieved positive outcomes for South Korea. The Lee government substantially scaled back economic and humanitarian support to the DPRK. Lee made clear that South Korea would be aligning Korea policy much more firmly with United States policy.

---

[18] Chanlett-Avery and Rinehart, *North Korea*.
[19] Chung-in Moon, *The Sunshine Policy: In Defense of Engagement as a Path to Peace in Korea* (Seoul: Yonsei University Press, 2012).

Lee called on the North Korean government to make firm commitments to de-nuclearisation before diplomatic, political and economic links would resume to any substantial level. South Korea demanded 'reciprocity' from North Korea before it would allow new negotiations but did not articulate a new strategy to achieve sustainable peace and long-term stability. Inter-Korean diplomacy was replaced by megaphone diplomacy on both sides. Suspension of multilateral diplomacy and freezing of North–South diplomatic relations was designed as a 'punishment' for the North Korean government's recalcitrance but it also closed off engagement channels and space for conflict resolution and permitted dangerous inflammation of every incident involving the two Koreas.[20] In 2010, when a South Korean corvette, the *Cheonan*, was sunk with heavy loss of life and with the blame pinned internationally on North Korea, diplomatic channels of communication were virtually non-existent and the conflict escalated dangerously.

Substantive talks between North Korea and South Korea did not take place during the Lee administration. In 2013 President Lee was succeeded by President Park Geun-hye, South Korea's first female president. President Park came to power with a declared policy of 'trustpolitik' to North Korea that encouraged the idea of reunification. Trustpolitik ran into difficulties, however, as the Park administration could not find a way to operationalise the policy.

With the United States and South Korea absenting themselves from North Korean security dynamics, and Japan unable to become involved because of its historic and contemporary estrangement, the political vacuum was filled by China. China's policy response was to encourage the DPRK into normalised economic and political relationships with the rest of the world so as to gradually integrate the DPRK and reduce

---

[20] Andrei Lankov, 'North Korea: The Logic of Survival', in Christoph Bluth and Hazel Smith (eds.), 'North Korea at the Crossroad', *Journal of International and Strategic Studies*, No. 5, 2012, p. 12. The South Korean government sponsored an international investigation of the *Cheonan* incident that concluded that North Korean forces were responsible. Not all were convinced with Russian analysts openly declaring their scepticism. See Tim Page, 'Russia's Northeast Asian Priorities: Where does North Korea fit in?', in Christoph Bluth and Hazel Smith (eds.), 'North Korea at the Crossroad', *Journal of International and Strategic Studies*, No. 5, 2012, p. 42. While international opinion was more supportive of the South Korean position, unequivocal conclusions blaming North Korea were not supported in the Presidential statement of the United Nations Security Council on the incident. For discussion see Kang Choi and Minsung Kim, 'An Assessment of the Security Environment and Challenges in the Post-Cheonan Era: A South Korean Perspective', *International Journal of Korean Unification Studies*, Vol. 19, No. 2, 2010, pp. 88–124. The point here, however, is that these incidents involved large-scale loss of life, yet there were virtually no diplomatic avenues left for conflict resolution.

the siege mentality of DPRK leaders. China repeatedly tried to bring the United States and North Korea back to the negotiating table but emphasised to the United States that only a diplomatic agreement that paid serious attention to the national security concerns of the DPRK would lead to long-term stability for the Korean peninsula. In line with its gradualist strategy of encouraging incremental progress, China maintained diplomatic, military and economic links with the new leadership of Kim Jong Un after the death of Kim Jong Il in December 2011.

The Obama administration, like its predecessor, had high expectation of China's role in Korea. The administration insisted that China and Russia join in punitive implementation of United Nations sanctions on North Korea but also relied on China to act as a conduit for global policy towards North Korea. At the same time, the United States reconfigured its defence and foreign policies in a 'pivot towards Asia' whose military aspects were understood by China as threatening to China's national interests.

Humanitarian assistance as an instrument of security policy

United States security planners calibrated the humanitarian assistance that North Koreans needed with the security imperatives of United States policy. The United States was not the only state to use food as a diplomatic instrument. During the 2000s South Korea conceived of the almost unconditional provision of food and fertilizer aid as part of a long-term strategy of opening towards North Korea.[21]

The 1994 Geneva Agreement had been hugely controversial within Washington as a sceptical and vocal Congress was not convinced that North Korea should be 'rewarded for bad behavior'. The Agreement did not have the status of a treaty and had not been ratified or endorsed by Congress, which had the power to block implementation. The United States was obligated under the terms of the Agreement to provide heavy fuel oil to the DPRK and Clinton officials tried to assure Congressional critics that the heavy fuel oil was 'aid' not economic assistance and was only to be used for heating and electricity generation; these purposes were made explicit and deliveries were closely monitored to ensure that the oil did indeed go for its intended purposes.[22] In the end the Clinton

---

[21] Moon, *The Sunshine Policy*.

[22] Gary L. Jones, *Nuclear Nonproliferation: Heavy Fuel Oil Delivered to North Korea under the Agreed Framework, GAO/T-RCED-00-20* (Washington, DC: General Accounting Office, 1999), available at http://gao.gov/assets/110/108176.pdf, accessed 24 September 2012.

administration supplied 200,000 metric tonnes of heavy fuel oil as aid to North Korea, but it was always delivered late and the administration had to set up a Special Fund authorised by the President because Clinton officials could not guarantee Congressional support for funding appropriations.[23] Clinton officials ran into more difficulties in 1999 when in order to gain access to a suspected missile development site at Kumchangri their only bargaining instrument was the provision of food aid; a massive 500,000 metric tonnes of the 695,154 metric tonnes allocated in 1999 for food aid was as a direct result of bargaining over United States access to the suspect site.[24] The United States recognised the existence of humanitarian need in the DPRK as the foundation for the provision of food aid, but Congressional and domestic hostility to doing deals with North Korea meant that United States administrations had few foreign policy instruments other than aid that would be politically acceptable to domestic critics.

United States official policy was to disassociate the provision of humanitarian assistance from security policy.[25] Indeed it was obliged to do so, given it was a signatory to various conventions on humanitarian policy. No country was obliged to provide humanitarian aid to another, but, if it did so, international legal norms prescribed that humanitarian aid must be provided solely on the basis of need and without regard to the politics of the receiving country. If provision of humanitarian aid was used as an inducement to security cooperation, it would not be a big step to threaten the withdrawal of humanitarian aid, irrespective of the demonstrable humanitarian need for aid. The logic of denying hungry people food for the purpose of obtaining a security deal from a recalcitrant government sat uneasily with the United States vision of itself as combining an ethical mission with the promotion of a realpolitik national interest.

The Bush administration delinked aid to North Korea from security concerns in the sense that such little progress took place on the security agenda that the small-scale food aid provided in 2002, 2003, 2004 and 2005 was clearly not a result of a quid pro quo in diplomatic negotiations. The United States completely withdrew food aid in 2006 and 2007. Food

---

[23] Ibid.; Mark Manyin and Mary Beth Nikitin, *Foreign Assistance to North Korea* (Washington, DC: Congressional Research Service, 2012), available at www.fas.org/sgp/crs/row/R40095.pdf, accessed 24 September 2012.

[24] Mark Manyin, *Foreign Assistance to North Korea* (Washington, DC: Congressional Research Service, 26 May 2005), p. 18, available at www.au.af.mil/au/awc/awcgate/crs/rl31785.pdf, accessed 5 November 2012.

[25] Hazel Smith, *Hungry for Peace: International Security, Humanitarian Assistance and Social Change in North Korea* (Washington, DC: United States Institute of Peace Press, 2005).

aid stopped because the North Korean government argued in 2005 that it no longer needed humanitarian assistance but that it required development aid to contribute towards long-term economic redevelopment. United States policy opposed development assistance as critics argued that the granting of concessional loans and grants would mean that the North Korean government was being rewarded for its flouting of international law. International NGOs continued to argue for the existence of humanitarian need in North Korea, although the debate became rather moot as the more conciliatory South Korean government of the early and mid-2000s provided large-scale and cheap 'loans' of fertiliser and food to North Korea. United States officials were not therefore faced with the problem of having to trade humanitarian aid for political gains during the first six years of the two Bush administrations.

The problem for the Bush administration was that after it entered into intensive negotiations with the DPRK in 2006, it suffered from the same lack of effective instruments that had confounded Clinton-era policy. United States policy-makers were left with few inducements with which to negotiate and without the ability to make economic sanctions effective. The result was a dramatic increase in humanitarian aid to North Korea.[26] Bush officials argued that the administration delinked humanitarian aid from security goals. A sceptical 2008 Congressional Research Service report commented that 'some argue that the timing for US pledges sometimes appears to be motivated also by a desire to influence talks over North Korea's nuclear program, and that the linkage between US donations and improvements in North Korea's cooperation with the WFP [World Food Programme] occasionally has been tenuous'.[27]

The Obama administration was more overt than its predecessors in linking both the provision and withdrawal of humanitarian food assistance to security negotiations. When the 'Leap Year' deal collapsed in March 2012 the *Los Angeles Times* reported that, 'The Obama administration says it has dropped plans to provide 240,000 metric tonnes of food aid for North Korea over Pyongyang's plans to launch what the US says is a missile – but which North Korea claims is a rocket designed to boost a satellite into space'.[28] The distinction between humanitarian aid and security instruments was explicitly elided.

---

[26] Bush second administration policy was articulated and vigorously defended by former National Security Council official Victor Cha, in *The Impossible State: North Korea Past and Future* (London: The Bodley Head, 2012).

[27] Manyin and Nikitin, *US Assistance to North Korea*, p. 4.

[28] Paul Richter, 'No Free Launch, Obama tells North Korea', *Los Angeles Times*, available at http://latimesblogs.latimes.com/world_now/2012/03/obama-to-.html., accessed 30 September 2012.

The politicisation of the human rights debate

Global perspectives on North Korean human rights ranged from those who argued that the only reason for North Korea's restrictions on its population was because of United States military and economic pressure that created a national security mentality in North Korea's leaders, through to those who argued that the North Korean government was an intrinsic abuser of human rights, and therefore regime change was the only viable policy to deal with systematic abuses.[29] The politicisation of debate on North Korean human rights rarely allowed qualified discussion to emerge into the scholarly or policy arena.[30] Those that sought to blame the United States for all North Korea's ills were unconvincing in the implication that North Korea was somehow a thwarted liberal democracy; only being prevented by United States policy from engaging in political transformation that would guarantee freedom of movement and assembly, and reduce state interference in the daily life to North Koreans. Those that argued that the North Korean government was unreformable failed to convince because of the blurring of the human rights agendas with regime change advocacy.[31]

[29] Rhoda Margesson, Emma Chanlett-Avery and Andorra Bruno, *North Korean Refugees in China and Human Rights Issues: International Response and US Policy Options* (Washington, DC: Congressional Research Service, 2007), pp. 22–3, available at www.dtic.mil/cgi-bin/GetTRDoc?Location=U2&doc=GetTRDoc.pdf&AD=ADA473619, accessed 6 November 2012.

[30] Richard Kagan, Matthew Oh and David Weissbrodt, *Human Rights in the Democratic People's Republic of Korea* (Minneapolis/Washington, DC: Minnesota Lawyers International Human Rights Committee/Asia Watch, 1988). Most commentary on North Korean human rights draws from this source, although it is rarely cited and its findings often used in an unqualified manner. Evaluations of the status of North Korean human rights have been issued annually since 1994 by the Korea Institute for National Unification. See, for example, Soo-am Kim, Kook-shin Kim, Soon-hee Lim, Hyun-joon Chon, Kyu-chang Lee and Jung-hyun Cho, *White Paper on Human Rights in North Korea 2012* (Seoul: Korea Institute for National Unification, 2012). These White Papers are useful documents but need to be read with care. Large sections are not substantiated or rely on uncorroborated testimony from individuals as the basis for very large generalisations. Even when more or less useful data are provided, the very sweeping assertions about what the data are supposed to mean are highly problematic in that they present themselves not as cumulative, carefully derived, scientific knowledge, but as the products of personal opinion or prior bias. An effort to fill the gap in terms of scholarly research in this area is the two-part special edition of *Critical Asian Studies* on 'Reframing North Korean Human Rights'. See Christine Hong and Hazel Smith (eds.), *Critical Asian Studies*, Vol. 45, No 4, December 2013 and Christine Hong and Hazel Smith (eds.), *Critical Asian Studies*, Vol. 46, No 1, March 2014.

[31] John Feffer, 'Human Rights in North Korea and the US Strategy of Linkage', *The Asia-Pacific Journal: Japan Focus*, 6 January 2006, available at www.japanfocus.org/-John-Feffer/1805, accessed 8 November 2014.

Defector accounts were routinely appropriated to support political agendas. In the 2000s, South Korea changed its approach to defectors to reduce the moral hazard of the system that had remunerated defectors more the more they could persuade South Korean intelligence agencies of the utility of the information they provided.[32] South Korea continued to financially support North Korean defectors but funding was delinked from intelligence 'value'.[33] The former close control by South Korean intelligence agencies over what North Korean defectors could do and say was reduced.[34] Not coincidentally, the information derived from defector accounts and defector surveys became more nuanced and therefore more credible.[35]

South Korean researchers had access to data, proximity to the North and intrinsic interest in producing scholarly work, but research was constrained due to the increased belligerence in North–South Korean relations from the late 2000s onwards. Scholars were wary of South Korea's National Security law, which made support for the North a criminal offence, and which could be interpreted as breached if researchers showed too much 'understanding' of the northern society. Systematic and careful investigation of North Korean human rights abuses included the meticulous 2006 account of North Korea's penal system by South Korean researcher, Soo-am Kim, but these careful analyses were not widely circulated.[36]

In 2004 the United Nations appointed a Special Rapporteur on Human Rights in the DPRK and the UN Human Rights Commission produced a series of reports on the DPRK.[37] The 2012 United Nations Human Rights Council report from the Special Rapporteur on North

---

[32] Jin-Heon Jung, *State and Church in the Making of Post-division Subjectivity: North Korean Migrants in South Korea*, MMG Working Paper 11–12 (Göttingen: Max Planck Institute for the Study of Religious and Ethnic Diversity, 2011).

[33] Ibid.   [34] Ibid.

[35] I interviewed several North Korean defectors in Seoul in 2012 to discuss economic transformation in the DPRK. These interviews were arranged through North Korean defector organisations. I was informed that I should offer an honorarium of which the going rate was $100 per interview. It is common practice in South Korea to offer honoraria for research participation and the majority of North Koreans living in South Korea were not well-off, so these were understood as standard practices. My view was that the opportunity of payment for interview provided an incentive to engage with foreigners but that there was no pressure on interviewees to conform to a pre-arranged script or to give answers I might have expected.

[36] For careful analysis, see Soo-am Kim, *The North Korean Penal Code, Criminal Procedures, and their Actual Applications* (Seoul: Korea Institute for National Unification, 2006).

[37] Human Rights Council, 'Report of the Special Rapporteur on the Situation of Human Rights in the Democratic People's Republic of Korea, A/HRC/19/65' in Human Rights Council, Nineteenth Session, Agenda Item 4, Human Rights Situations that Require the Council's Attention (Geneva: Human Rights Council, 13 February 2012), p. 14.

Korean Human Rights criticised North Korea's opaque legal and juridical system and the lack of independence of the judiciary as well as the state's use of the death penalty. The report called for full accounting for kidnapped foreign nationals and for an end to punishment and ill treatment, akin to torture in some cases, of North Korean asylum-seekers. The Special Rapporteur also called for both North and South Korea to make more progress on re-uniting families separated by the Korean War. The North Korean government was reminded that it needed to do more to improve its agriculture but other governments were also reminded of the need to provide humanitarian assistance with the caveat from the Rapporteur that assistance should not be 'made contingent upon any political requirements'.[38]

The report of the Special Rapporteur, Marzuki Darusman, to the United Nations Human Rights Council (UNHRC) of 1 February 2013, provided the foundation for the establishment of the Commission of Inquiry (COI) into human rights abuses in the DPRK.[39] The COI report expressed deep concern about human rights abuses in North Korea, especially in respect to politically motivated repression. The report was wide-ranging and the lack of transparency of the North Korean government combined with the systematic repetition of prison and judicial abuse meant that international campaigners had ample grounds to continue to pressurise military-first governments on human rights.

United Nations member states did not agree with the North Korean government that human rights concerns were being used solely as a political excuse to intervene in North Korea's sovereign jurisdiction. Some states were, however, unconvinced by the more lurid allegations against North Korea and were sceptical about the framing of North Korean human rights agendas that argued that the North was guilty of such systematic horrendous human rights abuses that the government's very existence constituted a moral abomination. In March 2014, China condemned the hard-hitting United Nations Human Rights Council COI report on North Korean human rights abuses as 'divorced from reality'.[40]

---

[38] Ibid.

[39] Human Rights Council, 'Report of the Special Rapporteur on the Situation of Human Rights in the Democratic People's Republic of Korea, Marzuki Darusman, A/HRC/22/57', in Human Rights Council, *Twenty-second Session, Agenda Item 4, Human Rights Situations that Require the Council's Attention* (Geneva: Human Rights Council, 1 February 2013).

[40] Tom Miles and Stephanie Nebehay, 'China Rejects N. Korean Crimes Report, Hits Chance of Prosecution', *Reuters*, 17 March 2014, available at http://in.reuters.com/article/2014/03/17/korea-north-un-idINDEEA2G07N20140317, accessed 11 May 2014.

Strategic paralysis

The United States succeeded in freezing North Korea's nuclear programme for seven years, from 1994 to 2001, and achieved a moratorium on the testing of medium and long-range missiles for four years, but after 9/11 the United States became less willing and less able to pursue proactive diplomacy with North Korea. North Korea was never important enough, when compared to say, the Iraq War, Afghanistan, international terrorism or, after worldwide recession in 2008, the economy, for presidents to sacrifice political capital to push controversial deals with North Korea through Congress and the Senate.

In a closely balanced Senate and Congress, where the majority would know little or nothing about North Korea, one or two seemingly well-informed voices could have a disproportionate influence over political agendas. While United States administrations were careful to separate out proliferation negotiations from wider concerns about North Korea, domestic pressure groups, especially those who viewed the thought of dealing with what they considered a morally abhorrent government as tantamount to offering sustenance to the regime, remained watchful of any concessions to North Korea. Those opposed to any deal with North Korea could not always prevent negotiations taking place but they could prevent or stall the implementation of agreements. United States Presidential authority was limited by the facts of political life at home and United States negotiators had to deal with sometimes vicious personal slanders if they appeared to be compromising too much with North Korea.[41]

The absence of sustained diplomatic initiatives had the unanticipated consequence of allowing North Korea to improve its capacity to produce nuclear weapons and develop increasingly sophisticated ballistic technology. The policy of strategic patience did not produce the hoped-for goals of human rights reform or denuclearisation, but it permitted China to fill the regional political vacuum caused by the absence of United States leadership on the most important on-going crisis in East Asia. Strategic patience morphed into paralysis as North Korea became a *de facto* nuclear armed state.

---

[41] Kerry, Executive Session.

15   North Koreans as agents of change

Government policy in North Korea hasn't changed much over the last twenty to thirty years; the mass mobilisation of the Kim Il Sung era morphed into military-first politics as the overriding objective of regime survival dominated domestic as well as foreign policies. Political freedoms remained non-existent and political reform off the political agenda. North Korean governments remained authoritarian and systematically subordinated individual human rights to regime security imperatives. Nevertheless, the breakdown in state capacity to reward acquiescence and punish dissent allowed North Koreans to carve out a space for the exercise of limited but important freedoms, especially in everyday economic decision-making.

The transformation of North Korea from a rigid command economy during the Cold War to the marketised society of today was not planned or foreseen but can be explained by understanding how North Korean people – not the government – took action by themselves, for themselves, in response to external and domestic exigencies. The self-directed activity of millions of small traders, led by women, who swapped, bartered, sold and generally engaged in the whole spectrum of non-state-directed, private economic transactions, transformed society from below and from inside; social change was not led from abroad.

In daily life, most people were forced into circumventing governmental regulations in order to find ways to survive and, in a few cases, prosper. The government's refusal to acknowledge the fundamental importance of marketisation in sustaining life and livelihoods increased the sense of dissonance between official pronouncements and real life. The failure to end economic hardship and the awareness of better living standards in China and South Korea combined to create a crisis of legitimacy for military-first governments. Strident government rhetoric directed against South Korea was partly designed to demonstrate to a domestic audience that even if North Korea was not as rich as the South, it was more legitimately Korean. Patriotism, as noted long ago by Disraeli, was the last resort of the scoundrel.

What gets lost in the ether?

In the sound and the fury that sometimes passes for reporting and comment on North Korea, what gets lost are the real tragedies: the mundane miseries of living without decent water and electricity supplies, medicines and good-quality food; the chance to be free to travel, read non-government-authorised books and magazines; to criticise the government; and to have a reasonable expectation that things might get better, if not for this generation then the next. These daily hardships are not unique to North Korea and represent a condition of life for many millions, especially women and girls, throughout the world. These quotidian realties of North Korean society are rarely discussed and reported as they are not sensationalist enough to sell newspapers, attract high ratings for television producers and drive hits on blogsites that must constantly up the ante with extremist vitriol if they are to be heard above the cacophony of internet traffic on North Korea.

The two censuses show that the North Korean population increased to 24 million in 2008 from just over 21 million in 1993 but who has reported what that means and why those figures suggest that the country is enmired in poverty but not uniquely so?[1] These demographic statistics make rather dry copy; they don't allow for headlines like 'three million dead' or 'North Koreans eating their babies' – both of which have graced broadsheet and tabloid coverage of North Korea. They should be news for an international media that is insatiable for North Korea stories; but for the fact that they don't confirm any of the clichés. They don't show a drop in population numbers across the country or in any of the ten provinces so the data cannot lend itself to other tropes that assert that one particular part of the country has been starved by the government to feed another part, whether this be geographical, usually the capital city, or social groups, usually the military and Party officials.[2] The data are perhaps even less newsworthy because the DPRK government admits they are true. In 1996, North Korean demographers reported that 'temporary economic difficulties' might cause slowdown in population growth and predicted that, at the bottom end of a possible range of scenarios, the population figures might be just over 24 million by 2010.[3]

---

[1] Figures derived from Sun Won Hong, *Analysis of 1993 Population Census Data DPR Korea* (Pyongyang: Population Center, DPRK, 1996); Chang Su Kim, *DPR Korea 2008 Population Census National Report* (Pyongyang: Central Bureau of Statistics Pyongyang, 2009).
[2] Ibid.
[3] Hong, *Analysis of 1993 Population Census*, pp. 135–6.

The demographic indicators do not provide much support for another favourite headline of lazy journalism – that Pyongyang is a Potemkin city where only the rich and privileged live and from which all others are excluded. The demographic data does not show dramatic differences between the provinces. Indeed, between 1993 and 2008 the provinces experienced similar levels of population growth. The capital's population growth was higher than the other provinces, at 1.25 per cent per year, but not markedly so.[4] Population growth ranged between 0.84 per cent and 0.96 per cent for the remaining nine provinces.[5] Pyongyang's total increase in population between the two census periods was about half a million compared to the next largest increases at 450,000 in the combined Nampo/South Pyongan province and 333,000 in South Hamgyong.[6]

Why these statistics should be reported is that they indicate increasing poverty for most of the population and show that North Korean society is undergoing a social process that is far from unique and very explicable. Slow rates of population growth in rich countries usually indicate a prosperous society that is actively choosing to have fewer children, but in North Korea slow rates of growth indicated the opposite. High maternal mortality, continuing maternal malnutrition, poor economic conditions and decision-making by women not to have children, despite the pro-natalist policy of governments, put the brakes on population growth during the military-first era.

North Korea is not unique

Military-first era policies and actions were far from uncommon. Many states privilege national security over individual rights. Even democratic states with long-standing commitments to government by the rule of law have sometimes been found wanting by international human rights bodies.[7] The illegal development of nuclear armaments outside the Nuclear Non-Proliferation Treaty (NPT) is also not idiosyncratic to North Korea – as witnessed by similar developments in India, Israel and Pakistan.

---

[4] Figures derived from ibid. and Kim, *DPR Korea 2008 Population Census*.
[5] Figures derived from Hong, *Analysis of 1993 Population Census*, and Kim, *DPR Korea 2008 Population Census*.
[6] Ibid.
[7] Brian Evans, 'The Fatal Flaws of Texas Justice', *Amnesty International, Human Rights Now Blog*, 31 October 2012, available at http://blog.amnestyusa.org/us/the-fatal-flaws-of-texas-justice, accessed 31 October 2012; Amnesty International, *Left in the Dark: The Use of Secret Evidence in the United Kingdom* (London: Amnesty International, 2012), available at www.amnesty.org/en/news/uk-new-report-slams-secret-justice-ahead-debate-controversial-bill-2012-10-15, accessed 31 October 2012.

North Korean society is remarkably similar to societies transiting from communism to capitalism; its politics can be explained by reference to communist institutionalist models and nationalist perspectives; it has a lot in common with militarised dictatorships everywhere and much of its political development can be understood fairly easily by anyone with a minimal knowledge of the transition from Maoism to market socialism. The trivial comments that insist on North Korea's 'uniqueness' do not understand that analytical frameworks work to compare and contrast; the issue is not empirical sameness but whether or not there are sufficiently adequate comparators so that useful analytical frameworks can be constructed such as to help explain specific cases. It is banal to assert that North Korea's political, economic and social trajectory is not identical to any other country; that is true for any and every country.

North Koreans as agents of change

Understanding North Koreans' sense of identity and history makes it easier to comprehend why North Koreans maintain a residual loyalty to the state they had created in 1948 and why they are not anxious to sublimate all aspects of their identity into becoming 'South Korean', especially when many are aware that South Korea is not always welcoming to North Koreans who migrate south. It also helps explain why political change in North Korea is much more likely to come about from within than from an external intervention against which the government could mobilise nationalist sentiments in its defence. North Korea, like all societies, is shaped by historical and cultural referents, not just by government policy. North Koreans, like people everywhere, have multiple social and personal interests, shaped by age, gender, occupation, class, geographical provenance – and many other factors. North Koreans are neither brainwashed nor stupid and are as capable as any other people of analysing their own problems. Like everyone else in the world, North Koreans are also perfectly capable of holding diverse, sometimes apparently contradictory, opinions all at the same time.

North Koreans know that the North Korean government is both inept and anachronistic, and that South Koreans and Chinese are prosperous and they are not, and yet maintain a sense of national pride that is founded within a specific history and identity. National pride is founded on the rebuilding of North Korea as a modern country after the utter devastation of the Korean War in which millions died, tens of thousands were orphaned and the county's civilian infrastructure, including dams, power stations, transport facilities and residential buildings, was literally bombed into small pieces. These historic achievements are widely understood as due to the involvement of all the population in the creation of a new life in the face of South Korean and foreign hostility and made possible by the leadership of Kim Il Sung. This sense of northern identity is not synonymous with government propaganda and is a tangible factor in understanding why many North Koreans continue to hold ambivalent views about their leadership and country.

The sense of northern national identity is difficult to comprehend by outsiders but it is fundamental in understanding why marketisation is understood by the government as a politically dangerous phenomenon that threatens regime security. Historically the government relied on consent as much as coercion to stave off threats. Marketisation is so dangerous for the political elite because it has been accompanied by the disassociation of the population from the government. In the Kim Il Sungist period, the population was bombarded by political messages and the government had the capacity to enforce compliance through economic rewards and penalties; but that was not the only reason for political acquiescence. During the Kim Il Sungist period, there was a sense that 'we are all in this together'. In the period of marketisation and military rule, the prevailing mood is of 'us against them'.

What next?

What is needed from outsiders is an end to ideological grandstanding and the development of a coherent global strategy to obtain a comprehensive settlement that includes denuclearisation of North Korea as a top priority. The potential of a nuclear accident arising from North Korea's 'make do and mend' approach to industrial development should provide a major impetus to get talks back on track. A comprehensive strategy would require security guarantees for the DPRK, enshrined in treaties, and would entail uncomfortable compromises with the North Korean leadership, but it would also demand transformation towards a liberalised society in the DPRK. The nearest analogous conflict may be that of Northern Ireland, where both sides came to the table after the realisation that neither could win on the battlefield; Conservative and Labour governments pardoned murderers and those they had inscribed in law as terrorists and reformed the police force to incorporate representatives across the sectarian divide proportionately and substantively. Nevertheless these compromises took place within the context of the strengthening of democratic processes in post-conflict society; the outcome was to reduce drastically the militarisation of society in Northern Ireland as well as the peaceful settlement of a very long-running and brutally prosecuted conflict.

The defunct six-party talks have too much negative baggage to serve as the foundation for fresh initiatives, although the United States, China, the DPRK, South Korea, Japan and Russia will continue to provide the key diplomatic players in Korean conflict resolution. Other states can be useful interlocutors; the United Kingdom and Germany are United States allies but they also have ambassadors based in the DPRK. Most importantly, the United States needs to re-engage and take the lead of a carefully calibrated diplomatic and economic initiative that would unite political forces across the aisle in American politics and bring American diplomatic leadership to the East Asian region.

None of these observations excuse the North Korean government from its responsibility to take action to reform itself. The North Korean government has the primary responsibility under international law to ensure that citizens are treated fairly and humanely. International organisations, states and non-governmental organisations are right to insist on denuclearisation by the North Korean government and morally correct to support a transformation to peace and freedom but, in the end, it is the twenty-four million population of North Korea that will effect that change. Instead of the victims or villains that populate the standard clichés, we should see North Koreans for what they are: the agents of change in North Korea.

Bibliography

Action Contre la Faim, *Nutritional Programme: North Hamgyong Province DPR of Korea, November 1999* (Pyongyang: Action Contre la Faim, 1999).

Aden, Nathaniel, 'North Korean Trade with China as Reported in Chinese Customs Statistics: Energy Trends and Implications', *The Korean Journal of Defense Analysis*, Vol. 23, No. 2, June 2011, pp. 231–55.

AFP, 'North Korea Resumes Massive Military Drills', Tuesday 19 September 1995.

Ahn, Choong-Yong (ed.), *North Korea Development Report 2003/2004* (Seoul: Korea Institute for International Economic Policy, 2003/4).

Al Suma, Hani, *The Ever-Shining Star of Korea* (Pyongyang: Foreign Languages Publishing House, 1986).

Amnesty International, *Starving North Koreans Forced to Survive on Diet of Grass and Tree Bark* (London: Amnesty International, 2010), available at www.amnesty.org/en/news-and-updates/starving-north-koreans-forced-survive-diet-grass-and-tree-bark-2010-07-14, accessed 17 July 2013.

Left in the Dark: The Use of Secret Evidence in the United Kingdom (London: Amnesty International, 2012), available at www.amnesty.org/en/news/uk-new-report-slams-secret-justice-ahead-debate-controversial-bill-2012-10-15, accessed 31 October 2012.

North Korea: New Satellite Images show Blurring of Political Prison Camp and Villages in North Korea (London: Amnesty International, 2013), available at www.amnesty.org/en/news/north-korea-new-images-show-blurring-prison-camps-and-villages-2013-03-07, accessed 27 July 2013.

Anderson, Benedict, *Imagined Communities: Reflections on the Origin and Spread of Nationalism* (London: Verso, 1983).

Armstrong, Charles K., *The North Korean Revolution 1945–1950* (Ithaca, NY: Cornell University Press, 2003).

'"Fraternal Socialism": The International Reconstruction of North Korea, 1953–62', *Cold War History*, Vol. 5, No. 2, May 2005, pp. 161–87.

'North Korea's South Korea Policy: Tactical Change, Strategic Consistency', in Sung Chull Kim and David C. Kang (eds.), *Engagement with North Korea: A Viable Alternative* (Albany: SUNY Press, 2009), pp. 225–44.

Associated Press (AP), 'North-Korea-Diplomacy', 19 September 1995.

Baik, Bong, *Kim Il Sung Biography (1)* (Beirut: Dar Al-Talia, 1973).

Baker, Don, *Korean Spirituality* (Honolulu: University of Hawai'i Press, 2008).

Banchev, Iuli, 'Prerogatives of the New Foreign Economic Policy Making',
    in Han S. Park (ed.), *North Korea: Ideology, Politics, Economy* (Englewood
    Cliffs: Prentice Hall, 1996), pp. 189–204.
Bank of Korea, *Gross Domestic Product of North Korea in 2009* (Seoul: Bank of
    Korea, 2010), available at www.nkeconwatch.com/nk-uploads/bok-dprk-
    gdp-2009.pdf, accessed 30 April 2011.
Barrett, Jasmine, 'The North Korean Healthcare System: On the Fine Line
    Between Resilience and Vulnerability', *Resilience: Interdisciplinary Perspectives
    on Science and Humanitarianism*, Vol. 2, March 2011, pp. 52–65.
Bazhanov, Evgeniy P., 'Russian Views of the Agreed Framework and the
    Four-Party Talks', in James Clay Moltz and Alexandre Y. Mansourov (eds.),
    *The North Korean Nuclear Program: Security, Strategy and New Perspectives
    from Russia* (London: Routledge, 2000), pp. 219–35.
Bazhanova, Natalya, 'North Korea's Decision to Develop an Independent
    Nuclear Program', in James Clay Moltz and Alexandre Y. Mansourov
    (eds.), *The North Korean Nuclear Program: Security, Strategy and New
    Perspectives from Russia* (London: Routledge, 2000), pp. 60–75.
BBC News, 'N Korean Ship Seized with Cuban Weapons Returns to Cuba',
    15 February 2014, available at www.bbc.co.uk/news/world-latin-america-
    26210187, accessed 30 May 2014.
BBC News Asia Pacific, 'North Korean Leader Kim Jong-Il's Son "made a
    general"', 28 September 2010, available at www.bbc.co.uk/news/world-
    asia-pacific-11417016, accessed 3 November 2014.
Bender, Klaus, 'The Mystery of the Supernotes', 11 January 2007, reproduced
    on the website of the Düsseldorfer Instituts für Außen-und
    Sicherheitspolitik (DIAS), available at www.dias-online.org/65.0.html,
    accessed 14 December 2012.
Bermudez, Joseph S., *North Korean Special Forces*, second edition (Annapolis:
    Naval Institute Press, 1998).
    'Information and the DPRK's Military and Power-holding Elite', in Kongdan
    Oh Hassig (ed.), *DPRK Policy Elites* (Alexandria, VA: Institute for Defense
    Analyses, 2004), unpaginated but pp. 15–58 on pdf; available at www.
    nkeconwatch.com/nk-uploads/dprkpolicyelites.pdf, accessed 2 November
    2014.
Bluth, Christoph, 'The North Korean Missile Program: Origins, Capabilities
    and Future Trajectories', mimeo (Leeds University, 2011).
Brady, James, *The Coldest War: A Memoir of Korea* (New York: Thomas Dunne
    Books, 1990).
Breen, Michael, *Kim Jong Il: North Korea's Dear Leader: Who he Is, What he
    Wants, What to Do about Him* (Chichester: John Wiley and Sons, 2004).
Brun, Ellen and Hersh, Jacques, *Socialist Korea: A Case Study in the Strategy of
    Economic Development* (London and New York: Monthly Review Press,
    1976).
Bryman, Alan, *Social Research Methods*, fourth edition (Oxford University
    Press, 2012).
Bulychev, Georgy, 'Korean Security Dilemmas: A Russian Perspective', in
    Hazel Smith (ed.), *Reconstituting Korean Security: A Policy Primer* (Tokyo:
    United Nations Press, 2007), pp. 182–212.

Buzo, Adrian, *The Guerilla Dynasty: Politics and Leadership in North Korea* (Boulder, CO: Westview Press, 1999).

Caritas, *Caritas and the DPRK – Building on 10 Years of Experience* (Hong Kong/ Rome: Caritas Hong Kong, 2006).

Carlin, Robert and Lewis, John W., *Negotiating with North Korea: 1993–2007* (Stanford: Center for International Security and Cooperation, January 2008).

Cathcart, Adam, 'Nationalism and Ethnic Identity in the Sino-Korean Border Region of Yanbian 1945–1950', *Korean Studies*, Vol. 34, 2010, pp. 25–53.

Central Bureau of Statistics, *Report on the DPRK Nutrition Assessment 2002* (Pyongyang: Central Bureau of Statistics, 20 November 2002).

DPRK 2004 Nutrition Assessment (Pyongyang: Central Bureau of Statistics, Institute of Child Nutrition, February 2005).

'2008 Census of Population of DPRK: Key Findings', available at www.unfpa. org/webdav/site/global/shared/documents/news/2010/dprk08_censuskey finds.pdf, accessed 22 June 2014.

Democratic People's Republic of Korea Preliminary Report of the National Nutrition Survey, October 2012 (Pyongyang: Central Bureau of Statistics, 2012).

Central Bureau of Statistics/UNDP, *Thematic Roundtable Meeting on Agricultural Recovery and Environmental Protection for the DPRK* (Pyongyang: UNDP, 1998).

Central Bureau of Statistics/UNICEF, *The Democratic People's Republic of Korea Multiple Indicator Cluster Survey Final Report 2009* (Pyongyang: CBS, 2010).

Cha, Victor, *The Impossible State: North Korea Past and Future* (London: The Bodley Head, 2012).

Chanlett-Avery, Emma, *North Korean Supporters in Japan: Issues for US Policy* (Washington, DC: Congressional Research Service, 7 November 2003), available at www.ncnk.org/resources/publications/CRS_Chosen_Soren_ 2003_RL32137.pdf, accessed 1 April 2014.

Chanlett-Avery, Emma and Rinehart, Ian E., *North Korea: US Relations, Nuclear Diplomacy, and Internal Situation* (Washington, DC: Congressional Research Service, January 2014), available at www.fas.org/sgp/crs/nuke/ R41259.pdf, accessed 27 April 2014.

Checa, Genaro Carnero, *Korea: Rice and Steel* (Pyongyang: Foreign Languages Publishing House, 1977).

Chen, Ching-chih, 'Police and Community Control Systems in the Empire', in Ramon H. Myers and Mark R. Peattie (eds.), *The Japanese Colonial Empire, 1895–1945* (Princeton University Press, 1984), pp. 213–39.

Chen, Jian, 'Limits of the "Lips and Teeth" Alliance: An Historical Review of Chinese–North Korean Relations', in Timothy Hildebrandt (ed.), *Uneasy Allies: Fifty Years of China–North Korea Relations* (Washington, DC: Woodrow Wilson Center Asia Program Special Report, September 2003), pp. 4–10.

Chestnut, Sheena E., 'The "Soprano State"? North Korean Involvement in Criminal Activity and Implications for International Security', undergraduate dissertation, mimeo (Stanford University, 2005).

China Daily, 'Tycoon Given 18 Years Behind Bars', 15 July 2003, reproduced online at 'China Through a Lens', www.china.org.cn/english/2003/Jul/69917.htm, accessed 15 December 2014.

'DPRK Students get in Sync with Technology', 14 July 2012, available at http://news.xinhuanet.com/english/culture/2012-07/14/c_131715635.htm, accessed 30 May 2014.

Cho, Jeong-Ah, *The Changes of Everyday Life in North Korea in the Aftermath of their Economic Difficulties* (Seoul: Korea Institute for National Unification, 2007).

Choe, Sang-Hun, 'New North Korean Missile is Called Into Question', *New York Times*, 27 April 2012, available at www.nytimes.com/2012/04/27/world/asia/new-north-korean-missile-is-called-into-question.html?_r=1&ref=northkorea, accessed 30 October 2012.

Choe, Sang-Hun, Doherty, Jake, Fararo, Kim, Gladstone, Rick, Kannapell, Andrea, Landler, Mark, Marsh, Bill and Sanger, David E., 'In Focus: North Korea's Nuclear Threats', *The New York Times*, updated 16 April 2013, available at www.nytimes.com/interactive/2013/04/12/world/asia/north-korea-questions.html?_r=0, accessed 15 September 2013.

Choe, Thae Sop, *Topics on Health*, English edition (Pyongyang: Korea Publications Exchange Association, 1999).

Choi, Bong Dae and Koo, Kab Woo 'The Development of Farmers' Markets in North Korean Cities', in Phillip H. Park (ed.), *The Dynamics of Change in North Korea: An Institutionalist Perspective* (Seoul: IFES Kyungnam University Press, 2009), pp. 75–134.

Choi, Jinwook, 'The North Korean Domestic Situation and its Impact on the Nuclear Crisis', *Ritsumeikan Annual Review of International Studies*, Vol. 5, 2006, pp. 1–18, available at www.ritsumei.ac.jp/acd/cg/ir/college/bulletin/e-vol.5/CHOI.pdf, accessed 5 January 2014.

Choi, Jinwook and Shaw, Meredith, 'The Rise of Kim Jong Eun and the Return of the Party', *International Journal of Korean Unification Studies*, Vol. 19, No. 2, 2010, pp. 175–202.

Choi, Kang and Kim, Minsung, 'An Assessment of the Security Environment and Challenges in the Post-Cheonan Era: A South Korean Perspective', *International Journal of Korean Unification Studies*, Vol. 19, No. 2, 2010, pp. 88–124.

Choi, Soo-Young, *A Study on the Structure of Industry in North Korea* (Seoul: Korea Institute of National Unification, 2006).

North Korea's Agricultural Reforms and Challenges in the Wake of the July 1 Measures (Seoul: Korea Institute for National Unification, 2007).

Chosun Ilbo, 'N. Korea's Underground Economy Booming', *Chosun Ilbo*, 8 February 2014, available at http://english.chosun.com/site/data/html_dir/2011/09/21/2011092101133.html, accessed 7 February 2014.

Christen, Roberto and Ahmed, Gamal M., *Agriculture in DPRK* (Pyongyang: FAO, undated but probably 2001).

Chung, Henry, *The Case of Korea* (New York: F. H. Revell Co., 1921).

Chung, Joseph Sang-hoon, *The North Korean Economy: Structure and Development* (Stanford: Hoover Institution Press, 1974).

Chung, Steven, 'The Split Screen: Sin Sang-ok in North Korea', in Sonia
    Ryang (ed.), *North Korea: Toward a Better Understanding* (Lanham:
    Lexington Books, 2009), pp. 85–107.
Clark, Donald N., *Living Dangerously in Korea: The Western Experience 1900–1950*
    (Norwalk, CT: Eastbridge, 2003).
Coalition to Stop the Use of Child Soldiers, *Child Soldiers Global Report 2008*
    (London: Coalition to Stop the Use of Child Soldiers, 2008), available at
    www.childsoldiersglobalreport.org/files/country_pdfs/FINAL_2008_
    Global_Report.pdf, accessed 27 January 2012.
Committee on Economic, Social and Cultural Rights, *Replies by the Government
    of the Democratic People's Republic of Korea to the List of Issues (E/C.12/Q/
    DPRK/1) to be taken up in Connection with the Consideration of the Second
    Periodic Reports of the Democratic People's Republic of Korea Concerning the
    Rights Referred to in Articles 1–15 of the International Covenant on Economic,
    Social and Cultural Rights (E/1990/6/Add. 35), HR/CESCR/NONE/2003/1*
    (Geneva: Committee on Economic, Social and Cultural Rights, 10–28
    November 2003).
Committee on the Elimination of Discrimination against Women, *Written
    Replies by the Democratic People's Republic of Korea Concerning the Responses
    to the List of Issues and Questions. PSWG/ 2005/II/CRP.2/Add.3* (New York:
    UN Women, 15 April 2005), available at www.un.org/womenwatch/daw/
    cedaw/cedaw33/responses/kor/kor-E.pdf, accessed 22 April 2014.
Compilation Committee of Kim Il Sung Encyclopaedia, 'On Improving the
    Guidance and Management of Industry to Fit the New Circumstances',
    in Compilation Committee of Kim Il Sung Encyclopaedia, *Kim Il Sung
    Encyclopaedia Volume One* (New Delhi: Vishwanath, 1992), pp. 538–39.
    Kim Il Sung Encyclopaedia Volume One (New Delhi: Vishwanath, 1992).
Cornell, Erik, *North Korea under Communism: Report of an Envoy to Paradise*
    (London: RoutledgeCurzon, 2002).
Creekmore, Marion, Jr., *A Moment of Crisis: Jimmy Carter, the Power of a
    Peacemaker, and North Korea's Nuclear Ambitions* (New York: Public Affairs,
    2006).
Cultural Relics Publishing House, *Tomb of King Tangun* (Pyongyang:
    Cultural Relics Publishing House, 1995).
Cumings, Bruce, 'Korea – the New Nuclear Flashpoint', *The Nation*, 7 April
    1984.
    The Origins of the Korean War, Vol. II: The Roaring of the Cataract 1947–1950
    (Princeton, NJ/Oxford: Princeton University Press, 1990).
    *The Origins of the Korean War, Vol. I: Liberation and the Emergence of Separate
    Regimes 1945–1947* (Seoul: Yuksabipyungsa, 2002).
    'Creating Korean Insecurity: The US Role', in Hazel Smith (ed.),
    Reconstituting Korean Security: A Policy Primer (Tokyo: United Nations Press,
    2007), pp. 21–42.
    The Korean War: A History (New York: Modern Library, 2010).
Cyrzyk, Loszek, 'Pyongyang's Reunification Policy', in Han S. Park (ed.),
    North Korea: Ideology, Politics, Economy (Englewood Cliffs: Prentice Hall,
    1996), pp. 205–19.

Davis, Mike, *Late Victorian Holocausts: El Niño Famines and the Making of the Third World* (London: Verso, 2001).

Délégation générale de la RPD de Corée en France, 'First-day sitting of First North-South High-Level Talks', in *Bulletin d'information, No. 11/990* (Paris: Délégation générale de la RPD de Corée en France, 7 September 1990).

'Keynote Speech of the Premier of the Administration Council of the DPRK at Third Inter-Korean High Talks', in *Bulletin d'information, Special Issue* (Paris: Délégation générale de la RPD de Corée en France, 14 December 1990).

Bulletin d'information, Special Issue No. 37/1097 (Paris: Délégation générale de la RPD de Corée en France, 28 January 1991).

'Statement of DPRK Foreign Ministry on the "Team Spirit 91"', in *Bulletin d'information, No. 2/191* (Paris: Délégation générale de la RPD de Corée en France, 28 January 1991).

Communiqué of the Supreme Command of the Korean People's Army (Paris: Délégation générale de la RPD de Corée en France, 26 February 1991).

Bulletin d'information, No. 11/591 (Paris: Délégation générale de la RPD de Corée en France, 28 May 1991).

'On the Measures Taken by the Government of the DPRK to Implement the Articles VI and VII of the Nuclear Non-Proliferation Treaty', in *Bulletin d'information, No. 11/591* (Paris: Délégation générale de la RPD de Corée en France, 28 May 1991).

'DPRK Welcomed President Bush's Announcement', in *Bulletin d'information, Special Issue No. 22/1091* (Paris: Délégation générale de la RPD de Corée en France, 1 October 1991).

'President Kim Il Sung Gives On-the-spot Guidance to Farms', in *Bulletin d'information, No. 15/0493* (Paris: Délégation générale de la RPD de Corée en France, 27 September 1993).

'Monument to Party Foundation completed', in *Bulletin d'information, No. 12/1195* (Paris: Délégation générale de la RPD de Corée en France, 17 November 1995).

Bulletin d'information, No. 14/0196 (Paris: Délégation générale de la RPD de Corée en France, 22 January 1996).

'Foreign Ministry Spokesman on Flood Damage in DPRK', in *Bulletin d'information, No. 22/0896* (Paris: Délégation générale de la RPD de Corée en France, 16 August 1996).

'Rajin-Sonbong Zone Appealing to Investor', in *Bulletin d'information, 25/1096* (Paris: Délégation générale de la RPD de Corée en France, 7 October 1996).

'Bright Future of "Golden Triangle"', in *Bulletin d'information, 28/0197* (Paris: Délégation générale de la RPD de Corée en France, 26 January 1997).

DeLisle, Guy, *Pyongyang: A Journey in North Korea* (Montreal: L'Association, 2005).

Democratic People's Republic of Korea Editorial Board, *Echoes of the Korean War* (Pyongyang: Foreign Languages Publishing House, 1996).

Kim Jong Il: Short Biography (Pyongyang: Foreign Languages Publishing House, 2001).

'Creators of Happiness', *Democratic People's Republic of Korea*, No. 660, April 2011.

Department of Public Information News and Media Division, *Resolution 1874 (2009) Strengthens Arms Embargo, Calls for Inspection of Cargo Vessels if States have 'Reasonable Grounds' to Believe Contain Prohibited Items* (New York: United Nations Security Council SC/9679, 2009), available at www.un.org/News/Press/docs/2009/sc9679.doc.htm, accessed 3 January 2013.

Dikötter, Frank, *Mao's Great Famine* (London: Bloomsbury, 2011).

DPRK Academy of Sciences, 'Information on the Disinterment of the Tomb of Tangun', *Tangun Founder-King of Korea* (Pyongyang: Foreign Languages Publishing House, 1994).

Tangun Founder-King of Korea (Pyongyang: Foreign Languages Publishing House, 1994).

DPRK Government, 'Statement of DPRK Government on Withdrawal from NPT', in Délégation générale de la RPD de Corée en France, *Bulletin d'information, No. 10/0393* (Paris: Délégation générale de la RPD de Corée en France, 12 March 1993).

'Second Periodic Reports of States Parties due in 1997: Democratic People's Republic of Korea, 05/11/2003, CRC/C/65/Add.24 (State Party Report)', *Committee on the Rights of the Child, Consideration of Reports Submitted by States Parties under Article 44 of the Convention* (Geneva: Office of the High Commissioner for Human Rights, 5 November 2003), available at www.refworld.org/pdfid/403a10a44.pdf, accessed 3 November 2014.

'Replies by the Government of the Democratic People's Republic of Korea to the List of Issues: Democratic People's Republic of Korea, 04/09/03', *Committee on Economic, Social and Cultural Rights, Thirty-first Session Item 6 of the Provisional Agenda* (Geneva: Office of the High Commissioner for Human Rights, 10–28 November 2003), available at www.bayefsky.com/issuesresp/rokorea_hr_cescr_none_2003_1.pdf, accessed 3 November 2014.

DPRK Ministry of Education, *The Development of Education: National Report of the Democratic People's Republic of Korea* (Pyongyang: Ministry of Education, 2004), available at www.ibe.unesco.org/International/ICE47/English/Natreps/reports/dprkorea.pdf, accessed 7 February 2014.

DPRK Ministry of Foreign Affairs, 'Statement of the Ministry of Foreign Affairs of the DPR of Korea on the Question of Signing the Nuclear Safeguards Accord', in Délégation générale de la RPD de Corée en France, *Bulletin d'information, Special Issue No. 26/1191* (Paris: Délégation générale de la RPD de Corée en France, 26 November, 1991).

'On the Truth of Nuclear Inspection by IAEA in DPRK', in Délégation générale de la RPD de Corée en France, *Bulletin d'information, No. 11/0393* (Paris: Délégation générale de la RPD de Corée en France, 5 March 1993).

DPRK official webpage, www.korea-dpr.com, accessed 14 December 2014.

Drennan, William, *A Comprehensive Resolution of the Korean War, Special Report* (Washington, DC: United States Institute of Peace, 2003), available at www.usip.org/publications/comprehensive-resolution-korean-war, accessed 18 April 2013.

Duncan, John. B., *'Hyanghwain*: Migration and Assimilation in Chosŏn Korea', in *Acta Koreana*, Vol. 3, July 2000, pp. 1–15.

Dürkop, Colin and Yeo, Min-Il, 'North Korea after Kim Jong Il: Political and Social Perspectives ahead of the Expected Change of Power', *KAS International Reports*, August 2011, available at www.kas.de/wf/doc/kas_23605-544-2-30.pdf?110811143245, accessed 29 August 2011.

Duus, Peter, *The Abacus and the Sword: The Japanese Penetration of Korea 1895–1910* (Berkeley: University of California Press, 1995).

Ebertstadt, Nicholas, *The End of North Korea* (Washington, DC: The American Enterprise Institute (AEI) Press, 1999).

'International Trade in Capital Goods, 1970–1995: Indications from "Mirror Statistics"', in Nicholas Eberstadt, *The North Korean Economy: Between Crisis and Catastrophe* (New Brunswick: Transaction Publishers, 2007), pp. 61–97.

Eberstadt, Nicholas and Banister, Judith, *The Population of North Korea* (Berkeley, CA: Institute of East Asian Studies, 1992).

Eckert, Carter, *Offspring of Empire: The Koch'ang Kims and the Colonial Origins of Korean Capitalism 1876–1945* (Seattle: University of Washington Press, 2003).

Eckert, Carter J., Lee, Ki-bail, Lew, Young Ick, Robinson, Michael and Wagner, Edward, *Korea Old and New: A History* (Cambridge, MA: Korea Institute, Harvard University/Ilchokak, 1990).

Economic and Social Council, 'Implementation of the International Covenant on Economic, Social and Cultural Rights, Second Periodic Report submitted by State Parties under Articles 16 and 17 of the Covenant: Addendum, Democratic People's Republic of Korea, E/1990/6/Add.35', mimeo, 15 May 2002.

'Report of the Special Rapporteur on Contemporary Forms of Racism, Racial Discrimination, Xenophobia and Related Intolerance; Doudou Diène, Addendum, Mission to Japan', in Commission on Human Rights, *Sixty-second Session Item 6 of the Provisional Agenda, E/CN.4/2006/16/Add.2* (Geneva: Economic and Social Council, 24 January 2006), available at http://web.archive.org/web/20061214115324/http://imadr.org/geneva/2006/G0610396.pdf, accessed 14 September 2013.

Em, Henry, 'Nationalism, Post-Nationalism and Shin Ch'ae-ho', *Korea Journal*, summer 1999, pp. 283–428.

The Great Enterprise: Sovereignty and Historiography in Modern Korea (Durham: Duke University Press, 2013).

'Commentary on Kim Heung-kyu's "A Community of Long Memories"', private communication to the author, May 2014.

Esselstrom, Erik, *Crossing Empire's Edge: Foreign Ministry Police and Japanese Expansionism in Northeast Asia* (Honolulu: University of Hawai'i Press, 2009).

EU, UNICEF and WFP in partnership with the Government of DPRK, *Nutrition Survey of the Democratic People's Republic of Korea* (Rome/Pyongyang: WFP, 1998).

Evans, Brian, 'The Fatal Flaws of Texas Justice', *Amnesty International, Human Rights Now Blog*, 31 October 2012, available at http://blog.amnestyusa.org/us/the-fatal-flaws-of-texas-justice, accessed 31 October 2012.

Everard, John, *Only Beautiful, Please: A British Diplomat in North Korea* (Stanford, CA: Asia/Pacific Research Center, Division of The Institute for International Studies, 2012).

'The Markets of Pyongyang', *Korea Economic Institute: Academic Paper Series*, Vol. 6, No. 1, January 2011, pp. 1–7, available at www.keia.org/ Communications/Programs/Everard/Everard.pdf, accessed 8 November 2014.

FAO/WFP, *Crop and Food Supply Assessment Mission to the Democratic People's Republic of Korea, Special Report* (Rome: FAO/WFP, 22 December 1995), available at www.fao.org/docrep/004/w0051e/w0051e00.htm, accessed 12 January 2014.

Crop and Food Supply Assessment Mission to the Democratic People's Republic of Korea, Special Alert, No. 267 (Rome: FAO/WFP, 16 May 1996), available at www.fao.org/docrep/004/w1302e/w1302e00.htm, accessed 8 November 2014.

Crop and Food Supply Assessment Mission to the Democratic People's Republic of Korea, Special Report (Pyongyang, FAO/WFP, 6 December 1996).

Crop and Food Supply Assessment Mission to the Democratic People's Republic of Korea, Special Alert, No. 275 (Rome: FAO/WFP, 3 June 1997).

Crop and Food Supply Assessment Mission to the Democratic People's Republic of Korea (Rome: FAO/WFP, 25 June 1998).

Crop and Food Supply Assessment Mission to the Democratic People's Republic of Korea, Special Report (Rome: FAO/WFP, 12 November 1998).

Crop and Food Supply Assessment Mission to the Democratic People's Republic of Korea, Special Report (Rome: FAO/WFP, 29 June 1999).

Democratic People's Republic of Korea Joint WFP/FAO Rapid Food Security Assessment Mission (Rome: FAO/WFP, 9–30 June 2008).

Crop and Food Supply Assessment Mission to the Democratic People's Republic of Korea, Special Report (Rome: FAO/WFP, 8 December 2008).

Crop and Food Supply Assessment Mission to the Democratic People's Republic of Korea, Special Report (Rome: FAO/WFP, 16 November 2010).

Crop and Food Supply Assessment Mission to the Democratic People's Republic of Korea, Special Report (Rome: FAO/WFP, 12 November 2012).

Crop and Food Supply Assessment Mission to the Democratic People's Republic of Korea Special Report (Rome: FAO, 28 November 2013).

Feffer, John, 'Human Rights in North Korea and the US Strategy of Linkage', *The Asia-Pacific Journal: Japan Focus*, 6 January 2006, available at www.japanfocus.org/-John-Feffer/1805, accessed 8 November 2014.

'The Right to Food: North Korea and the Politics of Famine and Human Rights', in Kie-Duck Park and Sang-Jin Han, *Human Rights in North Korea* (Seoul: The Sejong Institute, 2007), pp. 67–115.

Fendler, Karoly, 'Economic Assistance from Socialist Countries to North Korea in the Postwar Years: 1953–1963', in Han S. Park (ed.), *North Korea: Ideology, Politics, Economy* (Englewood Cliffs: Prentice Hall, 1996), pp. 161–73.

Fisher, Max, 'The Cannibals of North Korea', *The Washington Post*, 5 February 2013, available at www.washingtonpost.com/blogs/worldviews/wp/2013/02/05/the-cannibals-of-north-korea, accessed 13 September 2013.

Foreign Languages Publishing House, *Korean Paintings of Today* (Pyongyang: Foreign Languages Publishing House, 1980).

The Socialist Labour Law of the Democratic People's Republic of Korea, 18 April 1978 (Pyongyang: Foreign Languages Publishing House, 1986).

The Public Health Law of the Democratic People's Republic of Korea, 3 April 1980 (Pyongyang: Foreign Languages Publishing House, 1988).

100 Questions and Answers: Do you Know about Korea? (Pyongyang: Foreign Languages Publishing House, 1989).

Do you Know about Korea? Questions and Answers (Pyongyang: Foreign Languages Publishing House, 1989).

Korea Guidebook (Pyongyang: Foreign Languages Publishing House, 1989).

Mt. Kumgang (Pyongyang, Foreign Languages Publishing House, undated, probably 1990).

Intellectuals should Become Fighters True to the Party and the Socialist Cause: Report to the Conference of Korean Intellectuals (Pyongyang: Foreign Languages Publishing House, 1992).

Socialist Constitution of The Democratic People's Republic of Korea (Pyongyang: Foreign Languages Publishing House, 1993).

The Family Law of the Democratic People's Republic of Korea, 24 October 1990 (Pyongyang: Foreign Languages Publishing House, 1994).

The Family Law of the Democratic People's Republic of Korea (Pyongyang: Foreign Languages Publishing House, 1996).

Funabashi, Yoichi, *The Peninsula Question: A Chronicle of the Second Korean Nuclear Crisis* (Washington, DC: Brookings Institution Press, 2007).

Gause, Ken E., *North Korean Civil-Military Trends: Military-First Politics to a Point* (Carlisle, PA: Strategic Studies Institute, US Army War College, 2006), unpaginated but pp. 59–110 on pdf; available at www.nkeconwatch.com/nk-uploads/dprkpolicyelites.pdf, accessed 2 November 2014.

Gladstone, Rick and Sanger, David E., 'Panama Seizes Korean Ship, and Sugar-Coated Arms Parts', *The New York Times*, 16 July 2013, available at www.nytimes.com/2013/07/17/world/americas/panama-seizes-north-korea-flagged-ship-for-weapons.html?pagewanted=all, accessed 15 September 2013.

Goedde, Patricia, 'Law of "Our Own Style": The Evolution and Challenges of the North Korean Legal System', *Fordham International Law Journal*, Vol. 27, 2003–4, pp. 1265–88.

Gomà, Daniel, 'The Chinese-Korean Border Issue', *Asian Survey*, Vol. 46, No. 6, 2006, pp. 867–80.

Goodkind, Daniel and West, Loraine, 'The North Korean Famine and its Demographic Impact', *Population and Development Review*, Vol. 27, No. 2, June 2001, pp. 219–38.

Goodkind, Daniel, West, Loraine and Johnson, Peter, 'A Reassessment of Mortality in North Korea, 1993–2008', Annual Meeting of the Population Association of America, 31 March–2 April 2011, Washington, DC, 16 March 2011.

Gottingen, Johannes Reckel, *Korea and Manchuria: The Historical Links between Korea and the Ancestors of the Modern Manchus* (Seoul: The Royal Asiatic Society – Korea Branch, 8 November 2000), available at www.raskb.com/transactions/VOL76/VOL76.docx, accessed 18 January 2013.

Government Accountability Office, *Nonproliferation: US Agencies have Taken Some Steps, but More Effort is Needed to Strengthen and Expand the Proliferation Security Initiative, GAO-09-43* (Washington, DC: Government Accountability Office, November 2008).

Grajdanzev, Andrew J., *Modern Korea* (New York: Institute of Pacific Relations/ The John Day Company, 1944).

Granot, 'Oded, 'Background on North Korea-Iran Missile Deal', *MA'ARIV*, 14 April 1996, translated by US FBIS from Hebrew and reproduced online at www.fas.org/news/israel/tac95037.htm, accessed 8 November 2014.

Grayson, James Huntley, *Korea – A Religious History* (Abingdon: RoutledgeCurzon, 2002).

Grinker, Roy Richard, *Korea and its Futures: Unification and the Unfinished War* (London: Macmillan, 1998).

Haboush, Jahyun Kim (trans. and ed.), *The Memoirs of Lady Hyegyŏng* (Berkeley: University of California Press, 1996).

Haboush, Jahyun Kim and Deuchler, Martina (eds.), *Culture and State in Late Chosŏn Korea* (Cambridge: Harvard University Press, 1999).

Haggard, Stephan and Noland, Marcus, *Famine in North Korea: Markets, Aid and Reform* (New York: Columbia University Press, 2007).

Witness to Transformation: Refugee Insights into North Korea (Washington, DC: Peterson Institute for International Economics, 2011).

Halliday, Fred, *The Making of the Second Cold War*, second edition (London: Verso, 1986).

Cold War, Third World: An Essay on Soviet–American Relations (London: Hutchinson Radius, 1989).

Revolution and World Politics: the Rise and Fall of the Sixth Great Power (London: Macmillan, 1999).

Halliday, Jon, 'The North Korean Enigma', in Gordon White, Robin Murray and Christine White (eds.), *Revolutionary Socialist Development in the Third World* (Lexington: University Press of Kentucky, 1983).

'Anti-Communism and the Korean War (1950–1953)', *Socialist Register 1984: The Uses of Anti-Communism*, Vol. 21, pp. 130–63, available at http:// socialistregister.com/index.php/srv/article/view/5509/2407, accessed 8 November 2014.

'Women in North Korea: An Interview with the Korean Democratic Women's Union', *Bulletin of Concerned Asian Scholars*, Vol. 17, No. 3, Jul–Sep 1985, pp. 46–56, available at http://criticalasianstudies.org/assets/files/bcas/ v17n03.pdf, accessed 3 November 2014.

Halliday, Jon and Cumings, Bruce, *Korea: The Unknown War* (New York: Pantheon Books, 1988).

Han, Chungnim Choi, 'Social Organization of Upper Han Hamlet in Korea', doctoral dissertation (University of Michigan, June 1949).

Han, In Sup, 'The 2004 Revision of Criminal Law in North Korea: A Take-off?', *Santa Clara Journal of International Law*, Vol. 5, No. 1, 2006, pp. 122–33.

Hanley, Charles J., Choe, Sang-Hun, and Mendoza, Martha, *The Bridge at No Gun Ri* (New York: Henry Holt and Company, 2001).

Harrold, Michael, *Comrades and Strangers: Behind the Closed Doors of North Korea* (Chichester: John Wiley and Sons, 2004).

Hastings, Max, *The Korean War* (London: Michael Joseph, 1987).

Hawk, David R., *The Hidden Gulag: Exposing North Korea's Prison Camps: Prisoners' Testimonies and Satellite Photographs* (Washington, DC: US Committee for Human Rights in North Korea, 2003), available at www. hrnk.org/uploads/pdfs/The_Hidden_Gulag.pdf, accessed 8 November 2014.

Hawkins, Harry, 'Starving North Koreans are "Forced to Eat their Children"', *The Sun*, 28 January 2013, available at www.thesun.co.uk/sol/homepage/news/4765653/north-korean-parents-eating-their-children.html, accessed 17 July 2013.

He, Jiangcheng, 'Educational Reforms', in Han S. Park (ed.), *North Korea: Ideology, Politics, Economy* (Englewood Cliffs: Prentice Hall, 1996), pp. 33–50.

Helgesen, Geir and Christensen, Nis Høyrup, *North Korea 2007: Assisting Development and Change* (Copenhagen: Nordic Institute of Asian Studies 2007).

Hicks, George, *The Comfort Women: Japan's Brutal Regime of Enforced Prostitution in the Second World War* (New York: W. W. Norton and Company, 1997).

Ho, Jong Ho, Kang, Sok Hui, and Pak, Thae Ho, *The US Imperialists Started the Korean War* (Pyongyang: Foreign Languages Publishing House, 1993).

Hoare, J. E. and Pares, Susan, *North Korea in the 21st Century: An Interpretative Guide* (Folkestone: Global Oriental, 2005).

Hodgson, Geoffrey M., 'What Are Institutions?', *Journal of Economic Issues*, Vol. 40, No. 1, March 2006, pp. 1–25.

Hong, Christine and Smith, Hazel (eds.), *Critical Asian Studies*, Vol. 45, No 4, December 2013.

Critical Asian Studies, Vol. 46, No 1, March 2014.

Hong, Ihk-pyo, 'A Shift toward Capitalism? Recent Economic Reforms in North Korea', *East Asian Review*, Vol. 14, No. 4, Winter 2002, pp. 93–106.

Hong, Sun Won, *Analysis of 1993 Population Census Data DPR Korea* (Pyongyang: Population Center, 1996).

Howard, Keith, '*Juche* and Culture: What's New?', in Hazel Smith, Chris Rhodes, Diana Pritchard and Kevin Magill (eds.), *North Korea in the New World Order* (London: Macmillan Press, 1996), pp. 169–95.

Huh, Moon-Young, (ed.), *Basic Reading on Korean Unification* (Seoul: Korea Institute for National Unification, 2012).

Human Rights Council, 'National Report Submitted in Accordance with Paragraph 15 (A) of the Annex to Human Rights Council Resolution 5/1: Democratic People's Republic of Korea', Geneva, 30 November–11 December 2009.

'Report of the Special Rapporteur on the Situation of Human Rights in the Democratic People's Republic of Korea, A/HRC/19/65', in *Human Rights Council, Nineteenth Session, Agenda Item 4, Human Rights Situations that Require the Council's Attention* (Geneva: Human Rights Council, 13 February 2012).

'Report of the Special Rapporteur on the Situation of Human Rights in the Democratic People's Republic of Korea, Marzuki Darusman, A/HRC/22/57', in Human Rights Council, *Twenty-second Session, Agenda Item 4, Human Rights Situations that Require the Council's Attention* (Geneva: Human Rights Council, 1 February 2013).

'Situation of Human Rights in the Democratic People's Republic of Korea', in
    Human Rights Council, *Twenty-second Session, Agenda Item 4, Human Rights
    Situations that Require the Council's Attention* (Geneva: Human Rights
    Council, 9 April 2013).
Human Rights Watch, 'The Invisible Exodus: North Koreans in the People's
    Republic of China', *North Korea*, Vol. 145, No. 8, November 2002,
    pp. 1–37.
Hunter, Helen-Louise, *Kim Il Song's North Korea* (Westport: Praeger, 1999).
Hwang, Kyung Moon, 'From the Dirt to Heaven: Northern Korea in the Chosŏn
    and Early Modern Eras', *Harvard Journal of Asiatic Studies*, Vol. 62, No. 1,
    June 2002, pp. 135–78.
Beyond Birth: Social Status in the Emergence of Modern Korea (Cambridge,
    MA: Harvard University Asia Center, 2004).
'Citizenship, Social Equality and Government Reform: Changes in the
    Household Registration System in Korea, 1894–1910', *Modern Asian
    Studies*, Vol. 38, No. 2, 2004, pp. 355–87.
'Nation, State and the Modern Transformation of Korean Social Structure in
    the Early Twentieth Century', *History Compass*, Vol. 5, No. 2, 2007,
    pp. 330–46.
Hyder, Masood, 'The Status of Women in the DPRK' (Pyongyang: UN Office
    for the Coordination of Humanitarian Affairs, UNOCHA, 5 September
    2003), available at http://reliefweb.int/report/democratic-peoples-republic-
    korea/status-women-dprk, accessed 8 November 2014.
International Atomic Energy Agency (IAEA), *Fact Sheet on DPRK Nuclear
    Safeguards* (Vienna: IAEA, undated), available at www.iaea.org/newscenter/
    focus/iaeadprk/fact_sheet_may2003.shtml, accessed 4 January 2014.
International Fund for Agricultural Development (IFAD), *Upland Food Security
    Project, Report of Interim Evaluation Mission Agricultural Component*
    (Pyongyang: IFAD, April 2008).
Enabling Poor Rural People to Overcome Poverty in Vietnam (Rome: IFAD,
    2010), available at www.ifad.org/operations/projects/regions/Pi/factsheets/
    vn.pdf, accessed 8 November 2014.
International Institute of Strategic Studies (IISS), *The Military Balance
    2001–2002* (Oxford University Press, 2001).
The Military Balance 2011 (London: Routledge, 2011).
Jenkins, Charles Robert with Frederick, Jim, *The Reluctant Communist:
    My Desertion, Court-martial and Forty-year Imprisonment in North Korea*
    (Berkeley: University of California Press, 2008).
Jeung, Young-Tai, *North Korea's Civil-Military-Party Relations and Regime
    Stability* (Seoul: Korea Institute for National Unification, 2007).
Internal and External Perceptions of the North Korean Army (Seoul: Korea
    Institute for National Unification, 2008).
Jin, Wenhua, 'Sounds of Chinese Korean: A Variationist Approach', doctoral
    dissertation (University of Texas at Arlington, May 2008).
Jon, Chol Nam, *A Duel of Reason between Korea and US: Nuke, Missile
    and Artificial Satellite* (Pyongyang: Foreign Languages Publishing House,
    2000).

Jones, Gary L., *Nuclear Nonproliferation: Heavy Fuel Oil Delivered to North Korea under the Agreed Framework, GAO/T-RCED-00–20* (Washington, DC: General Accounting Office, 1999), available at http://gao.gov/assets/110/108176.pdf, accessed 24 September 2012.

Jong, Son Yong, 'The Korea Nation – A Homogeneous Nation Whose Founding Father Is Tangun', in DPRK Academy of Sciences (ed.), *Tangun: Founder-King of Korea* (Pyongyang: Foreign Languages Publishing House, 1994), pp. 132–40.

Joo, Hyung-min, 'Visualizing the Invisible Hands: The Shadow Economy in North Korea', *Economy and Society*, Vol. 39, No. 1, February 2010, pp. 110–45.

Ju, Kwang Il and Jong, Song Ui, *Korea's Tourist Map* (Pyongyang: Korea International Travel Company, 1995).

Jung, Jin-Heon, *State and Church in the Making of Post-division Subjectivity: North Korean Migrants in South Korea, MMG Working Paper 11–12* (Göttingen: Max Planck Institute for the Study of Religious and Ethnic Diversity, 2011).

Jung, Kyungja and Dalton, Bronwen, 'Rhetoric Versus Reality for the Women of North Korea: Mothers of the Revolution', *Asian Survey*, Vol. 46, No. 5 September/October 2006, pp. 741–60.

Kagan, Richard, Oh, Matthew and Weissbrodt, David, *Human Rights in the Democratic People's Republic of Korea* (Minneapolis/Washington, DC: Minnesota Lawyers International Human Rights Committee/Asia Watch, 1988).

Kallander, George L., *Salvation through Dissent: Tonghak Heterodoxy and Early Modern Korea* (Honolulu: University of Hawai'i Press, 2013).

Kan, Paul Rexton, Bechtol, Bruce E., Jr. and Collins, Robert M., *Criminal Sovereignty: Understanding North Korea's Illicit International Activities* (Carlisle, PA: US Army War College, 2010), available at www.strategicstudiesinstitute.army.mil/pdffiles/pub975.pdf, accessed 2 November 2014.

Kang, Chol-Hwan and Rigoulot, Pierre, translated by Yair Reiner, *Aquariums of Pyongyang: Ten Years in the North Korean Gulag* (New York: Basic Books, 2001).

Kang, Jin Woong, 'The Patriarchal State and Women's Status in Socialist North Korea', *Graduate Journal of Asia-Pacific Studies*, Vol. 6, No. 2, 2008, pp. 55–70, available at https://cdn.auckland.ac.nz/assets/arts/Departments/asian-studies/gjaps/docs-vol6-no2/Kang-vol6.pdf, accessed 8 November 2014.

Keck, Zachary, 'Eyeing Pipeline, Russia Forgives North Korean Debt', *The Diplomat*, 22 April 2014, available at http://thediplomat.com/2014/04/eyeing-pipeline-russia-forgives-north-korean-debt, accessed 27 April 2014.

Kerry, John, *Executive Session, Nomination of Christopher R. Hill to be Ambassador to Iraq, Congressional Record – Senate Vol. 155 Pr. 8* (Washington, DC: Congressional Record, Proceedings and Debates of the 111th Congress, First Session, 2012).

Khan, Dilawar Ali, *Improving the Quality of Basic Social Services for the Most Vulnerable Children and Women: Executive Summary* (Pyongyang: UNICEF, April 2001).

Kim, Byung-Yeon, 'Markets, Bribery, and Regime Stability in North Korea', working paper (Seoul: East Asia Institute Asia, April 2004), available at www.eai.or.kr/data/bbs/eng_report/2010040811122565.pdf, accessed 8 November 2014.

Kim, Byung-Yeon and Song, Dongho, 'The Participation of North Korean Households in the Informal Economy: Size, Determinants, and Effect', *Seoul Journal of Economics*, Vol. 21, No. 2, Summer 2008, pp. 361–85.

Kim, Chang Su, *DPR Korea 2008 Population Census National Report* (Pyongyang: Central Bureau of Statistics Pyongyang, 2009).

Kim, Chol U, *Songun Politics of Kim Jong Il* (Pyongyang: Foreign Languages Publishing House, 2008).

Kim, Chun Gun, 'Principles in Songun Revolution', *The Pyongyang Times*, 1 October 2011.

Kim, Han Gil, *Modern History of Korea* (Pyongyang: Foreign Languages Publishing House, 1979).

Kim, Il Sung, *On Improving and Strengthening the Training of Party Cadres* (Pyongyang: Foreign Languages Publishing House, 1975).

On the Three Principles of National Reunification (Pyongyang: Foreign Languages Publishing House, 1982).

Tasks of the People's Government in Modelling the Whole of Society on the Juche Idea (Pyongyang: Foreign Languages Publishing House, 1982).

'On Some Problems in Party Work and Economic Affairs', in Kim Il Sung, *Works, Vol. 23, October 1968–May 1969* (Pyongyang: Foreign Languages Publishing House, 1985), pp. 255–92.

Historical Experience of Building the Workers' Party of Korea (Pyongyang: Foreign Languages Publishing House, 1986).

The Non-Aligned Movement is a Mighty Anti-imperialist Revolutionary Force of our Times (Pyongyang: Foreign Languages Publishing House, 1986).

The Non-Aligned Movement and South–South Cooperation (Pyongyang: Foreign Languages Publishing House, 1987).

'Let us Further Develop Local Industry', in Kim Il Sung, *Works, Vol. 35* (Pyongyang: Foreign Languages Publishing House, 1989), pp. 159–69.

'Let us Implement the Public Health Law to the Letter', in Kim Il Sung, *Works, Vol. 35* (Pyongyang: Foreign Languages Publishing House, 1989), pp. 91–103.

'Let us Increase the Standard of Living of the People Through the Development of the Textile, Food and Consumer Goods Industries', in Kim Il Sung, *Works, Vol. 35* (Pyongyang: Foreign Languages Publishing House, 1989), pp. 77–90.

'On the Occasion of the 25th Anniversary of the Formation of the General Association of Korean Residents in Japan', in Kim Il Sung, *Works, Vol. 35* (Pyongyang: Foreign Languages Publishing House, 1989), pp. 136–9.

'On This Year's Experience in Farming and Next Year's Direction of Agricultural Work', in Kim Il Sung, *Works, Vol. 35* (Pyongyang: Foreign Languages Publishing House, 1989), pp. 232–68.

On the Proposal for Founding a Democratic Confederal Republic of Koryo
(Pyongyang: Foreign Languages Publishing House, 1990).

'The Role of Intellectuals in Building an Independent New Society', in Kim Il
Sung, *Works, Vol. 35* (Pyongyang: Foreign Languages Publishing House,
1990), pp. 222–31.

Works, Vol. 35 (Pyongyang: Foreign Languages Publishing House, 1990).

'Officials Must Become True Servants of the People', in Kim Il Sung,
Works, Vol. 44 (Pyongyang: Foreign Languages Publishing House, 1999),
pp. 19–33.

'On the Direction of Socialist Economic Construction for the Immediate
Period Ahead', in Kim Il Sung, *Works, Vol. 44* (Pyongyang: Foreign
Languages Publishing House, 1999), pp. 248–65.

Kim, Ilpyong J., 'China in North Korean Foreign Policy', in Samuel S. Kim,
North Korean Foreign Relations in the Post-Cold War Era (Oxford University
Press, 1998), pp. 742–67.

Kim, Jin-Ha, 'On the Threshold of Power, 2011/12 Pyongyang's Politics of
Transition', *International Journal of Korean Unification Studies*, Vol. 20,
No. 2, 2011, pp. 1–26.

Kim, Jin Wung, *A History of Korea: From 'Land of the Morning Calm' to States in
Conflict* (Bloomington: Indiana University Press, 2012).

Kim, Jong Il, *On the Juche Idea of our Party* (Pyongyang: Foreign Languages
Publishing House, 1985).

'Our Socialism for the People will not Perish', in Délégation générale de la
RPD de Corée en France, *Bulletin d'information, No. 10/591* (Paris:
Délégation générale de la RPD de Corée en France, 27 May 1991).

'Historical Lesson in Building Socialism and the General Line of our Party', in
Délégation générale de la RPD de Corée en France, *Bulletin d'information,
No. 02/0292* (Paris: Délégation générale de la RPD de Corée en France,
4 February 1992).

'Order of the Supreme Commander of the Korean People's Army', in
Délégation générale de la RPD de Corée en France, *Bulletin d'information,
No. 09/0393* (Paris: Délégation générale de la RPD de Corée en France,
8 March 1993).

'Respecting Seniors in the Revolution is a Noble Moral Obligation of
Revolutionaries', in Délégation générale de la RPD de Corée en France,
Bulletin d'information, Special Issue (Paris: Délégation générale de la RPD de
Corée en France, 27 December 1995).

'Let us Exalt the Brilliance of Comrade Kim Il Sung's Idea on the Youth
Movement and the Achievements Made under his Leadership', in
Délégation générale de la RPD de Corée en France, *Bulletin d'information,
Special Issue No. 23/0896* (Paris: Délégation générale de la RPD de Corée
en France, 31 August 1996).

*Let us Exalt the Brilliance of Comrade Kim Il Sung's Idea of the Youth Movement
and the Achievements Made under his Leadership* (Pyongyang: Foreign
Languages Publishing House, 1996).

'The Juche Philosophy is an Original Revolutionary Philosophy', *Kulloja*,
26 July 1996 (in English) (Paris: Délégation générale de la RPD de Corée en
France, 1996).

Kim, Jong Un, *Kim Jong Un Makes New Year Address* (Pyongyang: Korean
   Central News Agency, 1 January 2013), available at www.kcna.kp/goHome.
   do?lang=eng, accessed 3 January 2013.

Kim, Kook-shin, Cho, Hyun-joon, Lee, Keum-soon, Lim, Soon-hee, Lee,
   Kyu-chang and Hong, Woo-taek, *White Paper on Human Rights in North
   Korea 2011* (Seoul: Korea Institute for National Unification, 2011).

Kim, Kyu-won, 'North Korea Announces Education Reforms, Silent on
   Economy', *The Hankyoreh*, 26 September 2012, available at http://english.
   hani.co.kr/arti/english_edition/e_northkorea/553442.html, accessed
   27 February 2012.

Kim, Soo-am, *The North Korean Penal Code, Criminal Procedures, and their
   Actual Applications* (Seoul: Korea Institute for National Unification, 2006).

Kim, Soo-am, Kim, Kook-shin, Lim, Soon-hee, Chon, Hyun-joon, Lee,
   Kyu-chang and Cho, Jung-hyun, *White Paper on Human Rights in North
   Korea 2012* (Seoul: Korea Institute for National Unification, 2012).

Kim, Soo-am, Lee, Keum-Soon, Kim, Kook-Shin and Hong, Min, *Relations
   between Corruption and Human Rights in North Korea* (Seoul: Korea
   Institute for National Unification, 2013).

Kim, Sun Joo (ed.), *The Northern Region of Korea: History, Identity and Culture*
   (Seattle: University of Washington Press, 2010).

Kim, Sung Chull, *North Korea under Kim Jong Il: From Consolidation to Systemic
   Dissonance* (Albany: State University of New York Press, 2006).

Kim, Sung Ung (ed.), *Panorama of Korea* (Pyongyang: Foreign Languages
   Publishing House, 1999).

Kim, Suzy, 'Revolutionary Mothers: Women in the North Korean Revolution,
   1945–1950', *Comparative Studies in Society and History*, Vol. 52, No. 4, 2010,
   pp. 742–67.

   Everyday Life in the North Korean Revolution 1945-1950 (Ithaca, NY: Cornell
   University Press, 2013).

Kim, Woon-Keun, 'Recent Changes in North Korean Agriculture Policies and
   Projected Impacts on the Food Shortage', *East Asian Review*, Vol. 3, No. 3,
   Autumn 1999, pp. 93–110.

Kim, Young-Hoon, 'AREP Program and Inter-Korean Agricultural
   Cooperation', *East Asian Review*, Vol. 13, No. 4, Winter 2001,
   pp. 93–111, available at www.ieas.or.kr/vol13_4/13_4_6.pdf, accessed
   6 January 2014.

Kim, Young-Yoon, *Evaluation of South-North Economic Cooperation and Task for
   Success* (Seoul: Korea Institute for National Unification, 2005).

   A Study on the Reality and Prospect of Economic Reform in North Korea (Seoul:
   Korea Institute for National Unification, 2007).

Kim, Yung-Chung (ed.), *Women of Korea: A History from Ancient Times to 1945*
   (Seoul: Ewha Womans University Press, 1977).

King, Ross, 'Dialectical Variation in Korean', in Ho-Min Sohn (ed.), *Korean
   Language in Culture and Society* (Honolulu: University of Hawai'i Press,
   2006), pp. 264–80.

Koo, John H., 'Language', in John H. Koo and Andrew Nahm (eds.),
   An Introduction to Korean Culture (Elizabeth, NJ/Seoul: Hollym, 1997),
   pp. 99–117.

Koo, John H. and Nahm, Andrew (eds.), *An Introduction to Korean Culture* (Elizabeth, NJ; Seoul: Hollym, 1997).

Korea Institute for National Unification, *White Paper on Human Rights in North Korea 2007* (Seoul: Korea Institute for National Unification, 2007).

Korea Now, '80 Percent Post Profits in Inter-Korea Trade', *Korea Now*, Seoul, 24 August 2002.

'Peaceful Solutions First', *Korea Now*, 30 November 2002.

Korea Peninsula Energy Development Organization (KEDO), *Annual Report 2001* (New York: KEDO, 2001).

Korea Today, Editorial, 'Make this a Year of Brilliant Victory,' *Korea Today*, No. 3, 2004.

'*Chongmyong* and Related Customs', *Korea Today*, No. 4, 2011, p. 41.

'Songun Idea with Deep Roots', *Korea Today*, No. 4, 2011, pp. 24–5.

Korean Central News Agency (KCNA), 'On-the-spot Guidance of President Kim Il Sung', in Délégation générale de la RPD de Corée en France, *Bulletin d'information, No. 15/0493* (Paris: Délégation générale de la RPD de Corée en France, 7 April 1993).

'Kim Jong Un Inspects Command of KPA Unit 534', 12 January 2014, available at www.kcna.co.jp/index-e.htm, accessed 15 February 2014.

'Kim Jong Un Guides Night Exercise of KPA Paratroopers', 20 January 2014, available at www.kcna.co.jp/index-e.htm, accessed 15 February 2014.

'Kim Jong Un Guides Tactical Exercise of KPA Unit 323', 23 January 2014, available at www.kcna.co.jp/index-e.htm, accessed 15 February 2014.

Kuzio, Taras, 'Transition in Post-Communist States: Triple or Quadruple?', *Politics*, Vol. 21, Issue 3, 2001, pp. 168–77.

Kwon, Heonik and Chung, Byung-ho, *North Korea: Beyond Charismatic Politics* (Lanham: Rowman and Littlefield Publishers, 2012).

Kwon, Tae-Jin and Kim, Wook-Keun, 'Assessment of Food Supply in North Korea', *Journal of Rural Development*, Vol. 22, Winter 1999, pp. 47–66.

Kwon, Tae-Jin, Kim, Young-Hoon, Chung, Chung-Gil and Jeon, Hyoung-Jin, 'Research on North Korean Agriculture Development Planning: Executive Summary', undated but probably 2002.

Kwon, Tai-Hwan, 'Population Change and Development in Korea', *The Asia Society*, available at http://asiasociety.org/countries/population-change-and-development-korea, accessed 30 May 2014.

Lankov, Andrei, *North of the DMZ: Essays on Daily Life in North Korea* (Jefferson, MO: McFarland, 2007).

'North Korea in Transition: Changes in Internal Politics and the Logic of Survival', *International Journal of Korean Unification Studies*, Vol. 18, No. 1, 2009, pp. 1–27.

'Narco-Capitalism Grips North Korea', *Asia Times*, 18 March 2011, available at www.atimes.com/atimes/Korea/MC18Dg02.html, accessed 13 September 2013.

'North Korea: The Logic of Survival', in Christoph Bluth and Hazel Smith (eds.), 'North Korea at the Crossroad', *Journal of International and Strategic Studies*, No. 5, 2012, pp. 8–12, available at http://ceris.be/fileadmin/library/Publications/Journal-N5-E.pdf, accessed 2 November 2014.

The Real North Korea: Life and Politics in the Failed Stalinist Utopia (Oxford University Press, 2013).

Lankov, Andrei and Kim, Seok-hyang, 'North Korean Market Vendors: The Rise of Grassroots Capitalists in a Post-Stalinist Society', *Pacific Affairs*, Vol. 81, No. 1, Spring 2008, pp. 53–72.

Larsen, Kirk W., *Tradition, Treaties, and Trade: Qing Imperialism and Chosŏn Korea, 1850–1910* (Cambridge, MA: Harvard University Press, 2008).

Lee, Chae-Jin, *A Troubled Peace: US Policy and the Two Koreas* (Baltimore, MD: The Johns Hopkins University Press, 2006).

Lee, Chong-Sik, *The Korean Workers' Party: A Short History* (Stanford, CA: Hoover Institution Press, 1978).

Lee, Chulwoo, 'Modernity, Legality, and Power in Korea under Japanese Rule', in Gi-Wook Shin and Michael Robinson (eds.), *Colonial Modernity in Korea* (Cambridge, MA: Harvard University Press, 1999), pp. 21–51.

Lee, Dongmin, 'The Role of the North Korean Military in the Power-Transition Period', Background Paper Series 04 (Seoul: Ilmin International Relations Institute, July 2011).

Lee, Eun-Jung, 'Family Law and Inheritance Law in North Korea', *Journal of Korean Law*, Vol. 5, No. 1, 2005, pp. 172–93.

Lee, Hy-Sang, *North Korea: A Strange Socialist Fortress* (London: Praeger, 2001).

Lee, Jung-Chul, 'The Pseudo-Market Coordination Regime', in Phillip H. Park (ed.), *The Dynamics of Change in North Korea: An Institutionalist Perspective* (Boulder, CO: Lynne Rienner Publishers, 2009), pp. 181–213.

Lee, Kyo-Duk, Lee, Soon-Hee, Cho, Jeong-Ah and Song, Joung-Ho, *Study on the Power Elite of the Kim Jong Un Regime* (Seoul: Korea Institute for National Unification, 2013).

Lee, Kyo-Duk, Lim, Soon-Hee, Cho, Jeong-Ah, Lee, Gee-Dong and Lee, Young-Hoon, *Changes in North Korea as Revealed in the Testimonies of Saetomins* (Seoul: Korea Institute for National Unification, 2008).

Lee, Mun Woong, 'Rural North Korea under Communism: A Study of Sociocultural Change', doctoral dissertation (Houston: Rice University, 1975).

Lee, Peter W. and de Bary, Theodore Wm., *Sources of Korean Tradition Volume One: From Early Times Through the Sixteenth Century* (New York: Columbia University Press, 1997).

Lee, Soon-ho, 'Military Transformation on the Korean Peninsula: Technology versus Geography', doctoral dissertation (Department of Politics and International Studies, The University of Hull, 2011), available at https://hydra.hull.ac.uk/catalog/hull:5360, accessed 15 September 2013.

Lee, Suk, 'Food Shortages and Economic Institutions in the Democratic People's Republic of Korea', doctoral dissertation (Department of Economics, University of Warwick, January 2003).

Lee, Woo Young and Seo, Jungmin, '"Cultural Pollution" from the South?', in Kyung-Ae Park and Scott Snyder (eds.), *North Korea in Transition:*

Politics, Economy and Society (Lanham: Rowman and Littlefield, 2013), pp. 195–207.

Leipziger, Danny M., 'Thinking about the World Bank and North Korea', in Marcus Noland (ed.), *Economic Integration of the Korean Peninsula* (Washington, DC: Institute for International Economics, 1998), pp. 201–19.

Lerner, Mitchell B., *The Pueblo Incident: A Spy Ship and the Failure of American Foreign Policy* (Lawrence, KS: University Press of Kansas, 2002).

Li, Yong-Bok, *Education in the Democratic People's Republic of Korea* (Pyongyang: Foreign Languages Publishing House, 1986).

Lim, Dong-won, *Peacemaker: Twenty Years of Inter-Korean Relations and the North Korean Nuclear Issue* (Stanford, CA: Walter H. Shorenstein Asia-Pacific Research Center, 2012).

Lim, Kang-Taeg and Lim, Sung-Hoon, *Strategies for Development of a North Korean Special Economic Zone through Attracting Foreign Investment* (Seoul: Korea Institute for National Unification, 2005).

Lim, Phillip Wonhyuk, 'North Korea's Food Crisis', *Korea and World Affairs*, Winter 1997, pp. 568–85.

Lim, Soo-ho, 'North Korea's Currency Reform a Failure?', *SERI Quarterly*, April 2010, pp. 115–19.

Lim, Soon-Hee, *The Food Crisis and Life of Women in North Korea* (Seoul: Korea Institute for National Unification, 2005).

Value Changes of the North Korean New Generation and Prospects (Seoul: Korea Institute for National Unification, 2007).

Litwak, Robert S., *Rogue States and US Foreign Policy: Containment after the Cold War* (Washington, DC: Woodrow Wilson Center Press, 2000).

Outlier States: American Strategies to Change, Contain, or Engage Regimes (Washington, DC: Woodrow Wilson Center Press/Johns Hopkins University Press, 2012).

MacDonald, Callum, *Britain and the Korean War* (Oxford: Basil Blackwell, 1990).

'The Democratic People's Republic of Korea: An Historical Survey', in Hazel Smith, Chris Rhodes, Diana Pritchard and Kevin Magill (eds.), *North Korea in the New World Order* (London: Macmillan Press, 1996), pp. 1–16.

Mansourov, Alexandre Y., 'Inside North Korea's Black Box: Reversing the Optics', in Kongdan Oh and Ralph Hassig (eds.), *North Korean Policy Elites* (Alexandria, VA: Institute for Defense Analyses, 2004), unpaginated but pp. 159–226 on pdf, available at www.nkeconwatch.com/nk-uploads/dprkpolicyelites.pdf, accessed 2 November 2014.

'North Korea Stressed: Life on the Hamster Wheel', *International Journal of Korean Unification Studies*, Vol. 14, No. 2, 2005, pp. 85–114.

Manyin, Mark, *Foreign Assistance to North Korea* (Washington, DC: Congressional Research Service, 26 May 2005), available at www.au.af.mil/au/awc/awcgate/crs/rl31785.pdf, accessed 5 November 2012.

US Assistance to North Korea: Fact Sheet (Washington, DC: Congressional Research Service, 2005), updated 11 October 2006, available at http://assets.opencrs.com/rpts/RS21834_20061011.pdf, accessed 7 June 2012.

North Korea: Back on the Terrorism List? (Washington, DC: Congressional Research Service, 29 June 2010), available at www.fas.org/sgp/crs/row/RL30613.pdf, accessed 15 September 2013.

Manyin, Mark and Jun, Ryun, 'US Assistance to North Korea: Fact Sheet', CRS Report for Congress (Washington, DC: Congressional Research Service, 17 March 2003).

Manyin, Mark and Nikitin, Mary Beth, *Foreign Assistance to North Korea* (Washington, DC: Congressional Research Service, 2012), available at www.fas.org/sgp/crs/row/R40095.pdf, accessed 24 September 2012.

Margesson, Rhoda, Chanlett-Avery, Emma and Bruno, Andorra, *North Korean Refugees in China and Human Rights Issues: International Response and US Policy Options* (Washington, DC: Congressional Research Service, 2007), available at www.dtic.mil/cgi-bin/GetTRDoc?Location=U2&doc=GetTRDoc.pdf&AD=ADA473619, accessed 6 November 2012.

Martin, Bradley, 'The Koreas: Pyongyang Watch: The Riot Act?', *Asia Times Online*, 3 November 1999, available at www.atimes.com/koreas/AK03Dg01.html, accessed 15 December 2014.

Under the Loving Care of the Fatherly Leader: North Korea and the Kim Dynasty (New York: St. Martin's Press, 2006).

Matsusaka, Yoshihisa Tak, *The Making of Japanese Manchuria, 1904–1932* (Cambridge, MA: Harvard University Asia Center, 2003).

McCarthy, Thomas F., 'Managing Development Assistance in the DPRK', in E. Kwan Choi, E. Han Kim and Yesook Merrill (eds.), *North Korea in the World Economy* (London: RoutledegeCurzon, 2003), pp. 74–9.

McCormack, Gavan, 'Japan and North Korea – The Quest for Normalcy', in Hazel Smith (ed.), *Reconstituting Korean Security: A Policy Primer* (Tokyo: United Nations Press, 2007), pp. 162–81.

McCune, Shannon, 'Geographic Regions in Korea', *Geographical Review*, Vol. 39, No. 4, 1949, pp. 658–60.

McEachearn, Patrick, 'Inside the Red Box: North Korea's Post-Totalitarian Politics', doctoral dissertation (Louisiana State University and Agricultural and Mechanical College, May 2009).

Inside the Red Box: North Korea's Post Totalitarian Politics (New York: Columbia University Press, 2010).

McGowen, Tom, *The Korean War* (New York: Franklin Watts, 1992).

McGreal, Chris and Branigan, Tania, 'North Korea Pledges to Halt Nuclear Programme in Exchange for US Aid', *The Guardian*, 29 February 2012, available at www.guardian.co.uk/world/2012/feb/29/north-korea-moratorium-nuclear-programme, accessed 7 June 2012.

McKenzie, F. A., *Korea's Fight for Freedom* (New York: Fleming H. Revell Company, 1920).

Melman, Yossi, 'How the Mossad Killed a Deal with Kim Il-sung', *Haaretz*, 27 June 2006, available at www.haaretz.com/print-edition/features/how-the-mossad-killed-a-deal-with-kim-il-sung-1.191489, accessed 8 November 2014.

Michell, Anthony R., 'The Current North Korean Economy', in Marcus
Noland (ed.), *Economic Integration of the Korean Peninsula* (Washington, DC:
Institute for International Economics, 1998), pp. 137–63.

Michishita, Narushige, *North Korea's Military-Diplomatic Campaigns, 1966–2008*
(London: Routledge, 2010).

Mikheev, Vasily, 'Politics and Ideology in the post-Cold war era', in Han S. Park
(ed.), *North Korea: Ideology, Politics, Economy* (Englewood Cliffs: Prentice
Hall, 1996), pp. 87–104.

Miles, Tom and Nebehay, Stephanie, 'China Rejects N. Korean Crimes Report,
Hits Chance of Prosecution', *Reuters*, 17 March 2014, available at http://in.
reuters.com/article/2014/03/17/korea-north-un-
idINDEEA2G07N20140317, accessed 11 May 2014.

Min, Moosuk and Ahn, Jehee, *A Study of Education for Women in North Korea*
(Seoul: Korea Women's Development Institute, 2001), available at www.
kwdi.re.kr/data/02forum-4.pdf, accessed 22 June 2014.

Ministry of Atomic Energy of the Democratic People's Republic of Korea,
'Detailed report of the Ministry of Atomic Energy of the Democratic
People's Republic of Korea on Problems in Implementation of
Safeguards Agreement, Pyongyang, 21 February 1993', in Délégation
générale de la RPD de Corée en France, *Bulletin d'information, No. 05/0293*
(Paris: Délégation générale de la RPD de Corée en France, 22 February
1993).

Ministry of Defense, *2010 White Paper* (Seoul: Ministry of Defense, 2010),
available at www.nti.org/media/pdfs/2010WhitePaperAll_eng.pdf?_=
1340662780, accessed 8 November 2014.

Moltz, James Clay, 'The Renewal of Russian-North Korean Relations', in
James Clay Moltz and Alexandre Y. Mansourov (eds.), *The North Korean
Nuclear Program: Security, Strategy and New Perspectives from Russia*
(London: Routledge, 2000), pp. 197–209.

Moltz, James Clay and Mansourov, Alexandre Y. (eds.), *The North Korean
Nuclear Program: Security, Strategy and New Perspectives from Russia*
(New York: Routledge, 2000).

Moon, Chung-in, *The Sunshine Policy: In Defense of Engagement as a Path to
Peace in Korea* (Seoul: Yonsei University Press, 2012).

Moon, Chung-in and Lee, Sangkeun, 'Military Spending and the Arms
Race on the Korean Peninsula', *Asian Perspective*, Vol. 33, No. 4, 2009,
pp. 69–99.

Morris-Suzuki, Tessa, *Exodus to North Korea: Shadows from Japan's Cold War*
(Lanham: Rowman and Littlefield Publishers, 2007).

Myers, Ramon H. and Peattie, Mark R. (eds.), *The Japanese Colonial Empire,
1895–1945* (Princeton University Press, 1984).

Nahm, Andrew, *An Introduction to Korean History and Culture* (Elizabeth, NJ/
Seoul: Hollym, 1993).

Korea: Tradition and Transformation (Elizabeth, NJ/Seoul: Hollym, 1996).

'History: Pre-modern Korea', in John H. Koo and Andrew Nahm (eds.),
An Introduction to Korean Culture (Elizabeth, NJ/Seoul: Hollym, 1997),
pp. 53–72.

Introduction to Korean History and Culture (Elizabeth, NJ/Seoul: Hollym, 1997).

Nanchu with Hang, Xing, *In North Korea: An American Travels through an Imprisoned Nation* (London: McFarland and Company, 2003).

Nanto, Dick K. and Manyin, Mark E., *The Kaesong North-South Korean Industrial Complex* (Washington, DC: Congressional Research Service, 17 March 2011).

NAPSNet Daily Report, 2 November 1999.

Nathanail, Lola, *Food and Nutrition Assessment Democratic People's Republic of Korea, 16 March–24 April 1996* (Pyongyang: World Food Programme, 1996).

National EFA 2000 Assessment Group, *Democratic People's Republic of Korea, National EFA Assessment Report: The Implementation of the 'World Declaration on Education for All'* (Pyongyang: National EFA 2000 Assessment Group, 1999).

Natsios, Andrew S., *The Great North Korean Famine: Famine, Politics and Foreign Policy* (Washington, DC: United States Institute of Peace Press, 2001).

Nelson, Christine M., '"Opening" Pandora's Box: The Status of the Diplomatic Bag in International Relations', *Fordham International Law Journal*, Vol. 12, Issue 3, 1988, pp. 494–520.

New Focus International, 'Education in North Korea is a Lucrative Industry', *New Focus International*, 7 June 2013, available at http://newfocusintl.com/education-in-north-korea, accessed 7 February 2014.

'Insider Perspective: The Removal of Jang Song Taek (Update)' *New Focus International*, 9 December 2013, available at http://newfocusintl.com/insider-perspective-the-removal-of-jang-song-taek-update, accessed 14 January 2014.

'We have Just Witnessed a Coup in North Korea', *New Focus International*, 27 December 2013, available at http://newfocusintl.com/just-witnessed-coup-north-korea, accessed 14 January 2012.

'This is it: North Korea's Hidden Power System', *New Focus International*, 31 December 2013, available at http://newfocusintl.com/north-koreas-hidden-power-system/#comments, accessed 15 January 2014.

'Exclusive: in Conversation with North Korea's Highest-ranking Military Defector', *New Focus International*, 4 January 2014, available at http://newfocusintl.com/exclusive-conversation-north-koreas-highest-ranking-military-defector, accessed 23 January 2014.

Niksch, Larry A., *North Korea's Nuclear Weapons Development and Diplomacy* (Washington, DC: Congressional Research Service, 5 January 2010), available at www.fas.org/sgp/crs/nuke/RL33590.pdf, accessed 12 September 2013.

Nixson, Frederick and Collins, Paul, 'Economic Reform in North Korea', in Hazel Smith, Chris Rhodes, Diana Pritchard and Kevin Magill. (eds.), *North Korea in the New World Order* (London: Macmillan Press, 1996), pp. 154–68.

No author, 'Phase II DRK/92/WOI/A, Rationalizing Cottage Industry in Pyongyang', mimeo, undated but probably 2000.

Noland, Marcus, 'Prospects for the North Korean Economy', in Dae-Sook
    Suh and Chae-Jin Lee (eds.), *North Korea after Kim Il Sung* (Boulder, CO:
    Lynne Rienner, 1998), pp. 34–45.
North Korea Advisory Group, *Report to The Speaker, US House of
    Representatives* (Washington, DC: House of Representatives, 1999), available
    at www.fas.org/nuke/guide/dprk/nkag-report.htm, accessed 8 November
    2014.
Norton, Rebecca and Wallace, Jane, *Refugee Nutrition Information System
    (RNIS), No. 22 – Supplement – Report on the Nutrition Situation in the
    Democratic People's Republic of Korea* (Geneva: United Nations
    Administrative Committee on Coordination Sub-Committee on
    Nutrition, 1997), available at www.unsystem.org/scn/archives/
    rnis22sup_nkorea/s5115e.10.htm#Js5115e.10, accessed 8 November
    2014.
O'Carroll, Chad, 'North Korean Cargo of Gas Masks and Arms en-route to
    Syria', *NK*NewsPro*, 27 August 2013, available at www.nknews.org/2013/
    08/north-korean-arms-shipment-intercepted-en-route-to-syria, accessed
    15 September 2013.
Oberdorfer, Don, *The Two Koreas: A Contemporary History* (London: Warner
    Books, 1997).
Office of Public Information of the Republic of Korea, 'Population Survey of
    Korea', *Korean Survey*, Vol. 6, No. 6, Jun–Jul 1957, p. 11.
Oh, Kongdan and Hassig, Ralph C., *North Korea Through the Looking Glass*
    (Washington, DC: Brookings Institution Press, 2000).
Oh, Soo-chang, 'Economic Growth in P'yŏngan Province and the
    Development of Pyongyang in the Late Chosŏn Period', *Korean Studies*,
    Vol. 30, 2006, pp. 3–22.
Page, Tim, 'Russia's Northeast Asian Priorities: Where does North Korea fit
    in?', in Christoph Bluth and Hazel Smith (eds.), 'North Korea at the
    Crossroad', *Journal of International and Strategic Studies*, No. 5, Spring 2012,
    pp. 37–45, available at http://ceris.be/fileadmin/library/Publications/Journal-
    N5-E.pdf, accessed 2 November 2014.
Pai, Hyung Il, *Constructing 'Korean' Origins: A Critical Review of Archaeology,
    Historiography, and Racial Myth in Korean State-Formation Theories*
    (Cambridge, MA: Harvard University, 2000).
Pak, Chang-gon, 'Conversion from a Colonial Agricultural State into a Socialist
    Industrial State', in Ken'ichiro Hirano (ed.), *The State and Cultural
    Transformation: Perspectives from East Asia* (Tokyo: United Nations Press,
    1993), pp. 299–314.
Palais, James B., 'A Search for Korean Uniqueness', *Harvard Journal of Asiatic
    Studies*, Vol. 55, No. 2, December 1995, pp. 409–25.
Pang, Hwan Ju, *Korean Review* (Pyongyang: Foreign Languages Publishing
    House, 1987).
    National Culture of Korea (Pyongyang: Foreign Languages Publishing House,
    1988).
    Korean Folk Customs (Pyongyang: Foreign Languages Publishing House,
    1990).

Park, Byung-Kwang, 'China–North Korea Economic Relations during the Hu Jintao Era', in *International Journal of Korean Unification Studies*, Vol. 19, No. 2, 2010, pp. 125–50.

Park, Han S. (ed.), *North Korea: Ideology, Politics, Economy* (Englewood Cliffs: Prentice Hall, 1996).

Park, Hyeon-Sun, 'A Study on the Family System of Modern North Korea', doctoral dissertation (Ewha Womans University, 1999).

Park, Hyeong-Jung and Lee, Kyo-Duk, *Continuities and Changes in the Power Structure and the Role of Party Organizations under Kim Jong Il's Reign* (Seoul: Korea Institute for National Unification, 2005).

Park, Hyun Ok, *Two Dreams in One Bed: Empire, Social Life and the Origins of the North Korean Revolution in Manchuria* (Durham: Duke University Press, 2005).

Park, John S., *North Korea, Inc.*, working paper (Washington, DC: United States Institute of Peace, 2009), available at www.usip.org/files/resources/North%20Korea,%20Inc.PDF, accessed 15 February 2013.

Park, Kie-Duck and Han, Sang-Jin (eds.), *Human Rights in North Korea* (Seoul: The Sejong Institute, 2007).

Park, Kyung Ae, 'Ideology and Women in North Korea', in Han S. Park (ed.), *North Korea: Ideology, Politics, Economy* (Englewood Cliffs: Prentice Hall, 1996), pp. 71–85.

'Economic Crisis, Women's Changing Economic Roles, and their Implications for Women's Status in North Korea', *The Pacific Review*, Vol. 24, No. 2, May 2011, pp. 159–77.

Park, Phillip H. (ed.), *The Dynamics of Change in North Korea: An Institutionalist Perspective* (Boulder, CO: Lynne Rienner Publishers, 2009).

Park, Soon-Won, 'Colonial Industrial Growth and the Emergence of the Korean Working Class', in Gi-Wook Shin and Michael Robinson (eds.), *Colonial Modernity in Korea* (Cambridge, MA; Harvard University Press, 1999), pp. 128–60.

Colonial Industrialization and Labor in Korea: The Onoda Cement Factory (London: Harvard University Press, 1999).

Party History Research Institute, *History of Revolutionary Activities of the Great Leader Comrade Kim Il Sung* (Pyongyang: Foreign Languages Publishing House, 1983).

Peh, Kelvin S-H., 'Wildlife Protection: Seize Diplomats Smuggling Ivory', *Nature*, Vol. 500, 15 August 2013, p. 276.

Perl, Raphael S., *Drug Trafficking and North Korea: Issues for US Policy* (Washington, DC: Congressional Research Service, 2003), available at http://fpc.state.gov/documents/organization/27529.pdf, accessed 14 December 2012.

Drug Trafficking and North Korea: Issues for US Policy (Washington, DC: Congressional Research Service, 2005), available at http://digital.library.unt.edu/ark:/67531/metacrs6479, accessed 14 December 2012.

Drug Trafficking and North Korea: Issues for US Policy (Washington, DC: Congressional Research Service, 2007), available at www.fas.org/sgp/crs/row/RL32167.pdf, accessed 14 December 2012.

Perl, Raphael and Nanto, Dick, *North Korean Counterfeiting of US Currency* (Washington, DC: Congressional Research Service, 2006), available at www.nkeconwatch.com/nk-uploads/2006-3-22-north-korea-counterfeiting-us-currency.pdf, accessed 14 December 2012.

Person, James F. (ed.), *The Cuban Missile Crisis and the Origins of North Korea's Policy of Self-Reliance in National Defense, E-Dossier #12* (Washington, DC: Woodrow Wilson International Center for Scholars, 2012), available at www.wilsoncenter.org/sites/default/files/NKIDP_eDossier_12_North_ Korea_and_the_Cuban_Missile_Crisis_0.pdf, accessed 29 December 2013.

Peters, Richard and Li, Xiaobing, *Voices from the Korean War: Personal Stories of American, Korean and Chinese Soldiers* (Lexington: The University Press of Kentucky, 2005).

Pictorial Korea, 'Historical Pyongyang Meeting and Inter-Korean Summit Talks', *Democratic People's Republic of Korea No. 8*, August 2000.

Pollack, Jonathan D., *No Exit: North Korea, Nuclear Weapons and International Security* (Abingdon/London: Routledge/International Institute for Strategic Studies, 2011).

Pratt, Keith, *Everlasting Flower: A History of Korea* (London: Reaktion Books, 2006).

Pritchard, Charles L., *Failed Diplomacy: The Tragic Story of How North Korea Got the Bomb* (Washington, DC: Brookings Institution Press, 2007).

Pucek, Vladimir, 'The Impact of *Juche* upon Literature and Arts', in Han S. Park (ed.), *North Korea: Ideology, Politics, Economy* (Englewood Cliffs: Prentice Hall, 1996), pp. 51–70.

Puddington, Arch, *Freedom in the World 2012* (Washington, DC: Freedom House, 2012), available at www.freedomhouse.org/sites/default/files/FIW%202012%20Booklet_0.pdf, accessed 9 December 2012.

Ren, Xiao, 'Korean Security Dilemmas: Chinese Policies', in Hazel Smith (ed.), *Reconstituting Korean Security: A Policy Primer* (Tokyo: United Nations Press, 2007), pp. 145–61.

Rennack, Dianne E., *North Korea: Legislative Basis for US Economic Sanctions* (Washington, DC: Congressional Research Service, 2010).

Reuters, 'BC-Korea-Rice', 27 September 1995.

Ri, Hong Su, 'Songun Politics, Unique Mode of Politics', *The Pyongyang Times*, 19 November 2011, p. 3.

Richter, Paul, 'No Free Launch, Obama tells North Korea', *Los Angeles Times*, available at http://latimesblogs.latimes.com/world_now/2012/03/obama-to-.html, accessed 30 September 2012.

Robinson, W. Courtland, Lee, Myung Ken, Hill, Kenneth and Burnham, Gilbert M., 'Mortality in North Korean Migrant Households: A Retrospective Study', *The Lancet*, Vol. 354, No. 9175, Saturday 24 July 1999, pp. 291–5.

Robinson, W. Courtland, Lee, Myung Ken, Hill, Kenneth, Hsu, Edbert and Burnham, Gilbert, 'Demographic Methods to Assess Food Insecurity: A North Korean Case Study', *Prehospital and Disaster Medicine*, Vol. 15, No. 4, 2001, pp. 286–92.

Rodong Sinmun and *Kulloja*, 'Reject Imperialists' Ideological and Cultural Poisoning', *The Pyongyang Times*, 12 June 1999.

Rose, David, 'North Korea's Dollar Store', *Vanity Fair*, 5 August 2009, available at www.vanityfair.com/politics/features/2009/09/office-39-200909, accessed 15 September 2013.

Rufford, Nick, 'Iran Linked to Flood of Fake Dollars', *Sunday Times*, 17 July 1995.

Ruwitch, John and Park, Ju-min, 'Insight: North Korean Economy Surrenders to Foreign Currency Invasion', *Reuters*, 2 June 2013, available at www.reuters.com/article/2013/06/03/us-korea-north-money-idUSBRE9510E720130603, accessed 7 February 2013.

Ryang, Sonia, *North Koreans in Japan: Language, Ideology and Entity* (Boulder, CO: Westview, 1997).

'Gender in Oblivion: Women in the Democratic People's Republic of Korea (North Korea)', *Journal of African and Asian Studies*, Vol. 35, No. 3, August 2000, pp. 323–49.

Ryohaengsa, *Mt. Paektu* (Pyongyang: Korea International Travel Company, undated).

Sakai, Takashi, 'The Power Base of Kim Jong Il: Focusing on its Formation Process', in Han S. Park (ed.), *North Korea: Ideology, Politics, Economy* (Englewood Cliffs: Prentice Hall, 1996), pp. 105–22.

Samore, Gary, *North Korea's Weapons Programmes: A Net Assessment* (London: Macmillan Palgrave, 2004).

Samore, Gary and Ward, Adam, 'Living with Ambiguity: North Korea's Strategic Weapons Programmes', in Hazel Smith (ed.), *Reconstituting Korean Security: A Policy Primer* (Tokyo: United Nations Press, 2007), pp. 43–64.

Scalapino, Robert A., 'China and Korean Reunification – A Neighbour's Concerns', in Nicholas Eberstadt and Richard J. Ellings (eds.), *Korea's Future and the Great Powers* (Seattle: University of Washington Press, 2001), pp. 107–24.

Scalapino, Robert A. and Lee, Chong-Sik, *Communism in Korea: The Movement* (Berkeley: University of California Press, 1972).

Schiller, Markus and Schmucker, Robert H., 'A Dog and Pony Show: North Korea's New ICBM', 18 April 2012, available at http://lewis.armscontrolwonk.com/files/2012/04/KN-08_Analysis_Schiller_Schmucker.pdf, accessed 30 October 2012.

Schmid, Andre, *Korea Between Empires 1895–1919* (New York: Columbia University Press, 2002).

Sharwood, Anthony, 'Starved of Food, Starved of the Truth: How Kim Jong Un Suppresses his People', 9 April 2013, available at www.news.com.au/world-news/starved-of-food-starved-of-the-truth-how-kim-jong-un-suppresses-his-people/story-fndir2ev-1226616134393, accessed 17 July 2013.

Sherman, Wendy R., 'Talking to the North Koreans', *New York Times*, 7 March 2001, available at www.nytimes.com/2001/03/07/opinion/07SHER.html, accessed 19 April 2013.

Shim, Young-Hee, 'Human Rights of Women in North Korea: Factors and Present State', in Kie-Duck Park and Sang-Jin Han (eds.), *Human Rights in*

North Korea: Toward a Comprehensive Understanding (Sungnam: The Sejong Institute, 2007), pp. 171–208.

Shin, Eun-young, 'Ideology and Gender Equality: Women's Policies of North Korea and China', *East Asian Review*, Vol. 13, No. 3, Autumn 2001, pp. 81–104, available at www.ieas.or.kr/vol13_3/13_3_5.pdf, accessed 8 November 2014.

Shin, Gi-Wook, *Ethnic Nationalism in Korea: Genealogy, Politics, and Legacy* (Stanford University Press, 2006).

Shin, Gi-Wook and Robinson, Michael (eds.), *Colonial Modernity in Korea* (Cambridge, MA: Harvard University Asia Center, 1999).

Sigal, Leon D., *Disarming Strangers: Nuclear Diplomacy with North Korea* (Princeton University Press, 1998).

Singham, A. W. and Hune, Shirley, *Non-alignment in an Age of Alignments* (London: Zed, 1986).

Smith, Hazel, 'North Korean Foreign Policy in the 1990s: The Realist Approach', in Hazel Smith, Chris Rhodes, Diana Pritchard and Kevin Magill (eds.), *North Korea in the New World Order* (London: Macmillan, 1996), pp. 93–113.

'"Opening up" by Default: North Korea, the Humanitarian Community and the Crisis', *Pacific Review*, Vol. 12, No. 3, 1999, pp. 453–78.

WFP DPRK Programmes and Activities: A Gender Perspective (Pyongyang: WFP, December 1999).

'Bad, Mad, Sad or Rational Actor: Why the "Securitisation" Paradigm makes for Poor Policy Analysis of North Korea', *International Affairs*, Vol. 76, No. 3, July 2000, pp. 593–617.

'La Corée du Nord vers l'économie de marché: faux et vrais dilemmas', *Critique Internationale*, No. 15, April 2002, pp. 6–14.

Overcoming Humanitarian Dilemmas in the DPRK, Special Report No. 90 (Washington, DC: United States Institute of Peace, July 2002).

'Asymmetric Nuisance Value: The Border in China–Democratic People's Republic of Korea Relations', in Timothy Hildebrandt (ed.), *Uneasy Allies: Fifty Years of China– North Korea Relations* (Washington, DC: Woodrow Wilson Center Asia Program Special Report, September 2003), pp. 18–25.

'Brownback's Bill will not Help North Koreans', *Jane's Intelligence Review*, February 2004, pp. 42–5.

'Intelligence Matters: Improving Intelligence on North Korea', *Jane's Intelligence Review*, April 2004.

'Crime and Economic Instability: The Real Security Threat from North Korea and What to Do about it', *International Relations of the Asia Pacific*, Vol. 5, No. 2, 2005, pp. 235–49.

Food Security and Agricultural Production (Muscatine, IA/Berlin: Stanley Foundation/German Council on Foreign Relations, June 2005).

'How South Korean Means Support North Korean Ends: Crossed Purposes in Inter-Korean Cooperation', *International Journal of Korean Unification Studies*, Vol. 14, No. 2, 2005, pp. 21–51.

Hungry for Peace: International Security, Humanitarian Assistance and Social Change in North Korea (Washington, DC: United States Institute of Peace Press, 2005).

'North Koreans in China: Sorting Fact from Fiction', in Tsuneo Akaha and Anna Vassilieva (eds.), *Crossing National Borders: Human Migration Issues in Northeast Asia* (Tokyo: United Nations Press, 2005), pp. 165–90.

'North Korean Migrants Pose Long-term Challenge for China', *Jane's Intelligence Review*, June 2005, p. 35.

'The Disintegration and Reconstitution of the State in the DPRK', in Simon Chesterman, Michael Ignatieff and Ramesh Thakur (eds.), *Making States Work* (Tokyo: United Nations Press, 2005), pp. 167–92.

'Analysing Change in the DPR Korea', working paper (Bern: Swiss Agency for Development and Cooperation – East Asia Division, November 2006).

Caritas and the DPRK – Building on 10 Years of Experience (Hong Kong and Rome: Caritas, 2006).

(ed.), *Reconstituting Korean Security: A Policy Primer* (Tokyo: United Nations Press, 2007).

'North Korea as the Wicked Witch of the East: Social Science as Fairy Tale', *Asia Policy*, No. 5, January 2008, pp. 197–203.

'North Korean Shipping: A Potential for WMD Proliferation?', *Asia-Pacific Issues*, No. 87, February 2009.

'North Korea: Market Opportunity, Poverty and the Provinces', *New Political Economy*, Vol. 14, No. 3, June 2009, pp. 231–56.

'North Korea's Security Perspectives', in Andrew T. H. Tan (ed.), *East and South-East Asia: International Relations and Security Perspectives* (London: Routledge, 2013), pp. 121–32.

'Crimes Against Humanity? Unpacking the North Korean Human Rights Debate', in Christine Hong and Hazel Smith (eds.), *Critical Asian Studies, Reframing North Korean Human Rights*, Vol. 46, No. 1, March 2014, pp. 127–43.

Snyder, Scott, *Negotiating on the Edge: North Korean Negotiating Behavior* (Washington, DC: United States Institute of Peace Press, 1999).

Sok, Chang-sik, 'Experiences of State-building in the Democratic People's Republic of Korea', in Ken'ichiro Hirano (ed.), *The State and Cultural Transformation: Perspectives from East Asia* (Tokyo: United Nations Press, 1993), pp. 328–43.

Song, Un Hong, *Economic Development in the Democratic People's Republic of Korea, 18 April 1978* (Pyongyang: Foreign Languages Publishing House, 1990).

Sorensen, Clark, 'The Land, Climate, and People', in John H. Koo and Andrew Nahm (eds.), *An Introduction to Korean Culture* (Elizabeth, NJ/Seoul: Hollym, 1997), pp. 17–37.

Spina, Marion P., Jr., 'Brushes with the Law: North Korea and the Rule of Law', in *Academic Series Papers on Korea* (Washington, DC: Korea Economic Institute, 2008), pp. 75–97, available at www.keia.org/Publications/OnKorea/2008/08Spina.pdf, accessed 9 February 2014.

Stratfor.com Global Intelligence Update, 'Chinese Influence on the Rise in Pyongyang', *Sratfor.con Global Intelligence Update*, 5 November 1999, available at www.stratfor.com/sample/analysis/chinese-influence-rise-pyongyang, accessed 8 November 2014.

Standing Committee of the Supreme People's Assembly, *The Criminal Law of the Democratic People's Republic of Korea* (Pyongyang: Foreign Languages Publishing House, 1992).

The Civil Law of the Democratic People's Republic of Korea (Pyongyang: Foreign Languages Publishing House, 1994).

Stone, I. F., *The Hidden History of the Korean War* (Boston: Little, Brown and Company, 1988).

Strong, Anna Louise, *In North Korea: First Eye-Witness Report* (New York: Soviet Russia Today, 1949), available at www.marxists.org/reference/archive/strong-anna-louise/1949/in-north-korea/index.htm, accessed 12 October 2013.

Stueck, William, *The Korean War: An International History* (Princeton University Press, 1995).

Suh, Dae-Sook, *Kim Il Sung: The North Korean Leader* (New York: Columbia University Press, 1988).

Suh, Jae-Jean, *North Korea's Market Economy Society from Below* (Seoul: Korea Institute for National Unification, 2005).

'The Transformation of Class Structure and Class Conflict in North Korea', *International Journal of Korean Unification Studies*, Vol. 14, No. 2, 2005, pp. 53–84.

Economic Hardship and Regime Sustainability in North Korea (Seoul: Korea Institute for National Unification, 2008).

Supreme Command Korean People's Army, 'Press statement', *The Pyongyang Times*, 26 November 2011, p. 1.

Supreme People's Assembly, *DPRK's Socialist Constitution* (full text), amended and supplemented Socialist Constitution of the DPRK, adopted on 5 September 1998 (Pyongyang: DPRK Government, 1998), available at www.novexcn.com/dprk_constitution_98.html, accessed 23 January 2014.

Szalontai, Balázs, 'The Four Horsemen of the Apocalypse in North Korea', in Chris Springer (ed.), *North Korea Caught in Time: Images of War and Reconstruction* (Reading: Garnet Publishing, 2010), pp. ix–xxviii.

Takashi, Nada, *Korea in Kim Jong Il's Era* (Pyongyang: Foreign Languages Publishing House, 2000).

Taylor, Kathleen, 'Has Kim Jong-Il Brainwashed North Koreans?' *The Guardian*, 20 December 2011, available at www.theguardian.com/commentisfree/2011/dec/20/kim-jong-il-brainwashed-north-koreans, accessed 13 September 2013.

The Chosunilbo, 'Kim Jong-nam Says N. Korean Regime Won't Last Long', *The Chosunilbo*, 17 January 2012, available at http://english.chosun.com/site/data/html_dir/2012/01/17/2012011701790.html, accessed 25 January 2014.

The Institute for Far Eastern Studies, *North Korea to Become Strong in Science and Technology by Year 2022* (Seoul: The Institute for Far Eastern Studies, 21 December 2012), available at http://ifes.kyungnam.ac.kr/eng/FRM/FRM_0101V.aspx?code=FRM121221_0001, accessed 13 September 2013.

A Review of the Last Five Years of People-to-People Exchanges and Inter-Korean Economic Cooperation under the Lee Myung-bak Government (Seoul:

The Institute for Far Eastern Studies, 23 January 2013), available at http://
   ifes.kyungnam.ac.kr/eng/FRM/FRM_0101V.aspx?code=FRM130123_
   0001, accessed 13 September 2013.
The People's Korea, 'J. Kelly Failed to Produce "Evidence" in Pyongyang; Framed
   Up Admission Story', *People's Korea*, 19 January 2003, available at
   www.korea-np.co.jp/pk/188th_issue/2003013001.htm, accessed 9 June
   2012.
   'North, South Commemorate Accession Day of Nation's Founder', 2002,
   available at www1.korea-np.co.jp/pk/185th_issue/2002103113.htm,
   accessed 16 September 2013.
The Pyongyang Times, 'South–South Cooperation: Cause for Optimism',
   11 November 1995, p. 8.
The World Bank, 'Life Expectancy at Birth', available at http://data.worldbank.
   org/indicator/SP.DYN.LE00.IN/countries/KP?page=5&order=
   wbapi_data_value_2009%20wbapi_data_value%20wbapi_data_value-
   first&sort=asc&display=default, accessed 30 May 2014.
Thompson, Wayne and Nalty, Bernard C., *Within Limits: The US Air Force and
   the Korean War* (Washington, DC: Air Force Historical Studies Office, AF/
   HO,1190 Air Force Pentagon, 1996), available at www.dtic.mil/cgi-bin/
   GetTRDoc?AD=ADA440095&Location=U2&doc=GetTRDoc.pdf,
   accessed 8 November 2014.
Timmerman, Kenneth R., 'Iran and the Supernotes', Testimony on S.277 before
   Congressman Spencer Bachus Chairman, Subcommittee on General
   Oversight and Investigations of the Committee on Banking and Financial
   Services, 27 February 1996, reproduced on www.iran.org/tib/krt/960227sbc.
   htm, accessed 8 November 2014.
Toloraya, Georgy, *The Economic Future of North Korea: Will the Market Rule?*
   Academic Paper Series on North Korea: Vol. 2, No. 10 (Korea Economic
   Institute, 2008), available at www.keia.org/sites/default/files/publications/
   toloraya.pdf, accessed 8 November 2014.
Triangle Génération Humanitaire, *Annual Activity Report Year 2009*, available
   at www.trianglegh.org/ActionHumanitaire/PDF/PDF-Rapport-Activite/
   Rapport-TGH-2009-FR.pdf, accessed 22 June 2014.
Trigubenko, Marina Ye, 'Economic Characteristics and Prospect for
   Development: With Emphasis on Agriculture', in Han S. Park (ed.),
   North Korea: Ideology, Politics, Economy (Englewood Cliffs: Prentice Hall,
   1996), pp. 141–59.
Tumen Secretariat, *Tumen Update No. 3* (Beijing: Tumen Secretariat,
   October 2000).
Underwood, L. H., *Fifteen Years among the Top-Knots or Life in Korea*, second
   edition, revised and enlarged (Boston: American Tract Society, 1908).
United Nations, *Committee on the Rights of the Child Consideration of Reports
   Submitted by States Parties under Article 44 of the Convention, Second Periodic
   Reports of States Parties due in 1997 Addendum Democratic People's Republic of
   Korea, 16 May 2003, CRC/C/65/Add.24* (United Nations: New York,
   5 November 2003), p. 15, available at www.unhcr.org/refworld/country,,,
   STATEPARTIESREP, PRK,4562d8cf2,403a10a44,0.html, accessed
   27 January 2012.

United Nations, *DPR Korea Common Country Assessment 2002* (Pyongyang: UNOCHA, February 2003).

Strategic Framework for Cooperation Between the United Nations and the Government of the Democratic People's Republic of Korea 2007–2009 (Pyongyang: United Nations, September 2006).

United Nations Children's Fund (UNICEF), *Draft Situation Analysis DPR Korea 1997*, revised and edited (Pyongyang: UNICEF, 1997).

Background Situation Analysis on DPRK (Pyongyang: UNICEF, April 1998).

'An Analysis of the Situation of Children and Women in The Democratic People's Republic of Korea', draft, Pyongyang, May 1998.

DPRK Social Statistics (Pyongyang: UNICEF, 1998).

UNICEF Revised Funding Requirements: United Nations Consolidated Inter-Agency Appeal for the Democratic People's Republic of Korea: April 1997–March 1998 (Pyongyang: UNICEF, undated but 1998).

An Analysis of the Situation of Children and Women in the Democratic People's Republic of Korea 2000 (Pyongyang: UNICEF, 1999).

DPRK Social Statistics (Pyongyang: UNICEF, 1999).

Draft Master Plan of Operations (Pyongyang: UNICEF, 1999).

Situation Analysis of Women and Children in the DPRK (Pyongyang: UNICEF, 1999).

Annual Report 2000 Democratic People's Republic of Korea (Pyongyang: UNICEF, 2000).

Nutrition Situation in DPR Korea (Pyongyang: UNICEF, November 2000).

A Humanitarian Appeal for Children and Women (Pyongyang: UNICEF, 2002).

DPRK Donor Update (Pyongyang: UNICEF, 4 February 2002).

Country Programme of Cooperation between the Government of the Democratic People's Republic of Korea and the United Nations Children's Fund 2004–2006 Strategy Document (Pyongyang: UNICEF, February 2003).

DPRK at a Glance 2013 (Pyongyang: UNICEF, 2013), available at www.unicef.org/dprk/DPRK_at_a_glance_April_2013.pdf, accessed 7 February 2014.

The State of the World's Children 2013: Children with Disabilities (Geneva: UNICEF, 2013), available at www.unicef.org/sowc2013/files/SWCR2013_ENG_Lo_res_24_Apr_2013.pdf, accessed 20 April 2014.

United Nations Children's Fund (UNICEF)/World Health Organisation (WHO), *Immunization Summary: A Statistical Reference Containing Data Through 2010* (New York: UNICEF/World Health Organisation, 2012), available at www.childinfo.org/files/immunization_summary_en.pdf, accessed 22 June 2014.

United Nations Development Programme (UNDP), *Human Development Report 2004, Cultural Liberty in Today's Diverse World* (New York: UNDP, 2004).

United Nations Development Programme (UNDP) and DPRK government, *Report of the Thematic Roundtable on Agricultural Recovery and Environmental Protection in DPR Korea* (Geneva: UNDP, 28–9 May 1998).

Report of the First Thematic Round Table Conference for the Democratic People's Republic of Korea (Geneva: UNDP, 28–9 May 1998).

Report of the Thematic Round Table Conference for the Democratic People's Republic of Korea (Geneva: UNDP, June 2000).

United Nations Economic and Social Commission for Asia and the Pacific (UNESCAP), 'Report by the Delegation of the Democratic People's Republic of Korea', in Economic and Social Commission for Asia and the Pacific, 9–11 October 2007, available at http://globalaging.org/agingwatch/desa/aging/mipaa/Korea.pdf, accessed 8 November 2014.

United Nations Office for the Coordination of Humanitarian Affairs (UNOCHA), *Report* (Pyongyang: UNOCHA, 6 August 2002).

'Joint UNCT submission for the UN Compilation Report Universal Periodic Review–Democratic People's Republic of Korea (DPRK) 6th session (30 November–11 December 2009)', available at http://lib.ohchr.org/HRBodies/UPR/Documents/Session6/KP/UNCT_PRK_UPR_S06_2009.pdf, accessed 22 June 2014.

United Nations Population Fund (UNFPA) in the News, 'Democratic People's Republic of Korea: Census Finds Drop in Life Expectancy', 21 February 2010, available at http://inthenews.unfpa.org/?p=1005, accessed 8 November 2014.

United Nations Statistics Division, 'Growth Rate of GDP/Breakdown at Constant 2005 Prices in Percent (all countries)', National Accounts Main Aggregates Database, available at http://unstats.un.org/unsd/snaama/dnlList.asp, accessed 15 February 2014.

'Per Capita GDP at Current Prices in US Dollars (all countries)', National Accounts Main Aggregates Database, available at http://unstats.un.org/unsd/snaama/dnlList.asp, accessed 15 February 2014.

'Per Capita GNI at Current Prices in US Dollars (all countries)', National Accounts Main Aggregates Database, available at http://unstats.un.org/unsd/snaama/dnlList.asp, accessed 30 May 2014.

United States Department of State, *Country Reports on Terrorism 2010* (Washington, DC: United States Department of State, Office of the Coordinator for Counterterrorism, August 2011), available at www.state.gov/documents/organization/170479.pdf, accessed 15 September 2013.

Valencia, Mark J., 'The Proliferation Security Initiative: A Glass Half-Full', *Arms Control Today*, June 2007, available at www.armscontrol.org/act/2007_06/Valencia, accessed 8 November 2014.

Van Dyke, Jon, 'The Maritime Boundary between North and South Korea in the Yellow (West) Sea', *38 North* (US–Korea Institute, Johns Hopkins University School of Advanced International Studies, 29 July 2010), available at www.38north.org/?p=1232, accessed 8 November 2014.

Von Hippel, David F. and Hayes, Peter, 'North Korean Energy Sector: Current Status and Scenarios from 2000 and 2005', in Marcus Noland (ed.), *Economic Integration of the Korean Peninsula* (Washington, DC: Institute for International Economics, 1998), pp. 77–117.

Walsh, Jim, 'Three States, Three Stories: Comparing Iran, Syria and North Korea's Nuclear Programs', in Jung-Ho Bae and Jae H. Ku (eds.), *Nuclear*

Security 2012: Challenges of Proliferation and Implication [*sic*] *for the Korean Peninsula* (Seoul: Korea Institute for National Unification, 2012), pp. 123–49.

Washburn, John N., 'Russia Looks at Northern Korea', *Pacific Affairs*, Vol. 20, No. 2, June 1947, pp. 152–60.

Watts, Jonathan, 'South Korean Tourist Shot Dead in North Korea', *The Guardian*, 11 July 2008, available at www.guardian.co.uk/world/2008/jul/11/korea, accessed 22 June 2014.

White, Gordon, 'North Korean *Chuch'e:* The Political Economy of Independence', *Bulletin of Concerned Asian Scholars*, Vol. 7, No. 2, pp. 44–54, available at http://criticalasianstudies.org/assets/files/bcas/v07n02.pdf, accessed 8 November 2014.

Williams, Paul D. (ed.), *Security Studies: An Introduction* (London: Routledge, 2008).

Wit, Joel S., Poneman, Daniel B. and Gallucci, Robert L., *Going Critical: The First North Korean Nuclear Crisis* (Washington, DC: Brookings Institution Press, 2005).

Worden, William L., *General Dean's Story* (New York: The Viking Press, 1954).

World Food Programme (WFP), 'Emergency Operation DPR Korea No. 5710.00: Emergency Food Assistance for Flood Victims', in WFP, *WFP Operations in DPR Korea as of 14 July 1999* (Rome: WFP, undated but 1999).

Nutritional Survey of the DPRK (Rome: WFP, January 1999).

'Protracted Relief and Recovery Operation – DPR Korea 6157.00', in WFP, *Projects for Executive Board Approval, Agenda Item 7, 19–22 October 1999* (Rome: WFP, 1999).

Report on the Nutrition Survey of the DPRK (Pyongyang: WFP, 1999).

'Emergency operation DPR Korea No. 5959.02, Emergency Assistance for Vulnerable Groups' (Pyongyang: WFP, 2000)

Full Report of the Evaluation of DPRK EMOPs 5959.00 and 5959.01 'Emergency Assistance to Vulnerable Groups' 20 March–10 April 2000 (Rome: WFP, 2000).

Pyongyang Province (Pyongyang: WFP, 2001).

Statistics of DPRK Population 2002 (Pyongyang: WFP, 2003).

Emergency Operation (EMOP 200266): Emergency Food Assistance to Vulnerable Groups in the Democratic People's Republic of Korea (Rome: WFP, undated but 2011), available at http://reliefweb.int/sites/reliefweb.int/files/resources/Full_Report_454.pdf, accessed 8 November 2014.

Overview of Needs and Assistance in DPRK 2012 (Rome: World Food Programme, 2012).

WFP/FAO/UNICEF, *Special Report: Rapid Food Security Assessment Mission to the Democratic People's Republic of Korea, 24 March 2011* (Rome: WFP, 2011), available at http://ko.wfp.org/sites/default/files/english_rfsa.pdf, accessed 22 June 2014.

WFP/FAO/UNICEF/Save the Children Fund UK, *Nutritional Assessment Mission to the Democratic People's Republic of Korea* (Pyongyang/Rome: WFP, November 1997).

World Health Organisation (WHO), *Democratic People's Republic of Korea: National Health System Profile* (Pyongyang: WHO, undated but probably 2006).

World Malaria Report 2010 (Geneva: World Health Organisation, 2010).

Global Tuberculosis Control: WHO Report 2011 (Geneva: World Health Organisation, 2011).

Wright, David C. and Kadyshev, Timur, 'An Analayis of the North Korean Nodong Missile', *Science and Global Security*, Vol. 4, No. 2, 1994, pp. 129–60.

Yang, Ryon Hui, 'Taehongdan County Integrated Farm on Paektu Plateau', *The Pyongyang Times*, 13 August 1994.

Yang, Sung Chul, *The North and South Korean Political Systems: A Comparative Analysis*, revised edition (Elizabeth, NJ: Hollym, 1999).

Yoon, Dae-Kyu, 'Economic Reform and Institutional Transformation', Phillip H. Park (ed.), *The Dynamics of Change in North Korea* (Seoul: Institute for Far Eastern Studies, 2009), pp. 43–73.

'The Constitution of North Korea: Its Changes and Implications', *Fordham International Law Journal*, Vol. 27, No. 4, April 2004, pp. 1289–305, available at http://ir.lawnet.fordham.edu/cgi/viewcontent.cgi?article=1934&context=ilj, accessed 9 February 2014.

Young, Soogil, Lee, Chang-Jae and Zang, Hyoungsoo, 'Preparing for the Economic Integration of Two Koreas: Policy Challenges to South Korea', in Marcus Noland (ed.), *Economic Integration of the Korean Peninsula* (Washington, DC: Institute for International Economics, 1998), pp. 251–71.

Zacek, Jane Shapiro, 'Russia in North Korean Foreign Policy', in Samuel S. Kim, *North Korean Foreign Relations in the Post-Cold War Era* (Oxford University Press, 1998), pp. 75–93.

Zhu, Jieming, 'Urban Development under Ambiguous Property Rights: A Case of China's Transition Economy', *International Journal of Urban and Regional Research* , Vol. 26, Issue 1, 2002, pp. 33–50.

Index